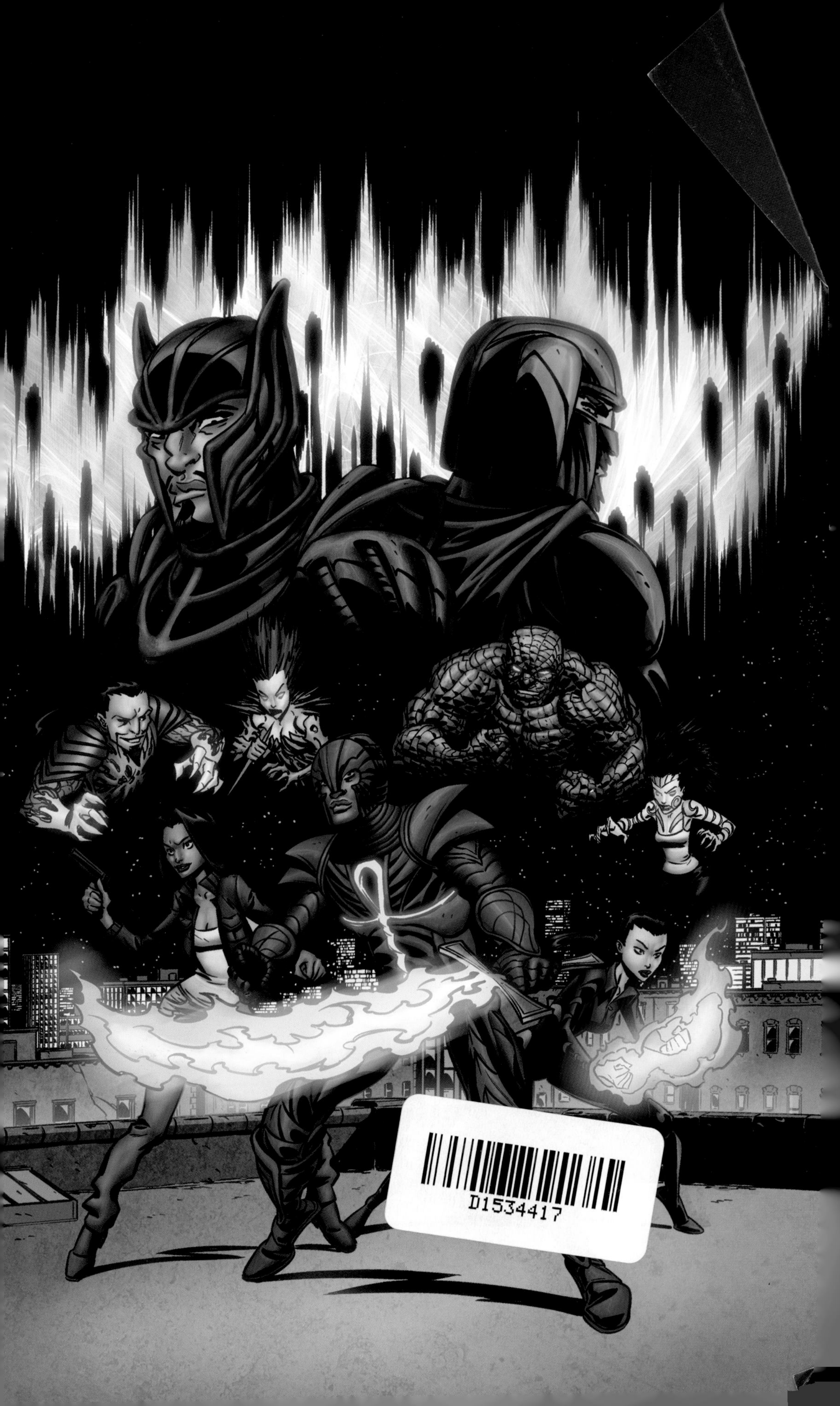

PREVIOUSLY IN...

LEGEND OF THE MANTAMAJI™

Elijah Alexander, a New York A.D.A., learned he was the last of a race of mystical knights called the Mantamaji. Noah, the only other surviving Mantamaji, informed Elijah that Sirach, an evil Mantamaji who betrayed their race three thousand years ago, had been resurrected in New York City, and is now posing as Brother Hope, a prominent religious leader with a secret criminal gang called the New World Knights. Elijah and his mother were preserved for millennia in enchanted slumber by his father and female mystic warriors called Sanctuants.

While his detective girlfriend Sydney raced to uncover the truth about Brother Hope at the wharf, Elijah's mother Mariah also tried to reason with Brother Hope there. With both his loved ones in danger, Elijah went with Noah to save them. Sydney was knocked unconscious, and an outmanned Noah and Elijah watched Sirach stab Mariah through the heart with his flaming sword.

Motivated now by revenge, Elijah has agreed to let Noah train him so he can use his Mantamaji powers to take down Sirach and his army of followers.

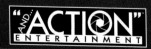

"AND..." ACTION" ENTERTAINMENT

"And... Action!" Entertainment © ™ All Eyes On E, Inc.

10061 Riverside Drive, Suite 296 Toluca Lake, California 91602

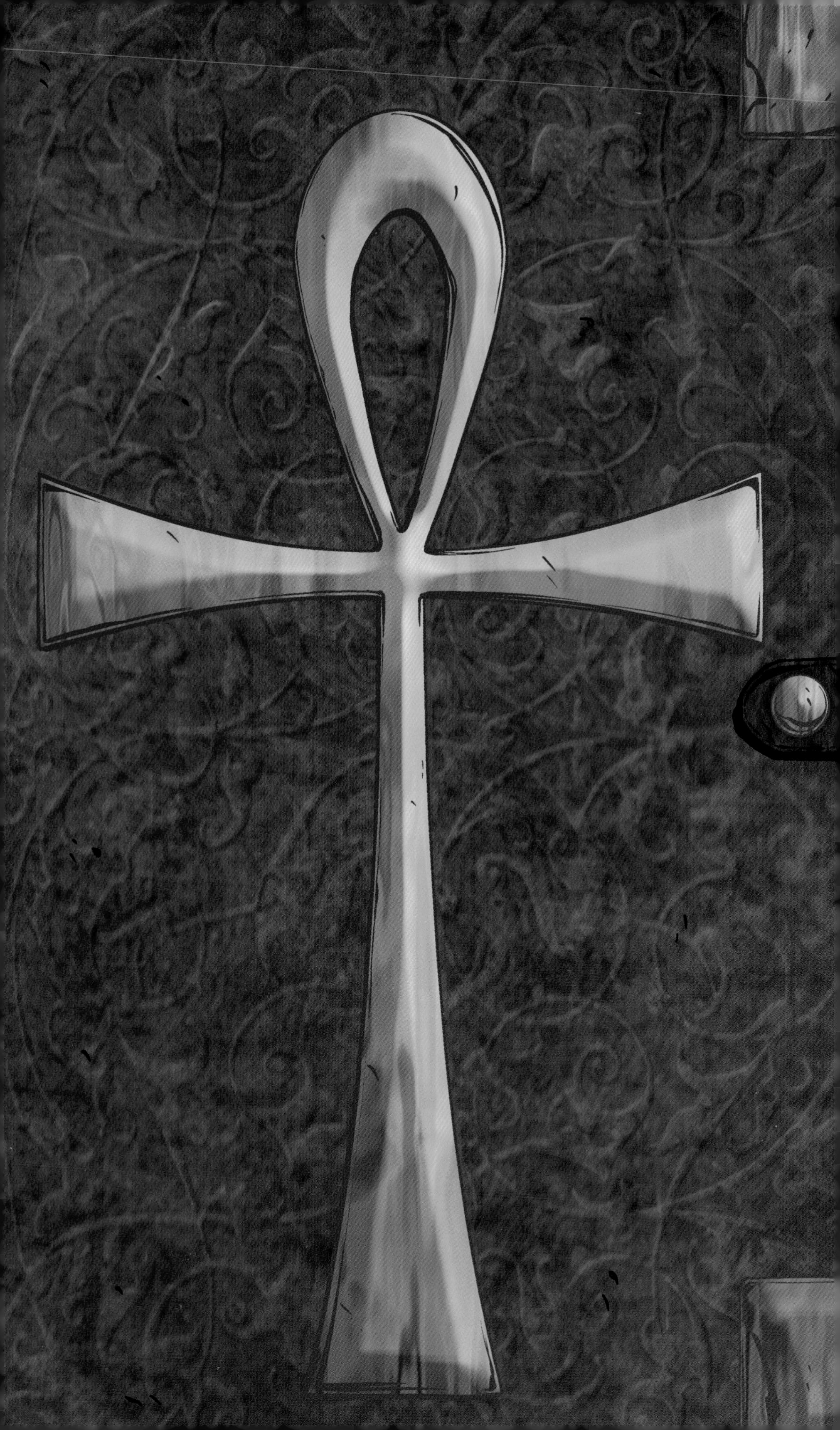

CHAPTER 7

My golden-hearted son, I must tell you an ancient tale, about a race of people with divine purpose and with magical gifts. Their appearance was like an eclipse or a murmuration of birds: it was a sign that change was coming.

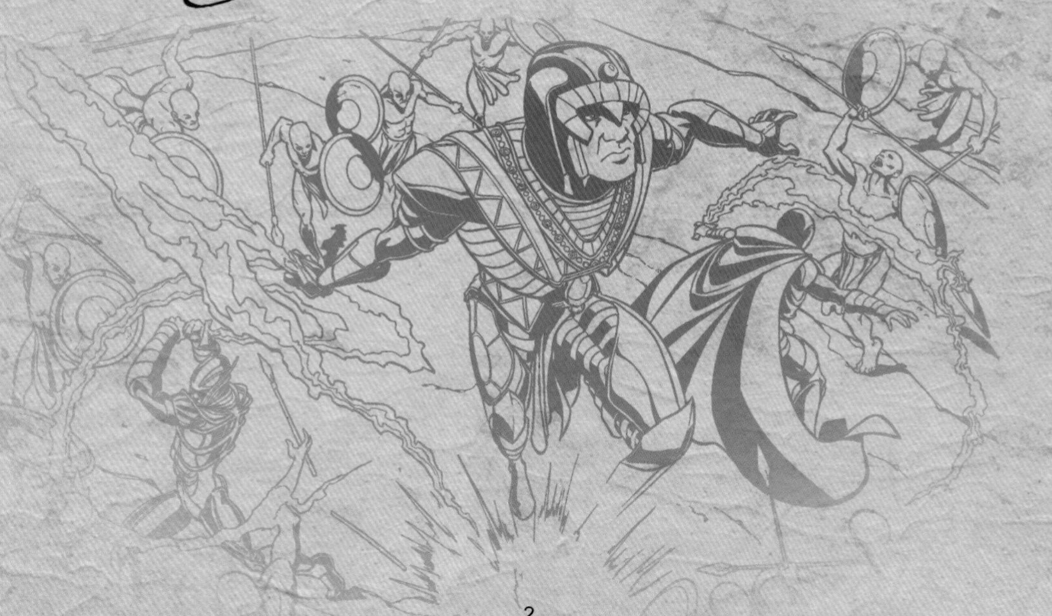

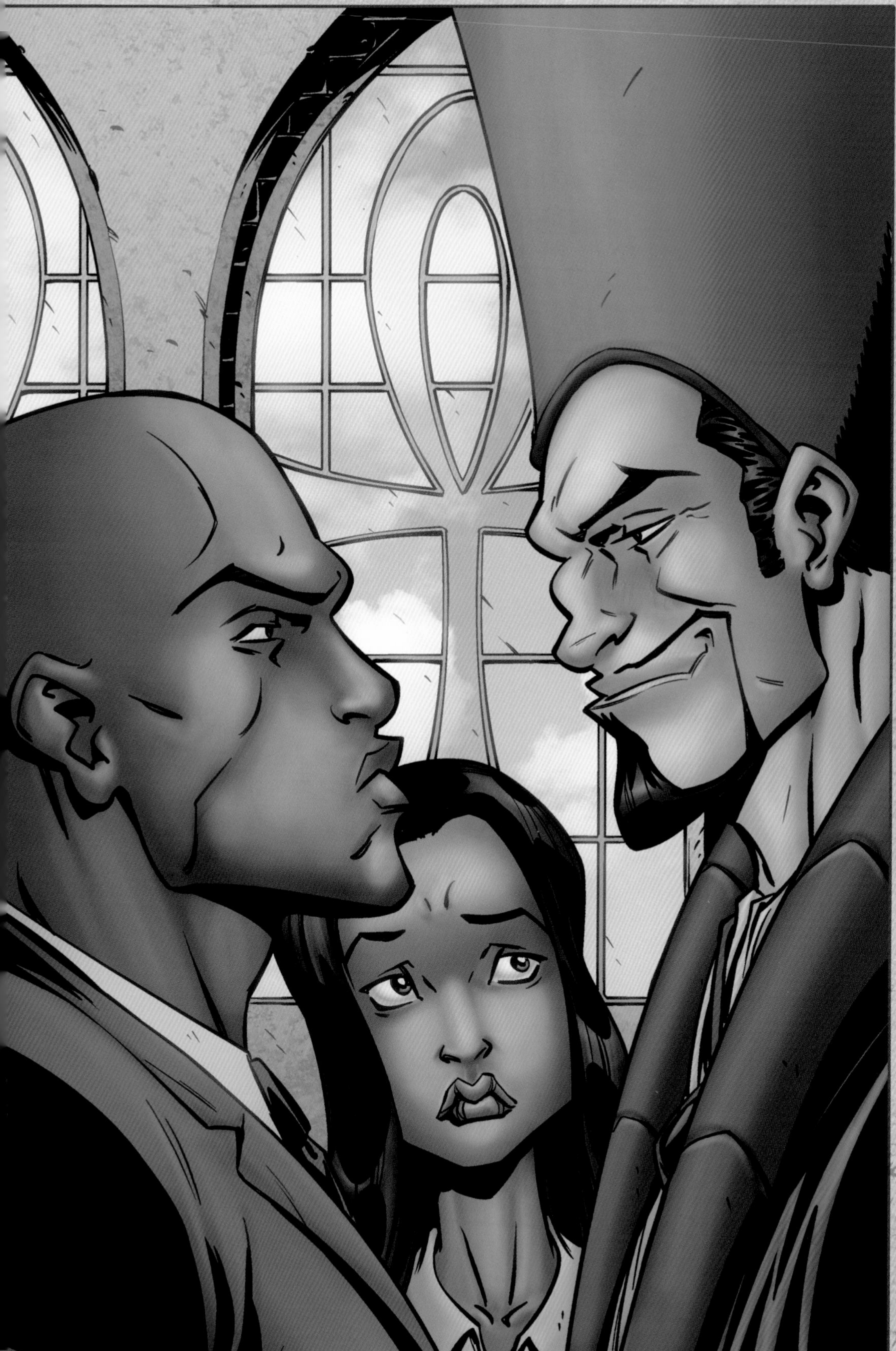

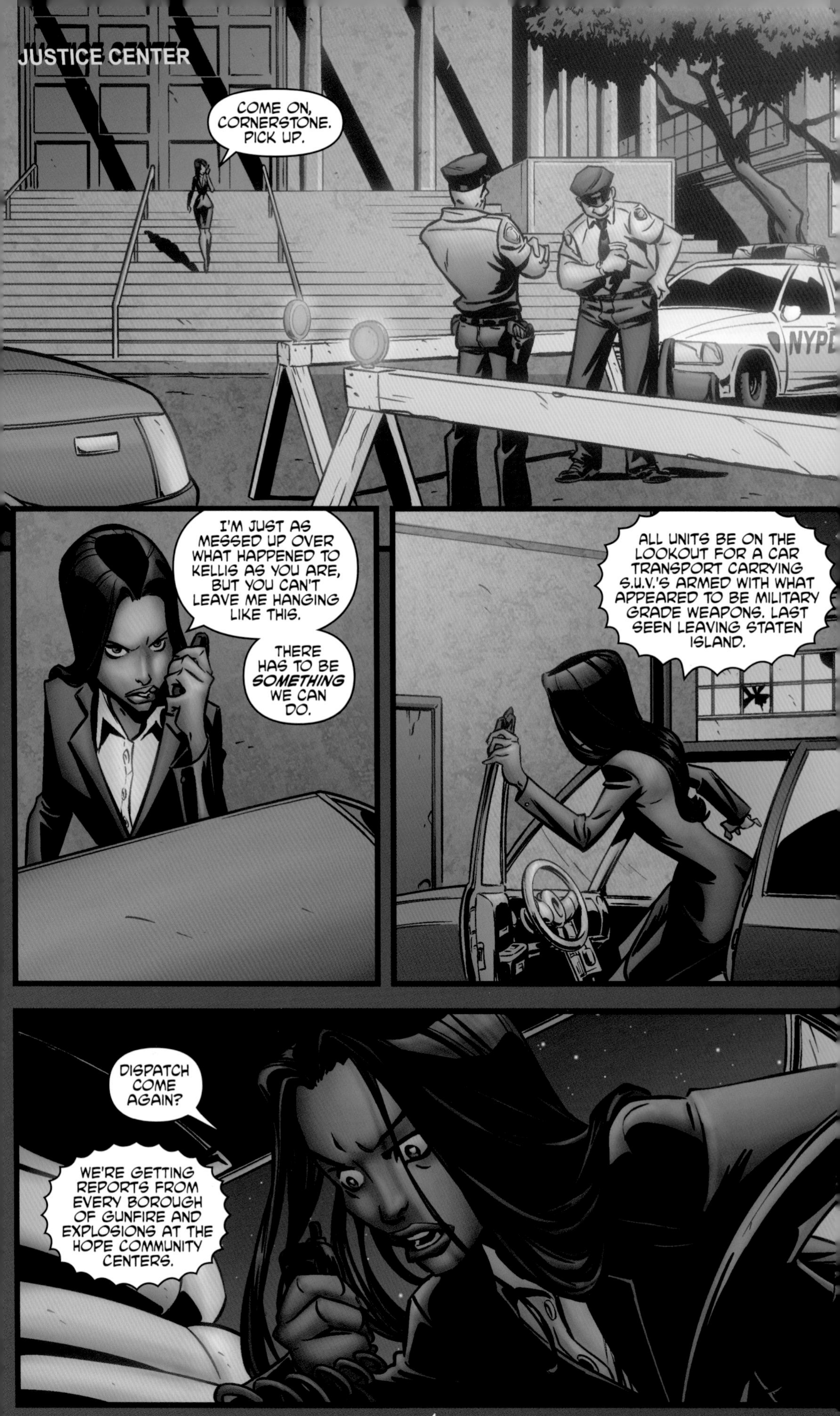
JUSTICE CENTER
COME ON, CORNERSTONE. PICK UP.
I'M JUST AS MESSED UP OVER WHAT HAPPENED TO KELLIS AS YOU ARE, BUT YOU CAN'T LEAVE ME HANGING LIKE THIS.
THERE HAS TO BE *SOMETHING* WE CAN DO.
ALL UNITS BE ON THE LOOKOUT FOR A CAR TRANSPORT CARRYING S.U.V.'S ARMED WITH WHAT APPEARED TO BE MILITARY GRADE WEAPONS. LAST SEEN LEAVING STATEN ISLAND.
DISPATCH COME AGAIN?
WE'RE GETTING REPORTS FROM EVERY BOROUGH OF GUNFIRE AND EXPLOSIONS AT THE HOPE COMMUNITY CENTERS.

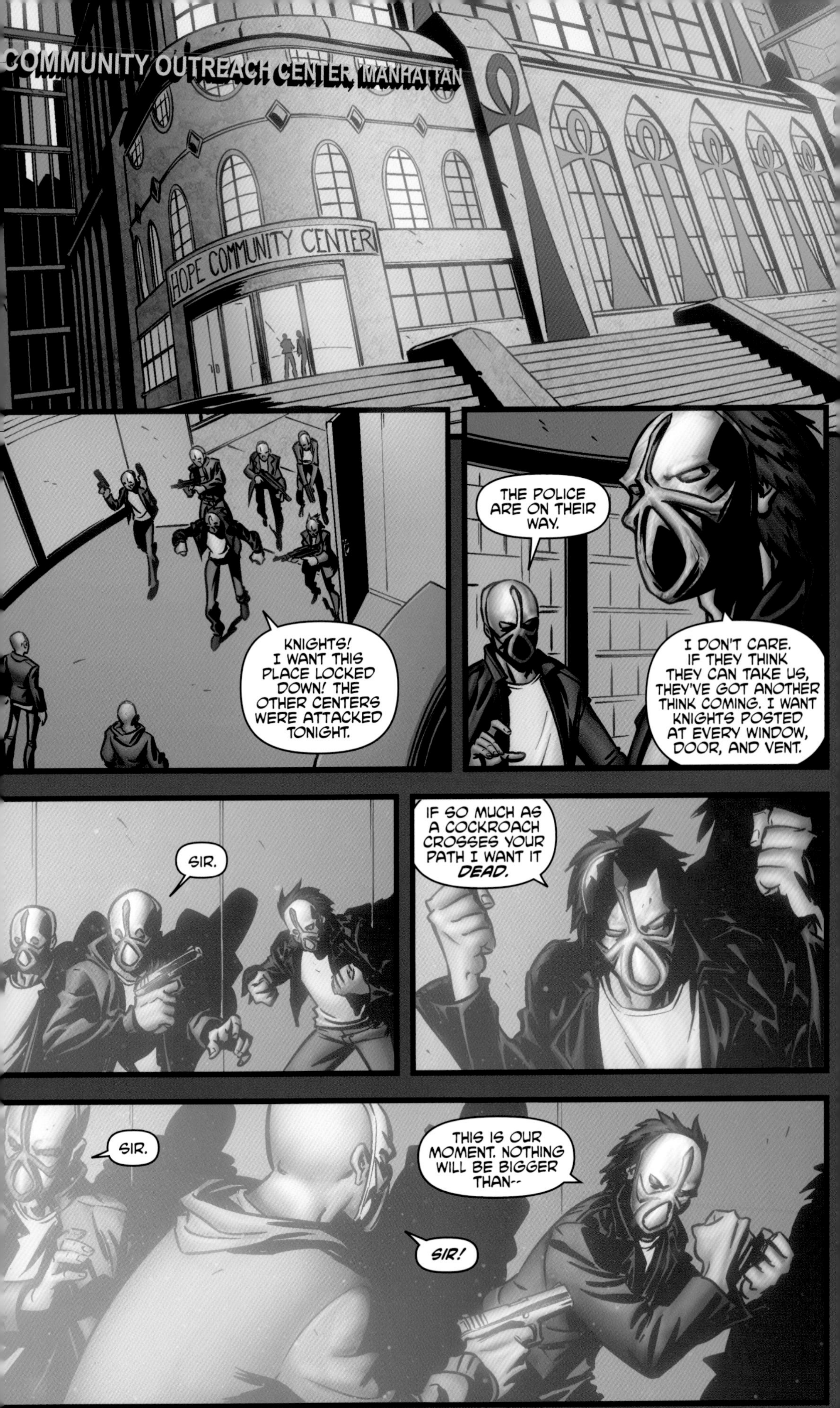
COMMUNITY OUTREACH CENTER, MANHATTAN
HOPE COMMUNITY CENTER
KNIGHTS! I WANT THIS PLACE LOCKED DOWN! THE OTHER CENTERS WERE ATTACKED TONIGHT.
THE POLICE ARE ON THEIR WAY.
I DON'T CARE. IF THEY THINK THEY CAN TAKE US, THEY'VE GOT ANOTHER THINK COMING. I WANT KNIGHTS POSTED AT EVERY WINDOW, DOOR, AND VENT.
SIR.
IF SO MUCH AS A COCKROACH CROSSES YOUR PATH I WANT IT *DEAD.*
SIR.
THIS IS OUR MOMENT. NOTHING WILL BE BIGGER THAN--
SIR!

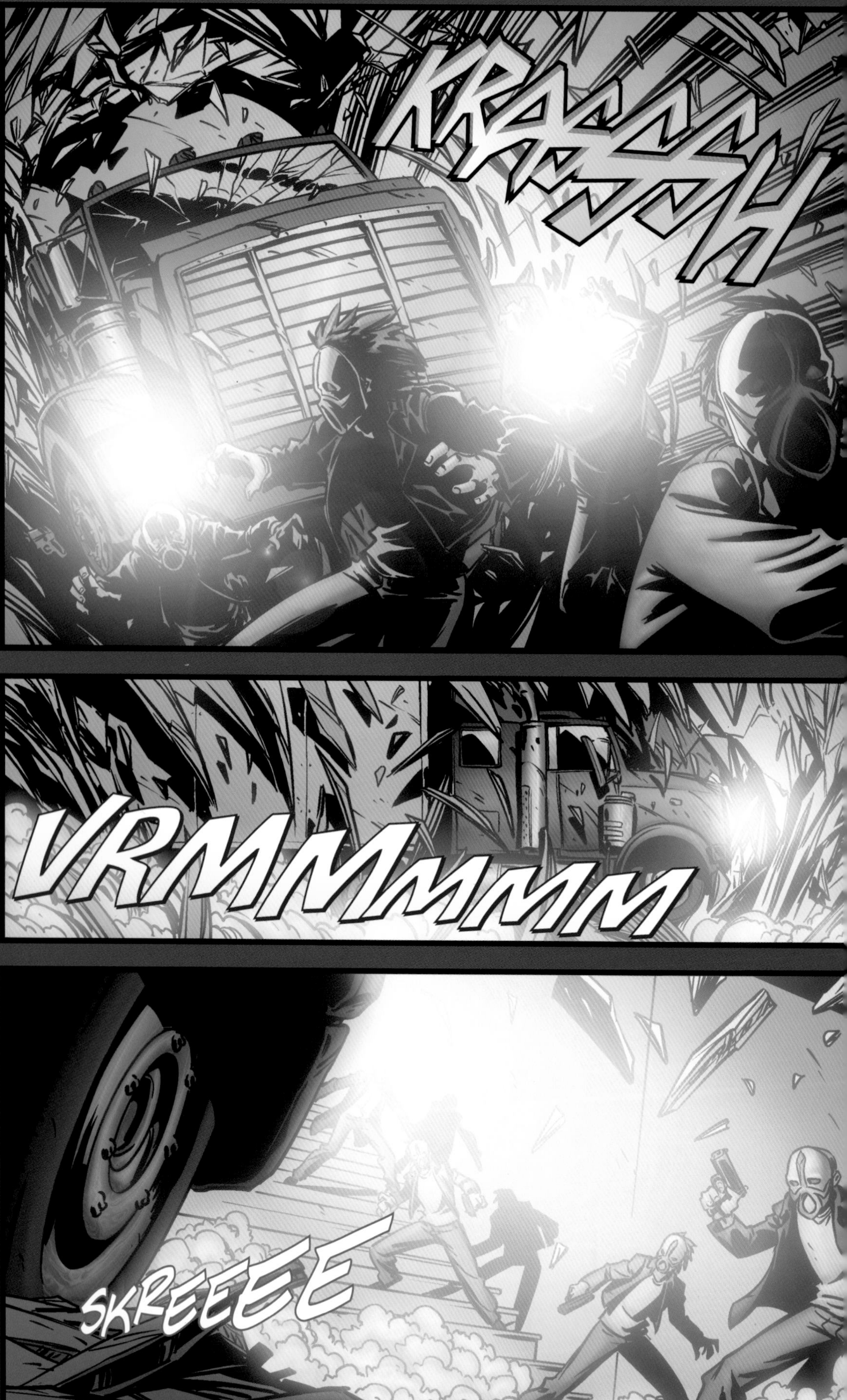
KRAAASSSH
VRMMMMMM
SKREEEE

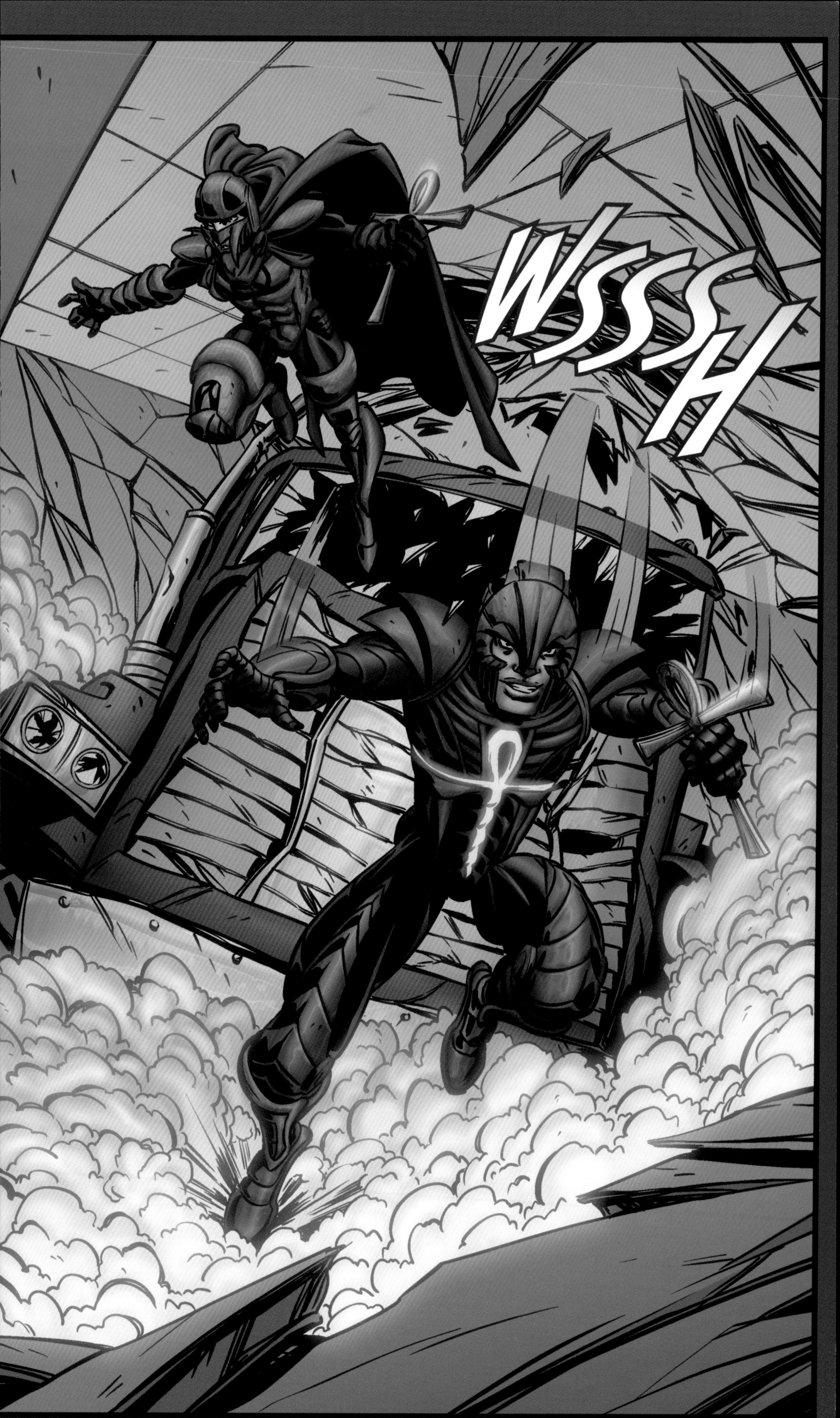
WSSSH

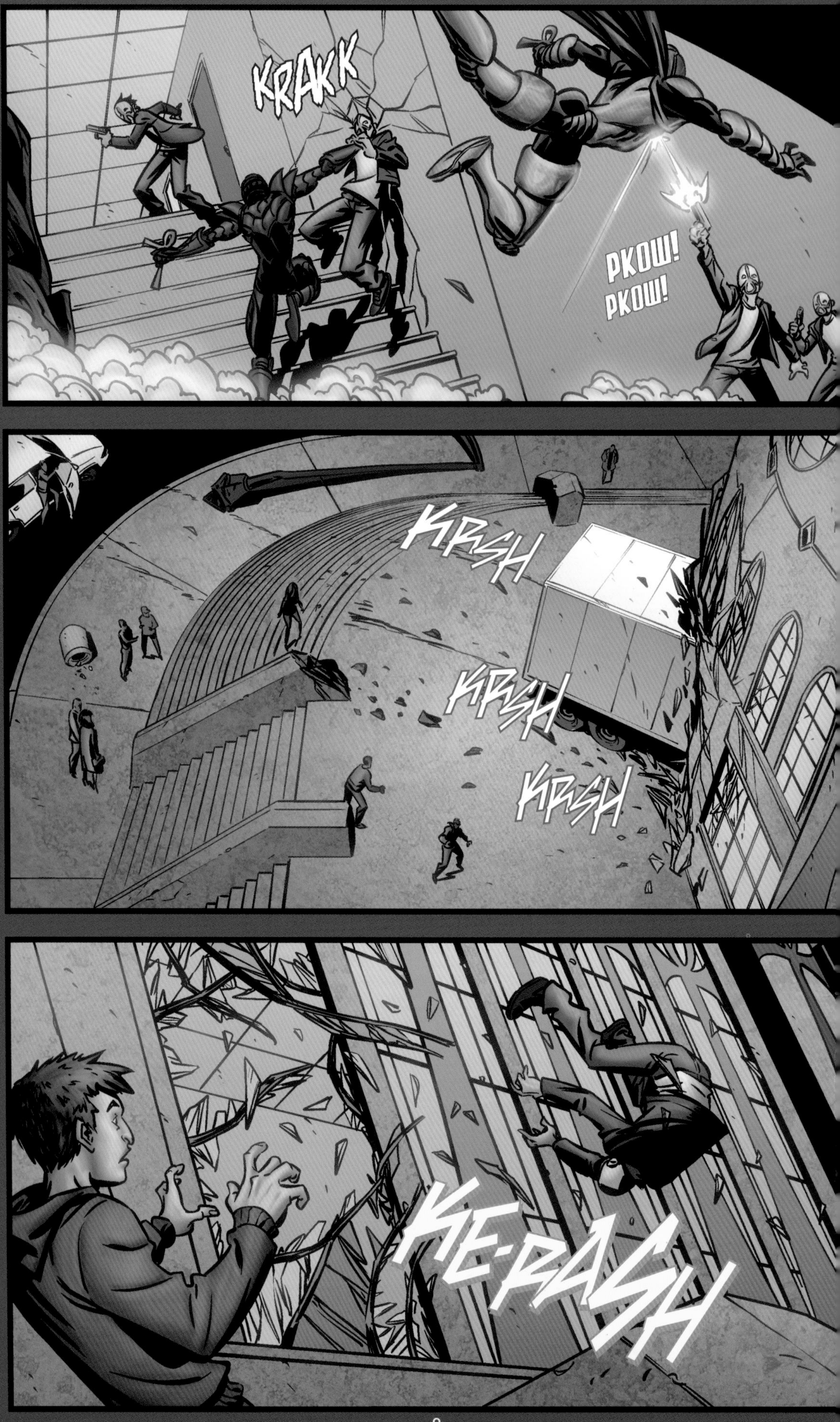
KRAKK
PKOW!
PKOW!
KRSH
KRSH
KRSH
KE-RASH

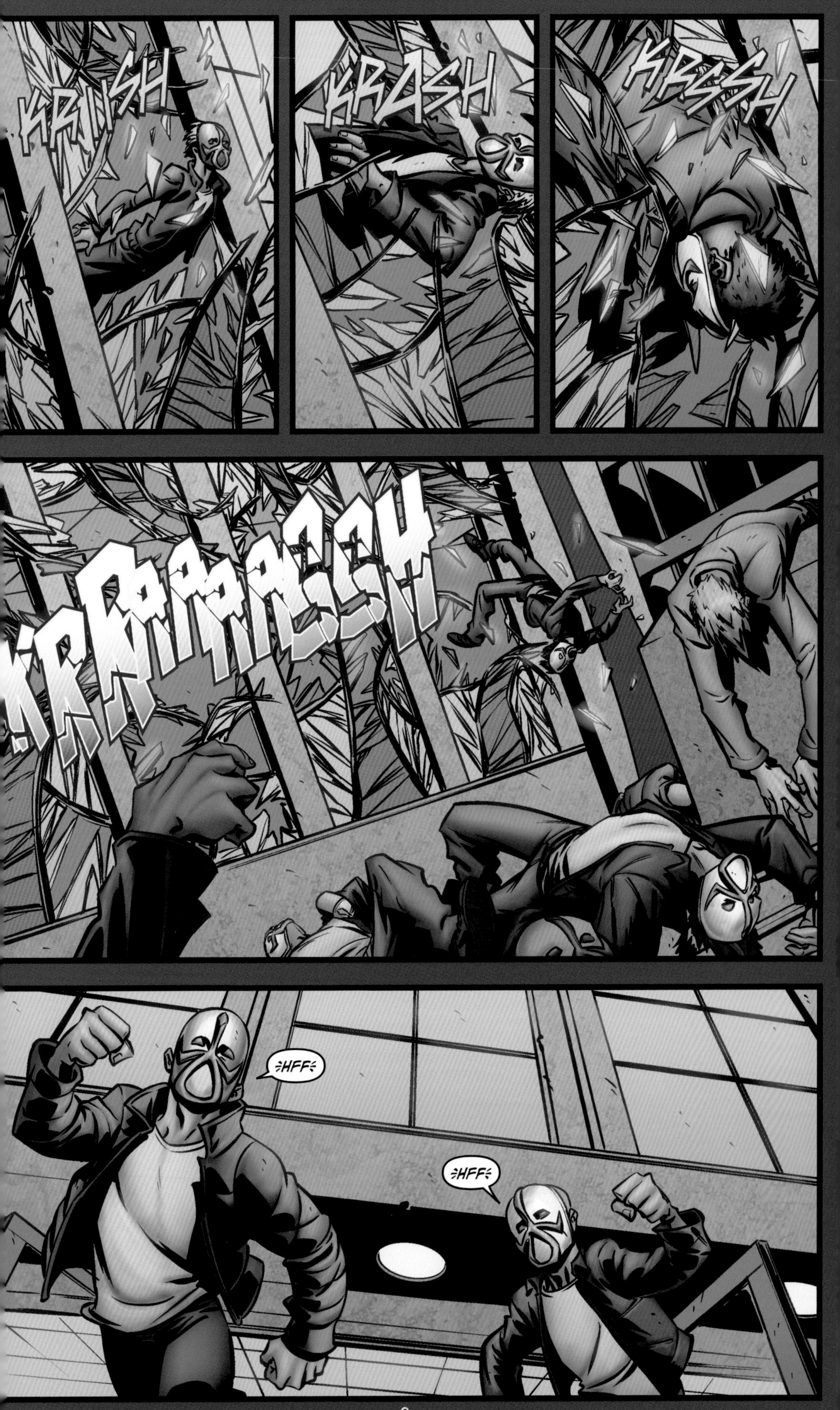
KRASH
KRASH
KRASH
KRRAAAAASSH
HFF
HFF

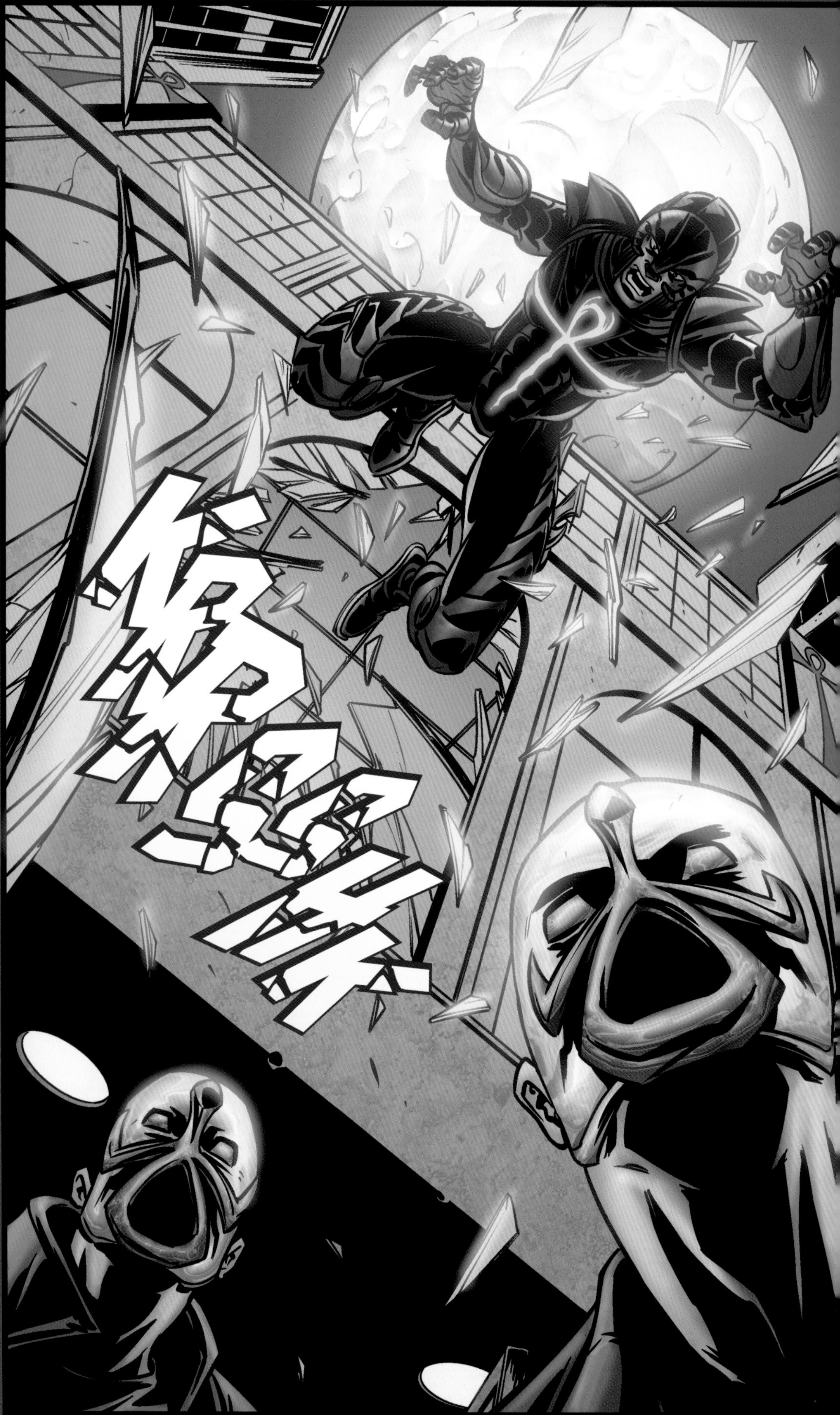

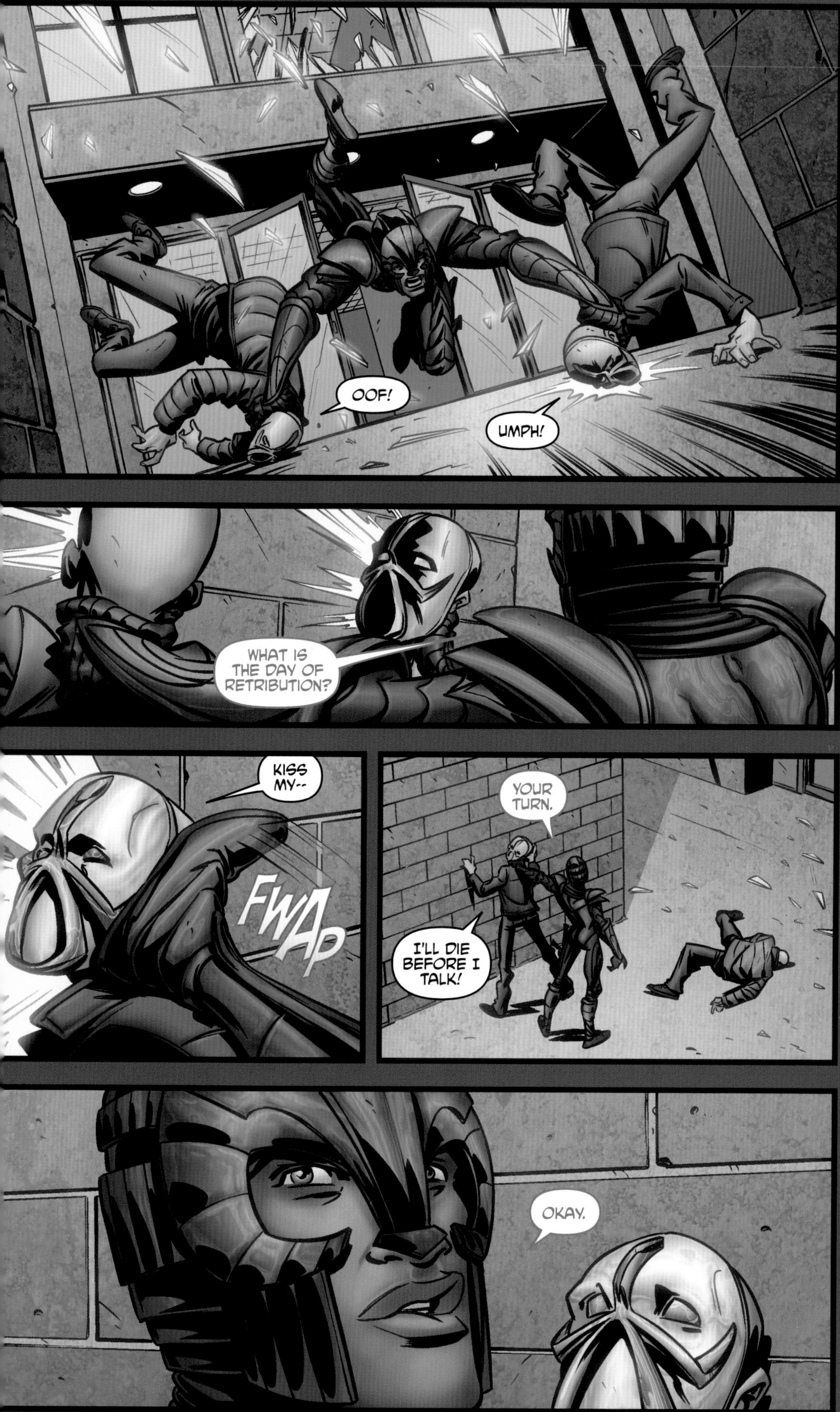
OOF!
UMPH!
WHAT IS THE DAY OF RETRIBUTION?
KISS MY--
FWAP
YOUR TURN.
I'LL DIE BEFORE I TALK!
OKAY.

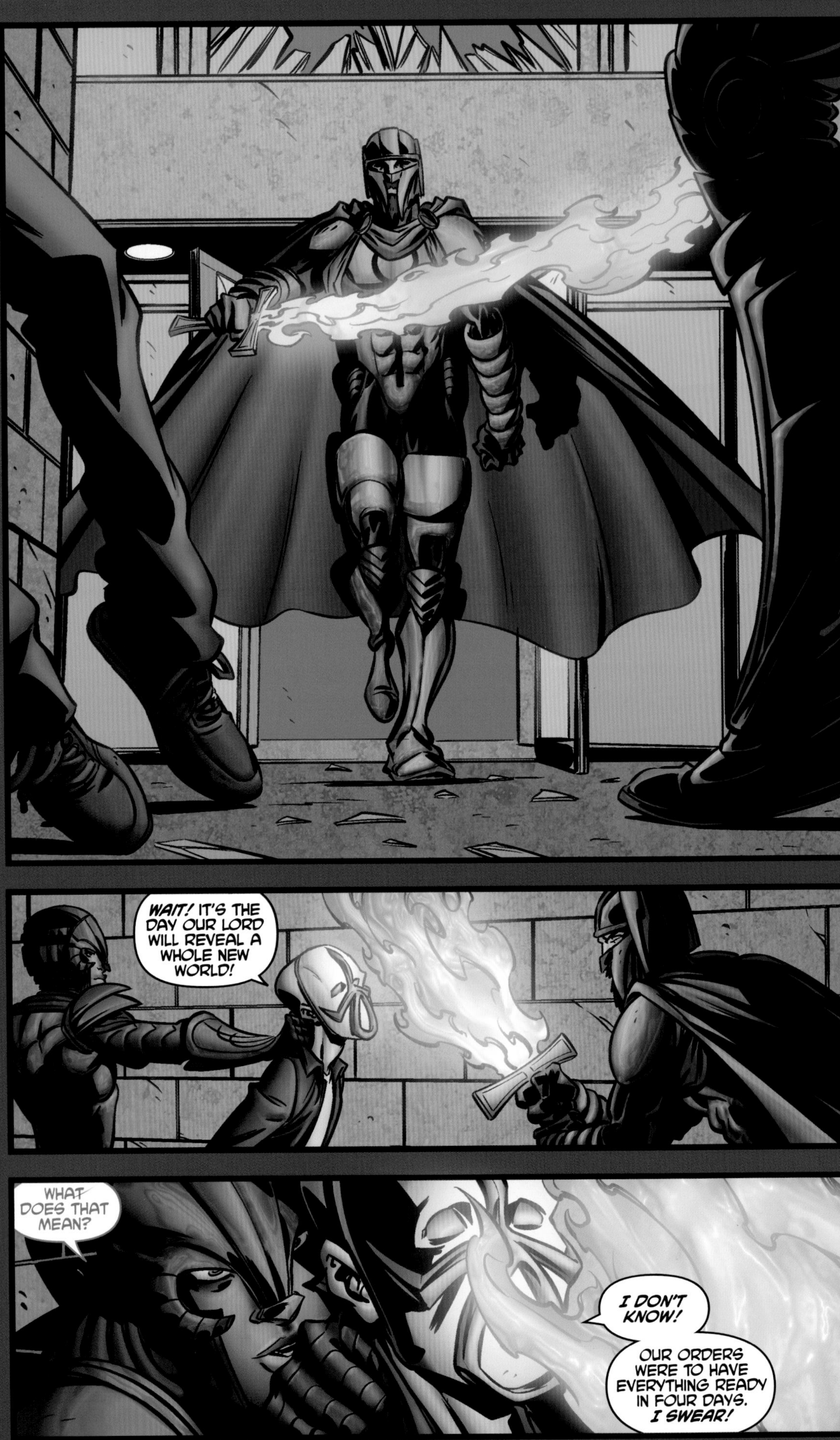
WAIT! IT'S THE DAY OUR LORD WILL REVEAL A WHOLE NEW WORLD!
WHAT DOES THAT MEAN?
I DON'T KNOW!
OUR ORDERS WERE TO HAVE EVERYTHING READY IN FOUR DAYS. I SWEAR!

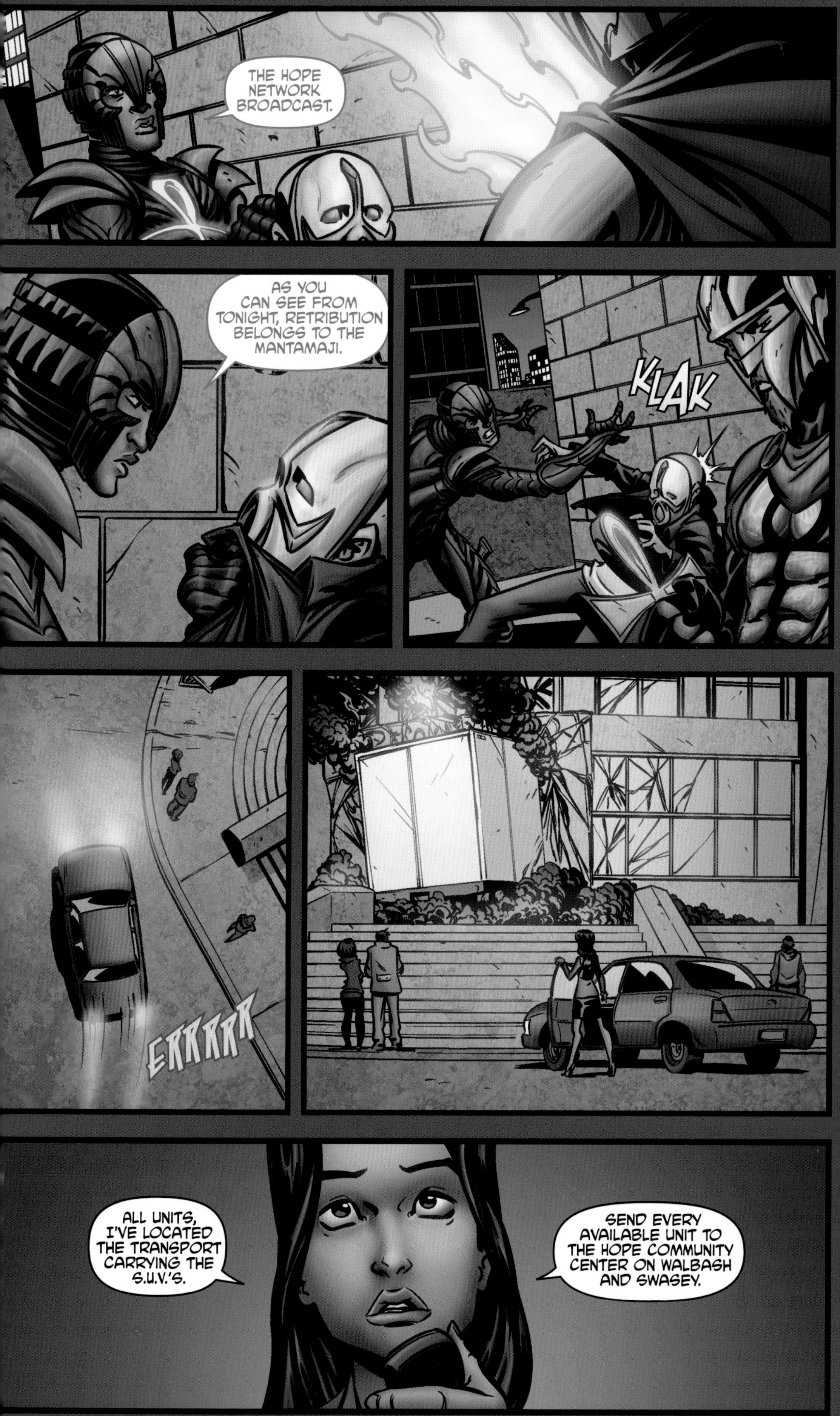
THE HOPE NETWORK BROADCAST.
AS YOU CAN SEE FROM TONIGHT, RETRIBUTION BELONGS TO THE MANTAMAJI.
KLAK
ERRRRR
ALL UNITS, I'VE LOCATED THE TRANSPORT CARRYING THE S.U.V.'S.
SEND EVERY AVAILABLE UNIT TO THE HOPE COMMUNITY CENTER ON WALBASH AND SWASEY.

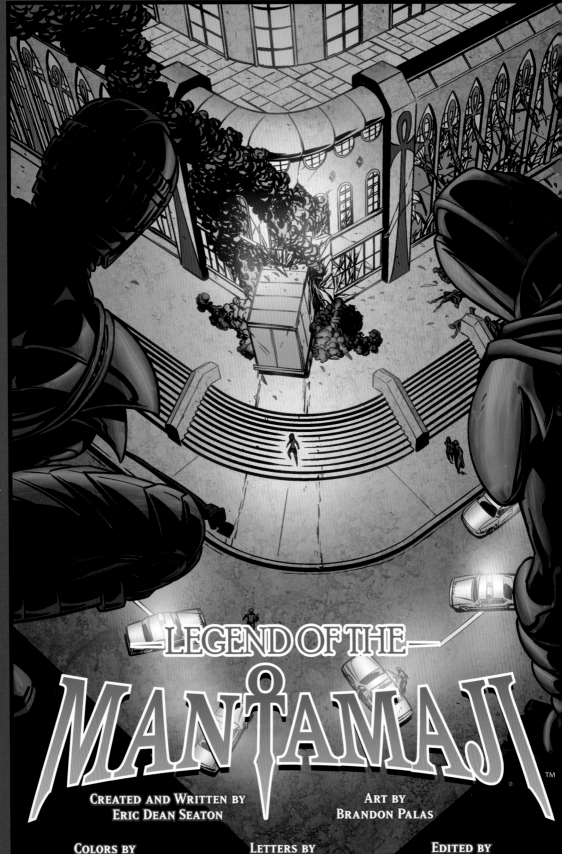

LEGEND OF THE
MANTAMAJI ™

CREATED AND WRITTEN BY
ERIC DEAN SEATON

ART BY
BRANDON PALAS

COLORS BY
ANDREW DALHOUSE

LETTERS BY
DERON BENNETT

EDITED BY
DAVID ELLIS DICKERSON

10061 Riverside Drive, Suite 296 Toluca Lake, California 91602. Legend of the Mantamaji and its related characters are ™ and
© 2014 of Nighthawk Entertainment, Inc. All rights reserved. Published by "And... Action!" Entertainment © ™ All Eyes On E, Inc.
Any similarities to persons living or dead is purely coincidental. None of the publication may be reprinted, copied or quoted
without the written consent of Nighthawk Entertainment, Inc. Printed in Korea. ISBN 978-1-930315-37-2

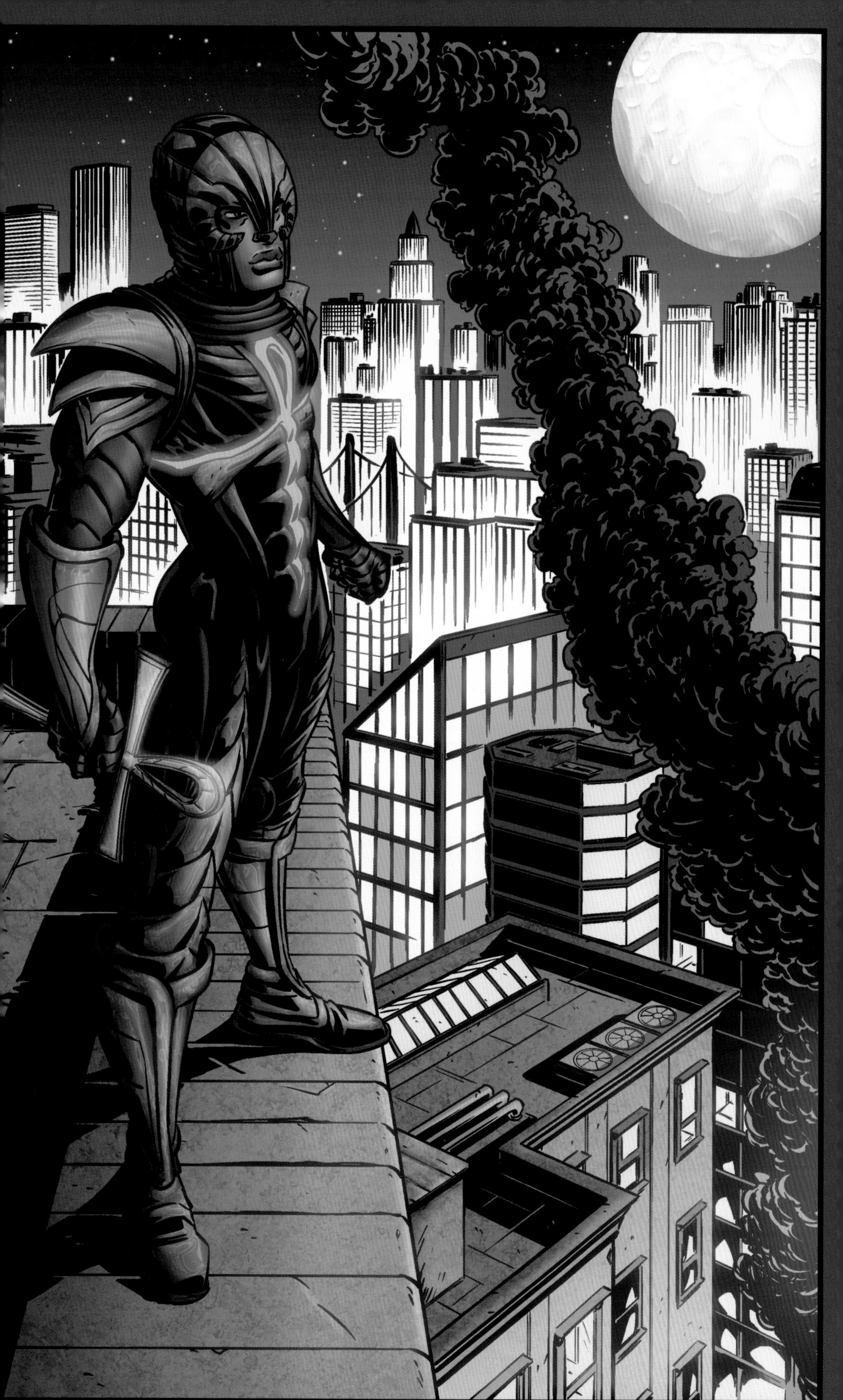

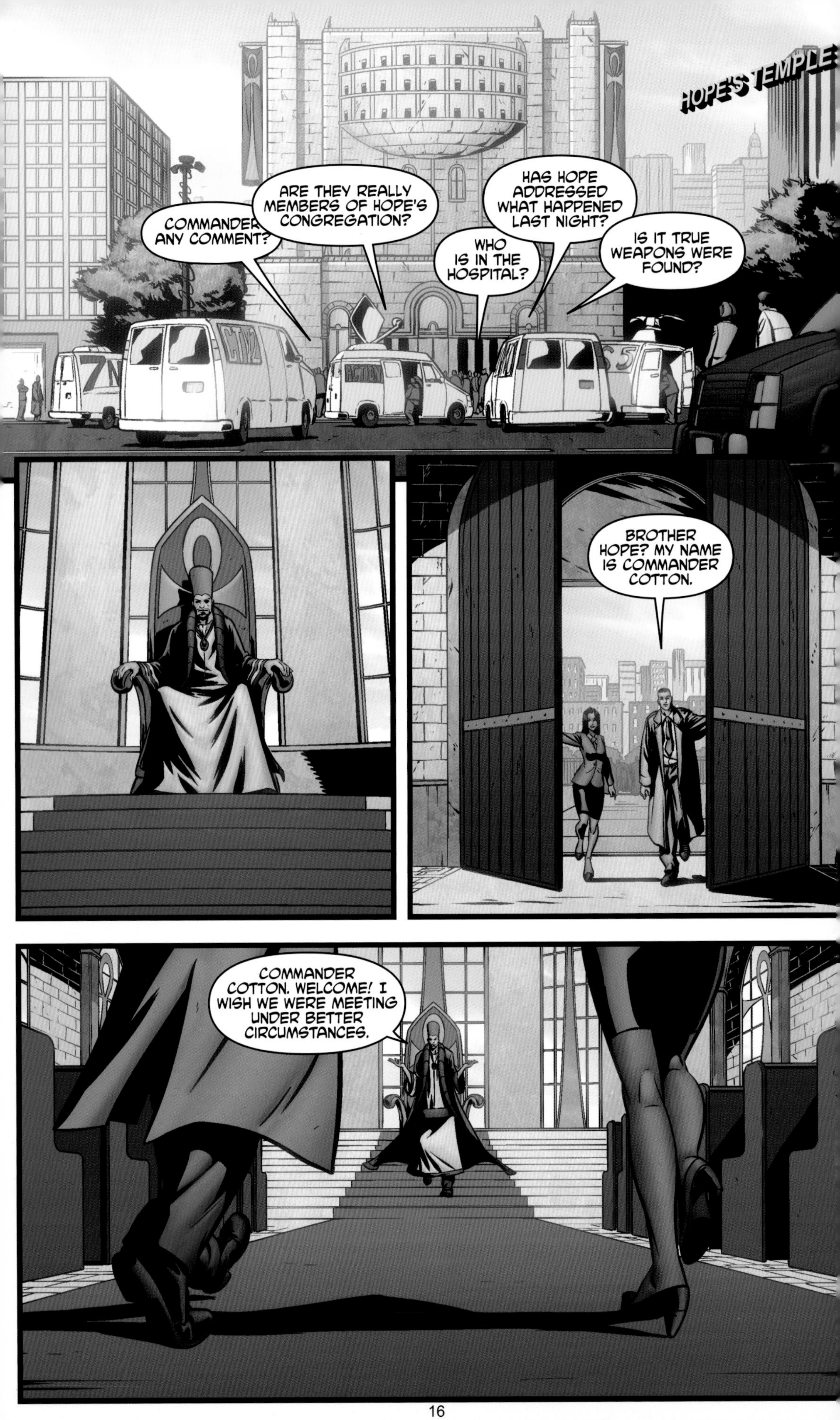
HOPE'S TEMPLE
COMMANDER, ANY COMMENT?
ARE THEY REALLY MEMBERS OF HOPE'S CONGREGATION?
WHO IS IN THE HOSPITAL?
HAS HOPE ADDRESSED WHAT HAPPENED LAST NIGHT?
IS IT TRUE WEAPONS WERE FOUND?
CTV12
7N
ACTION
BROTHER HOPE? MY NAME IS COMMANDER COTTON.
COMMANDER COTTON. WELCOME! I WISH WE WERE MEETING UNDER BETTER CIRCUMSTANCES.

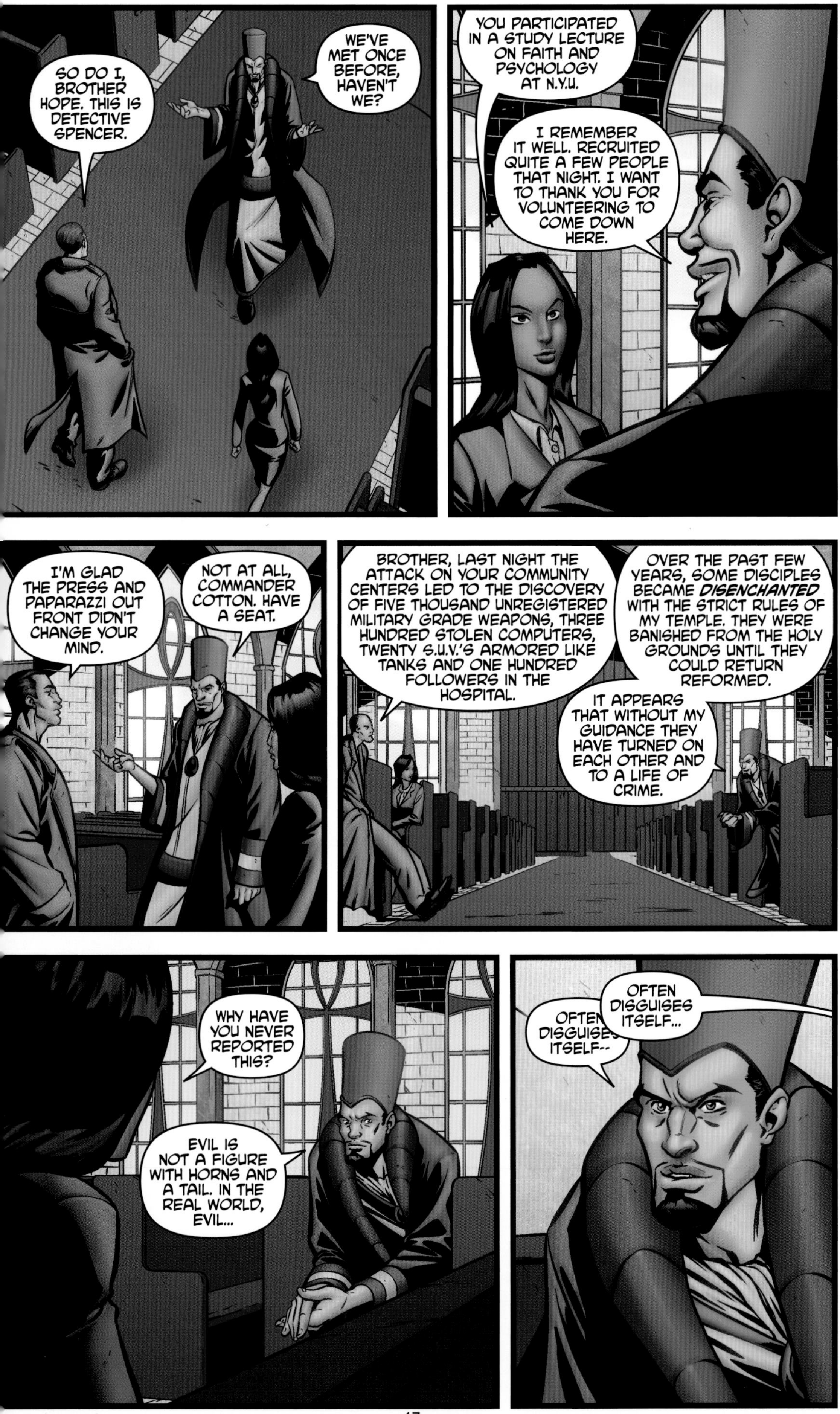
SO DO I, BROTHER HOPE. THIS IS DETECTIVE SPENCER.
WE'VE MET ONCE BEFORE, HAVEN'T WE?
YOU PARTICIPATED IN A STUDY LECTURE ON FAITH AND PSYCHOLOGY AT N.Y.U.
I REMEMBER IT WELL. RECRUITED QUITE A FEW PEOPLE THAT NIGHT. I WANT TO THANK YOU FOR VOLUNTEERING TO COME DOWN HERE.
I'M GLAD THE PRESS AND PAPARAZZI OUT FRONT DIDN'T CHANGE YOUR MIND.
NOT AT ALL, COMMANDER COTTON. HAVE A SEAT.
BROTHER, LAST NIGHT THE ATTACK ON YOUR COMMUNITY CENTERS LED TO THE DISCOVERY OF FIVE THOUSAND UNREGISTERED MILITARY GRADE WEAPONS, THREE HUNDRED STOLEN COMPUTERS, TWENTY S.U.V.'S ARMORED LIKE TANKS AND ONE HUNDRED FOLLOWERS IN THE HOSPITAL.
OVER THE PAST FEW YEARS, SOME DISCIPLES BECAME *DISENCHANTED* WITH THE STRICT RULES OF MY TEMPLE. THEY WERE BANISHED FROM THE HOLY GROUNDS UNTIL THEY COULD RETURN REFORMED.
IT APPEARS THAT WITHOUT MY GUIDANCE THEY HAVE TURNED ON EACH OTHER AND TO A LIFE OF CRIME.
WHY HAVE YOU NEVER REPORTED THIS?
EVIL IS NOT A FIGURE WITH HORNS AND A TAIL. IN THE REAL WORLD, EVIL...
OFTEN DISGUISES ITSELF...
OFTEN DISGUISES ITSELF--

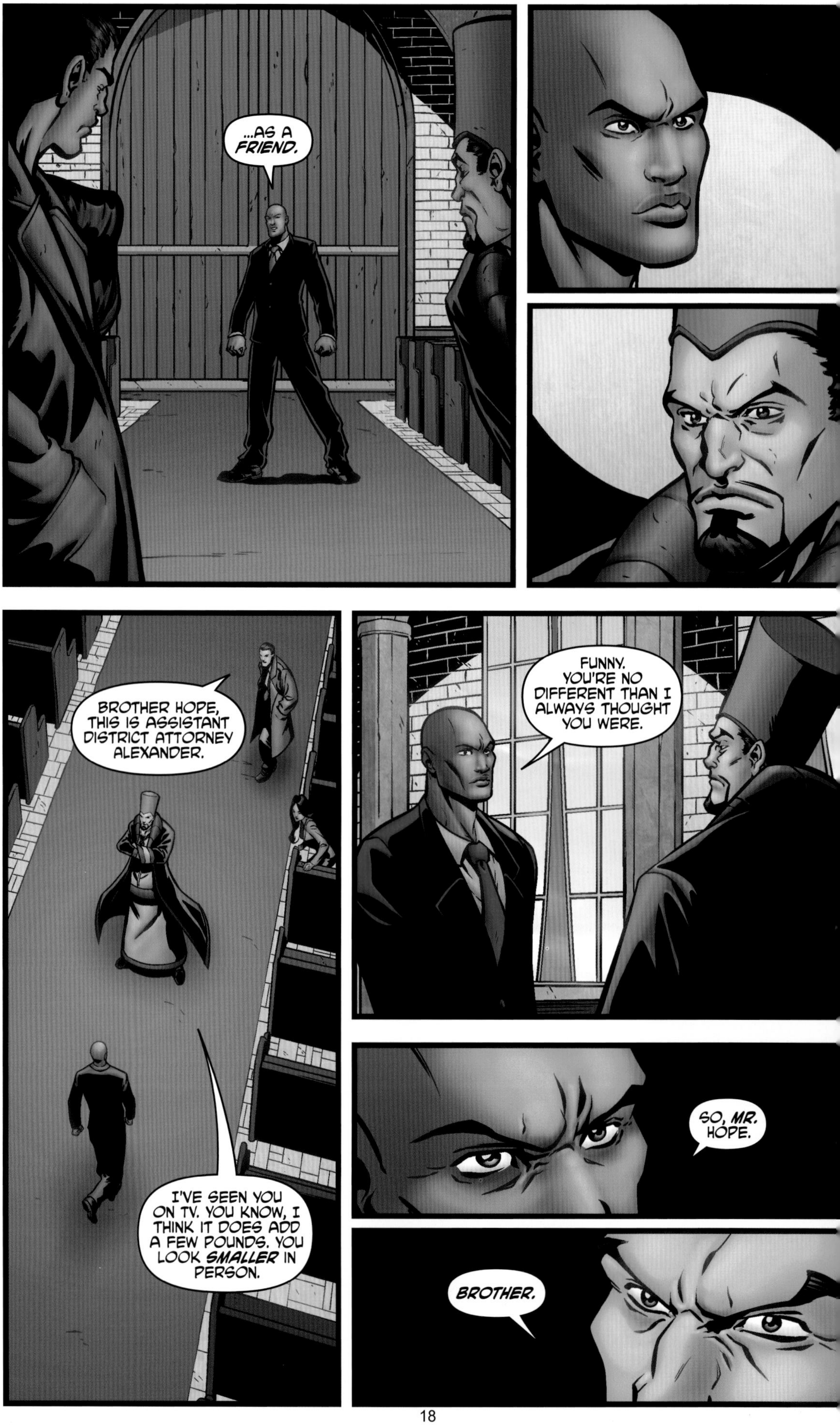
...AS A FRIEND.
BROTHER HOPE, THIS IS ASSISTANT DISTRICT ATTORNEY ALEXANDER.
I'VE SEEN YOU ON TV. YOU KNOW, I THINK IT DOES ADD A FEW POUNDS. YOU LOOK SMALLER IN PERSON.
FUNNY. YOU'RE NO DIFFERENT THAN I ALWAYS THOUGHT YOU WERE.
SO, MR. HOPE.
BROTHER.

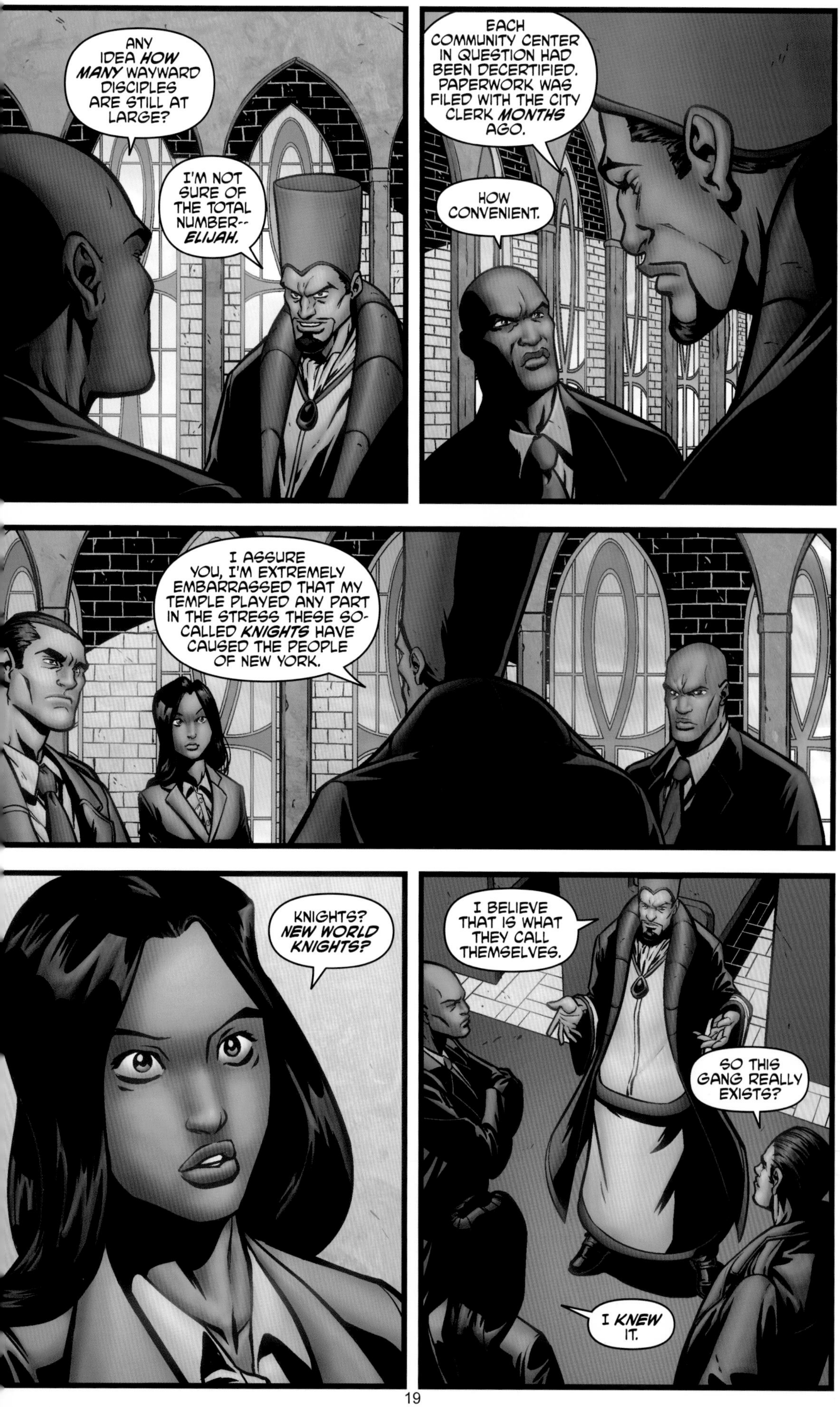
ANY IDEA *HOW MANY* WAYWARD DISCIPLES ARE STILL AT LARGE?
I'M NOT SURE OF THE TOTAL NUMBER-- *ELIJAH.*
EACH COMMUNITY CENTER IN QUESTION HAD BEEN DECERTIFIED. PAPERWORK WAS FILED WITH THE CITY CLERK *MONTHS* AGO.
HOW CONVENIENT.
I ASSURE YOU, I'M EXTREMELY EMBARRASSED THAT MY TEMPLE PLAYED ANY PART IN THE STRESS THESE SO-CALLED *KNIGHTS* HAVE CAUSED THE PEOPLE OF NEW YORK.
KNIGHTS? *NEW WORLD KNIGHTS?*
I BELIEVE THAT IS WHAT THEY CALL THEMSELVES.
SO THIS GANG REALLY EXISTS?
I *KNEW* IT.

YOUR *KNIGHTS* HAVE BEEN INVOLVED IN *TWENTY THREE* MAJOR FELONY CASES IN THE LAST EIGHTEEN MONTHS.

THEY ARE NOT *MY KNIGHTS.* HAD I KNOWN THIS EVIL WAS MANIFESTING I WOULD HAVE ACTED IMMEDIATELY.

BUT MY POWER LIES IN *FAITH,* NOT VIOLENCE.

THEN PERHAPS YOUR *FAITH* IS *LACKING*--MR. HOPE.

FAITH IS THE EXTENSION OF HOPE INTO THE REALM OF THE UNKNOWABLE.

IT'S, IN A SENSE, THE BEGINNING OF A MAN'S SOUL. I ASSURE YOU, MY SOUL'S INTACT.

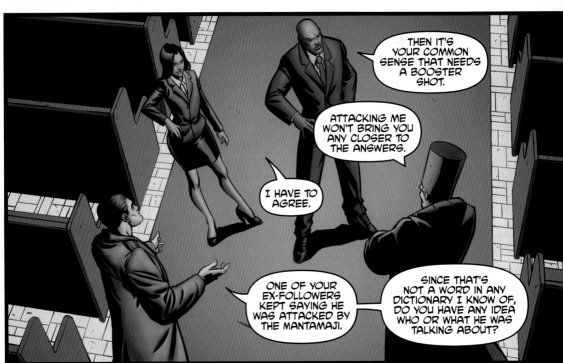

THEN IT'S YOUR COMMON SENSE THAT NEEDS A BOOSTER SHOT.

ATTACKING ME WON'T BRING YOU ANY CLOSER TO THE ANSWERS.

I HAVE TO AGREE.

ONE OF YOUR EX-FOLLOWERS KEPT SAYING HE WAS ATTACKED BY THE MANTAMAJI.

SINCE THAT'S NOT A WORD IN ANY DICTIONARY I KNOW OF, DO YOU HAVE ANY IDEA WHO OR WHAT HE WAS TALKING ABOUT?

THAT IS NOT A NAME I AM FAMILIAR WITH. I'M EVERY BIT IN THE DARK AS YOU ARE.

I'LL REMEMBER TO TELL THAT TO ANYONE HURT BY THESE NEW WORLD KNIGHTS. THAT WOULD INCLUDE ALL THE PEOPLE THAT ARE IN JAIL BASED ON CRIMES THE KNIGHTS MAY HAVE COMMITTED.

THEY HAVE MY CONDOLENCES. ALLOW ME TO OFFER COUNSELING.

THEIR GRIEF DOESN'T NEED *COUNSELING*. RETRIBUTION IS MORE IN ORDER.

A RECKONING? THAT TOO MAY COME.

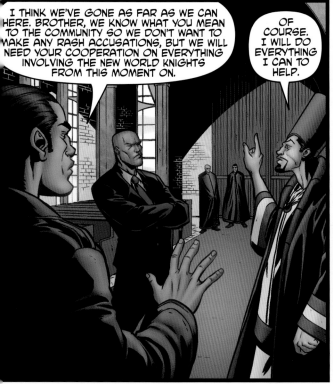

I THINK WE'VE GONE AS FAR AS WE CAN HERE. BROTHER, WE KNOW WHAT YOU MEAN TO THE COMMUNITY SO WE DON'T WANT TO MAKE ANY RASH ACCUSATIONS, BUT WE WILL NEED YOUR COOPERATION ON EVERYTHING INVOLVING THE NEW WORLD KNIGHTS FROM THIS MOMENT ON.

OF COURSE. I WILL DO EVERYTHING I CAN TO HELP.

I WILL START BY SPEAKING TO THE PRESS. COMMANDER, WILL YOU JOIN ME? MAYBE MY WORDS CAN HELP BRING ORDER.

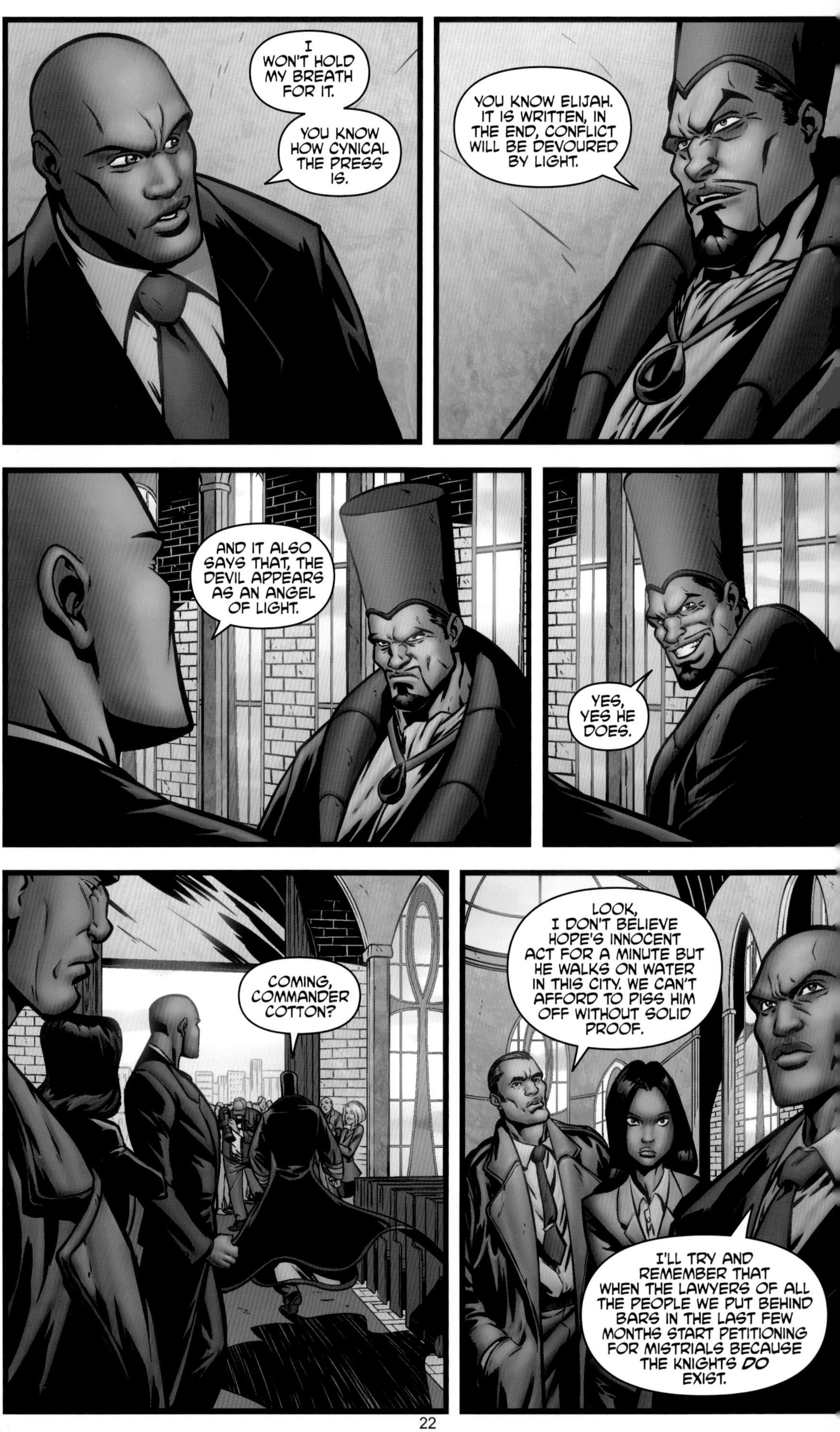
I WON'T HOLD MY BREATH FOR IT.
YOU KNOW HOW CYNICAL THE PRESS IS.
YOU KNOW ELIJAH. IT IS WRITTEN, IN THE END, CONFLICT WILL BE DEVOURED BY LIGHT.
AND IT ALSO SAYS THAT, THE DEVIL APPEARS AS AN ANGEL OF LIGHT.
YES, YES HE DOES.
COMING, COMMANDER COTTON?
LOOK, I DON'T BELIEVE HOPE'S INNOCENT ACT FOR A MINUTE BUT HE WALKS ON WATER IN THIS CITY. WE CAN'T AFFORD TO PISS HIM OFF WITHOUT SOLID PROOF.
I'LL TRY AND REMEMBER THAT WHEN THE LAWYERS OF ALL THE PEOPLE WE PUT BEHIND BARS IN THE LAST FEW MONTHS START PETITIONING FOR MISTRIALS BECAUSE THE KNIGHTS *DO* EXIST.

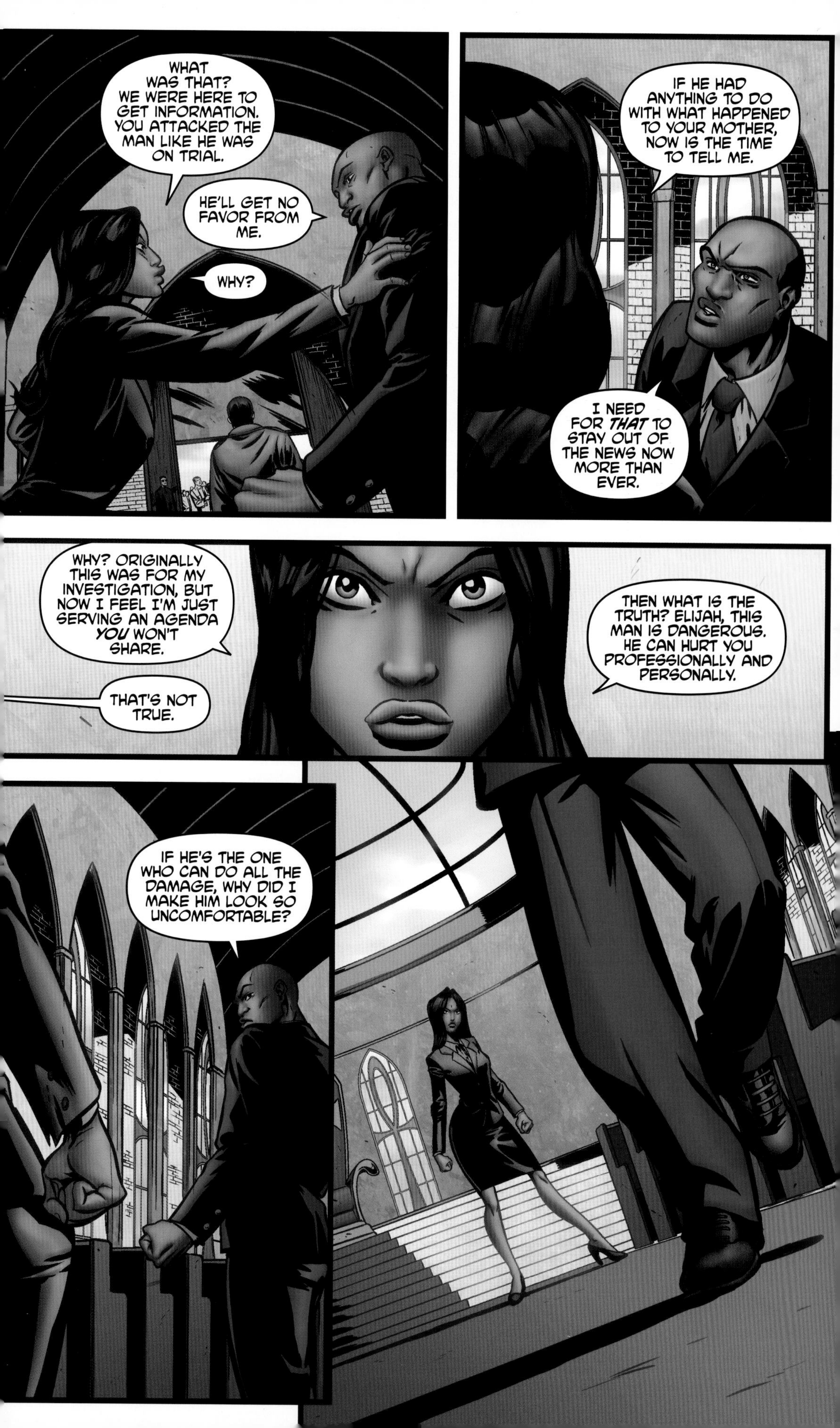
WHAT WAS THAT? WE WERE HERE TO GET INFORMATION. YOU ATTACKED THE MAN LIKE HE WAS ON TRIAL.
HE'LL GET NO FAVOR FROM ME.
WHY?
IF HE HAD ANYTHING TO DO WITH WHAT HAPPENED TO YOUR MOTHER, NOW IS THE TIME TO TELL ME.
I NEED FOR THAT TO STAY OUT OF THE NEWS NOW MORE THAN EVER.
WHY? ORIGINALLY THIS WAS FOR MY INVESTIGATION, BUT NOW I FEEL I'M JUST SERVING AN AGENDA YOU WON'T SHARE.
THAT'S NOT TRUE.
THEN WHAT IS THE TRUTH? ELIJAH, THIS MAN IS DANGEROUS. HE CAN HURT YOU PROFESSIONALLY AND PERSONALLY.
IF HE'S THE ONE WHO CAN DO ALL THE DAMAGE, WHY DID I MAKE HIM LOOK SO UNCOMFORTABLE?

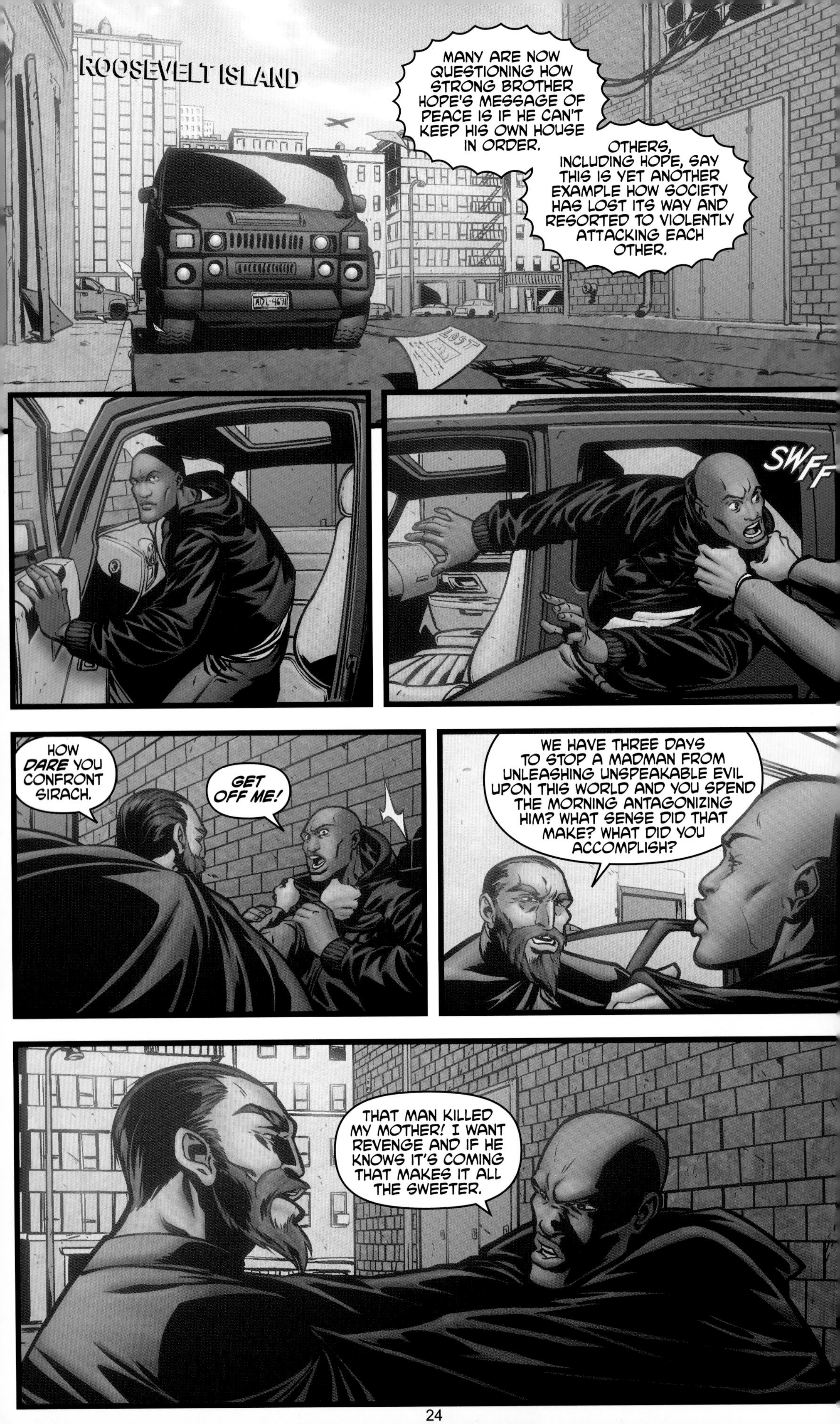
ROOSEVELT ISLAND
MANY ARE NOW QUESTIONING HOW STRONG BROTHER HOPE'S MESSAGE OF PEACE IS IF HE CAN'T KEEP HIS OWN HOUSE IN ORDER.
OTHERS, INCLUDING HOPE, SAY THIS IS YET ANOTHER EXAMPLE HOW SOCIETY HAS LOST ITS WAY AND RESORTED TO VIOLENTLY ATTACKING EACH OTHER.
LOST
SWFF
HOW *DARE* YOU CONFRONT SIRACH.
GET OFF ME!
WE HAVE THREE DAYS TO STOP A MADMAN FROM UNLEASHING UNSPEAKABLE EVIL UPON THIS WORLD AND YOU SPEND THE MORNING ANTAGONIZING HIM? WHAT SENSE DID THAT MAKE? WHAT DID YOU ACCOMPLISH?
THAT MAN KILLED MY MOTHER! I WANT REVENGE AND IF HE KNOWS IT'S COMING THAT MAKES IT ALL THE SWEETER.

YOU MUST UNDERSTAND, THE OBSTACLES IN EVERY MAN'S PATH ARE TO RELEASE HIS PERSONAL GOALS AND TAKE HOLD OF HIS GREATER DESTINY.

YOU CAN RECITE ALL THE PHILOSOPHICAL BABBLE YOU WANT, BUT THIS IS ABOUT *REVENGE.* THE MOMENT I HAVE IT, I'M *DONE.*

DO YOU THINK JUST BECAUSE I OPENED YOUR MIND YOU ARE SOME *INDESTRUCTIBLE FIGHTING MACHINE?*

YOUR FATHER WOULD NEVER BE SO PUGNACIOUS.

MY FATHER? I DON'T KNOW THE MAN. HE'S JUST A MYTH. THE PERFECT HERO FROM A FAIRY TALE. I CAN'T BE THAT.

CANDOR WAS FAR FROM PERFECT BUT HE ALWAYS TRIED TO DO THE RIGHT THING.

AND SO DO I.

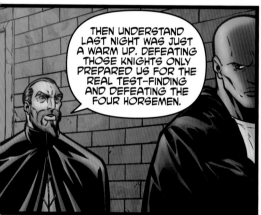

THEN UNDERSTAND LAST NIGHT WAS JUST A WARM UP. DEFEATING THOSE KNIGHTS ONLY PREPARED US FOR THE REAL TEST-FINDING AND DEFEATING THE FOUR HORSEMEN.

WHO ARE THE FOUR HORSEMEN?

THREE THOUSAND YEARS AGO, IN ORDER TO EXTEND HIS POWER-SINCE HE COULDN'T BE EVERYWHERE-SIRACH SHARED HIS GREATEST ABILITIES WITH FOUR ESPECIALLY DEVOUT FOLLOWERS.

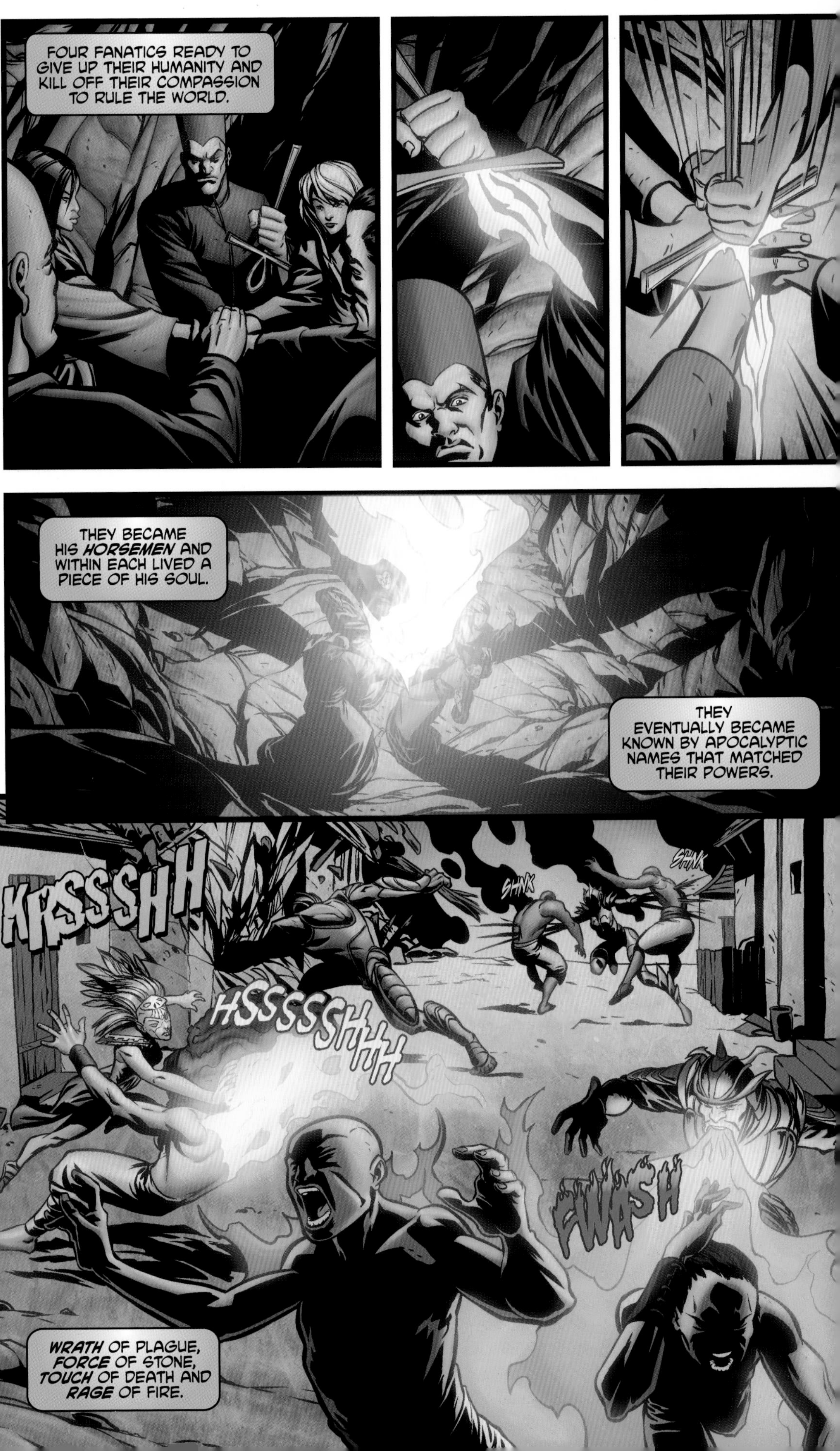
FOUR FANATICS READY TO GIVE UP THEIR HUMANITY AND KILL OFF THEIR COMPASSION TO RULE THE WORLD.
THEY BECAME HIS *HORSEMEN* AND WITHIN EACH LIVED A PIECE OF HIS SOUL.
THEY EVENTUALLY BECAME KNOWN BY APOCALYPTIC NAMES THAT MATCHED THEIR POWERS.
KRSSSHH
SHNK
SHNK
HSSSSSHHH
FWASH
WRATH OF PLAGUE, *FORCE* OF STONE, *TOUCH* OF DEATH AND *RAGE* OF FIRE.

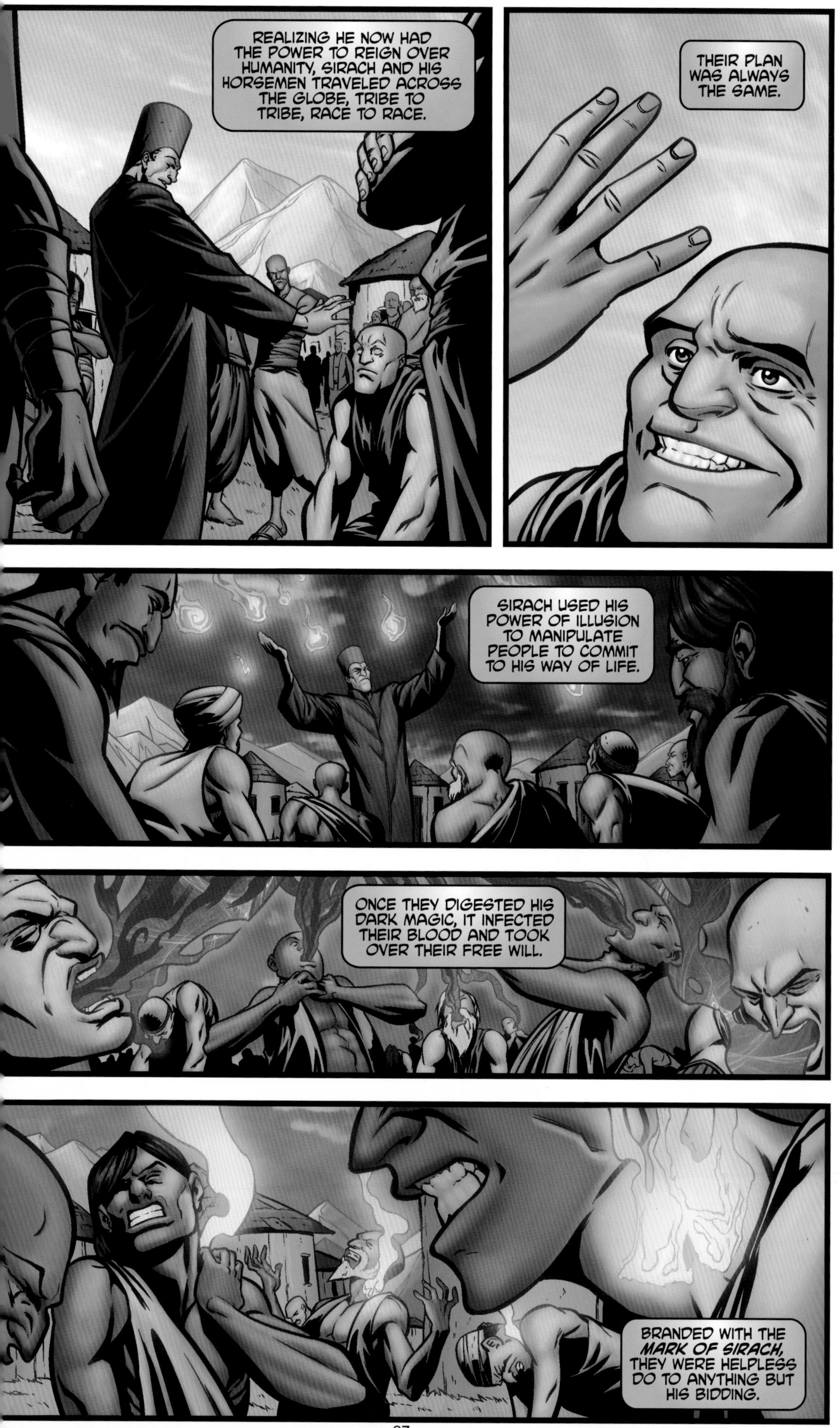
REALIZING HE NOW HAD THE POWER TO REIGN OVER HUMANITY, SIRACH AND HIS HORSEMEN TRAVELED ACROSS THE GLOBE, TRIBE TO TRIBE, RACE TO RACE.
THEIR PLAN WAS ALWAYS THE SAME.
SIRACH USED HIS POWER OF ILLUSION TO MANIPULATE PEOPLE TO COMMIT TO HIS WAY OF LIFE.
ONCE THEY DIGESTED HIS DARK MAGIC, IT INFECTED THEIR BLOOD AND TOOK OVER THEIR FREE WILL.
BRANDED WITH THE *MARK OF SIRACH,* THEY WERE HELPLESS DO TO ANYTHING BUT HIS BIDDING.

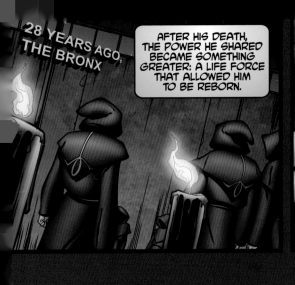

28 YEARS AGO, THE BRONX

AFTER HIS DEATH, THE POWER HE SHARED BECAME SOMETHING GREATER: A LIFE FORCE THAT ALLOWED HIM TO BE REBORN.

THE ORIGINAL HORSEMEN DIED IN THE GREAT WAR, BUT SIRACH'S DARK MAGIC LIVED ON.

WE COMMIT OUR SOULS TO YOU, RISE UP AND BE MADE WHOLE.

PASSED DOWN FROM PARENT TO CHILD, GENERATION TO GENERATION, IN THE BLOOD OF THEIR DESCENDANTS.

WE COMMIT OUR SOULS TO YOU, RISE UP AND BE MADE WHOLE.

WE COMMIT OUR SOULS TO YOU, RISE UP AND BE MADE WHOLE.

SIRACH!

SIRACH!

SIRACH!

SPLOOSH

SIRACH!

SIRACH!

SIRACH!

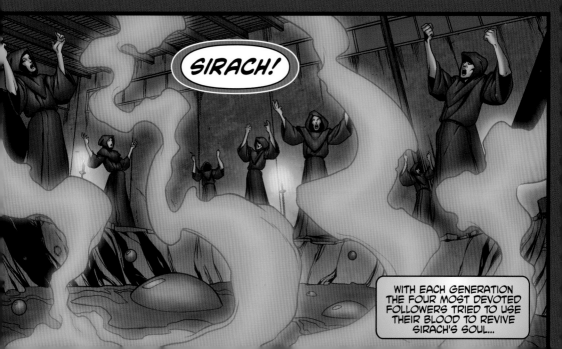

SIRACH!

WITH EACH GENERATION THE FOUR MOST DEVOTED FOLLOWERS TRIED TO USE THEIR BLOOD TO REVIVE SIRACH'S SOUL...

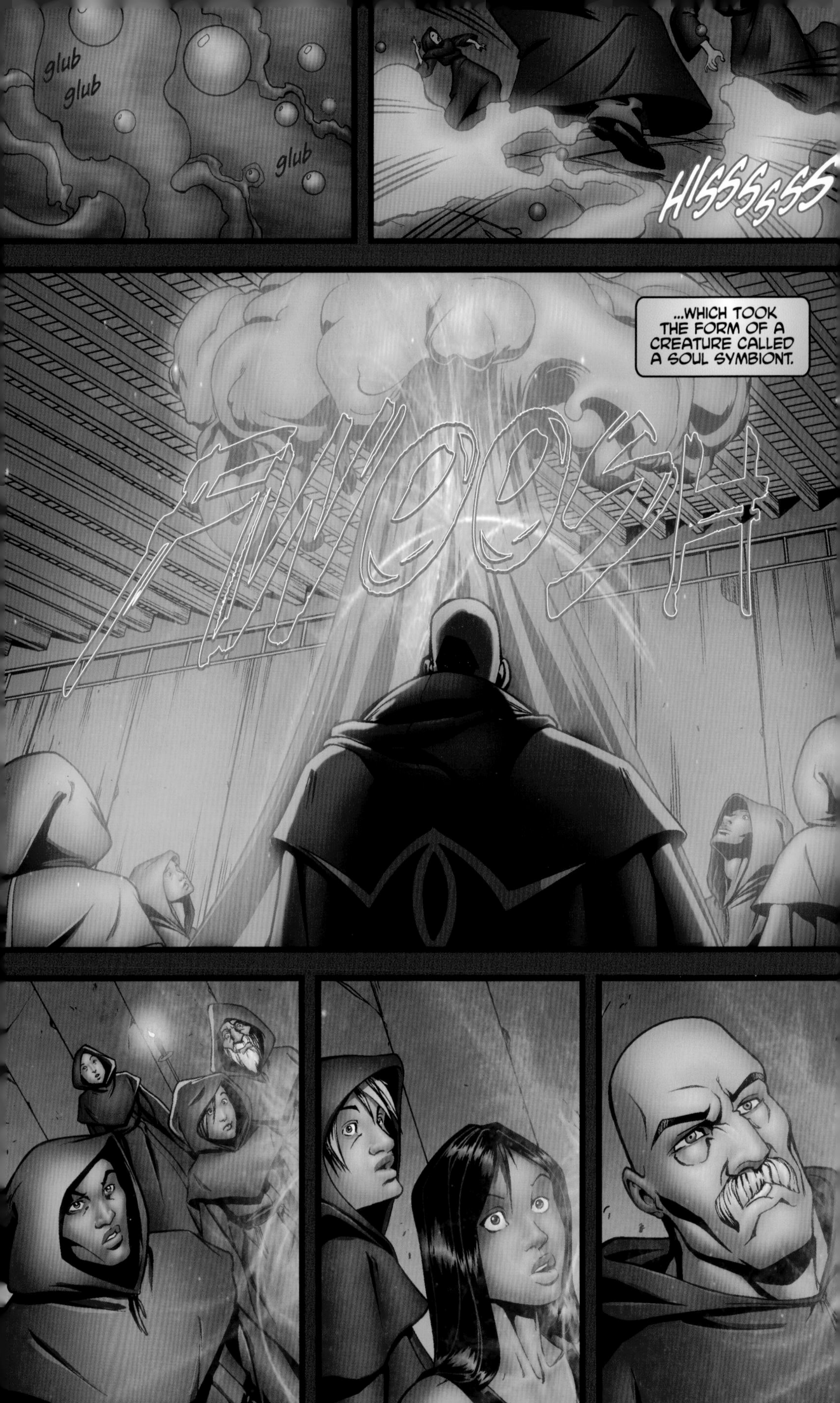
glub
glub
glub
HISSSSSS
...WHICH TOOK THE FORM OF A CREATURE CALLED A SOUL SYMBIONT.
FWOOSH

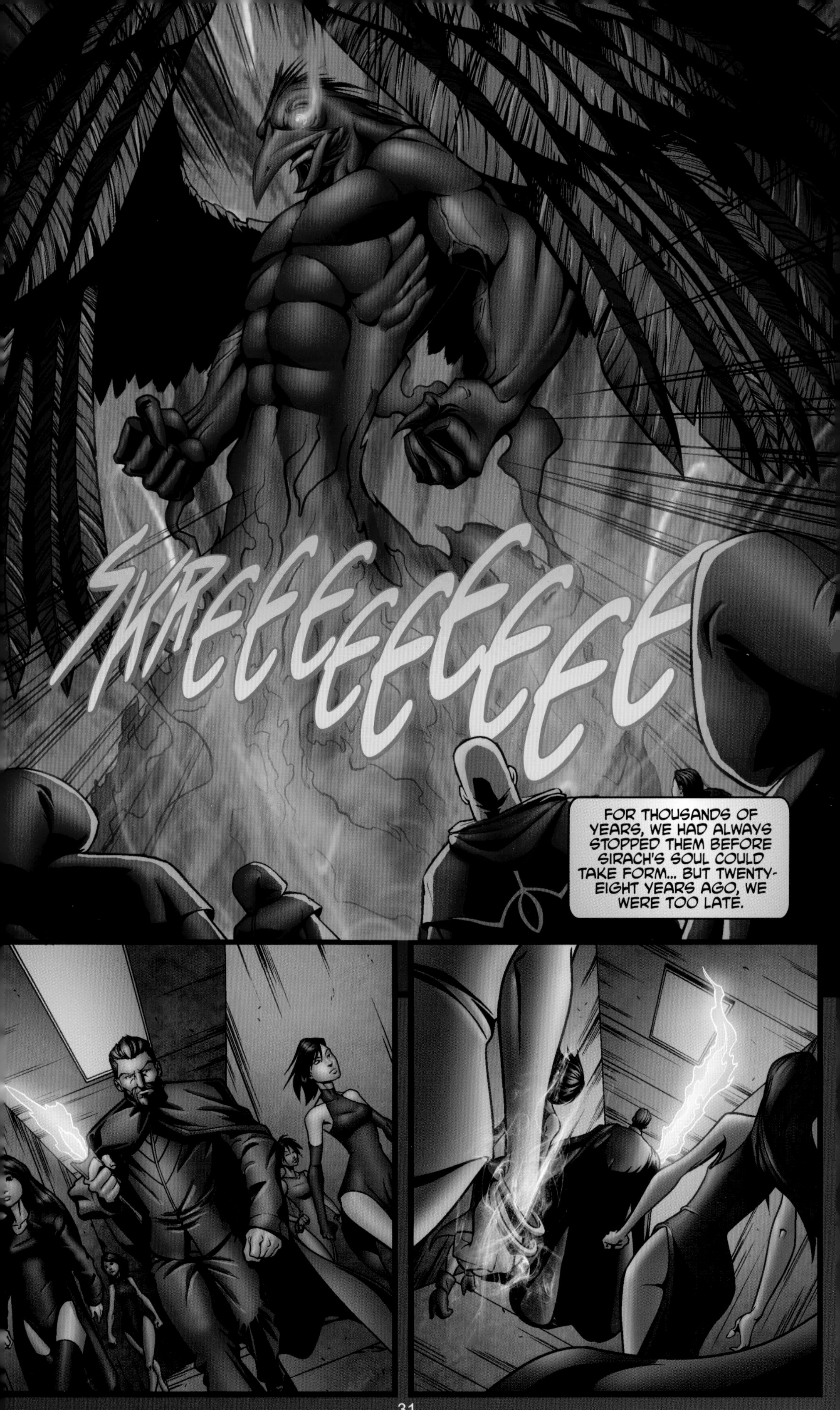
SKREEEEEEEEEE
FOR THOUSANDS OF YEARS, WE HAD ALWAYS STOPPED THEM BEFORE SIRACH'S SOUL COULD TAKE FORM... BUT TWENTY-EIGHT YEARS AGO, WE WERE TOO LATE.

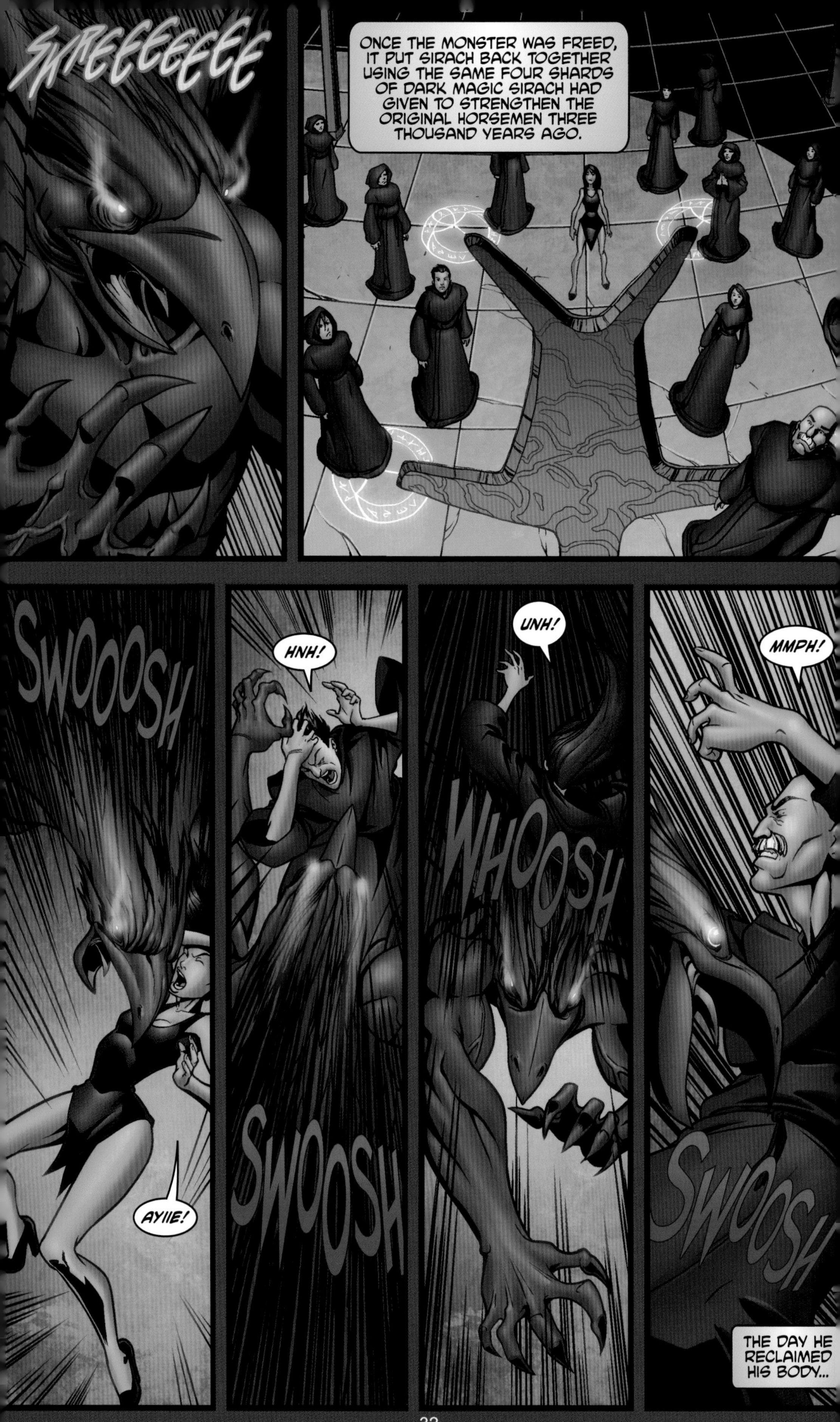
SKREEEEEEEE
ONCE THE MONSTER WAS FREED, IT PUT SIRACH BACK TOGETHER USING THE SAME FOUR SHARDS OF DARK MAGIC SIRACH HAD GIVEN TO STRENGTHEN THE ORIGINAL HORSEMEN THREE THOUSAND YEARS AGO.
SWOOOSH
AYIIE!
HNH!
SWOOSH
UNH!
WHOOSH
MMPH!
SWOOSH
THE DAY HE RECLAIMED HIS BODY...

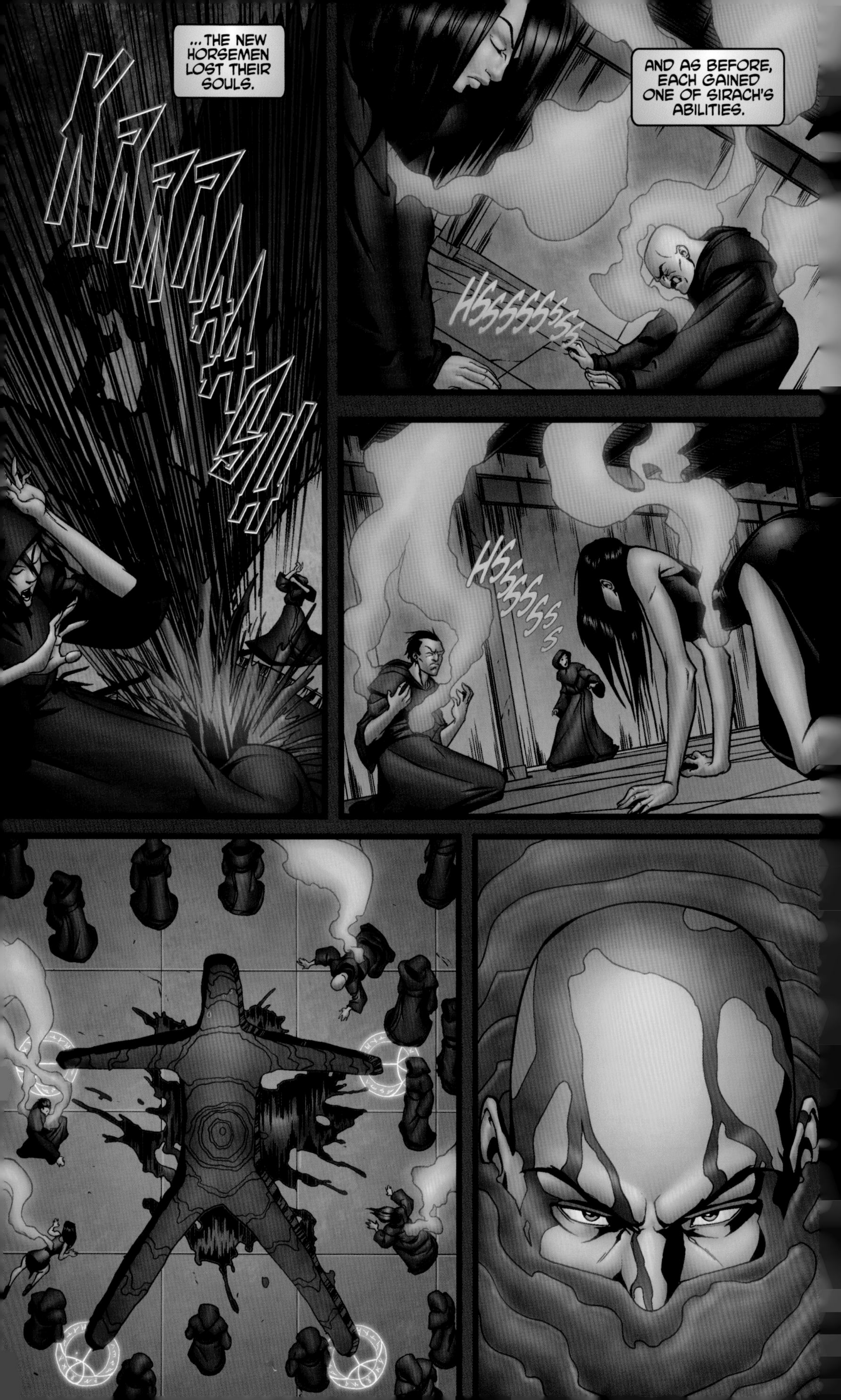
...THE NEW HORSEMEN LOST THEIR SOULS.
AND AS BEFORE, EACH GAINED ONE OF SIRACH'S ABILITIES.

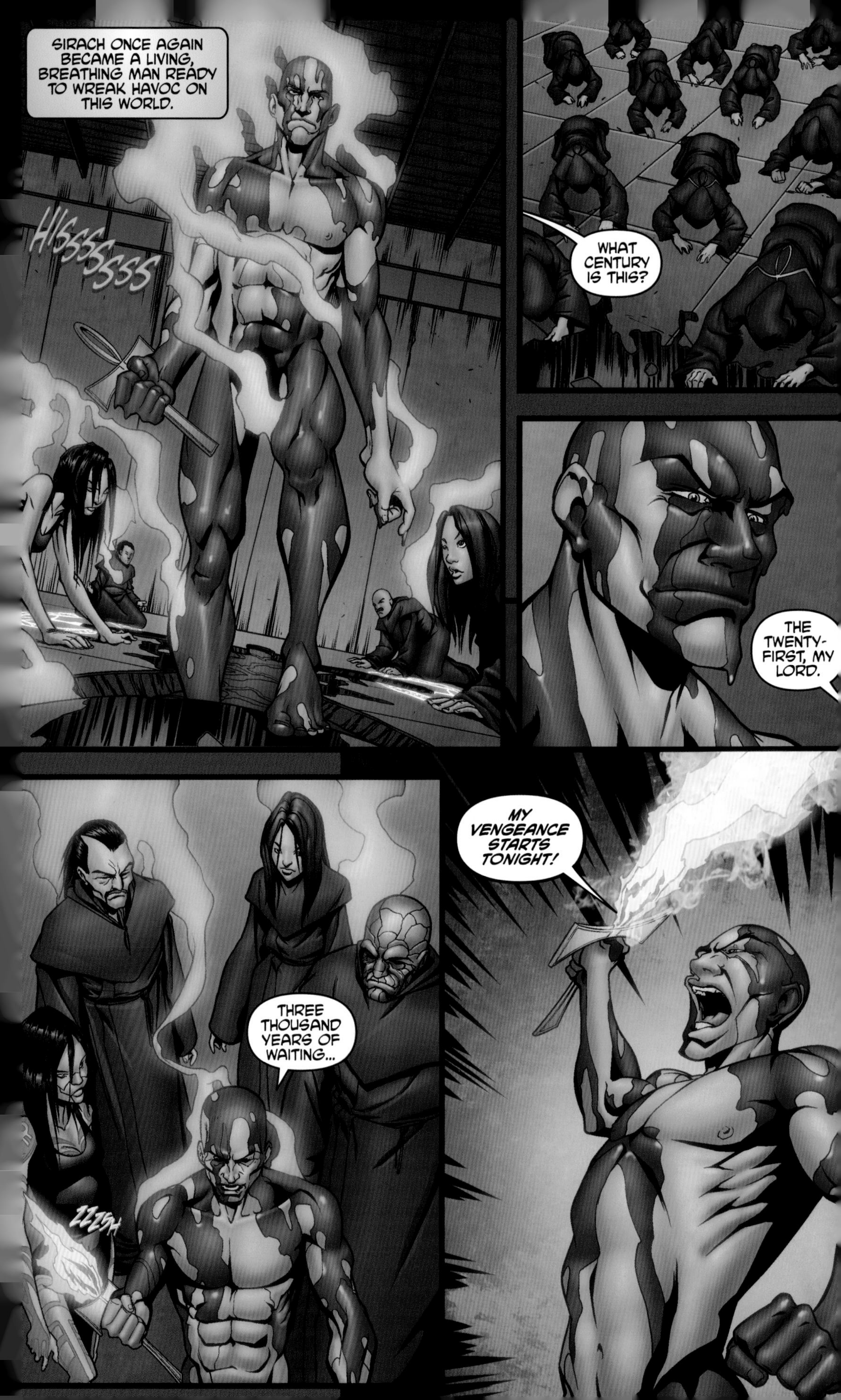
SIRACH ONCE AGAIN BECAME A LIVING, BREATHING MAN READY TO WREAK HAVOC ON THIS WORLD.
HISSSSSSS
WHAT CENTURY IS THIS?
THE TWENTY-FIRST, MY LORD.
THREE THOUSAND YEARS OF WAITING...
ZZZSH
MY VENGEANCE STARTS TONIGHT!

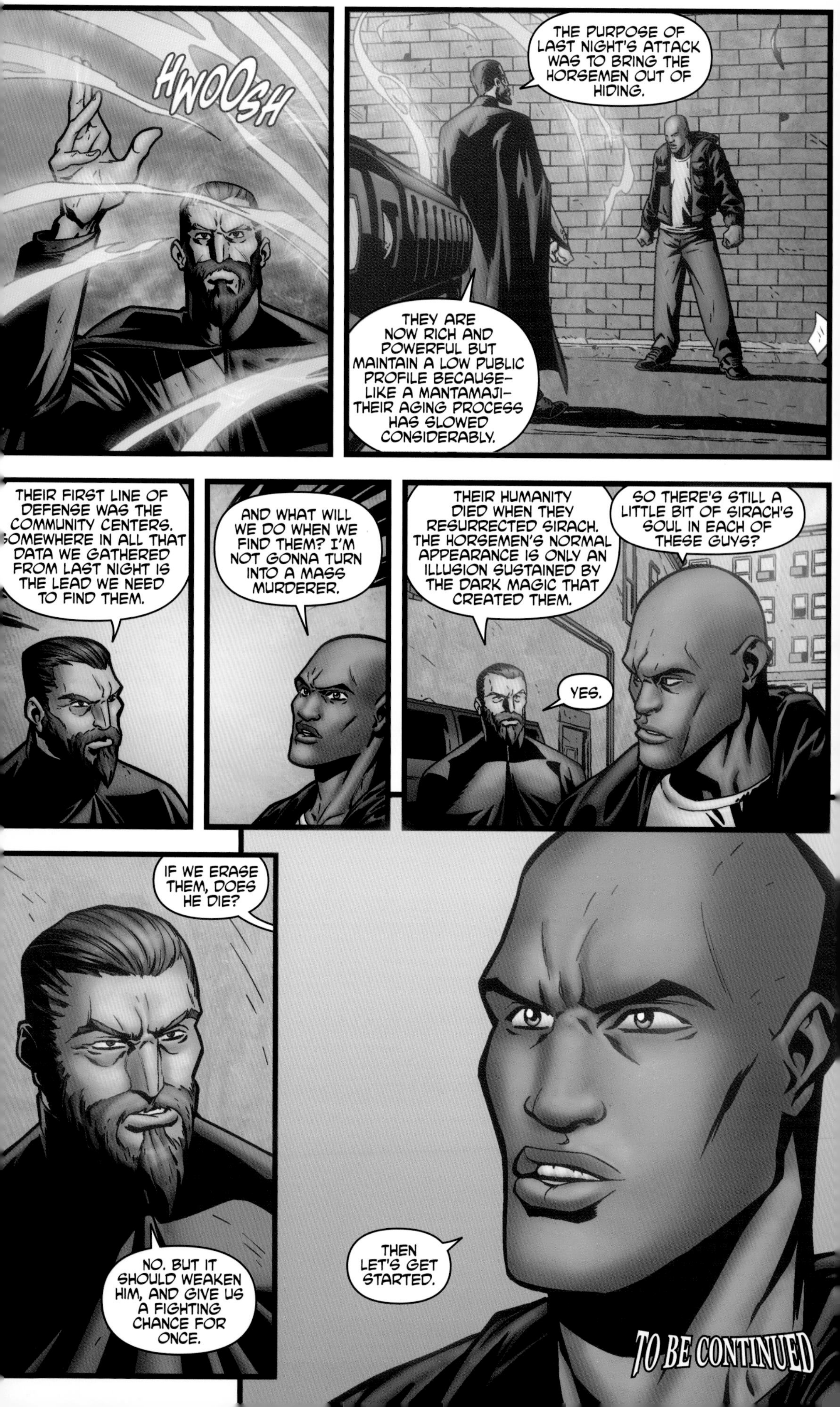
HWOOSH
THE PURPOSE OF LAST NIGHT'S ATTACK WAS TO BRING THE HORSEMEN OUT OF HIDING.
THEY ARE NOW RICH AND POWERFUL BUT MAINTAIN A LOW PUBLIC PROFILE BECAUSE-LIKE A MANTAMAJI-THEIR AGING PROCESS HAS SLOWED CONSIDERABLY.
THEIR FIRST LINE OF DEFENSE WAS THE COMMUNITY CENTERS. SOMEWHERE IN ALL THAT DATA WE GATHERED FROM LAST NIGHT IS THE LEAD WE NEED TO FIND THEM.
AND WHAT WILL WE DO WHEN WE FIND THEM? I'M NOT GONNA TURN INTO A MASS MURDERER.
THEIR HUMANITY DIED WHEN THEY RESURRECTED SIRACH. THE HORSEMEN'S NORMAL APPEARANCE IS ONLY AN ILLUSION SUSTAINED BY THE DARK MAGIC THAT CREATED THEM.
SO THERE'S STILL A LITTLE BIT OF SIRACH'S SOUL IN EACH OF THESE GUYS?
YES.
IF WE ERASE THEM, DOES HE DIE?
NO. BUT IT SHOULD WEAKEN HIM, AND GIVE US A FIGHTING CHANCE FOR ONCE.
THEN LET'S GET STARTED.
TO BE CONTINUED

CHAPTER 8

Sanctuants were women with great mystical powers. They fought alongside the Mantamaji and were treated as equals—yes, even in that ancient time. For equality is not a new idea, but rather an old one that has been forgotten, like a beautiful temple buried by mere sand.

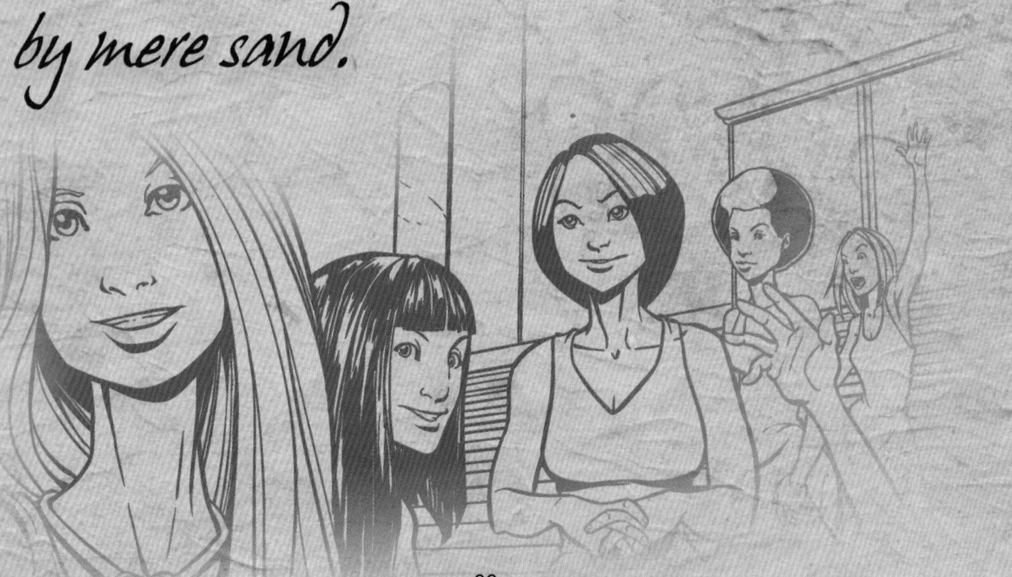

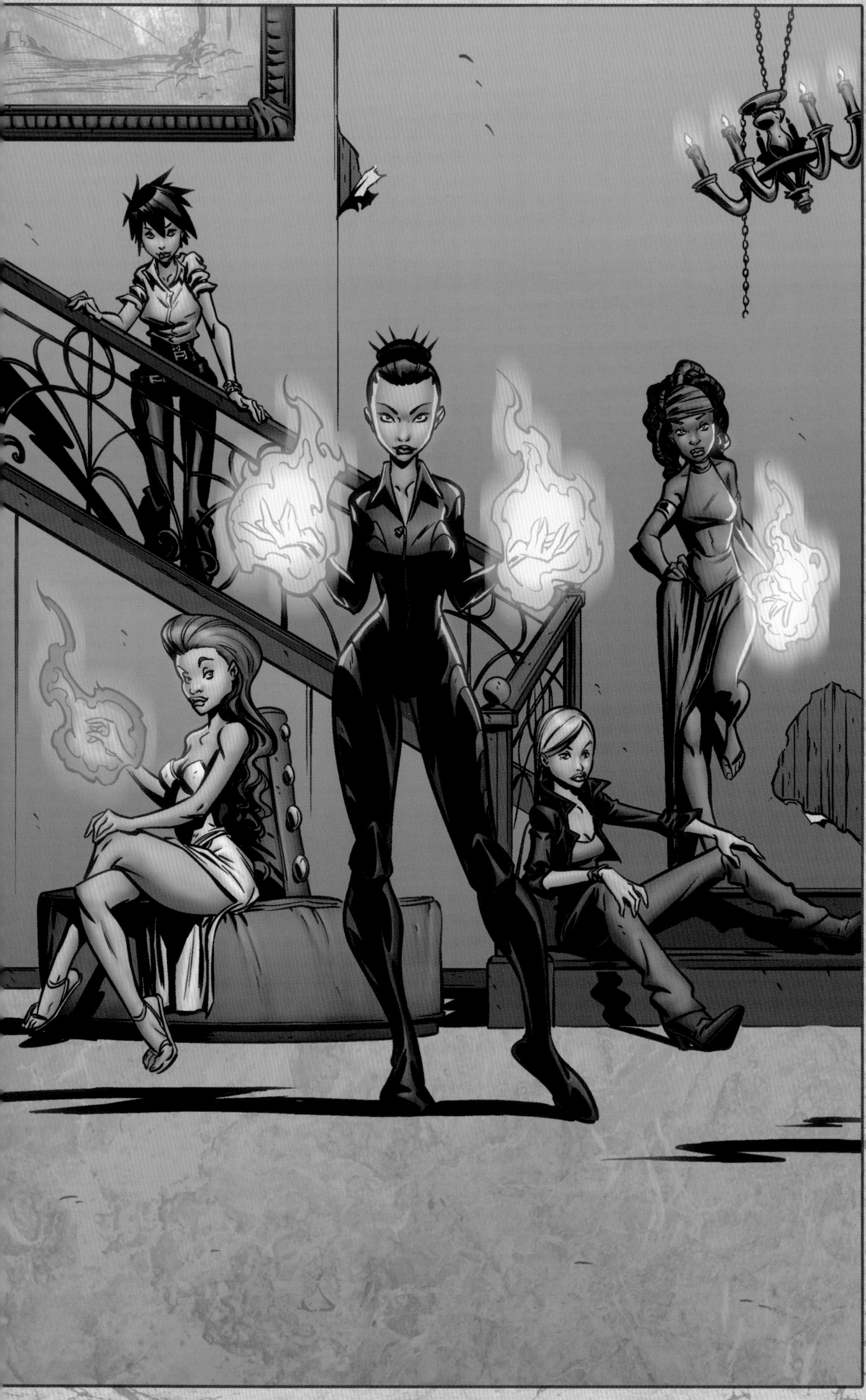

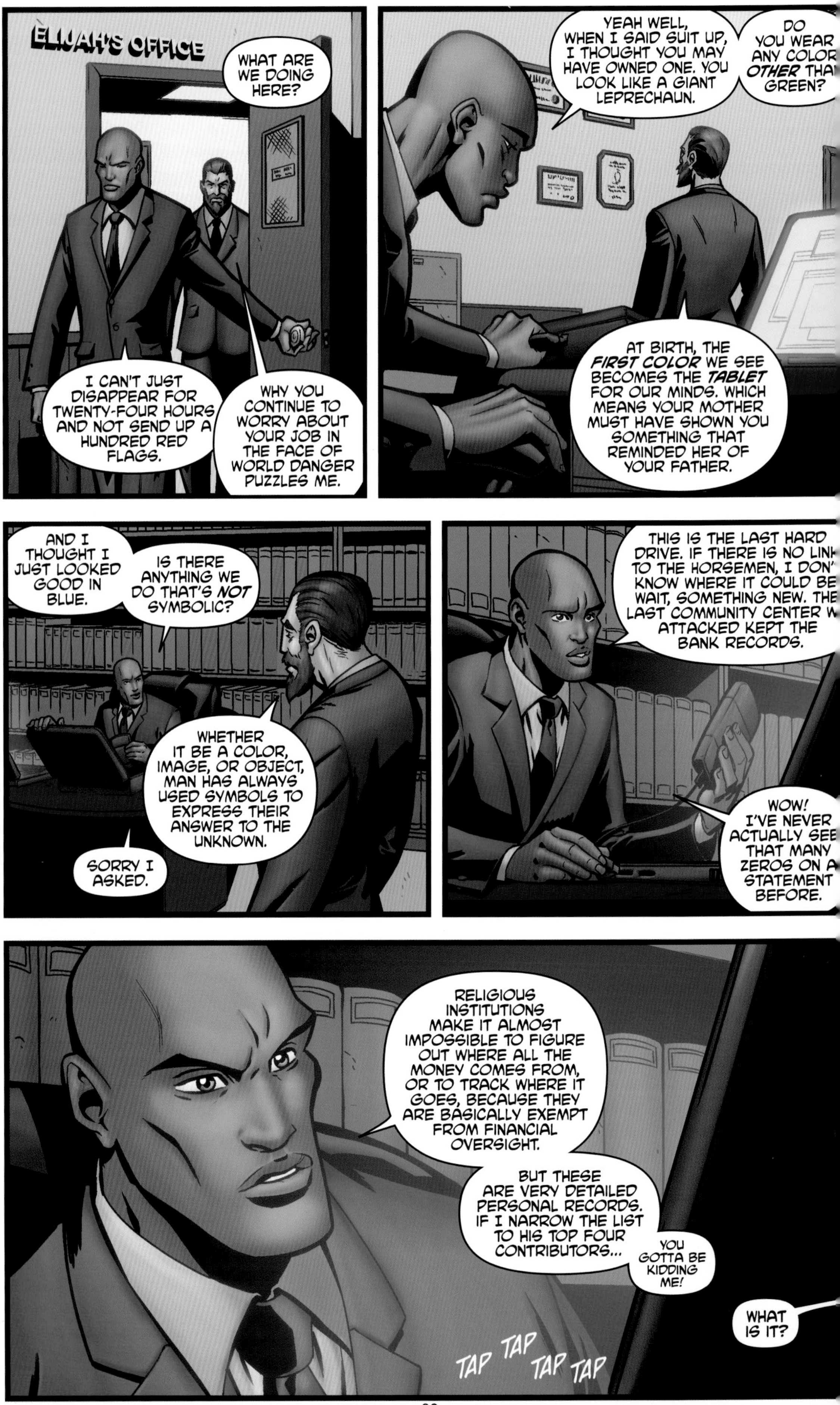
ELIJAH'S OFFICE
WHAT ARE WE DOING HERE?
I CAN'T JUST DISAPPEAR FOR TWENTY-FOUR HOURS AND NOT SEND UP A HUNDRED RED FLAGS.
WHY YOU CONTINUE TO WORRY ABOUT YOUR JOB IN THE FACE OF WORLD DANGER PUZZLES ME.
YEAH WELL, WHEN I SAID SUIT UP, I THOUGHT YOU MAY HAVE OWNED ONE. YOU LOOK LIKE A GIANT LEPRECHAUN.
DO YOU WEAR ANY COLOR *OTHER* THA GREEN?
AT BIRTH, THE *FIRST COLOR* WE SEE BECOMES THE *TABLET* FOR OUR MINDS. WHICH MEANS YOUR MOTHER MUST HAVE SHOWN YOU SOMETHING THAT REMINDED HER OF YOUR FATHER.
AND I THOUGHT I JUST LOOKED GOOD IN BLUE.
IS THERE ANYTHING WE DO THAT'S *NOT* SYMBOLIC?
WHETHER IT BE A COLOR, IMAGE, OR OBJECT, MAN HAS ALWAYS USED SYMBOLS TO EXPRESS THEIR ANSWER TO THE UNKNOWN.
SORRY I ASKED.
THIS IS THE LAST HARD DRIVE. IF THERE IS NO LIN TO THE HORSEMEN, I DON KNOW WHERE IT COULD BE WAIT, SOMETHING NEW. THE LAST COMMUNITY CENTER W ATTACKED KEPT THE BANK RECORDS.
WOW! I'VE NEVER ACTUALLY SEE THAT MANY ZEROS ON A STATEMENT BEFORE.
RELIGIOUS INSTITUTIONS MAKE IT ALMOST IMPOSSIBLE TO FIGURE OUT WHERE ALL THE MONEY COMES FROM, OR TO TRACK WHERE IT GOES, BECAUSE THEY ARE BASICALLY EXEMPT FROM FINANCIAL OVERSIGHT.
BUT THESE ARE VERY DETAILED PERSONAL RECORDS. IF I NARROW THE LIST TO HIS TOP FOUR CONTRIBUTORS...
YOU GOTTA BE KIDDING ME!
WHAT IS IT?
TAP TAP TAP TAP

ONE OF THEM IS THE PARTNER FOR THE LAW FIRM THAT OFFERED ME A JOB!

NOT ONLY DID I HELP PUT PEOPLE IN JAIL THAT DON'T BELONG, BUT I WAS BUSTING MY BUTT TO GET A JOB WORKING FOR A REAL CRIMINAL.

MY CAREER IS OVER.

OR PERHAPS YOUR DESTINY DREW YOU TO THIS PARTICULAR DANGER, THIS EXACT FIGHT.

YEAH, THAT'S NOT GOING TO CHEER ME UP.

OKAY, SO HERE'S WHAT WE'RE LOOKING AT. RECOGNIZE HIM?

RAGE OF FIRE.

HE GOES BY THE NAME ARGO YAMATO.

Unity Inc.: Fielding Hope in Our Future
Founded 23 years ago in Gernwich Village

Founding member ARGO YAMATO. Born in Kyoto, Japan Argo Yamato has built has built an empire with his business Blazer Star Esports

Argo Yamato

click here for link

HE WAS AN EXPELLED MEMBER OF THE RED NINJA DRAGON CLAN OF JAPAN. HE HAS BEEN IN CHARGE OF THE NEW WORLD KNIGHTS' COMBAT TRAINING AND IS A MASTER IN ALL FORMS OF MARTIAL ARTS.

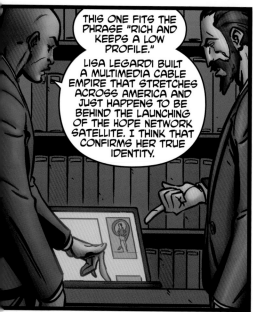

THIS ONE FITS THE PHRASE "RICH AND KEEPS A LOW PROFILE."

LISA LEGARDI BUILT A MULTIMEDIA CABLE EMPIRE THAT STRETCHES ACROSS AMERICA AND JUST HAPPENS TO BE BEHIND THE LAUNCHING OF THE HOPE NETWORK SATELLITE. I THINK THAT CONFIRMS HER TRUE IDENTITY.

HMMM, RED HAIR. SHE COULD BE WRATH OF PLAGUE BUT I'VE NEVER SEEN HER IN THIS FORM BEFORE.

WHAT DOES SHE USUALLY LOOK LIKE?

AN ABOMINATION.

OKAY...

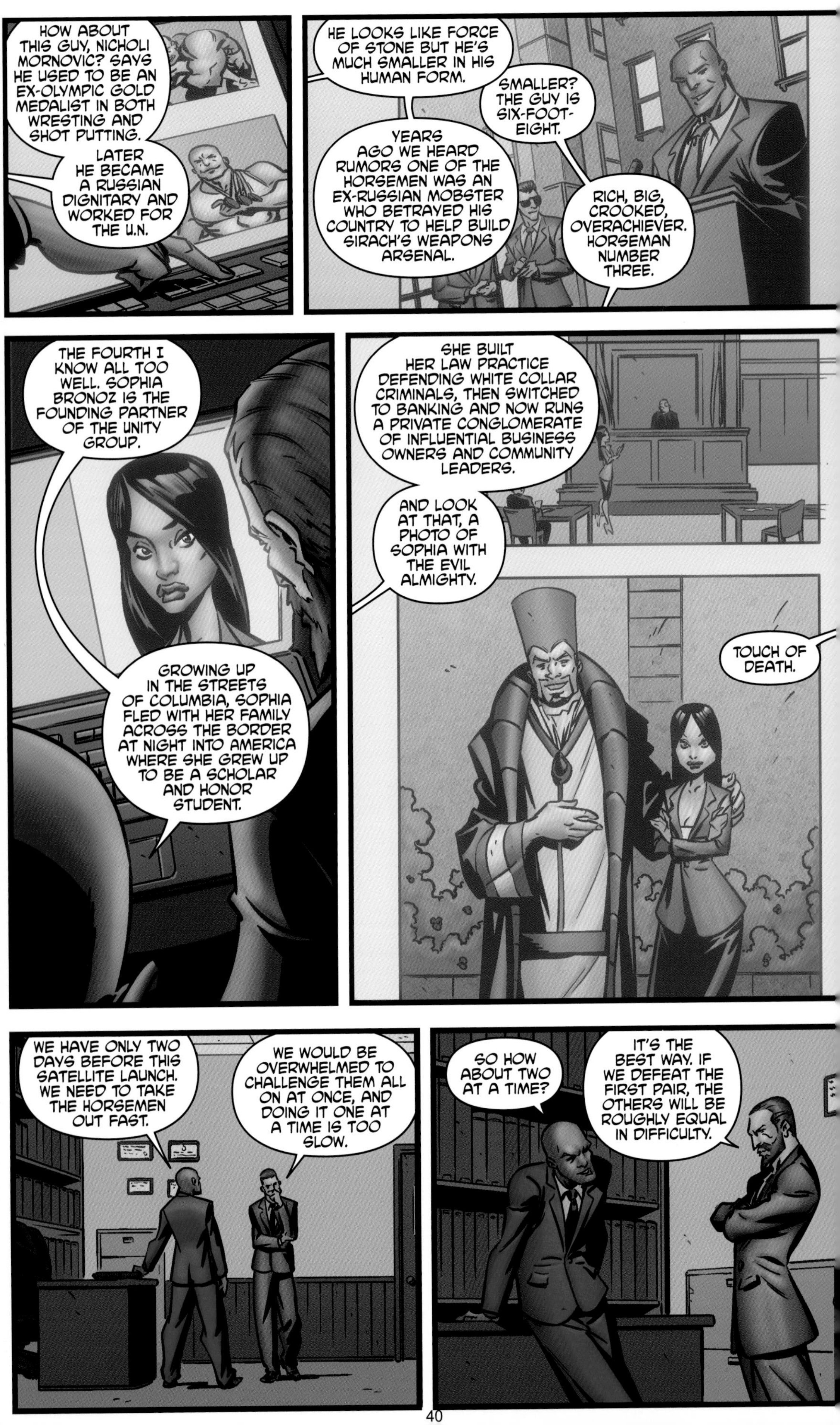
HOW ABOUT THIS GUY, NICHOLI MORNOVIC? SAYS HE USED TO BE AN EX-OLYMPIC GOLD MEDALIST IN BOTH WRESTING AND SHOT PUTTING.
LATER HE BECAME A RUSSIAN DIGNITARY AND WORKED FOR THE U.N.
HE LOOKS LIKE FORCE OF STONE BUT HE'S MUCH SMALLER IN HIS HUMAN FORM.
SMALLER? THE GUY IS SIX-FOOT-EIGHT.
YEARS AGO WE HEARD RUMORS ONE OF THE HORSEMEN WAS AN EX-RUSSIAN MOBSTER WHO BETRAYED HIS COUNTRY TO HELP BUILD SIRACH'S WEAPONS ARSENAL.
RICH, BIG, CROOKED, OVERACHIEVER. HORSEMAN NUMBER THREE.
THE FOURTH I KNOW ALL TOO WELL. SOPHIA BRONOZ IS THE FOUNDING PARTNER OF THE UNITY GROUP.
GROWING UP IN THE STREETS OF COLUMBIA, SOPHIA FLED WITH HER FAMILY ACROSS THE BORDER AT NIGHT INTO AMERICA WHERE SHE GREW UP TO BE A SCHOLAR AND HONOR STUDENT.
SHE BUILT HER LAW PRACTICE DEFENDING WHITE COLLAR CRIMINALS, THEN SWITCHED TO BANKING AND NOW RUNS A PRIVATE CONGLOMERATE OF INFLUENTIAL BUSINESS OWNERS AND COMMUNITY LEADERS.
AND LOOK AT THAT, A PHOTO OF SOPHIA WITH THE EVIL ALMIGHTY.
TOUCH OF DEATH.
WE HAVE ONLY TWO DAYS BEFORE THIS SATELLITE LAUNCH. WE NEED TO TAKE THE HORSEMEN OUT FAST.
WE WOULD BE OVERWHELMED TO CHALLENGE THEM ALL ON AT ONCE, AND DOING IT ONE AT A TIME IS TOO SLOW.
SO HOW ABOUT TWO AT A TIME?
IT'S THE BEST WAY. IF WE DEFEAT THE FIRST PAIR, THE OTHERS WILL BE ROUGHLY EQUAL IN DIFFICULTY.

I GUESS I SHOULDN'T HAVE CONFRONTED SIRACH TODAY.

IF YOU ARE NOW WORRIED THAT HE KNOWS WHO YOU ARE, HE DOESN'T.

HOW COULD YOU KNOW THAT?

BECAUSE WE ARE IN YOUR OFFICE. IF HE TOLD THE HORSEMEN AND IF THEY KNEW YOUR IDENTITY, THEY WOULD HAVE BEEN WAITING FOR US HERE.

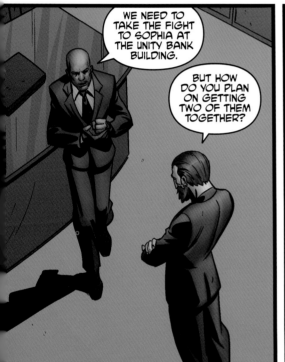

WE NEED TO TAKE THE FIGHT TO SOPHIA AT THE UNITY BANK BUILDING.

BUT HOW DO YOU PLAN ON GETTING TWO OF THEM TOGETHER?

WITH TWO DAYS BEFORE THEY EXECUTE WHATEVER IT IS THEY ARE PLANNING THEY NEED TO COORDINATE THEIR EFFORTS.

SINCE SOPHIA WILL BE THERE ALREADY, I'LL JUST CHARM MY WAY INTO THE UNITY GROUP AND LATE IN THE DAY SOMEONE FROM HER OFFICE WILL INVITE ONE OF THE OTHER HORSEMEN DOWN TO GO OVER THE PLANS.

WHY WOULD SHE LET YOU HANG AROUND HER OFFICES?

FOR A THREE THOUSAND YEAR OLD MAN YOU DON'T KNOW WHOLE LOT ABOUT WOMEN.

41

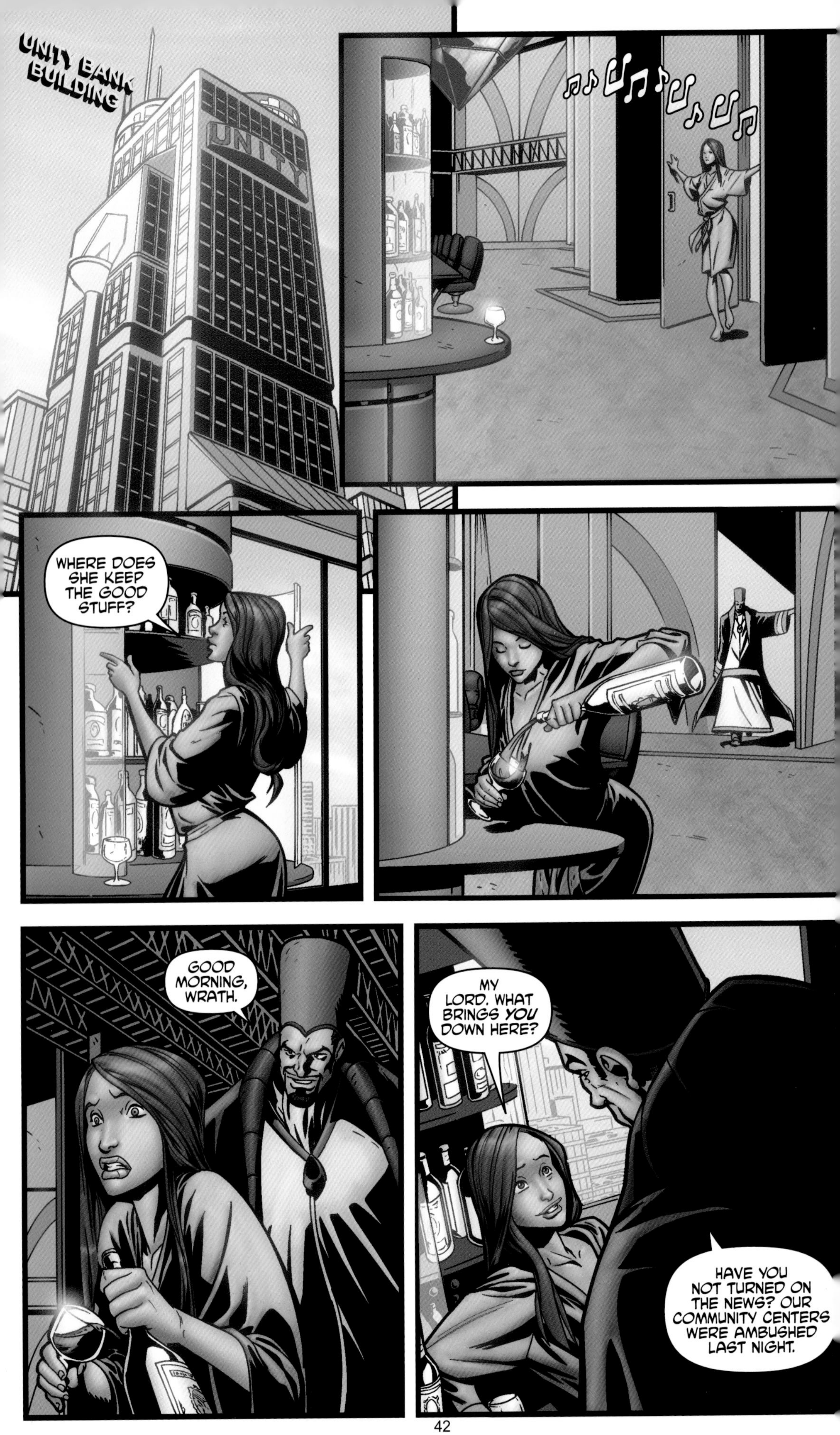
UNITY BANK BUILDING
UNITY
WHERE DOES SHE KEEP THE GOOD STUFF?
GOOD MORNING, WRATH.
MY LORD. WHAT BRINGS *YOU* DOWN HERE?
HAVE YOU NOT TURNED ON THE NEWS? OUR COMMUNITY CENTERS WERE AMBUSHED LAST NIGHT.

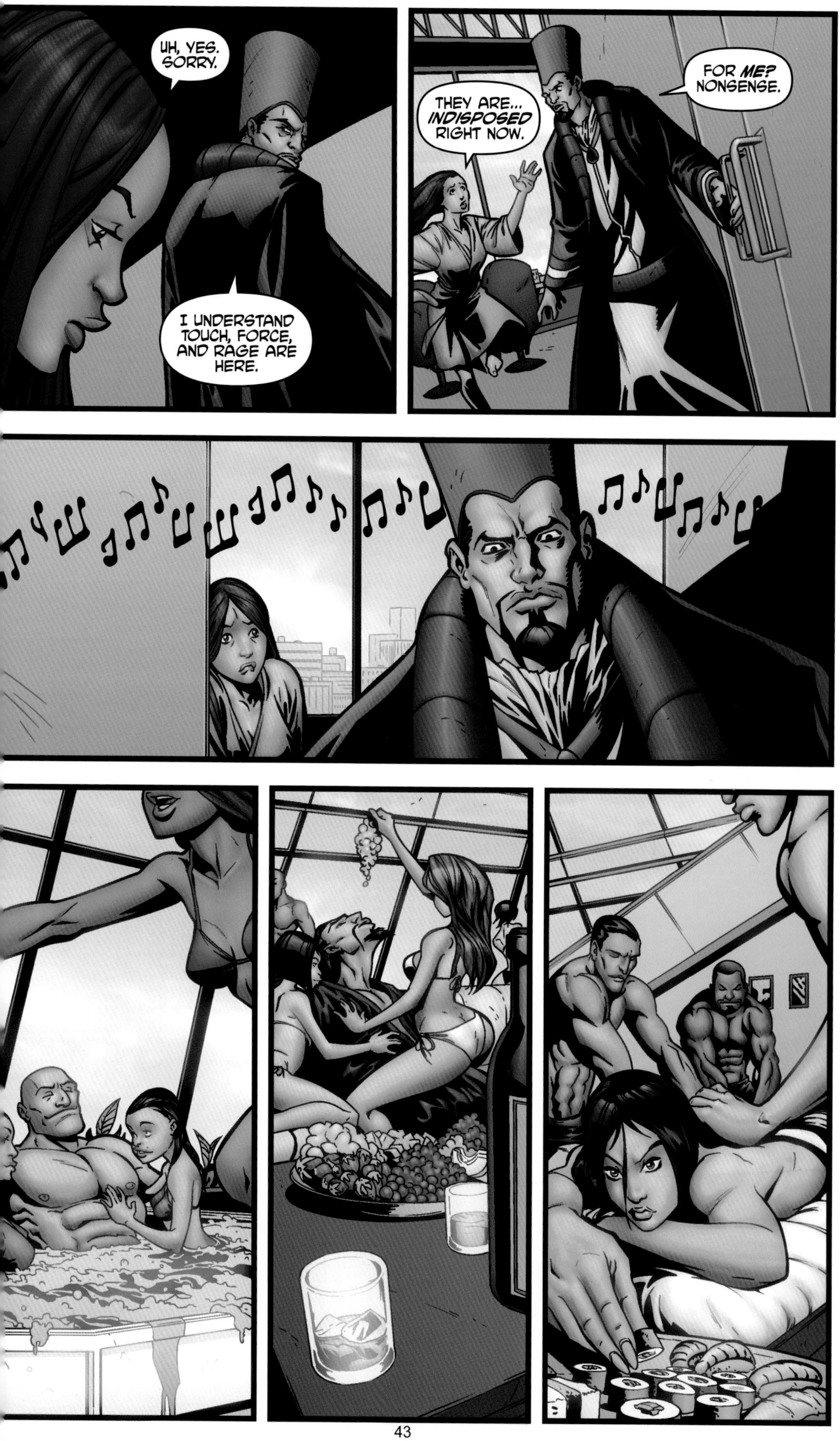
UH, YES. SORRY.
I UNDERSTAND TOUCH, FORCE, AND RAGE ARE HERE.
THEY ARE... INDISPOSED RIGHT NOW.
FOR ME? NONSENSE.

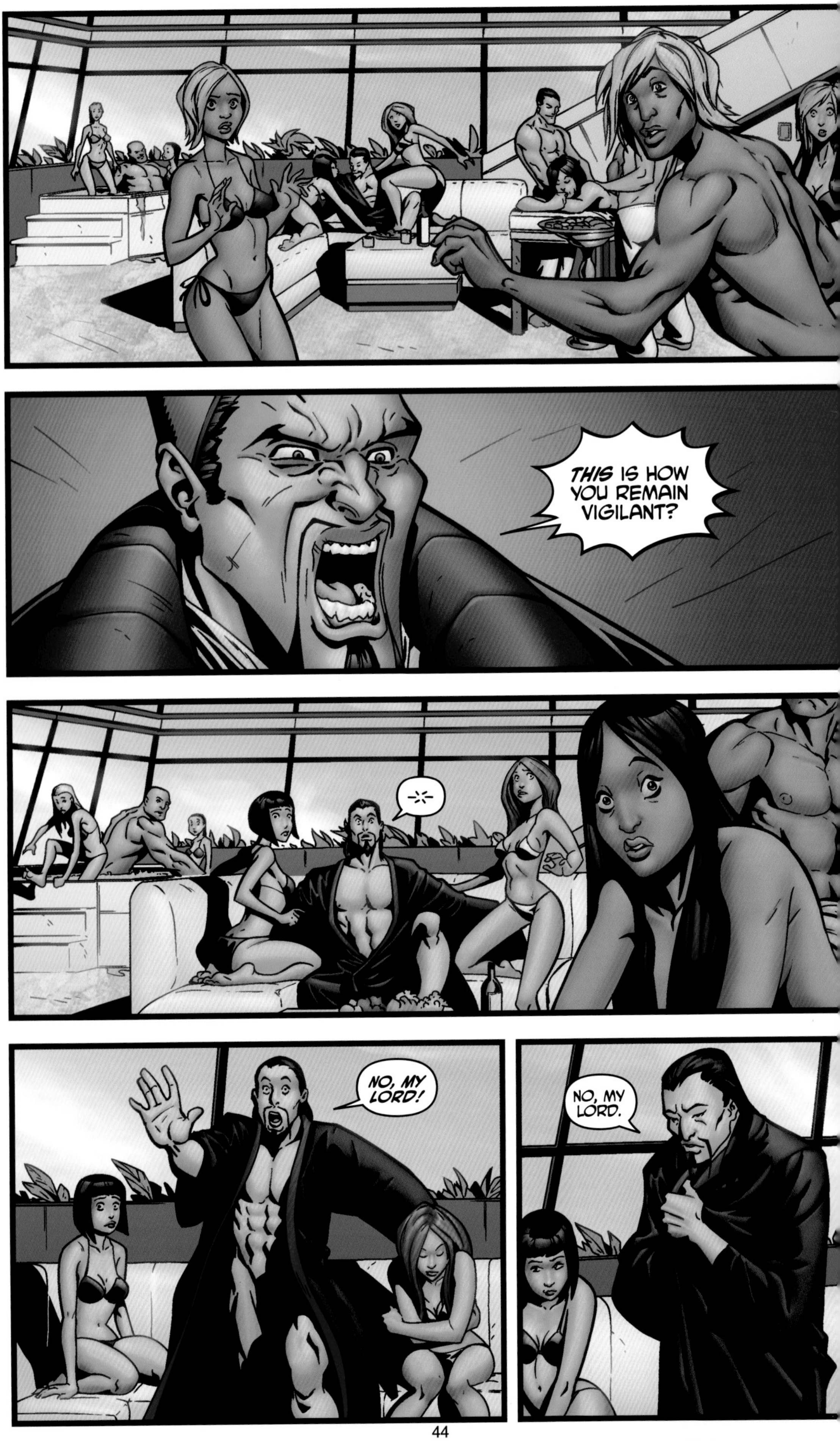
THIS IS HOW YOU REMAIN VIGILANT?
-:-
NO, MY LORD!
NO, MY LORD.

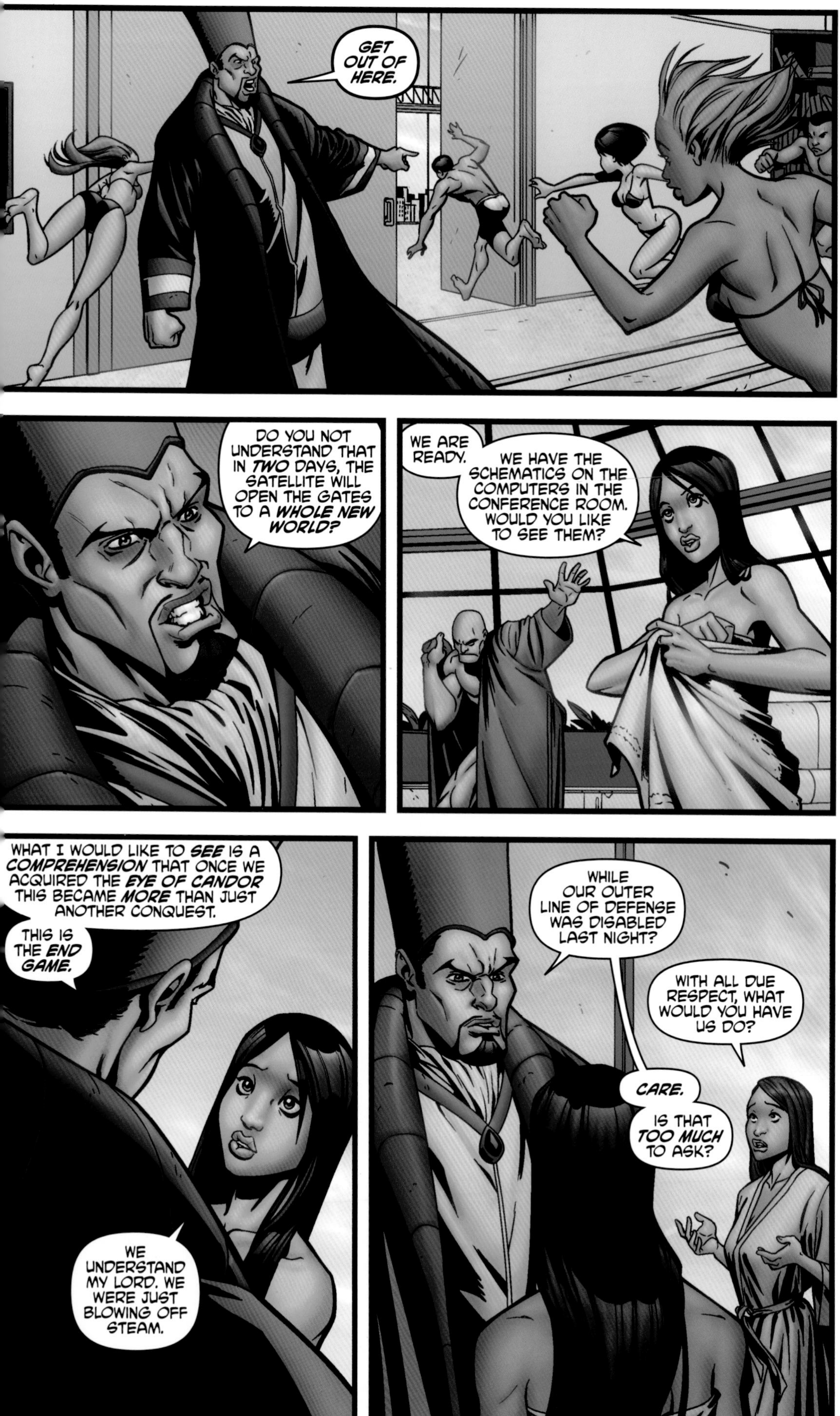
GET OUT OF HERE.
DO YOU NOT UNDERSTAND THAT IN TWO DAYS, THE SATELLITE WILL OPEN THE GATES TO A WHOLE NEW WORLD?
WE ARE READY.
WE HAVE THE SCHEMATICS ON THE COMPUTERS IN THE CONFERENCE ROOM. WOULD YOU LIKE TO SEE THEM?
WHAT I WOULD LIKE TO SEE IS A COMPREHENSION THAT ONCE WE ACQUIRED THE EYE OF CANDOR THIS BECAME MORE THAN JUST ANOTHER CONQUEST.
THIS IS THE END GAME.
WE UNDERSTAND MY LORD. WE WERE JUST BLOWING OFF STEAM.
WHILE OUR OUTER LINE OF DEFENSE WAS DISABLED LAST NIGHT?
WITH ALL DUE RESPECT, WHAT WOULD YOU HAVE US DO?
CARE.
IS THAT TOO MUCH TO ASK?

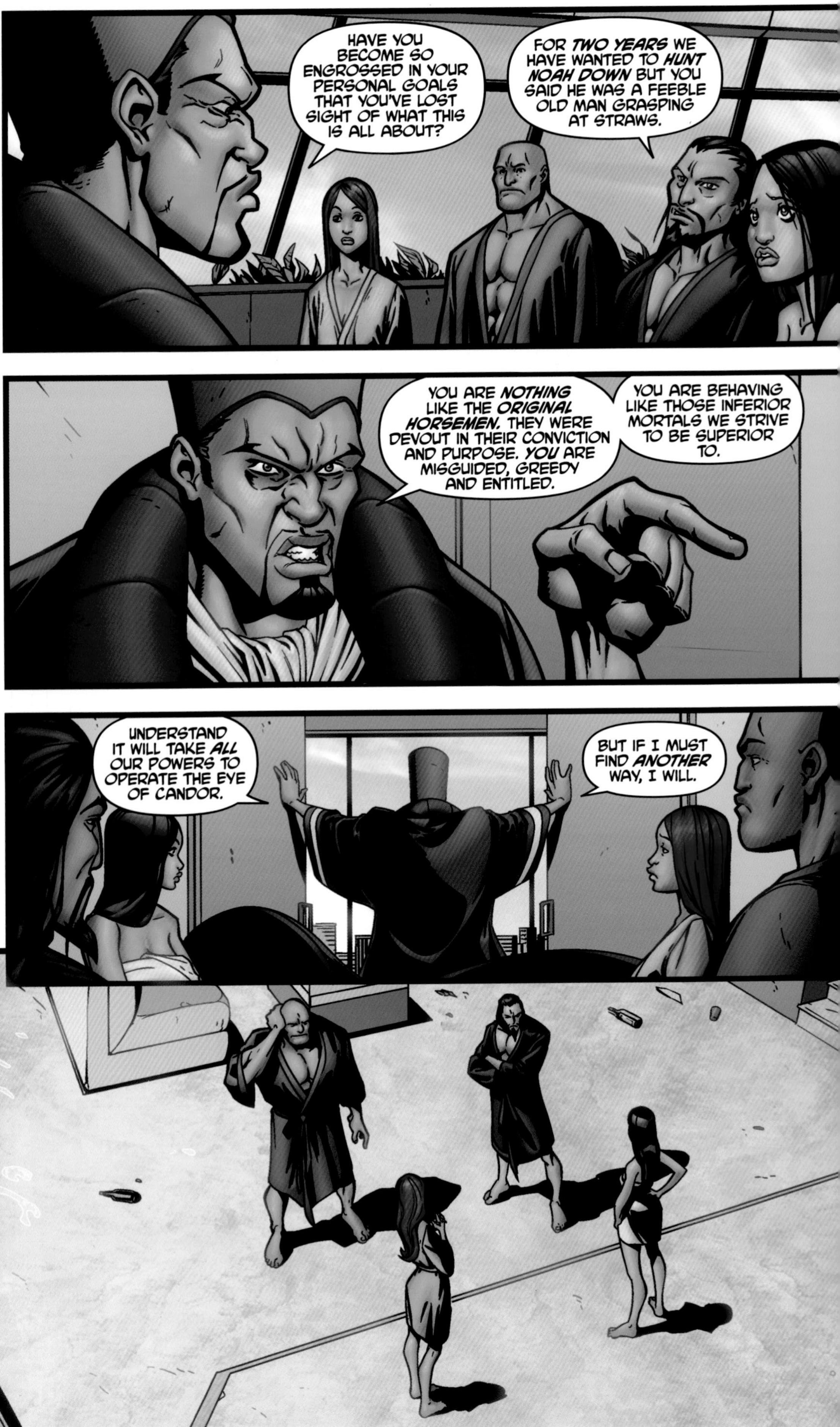
HAVE YOU BECOME SO ENGROSSED IN YOUR PERSONAL GOALS THAT YOU'VE LOST SIGHT OF WHAT THIS IS ALL ABOUT?
FOR TWO YEARS WE HAVE WANTED TO HUNT NOAH DOWN BUT YOU SAID HE WAS A FEEBLE OLD MAN GRASPING AT STRAWS.
YOU ARE NOTHING LIKE THE ORIGINAL HORSEMEN. THEY WERE DEVOUT IN THEIR CONVICTION AND PURPOSE. YOU ARE MISGUIDED, GREEDY AND ENTITLED.
YOU ARE BEHAVING LIKE THOSE INFERIOR MORTALS WE STRIVE TO BE SUPERIOR TO.
UNDERSTAND IT WILL TAKE ALL OUR POWERS TO OPERATE THE EYE OF CANDOR.
BUT IF I MUST FIND ANOTHER WAY, I WILL.

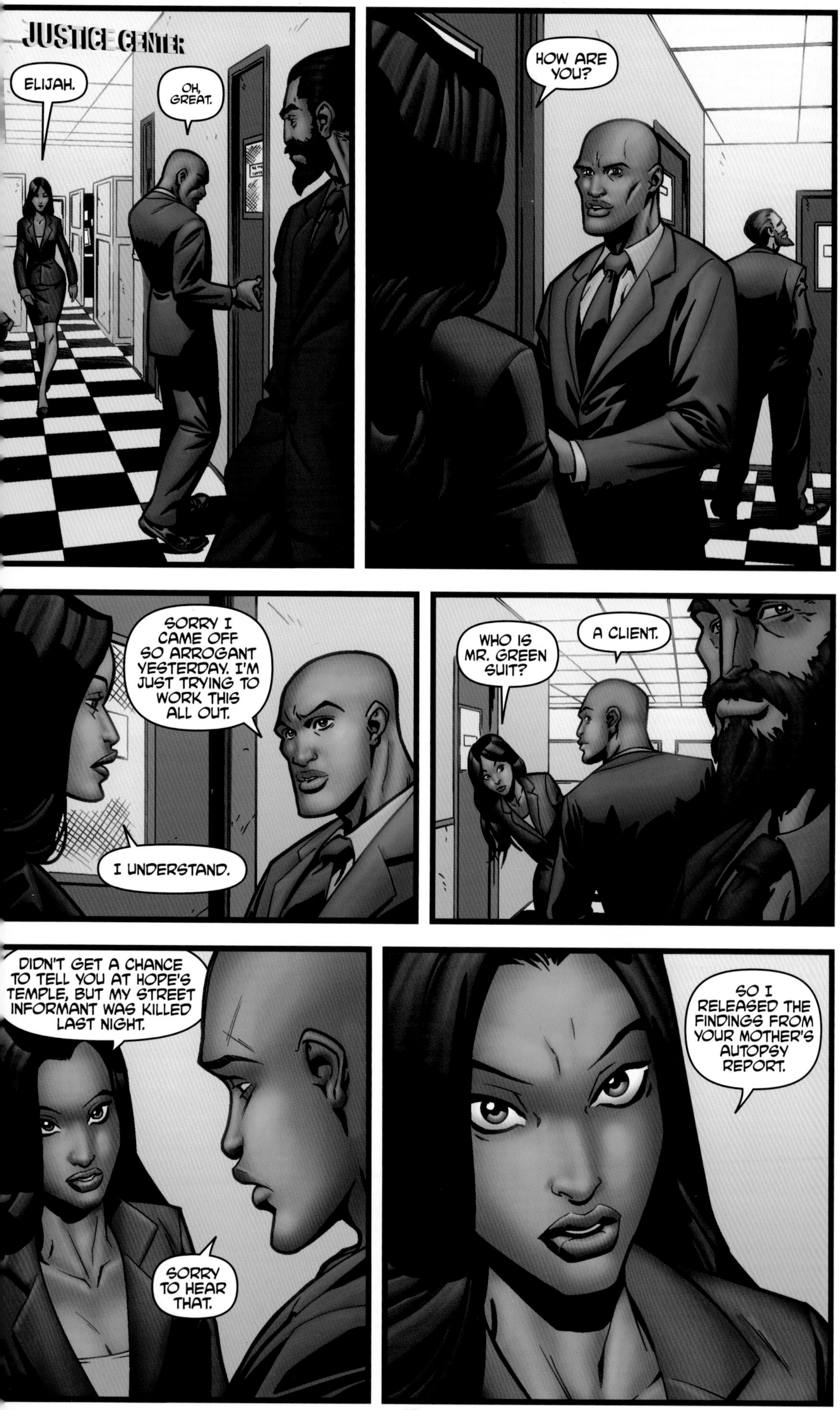
JUSTICE CENTER
ELIJAH.
OH, GREAT.
HOW ARE YOU?
SORRY I CAME OFF SO ARROGANT YESTERDAY. I'M JUST TRYING TO WORK THIS ALL OUT.
I UNDERSTAND.
WHO IS MR. GREEN SUIT?
A CLIENT.
DIDN'T GET A CHANCE TO TELL YOU AT HOPE'S TEMPLE, BUT MY STREET INFORMANT WAS KILLED LAST NIGHT.
SORRY TO HEAR THAT.
SO I RELEASED THE FINDINGS FROM YOUR MOTHER'S AUTOPSY REPORT.

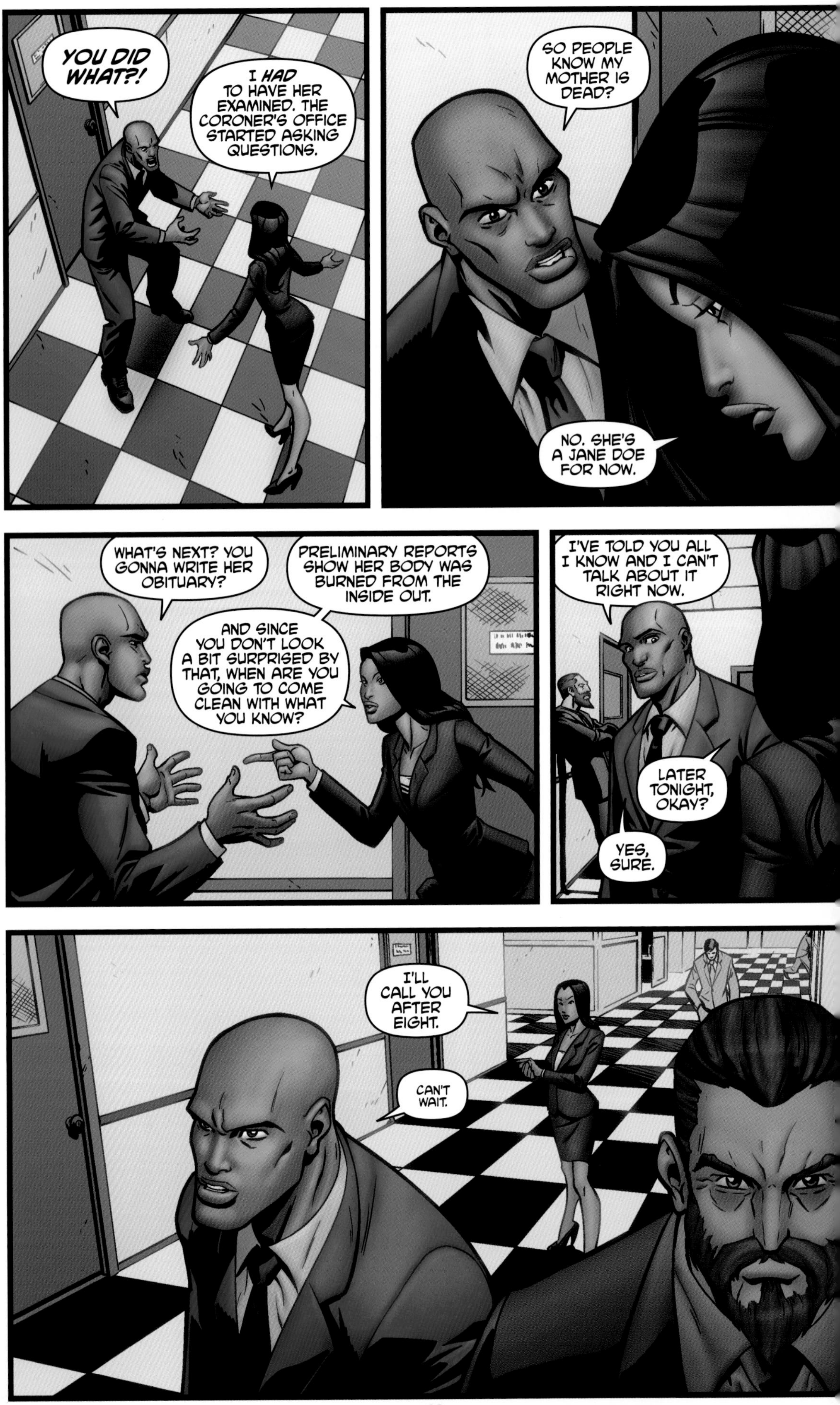
YOU DID WHAT?!
I HAD TO HAVE HER EXAMINED. THE CORONER'S OFFICE STARTED ASKING QUESTIONS.
SO PEOPLE KNOW MY MOTHER IS DEAD?
NO. SHE'S A JANE DOE FOR NOW.
WHAT'S NEXT? YOU GONNA WRITE HER OBITUARY?
PRELIMINARY REPORTS SHOW HER BODY WAS BURNED FROM THE INSIDE OUT.
AND SINCE YOU DON'T LOOK A BIT SURPRISED BY THAT, WHEN ARE YOU GOING TO COME CLEAN WITH WHAT YOU KNOW?
I'VE TOLD YOU ALL I KNOW AND I CAN'T TALK ABOUT IT RIGHT NOW.
LATER TONIGHT, OKAY?
YES, SURE.
I'LL CALL YOU AFTER EIGHT.
CAN'T WAIT.

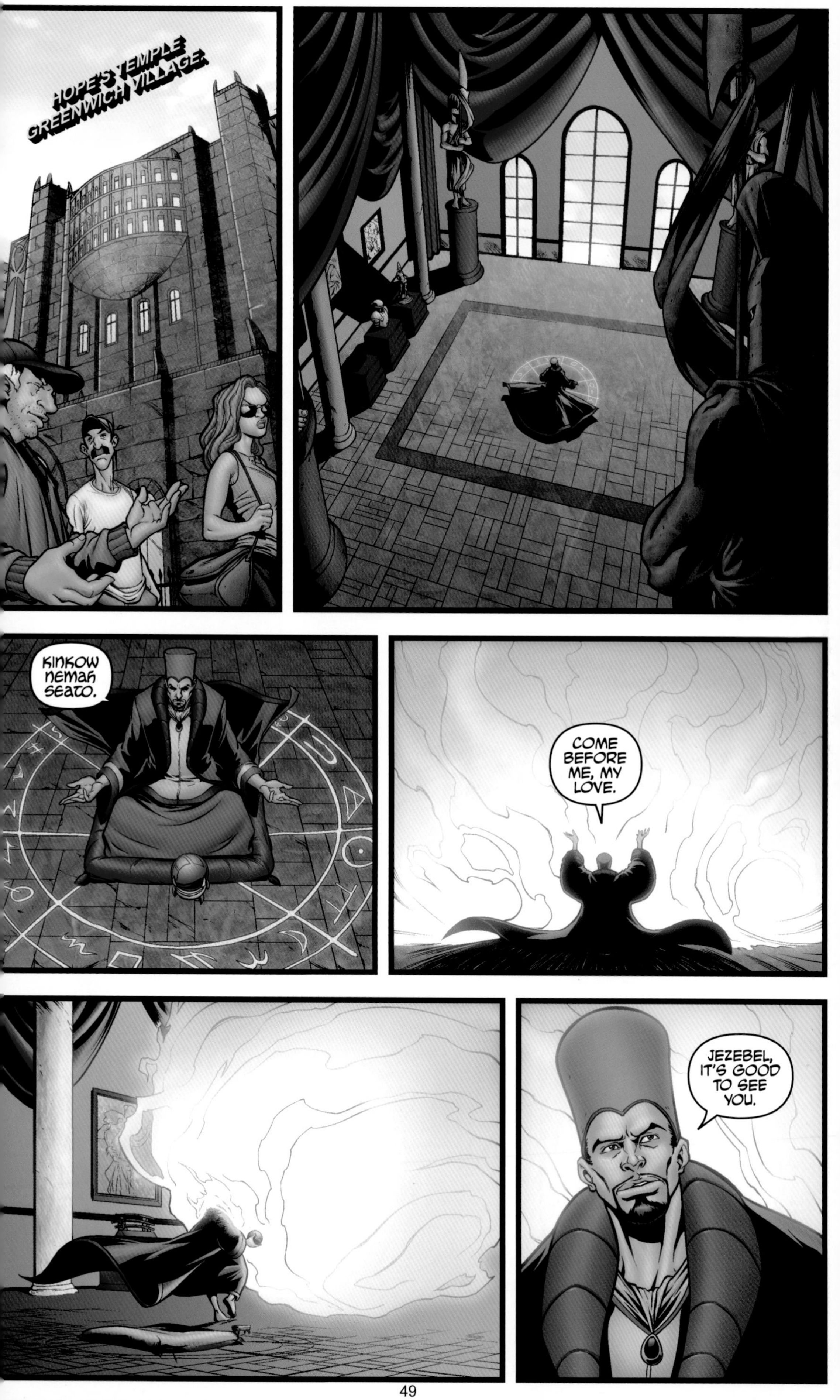
HOPE'S TEMPLE
GREENWICH VILLAGE.
KINKOW NEMAH SEATO.
COME BEFORE ME, MY LOVE.
JEZEBEL, IT'S GOOD TO SEE YOU.

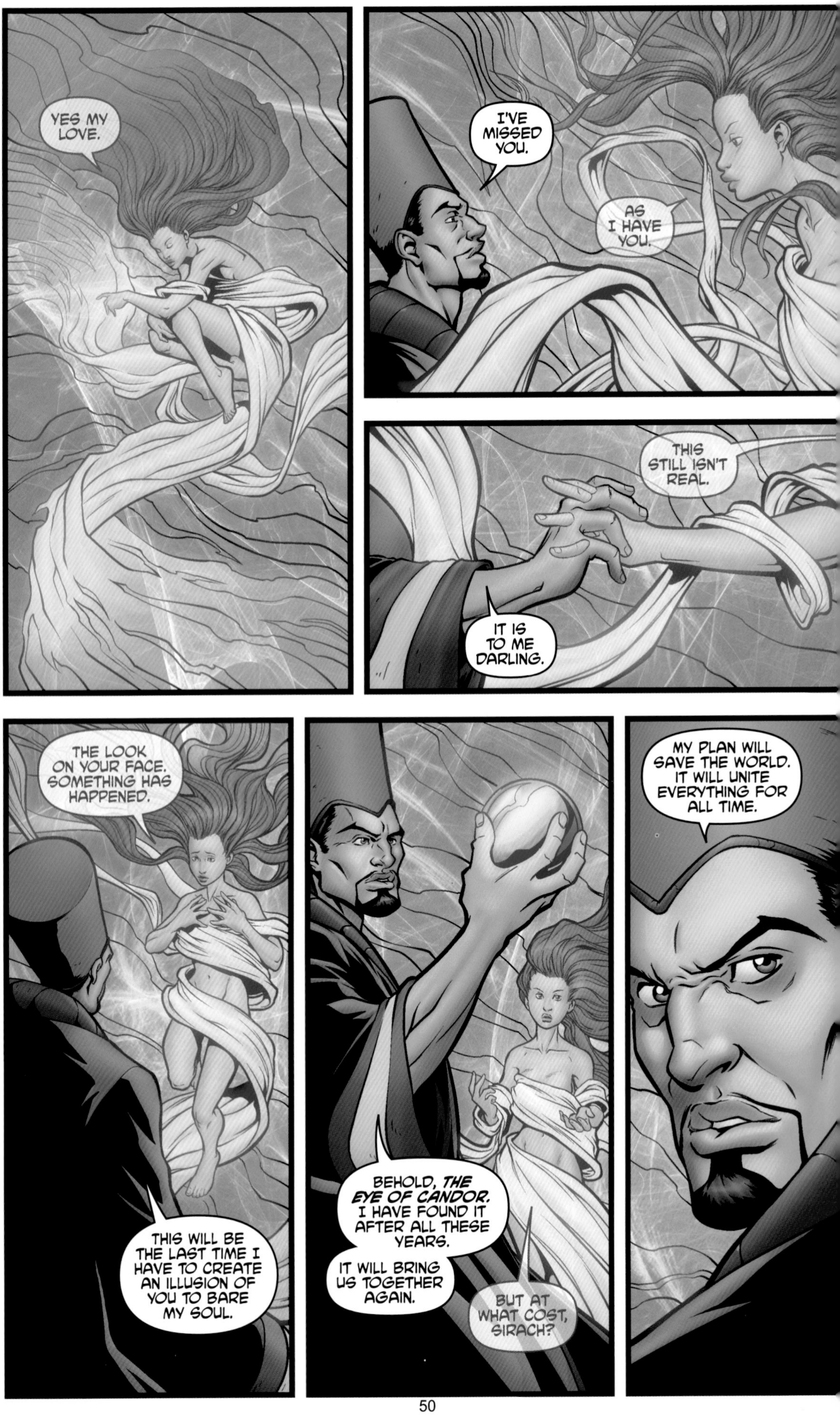
YES MY LOVE.
I'VE MISSED YOU.
AS I HAVE YOU.
THIS STILL ISN'T REAL.
IT IS TO ME DARLING.
THE LOOK ON YOUR FACE. SOMETHING HAS HAPPENED.
THIS WILL BE THE LAST TIME I HAVE TO CREATE AN ILLUSION OF YOU TO BARE MY SOUL.
BEHOLD, *THE EYE OF CANDOR.* I HAVE FOUND IT AFTER ALL THESE YEARS.
IT WILL BRING US TOGETHER AGAIN.
BUT AT WHAT COST, SIRACH?
MY PLAN WILL SAVE THE WORLD. IT WILL UNITE EVERYTHING FOR ALL TIME.

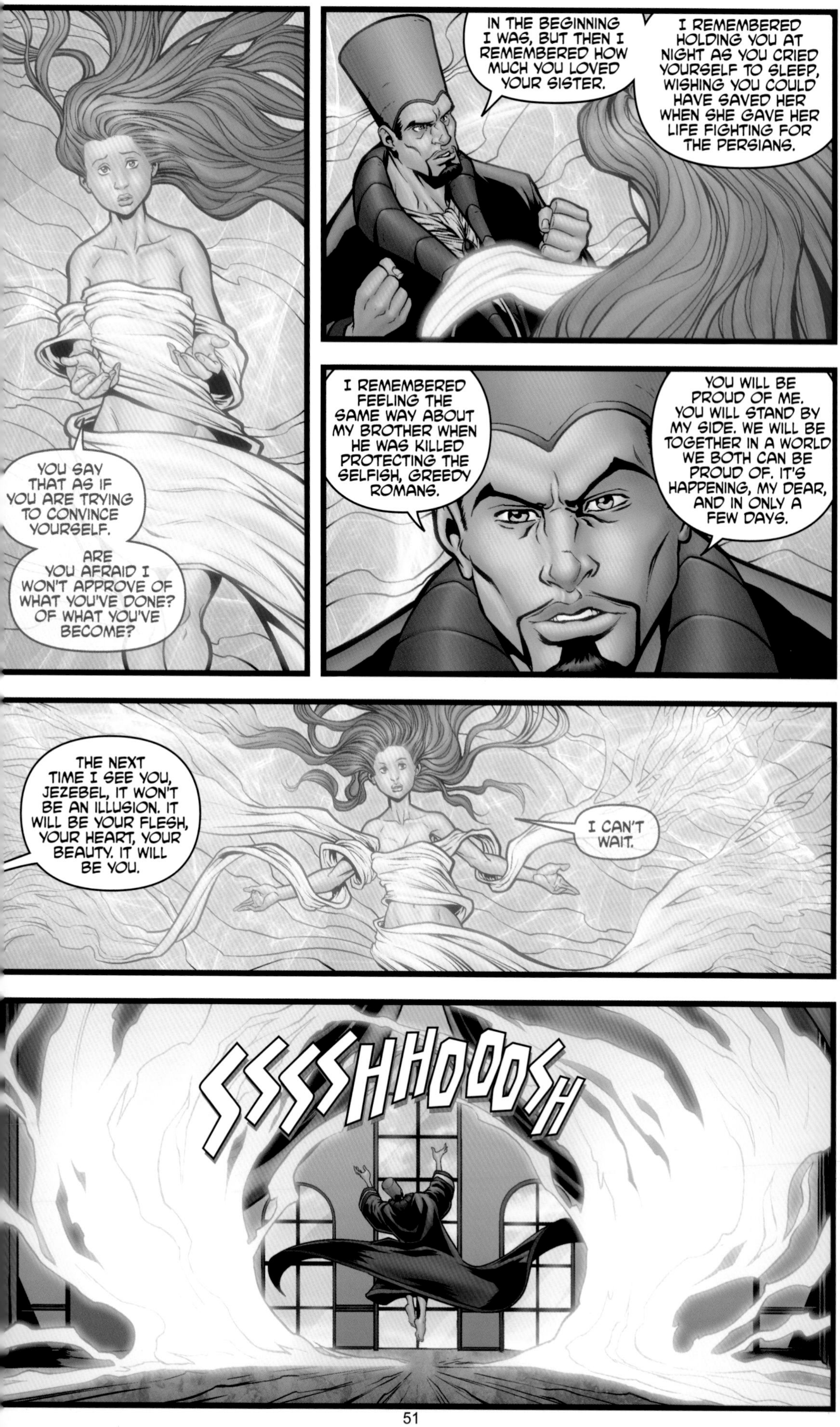
IN THE BEGINNING I WAS, BUT THEN I REMEMBERED HOW MUCH YOU LOVED YOUR SISTER.
I REMEMBERED HOLDING YOU AT NIGHT AS YOU CRIED YOURSELF TO SLEEP, WISHING YOU COULD HAVE SAVED HER WHEN SHE GAVE HER LIFE FIGHTING FOR THE PERSIANS.
YOU SAY THAT AS IF YOU ARE TRYING TO CONVINCE YOURSELF.
ARE YOU AFRAID I WON'T APPROVE OF WHAT YOU'VE DONE? OF WHAT YOU'VE BECOME?
I REMEMBERED FEELING THE SAME WAY ABOUT MY BROTHER WHEN HE WAS KILLED PROTECTING THE SELFISH, GREEDY ROMANS.
YOU WILL BE PROUD OF ME. YOU WILL STAND BY MY SIDE. WE WILL BE TOGETHER IN A WORLD WE BOTH CAN BE PROUD OF. IT'S HAPPENING, MY DEAR, AND IN ONLY A FEW DAYS.
THE NEXT TIME I SEE YOU, JEZEBEL, IT WON'T BE AN ILLUSION. IT WILL BE YOUR FLESH, YOUR HEART, YOUR BEAUTY. IT WILL BE YOU.
I CAN'T WAIT.
SSSSHHOOOSH

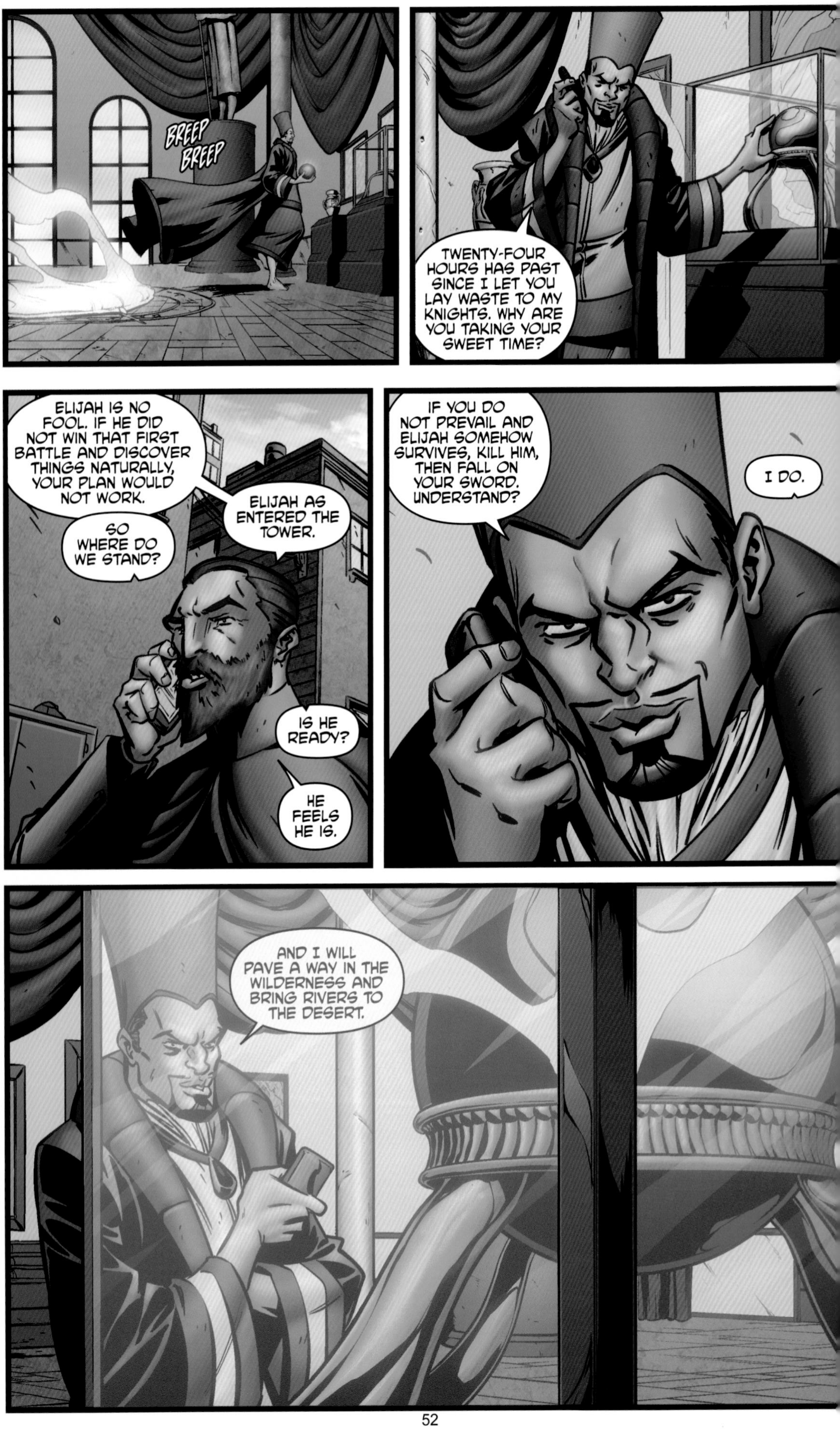
BREEP BREEP
TWENTY-FOUR HOURS HAS PAST SINCE I LET YOU LAY WASTE TO MY KNIGHTS. WHY ARE YOU TAKING YOUR SWEET TIME?
ELIJAH IS NO FOOL. IF HE DID NOT WIN THAT FIRST BATTLE AND DISCOVER THINGS NATURALLY, YOUR PLAN WOULD NOT WORK.
SO WHERE DO WE STAND?
ELIJAH AS ENTERED THE TOWER.
IS HE READY?
HE FEELS HE IS.
IF YOU DO NOT PREVAIL AND ELIJAH SOMEHOW SURVIVES, KILL HIM, THEN FALL ON YOUR SWORD. UNDERSTAND?
I DO.
AND I WILL PAVE A WAY IN THE WILDERNESS AND BRING RIVERS TO THE DESERT.

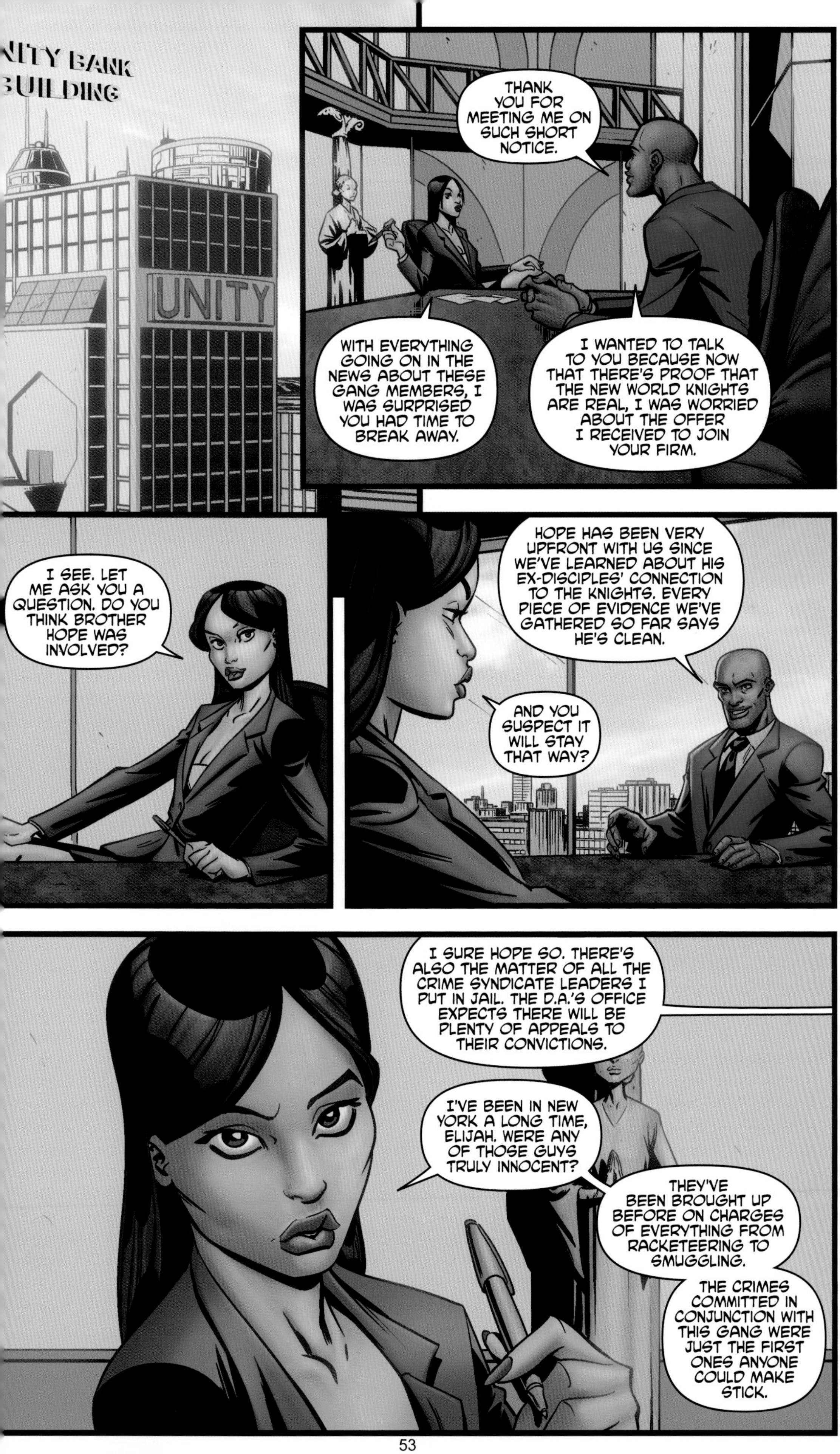
UNITY BANK BUILDING
UNITY
THANK YOU FOR MEETING ME ON SUCH SHORT NOTICE.
WITH EVERYTHING GOING ON IN THE NEWS ABOUT THESE GANG MEMBERS, I WAS SURPRISED YOU HAD TIME TO BREAK AWAY.
I WANTED TO TALK TO YOU BECAUSE NOW THAT THERE'S PROOF THAT THE NEW WORLD KNIGHTS ARE REAL, I WAS WORRIED ABOUT THE OFFER I RECEIVED TO JOIN YOUR FIRM.
I SEE. LET ME ASK YOU A QUESTION. DO YOU THINK BROTHER HOPE WAS INVOLVED?
HOPE HAS BEEN VERY UPFRONT WITH US SINCE WE'VE LEARNED ABOUT HIS EX-DISCIPLES' CONNECTION TO THE KNIGHTS. EVERY PIECE OF EVIDENCE WE'VE GATHERED SO FAR SAYS HE'S CLEAN.
AND YOU SUSPECT IT WILL STAY THAT WAY?
I SURE HOPE SO. THERE'S ALSO THE MATTER OF ALL THE CRIME SYNDICATE LEADERS I PUT IN JAIL. THE D.A.'S OFFICE EXPECTS THERE WILL BE PLENTY OF APPEALS TO THEIR CONVICTIONS.
I'VE BEEN IN NEW YORK A LONG TIME, ELIJAH. WERE ANY OF THOSE GUYS TRULY INNOCENT?
THEY'VE BEEN BROUGHT UP BEFORE ON CHARGES OF EVERYTHING FROM RACKETEERING TO SMUGGLING.
THE CRIMES COMMITTED IN CONJUNCTION WITH THIS GANG WERE JUST THE FIRST ONES ANYONE COULD MAKE STICK.

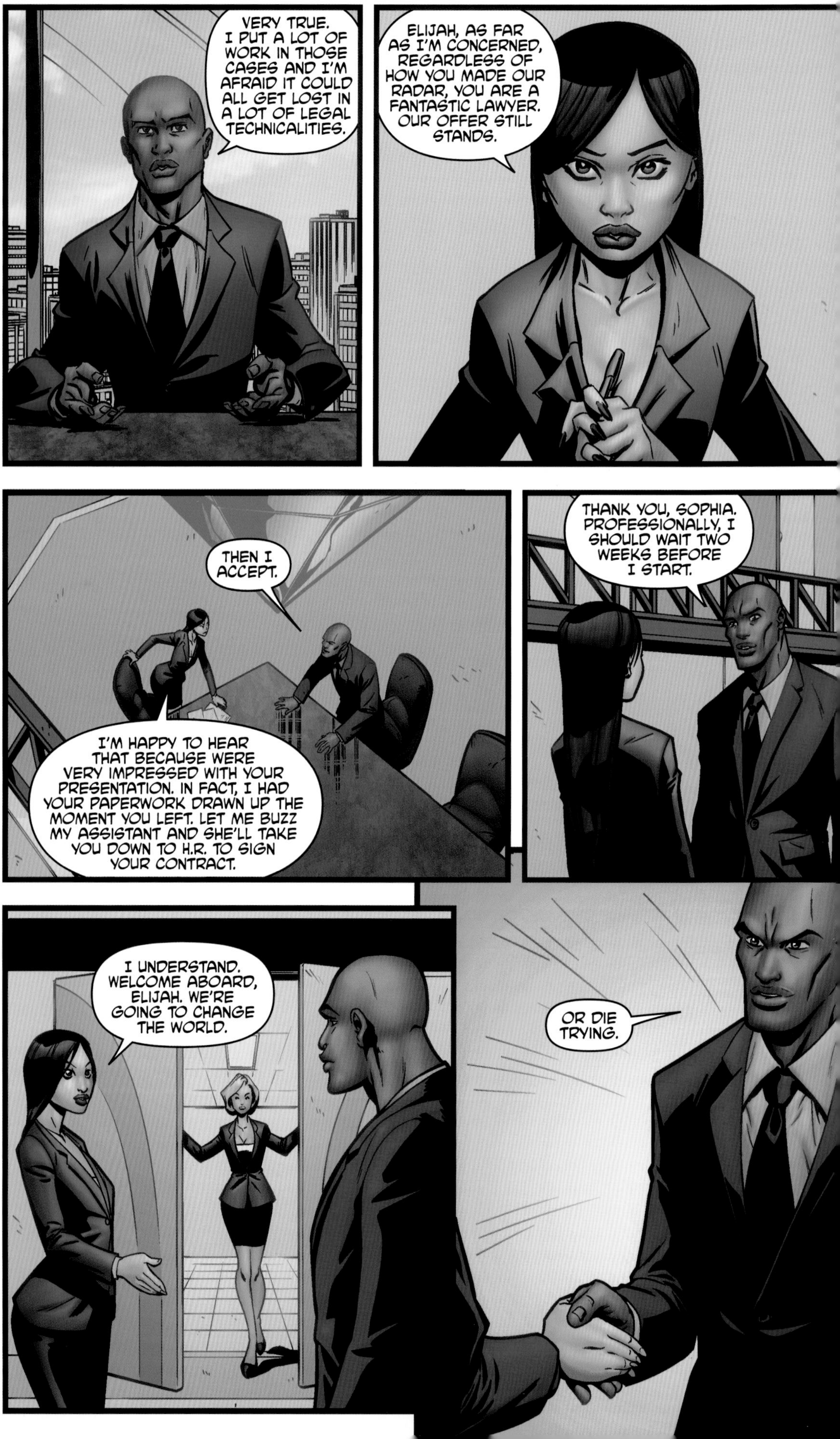
VERY TRUE. I PUT A LOT OF WORK IN THOSE CASES AND I'M AFRAID IT COULD ALL GET LOST IN A LOT OF LEGAL TECHNICALITIES.
ELIJAH, AS FAR AS I'M CONCERNED, REGARDLESS OF HOW YOU MADE OUR RADAR, YOU ARE A FANTASTIC LAWYER. OUR OFFER STILL STANDS.
THEN I ACCEPT.
I'M HAPPY TO HEAR THAT BECAUSE WERE VERY IMPRESSED WITH YOUR PRESENTATION. IN FACT, I HAD YOUR PAPERWORK DRAWN UP THE MOMENT YOU LEFT. LET ME BUZZ MY ASSISTANT AND SHE'LL TAKE YOU DOWN TO H.R. TO SIGN YOUR CONTRACT.
THANK YOU, SOPHIA. PROFESSIONALLY, I SHOULD WAIT TWO WEEKS BEFORE I START.
I UNDERSTAND. WELCOME ABOARD, ELIJAH. WE'RE GOING TO CHANGE THE WORLD.
OR DIE TRYING.

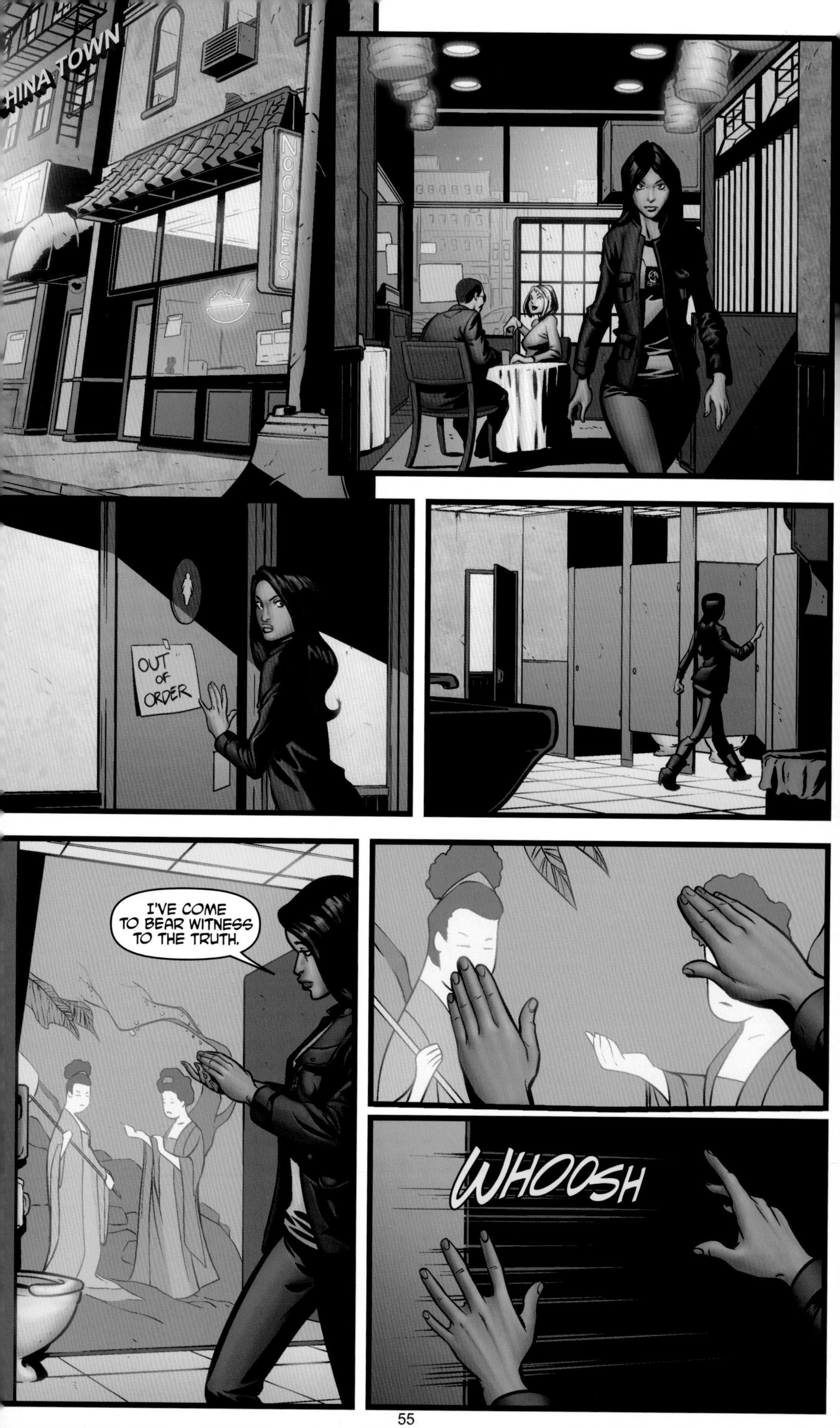
CHINA TOWN
NOODLES
OUT OF ORDER
I'VE COME TO BEAR WITNESS TO THE TRUTH.
WHOOSH

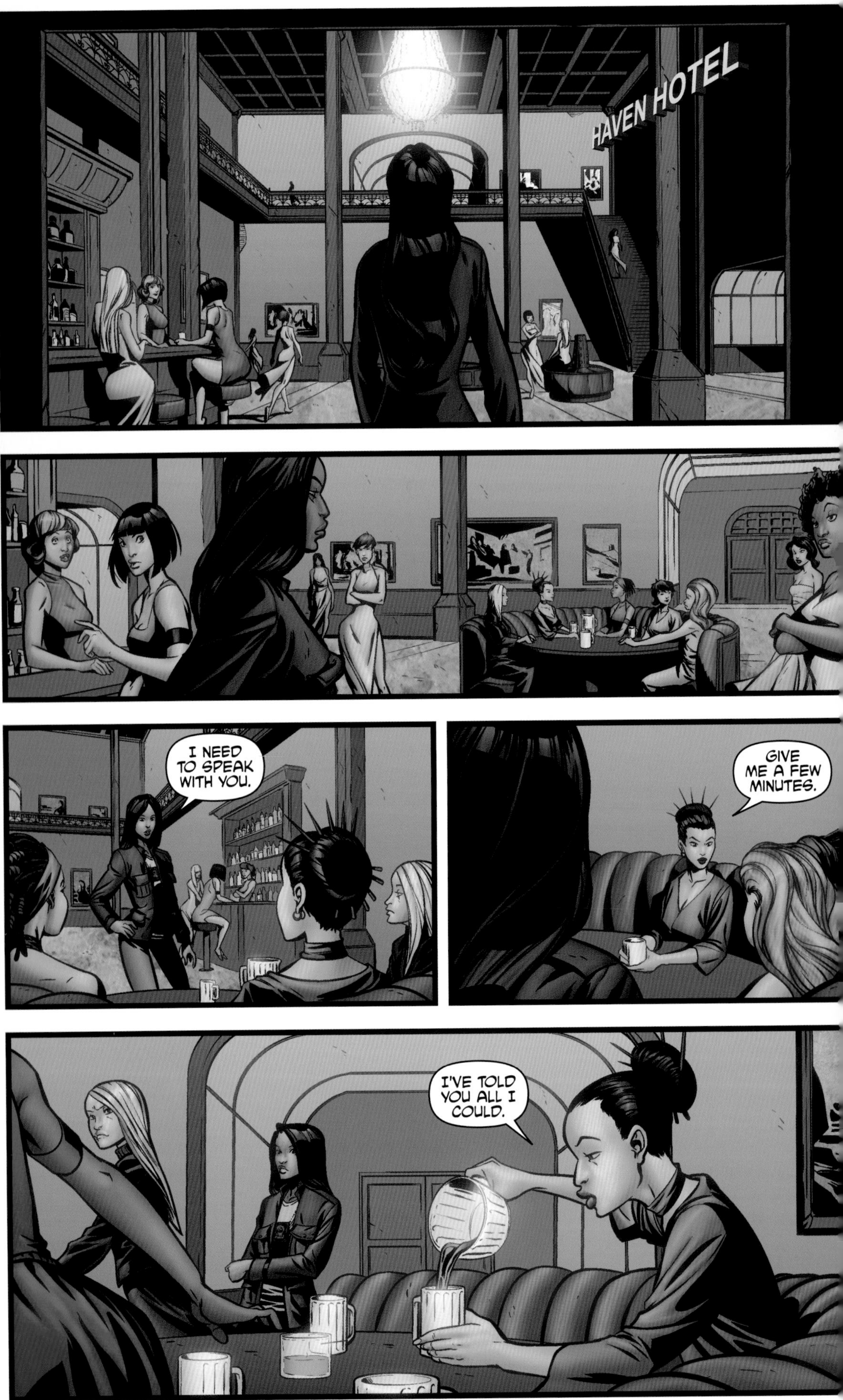
HAVEN HOTEL
I NEED TO SPEAK WITH YOU.
GIVE ME A FEW MINUTES.
I'VE TOLD YOU ALL I COULD.

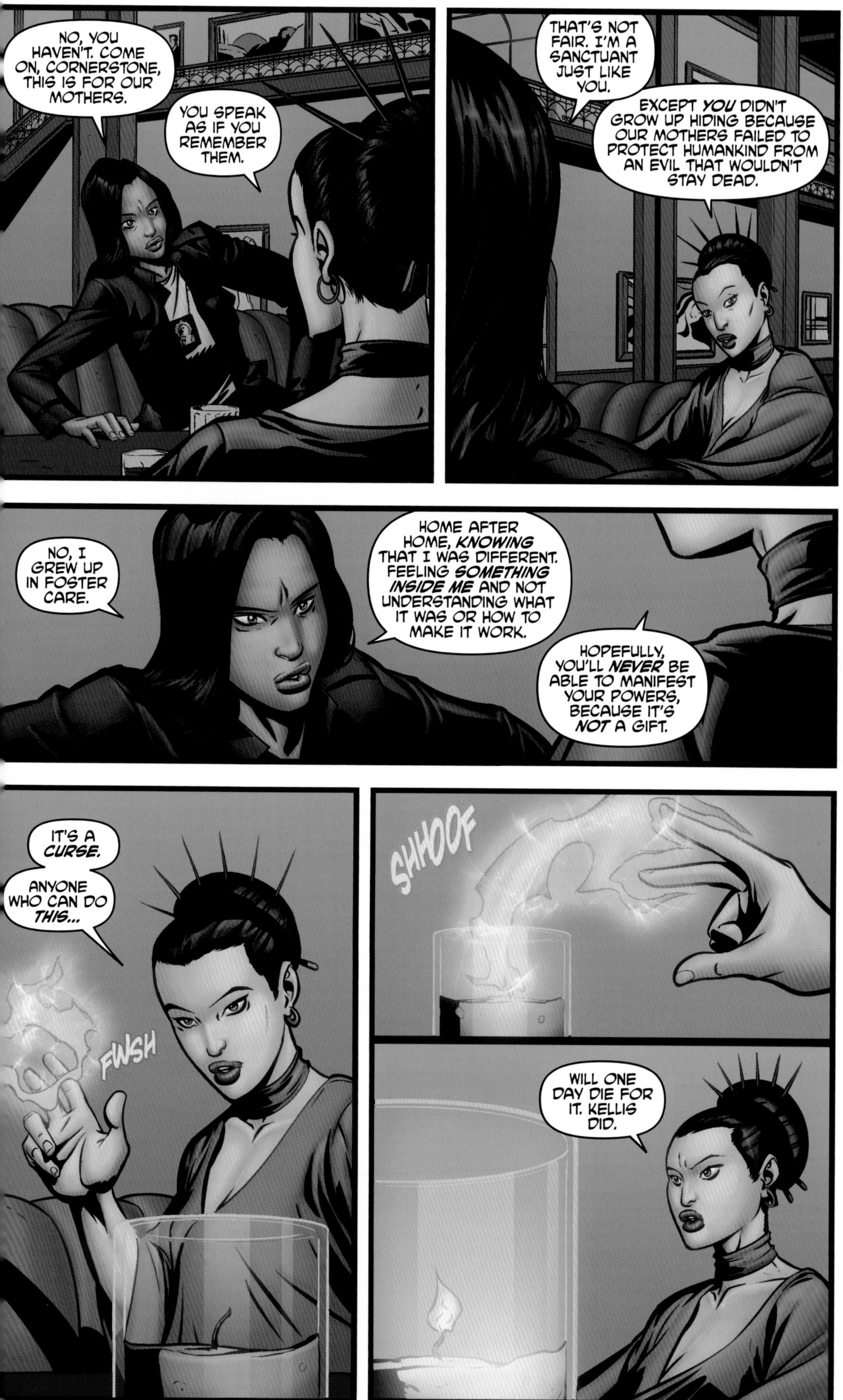
NO, YOU HAVEN'T. COME ON, CORNERSTONE, THIS IS FOR OUR MOTHERS.
YOU SPEAK AS IF YOU REMEMBER THEM.
THAT'S NOT FAIR. I'M A SANCTUANT JUST LIKE YOU.
EXCEPT *YOU* DIDN'T GROW UP HIDING BECAUSE OUR MOTHERS FAILED TO PROTECT HUMANKIND FROM AN EVIL THAT WOULDN'T STAY DEAD.
NO, I GREW UP IN FOSTER CARE.
HOME AFTER HOME, *KNOWING* THAT I WAS DIFFERENT. FEELING *SOMETHING INSIDE ME* AND NOT UNDERSTANDING WHAT IT WAS OR HOW TO MAKE IT WORK.
HOPEFULLY, YOU'LL *NEVER* BE ABLE TO MANIFEST YOUR POWERS, BECAUSE IT'S *NOT* A GIFT.
IT'S A *CURSE.*
ANYONE WHO CAN DO *THIS...*
FWSH
SHHOOF
WILL ONE DAY DIE FOR IT. KELLIS DID.

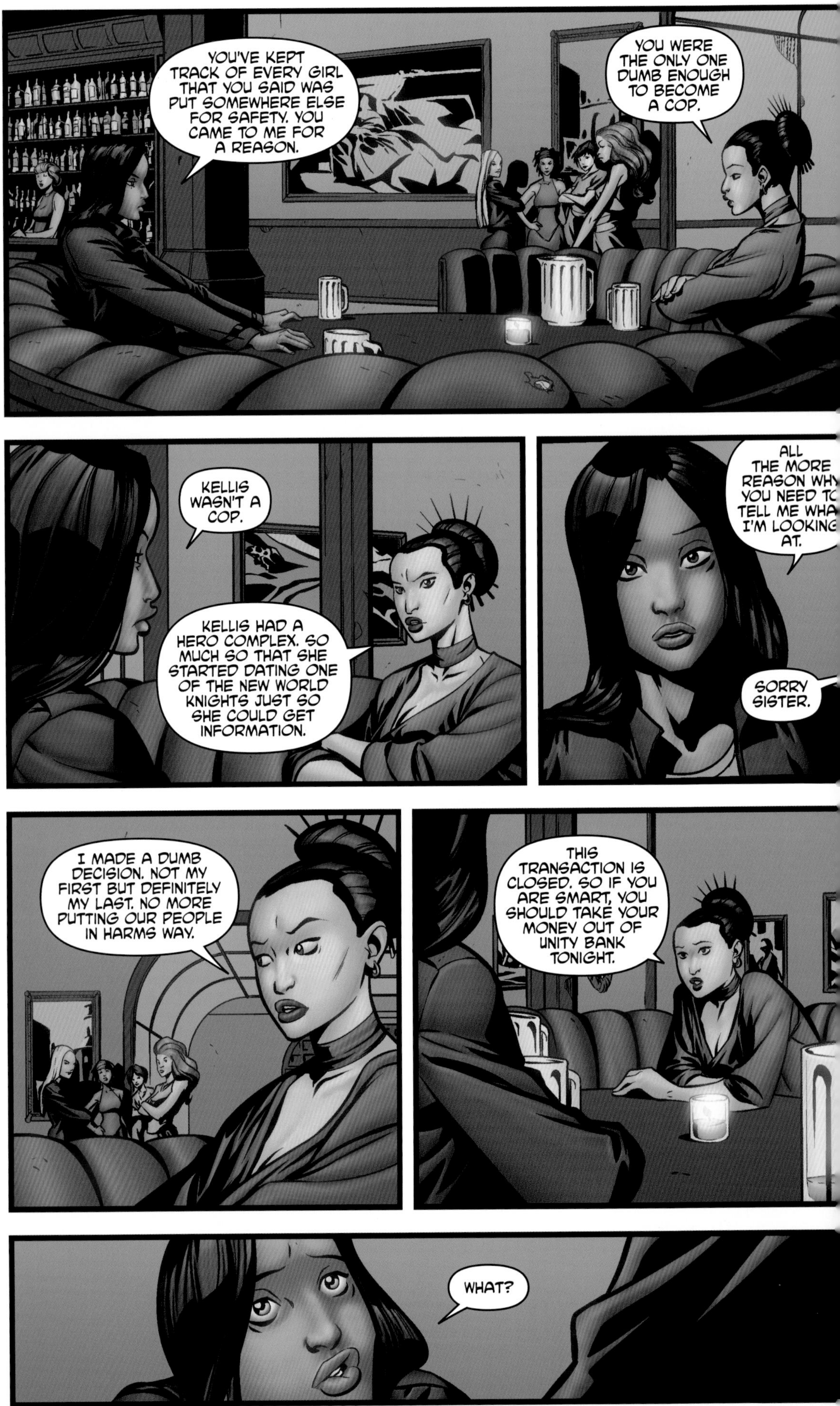
YOU'VE KEPT TRACK OF EVERY GIRL THAT YOU SAID WAS PUT SOMEWHERE ELSE FOR SAFETY. YOU CAME TO ME FOR A REASON.
YOU WERE THE ONLY ONE DUMB ENOUGH TO BECOME A COP.
KELLIS WASN'T A COP.
KELLIS HAD A HERO COMPLEX. SO MUCH SO THAT SHE STARTED DATING ONE OF THE NEW WORLD KNIGHTS JUST SO SHE COULD GET INFORMATION.
ALL THE MORE REASON WHY YOU NEED TO TELL ME WHAT I'M LOOKING AT.
SORRY SISTER.
I MADE A DUMB DECISION. NOT MY FIRST BUT DEFINITELY MY LAST. NO MORE PUTTING OUR PEOPLE IN HARMS WAY.
THIS TRANSACTION IS CLOSED. SO IF YOU ARE SMART, YOU SHOULD TAKE YOUR MONEY OUT OF UNITY BANK TONIGHT.
WHAT?

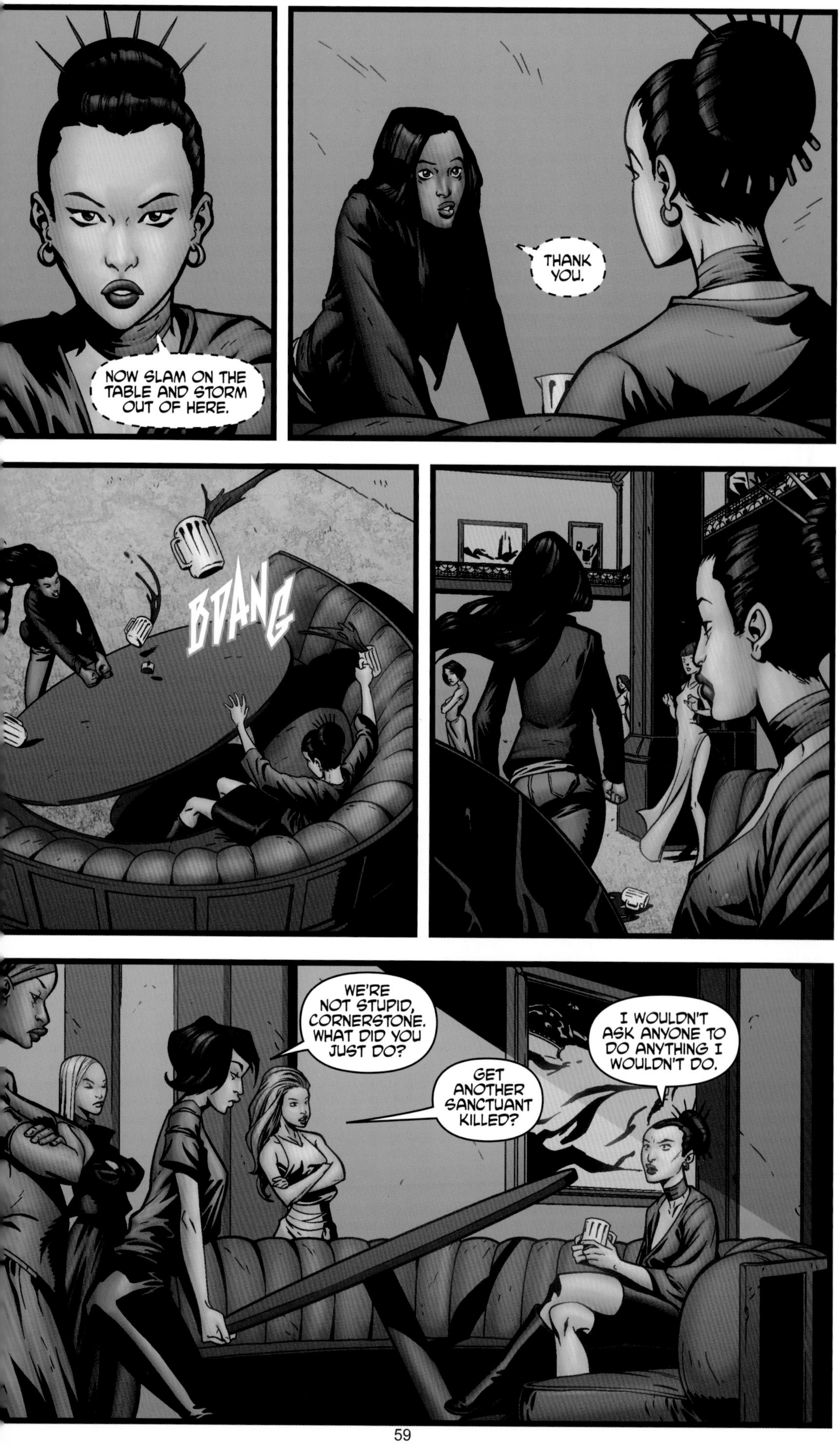
NOW SLAM ON THE TABLE AND STORM OUT OF HERE.
THANK YOU.
BDANG
WE'RE NOT STUPID, CORNERSTONE. WHAT DID YOU JUST DO?
GET ANOTHER SANCTUANT KILLED?
I WOULDN'T ASK ANYONE TO DO ANYTHING I WOULDN'T DO.

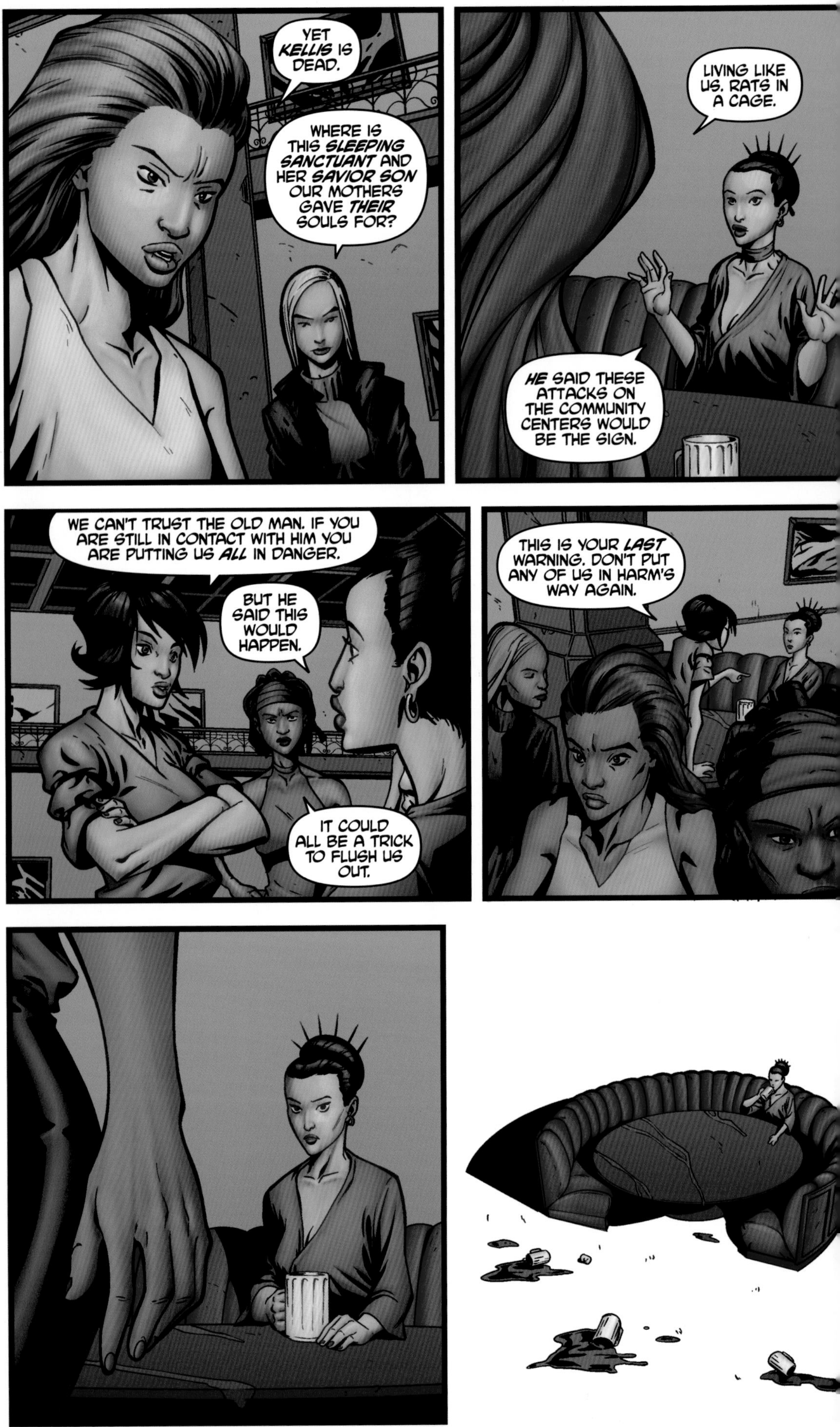
YET KELLIS IS DEAD.
WHERE IS THIS SLEEPING SANCTUANT AND HER SAVIOR SON OUR MOTHERS GAVE THEIR SOULS FOR?
LIVING LIKE US. RATS IN A CAGE.
HE SAID THESE ATTACKS ON THE COMMUNITY CENTERS WOULD BE THE SIGN.
WE CAN'T TRUST THE OLD MAN. IF YOU ARE STILL IN CONTACT WITH HIM YOU ARE PUTTING US ALL IN DANGER.
BUT HE SAID THIS WOULD HAPPEN.
IT COULD ALL BE A TRICK TO FLUSH US OUT.
THIS IS YOUR LAST WARNING. DON'T PUT ANY OF US IN HARM'S WAY AGAIN.

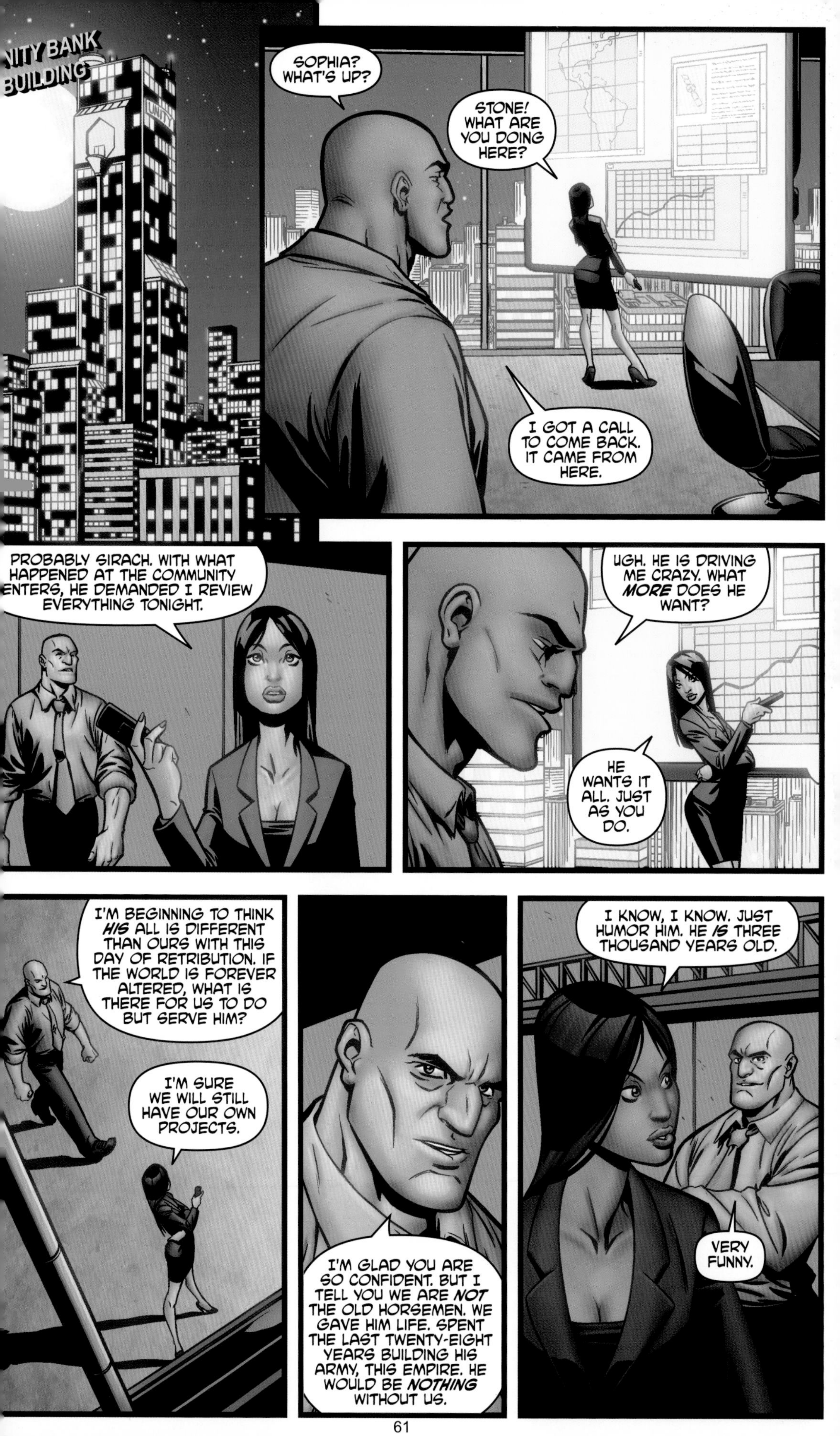
NITY BANK BUILDING
SOPHIA? WHAT'S UP?
STONE! WHAT ARE YOU DOING HERE?
I GOT A CALL TO COME BACK. IT CAME FROM HERE.
PROBABLY SIRACH. WITH WHAT HAPPENED AT THE COMMUNITY ENTERS, HE DEMANDED I REVIEW EVERYTHING TONIGHT.
UGH. HE IS DRIVING ME CRAZY. WHAT MORE DOES HE WANT?
HE WANTS IT ALL. JUST AS YOU DO.
I'M BEGINNING TO THINK HIS ALL IS DIFFERENT THAN OURS WITH THIS DAY OF RETRIBUTION. IF THE WORLD IS FOREVER ALTERED, WHAT IS THERE FOR US TO DO BUT SERVE HIM?
I'M SURE WE WILL STILL HAVE OUR OWN PROJECTS.
I'M GLAD YOU ARE SO CONFIDENT. BUT I TELL YOU WE ARE NOT THE OLD HORSEMEN. WE GAVE HIM LIFE. SPENT THE LAST TWENTY-EIGHT YEARS BUILDING HIS ARMY, THIS EMPIRE. HE WOULD BE NOTHING WITHOUT US.
I KNOW, I KNOW. JUST HUMOR HIM. HE IS THREE THOUSAND YEARS OLD.
VERY FUNNY.

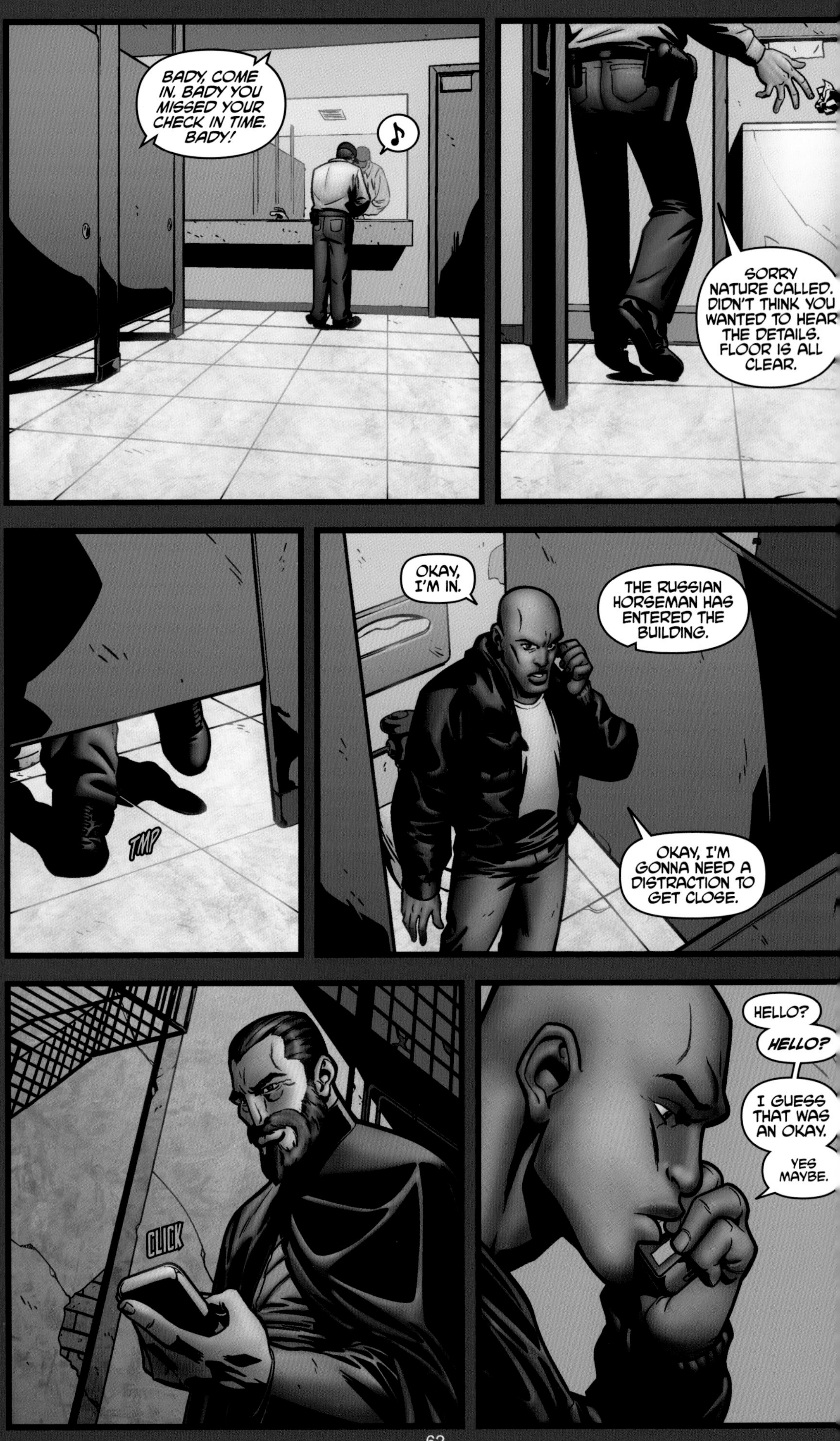
BADY, COME IN. BADY YOU MISSED YOUR CHECK IN TIME. BADY!
♪
SORRY NATURE CALLED. DIDN'T THINK YOU WANTED TO HEAR THE DETAILS. FLOOR IS ALL CLEAR.
TMP
OKAY, I'M IN.
THE RUSSIAN HORSEMAN HAS ENTERED THE BUILDING.
OKAY, I'M GONNA NEED A DISTRACTION TO GET CLOSE.
CLICK
HELLO?
HELLO?
I GUESS THAT WAS AN OKAY.
YES MAYBE.

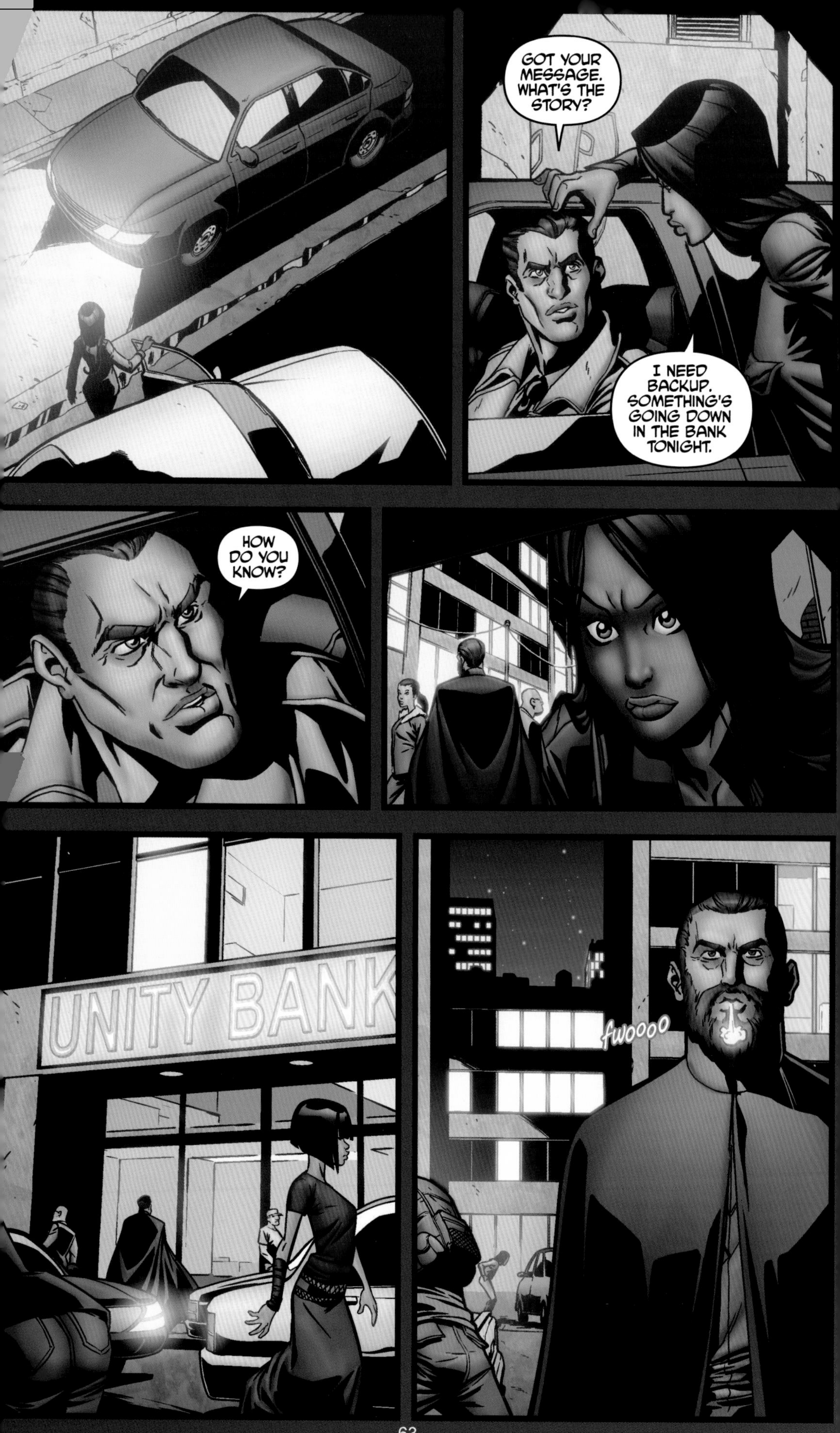
GOT YOUR MESSAGE. WHAT'S THE STORY?
I NEED BACKUP. SOMETHING'S GOING DOWN IN THE BANK TONIGHT.
HOW DO YOU KNOW?
UNITY BANK
fwoooo

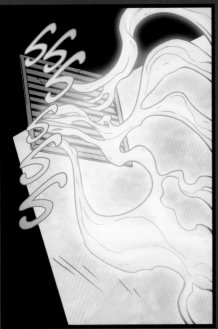

WHAT IS *THAT?*

RRIING
RRIING

ARE YOU SEEING THIS?

SEEING WHAT?

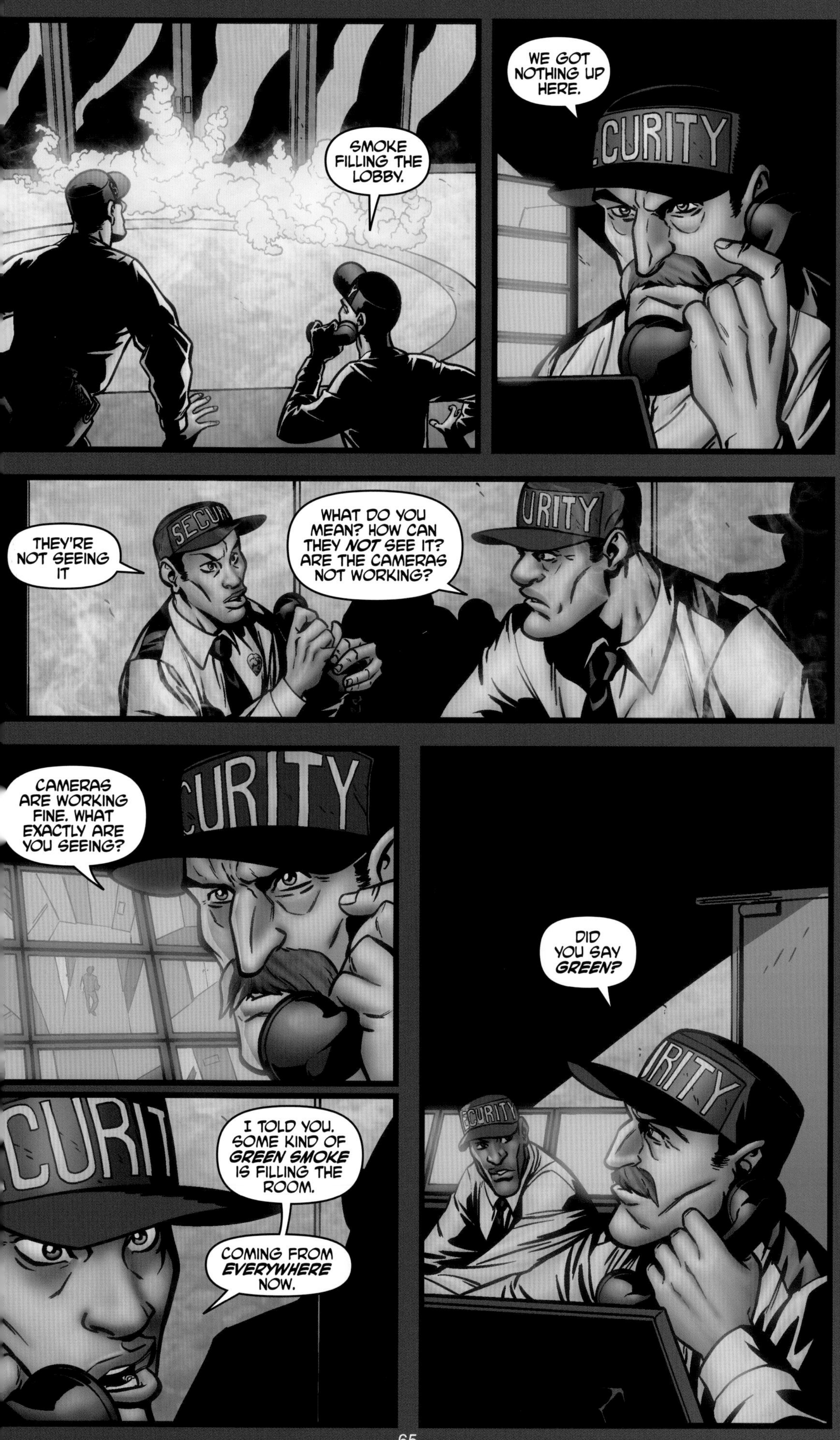
SMOKE FILLING THE LOBBY.
WE GOT NOTHING UP HERE.
THEY'RE NOT SEEING IT
WHAT DO YOU MEAN? HOW CAN THEY NOT SEE IT? ARE THE CAMERAS NOT WORKING?
CAMERAS ARE WORKING FINE. WHAT EXACTLY ARE YOU SEEING?
I TOLD YOU. SOME KIND OF GREEN SMOKE IS FILLING THE ROOM.
COMING FROM EVERYWHERE NOW.
DID YOU SAY GREEN?

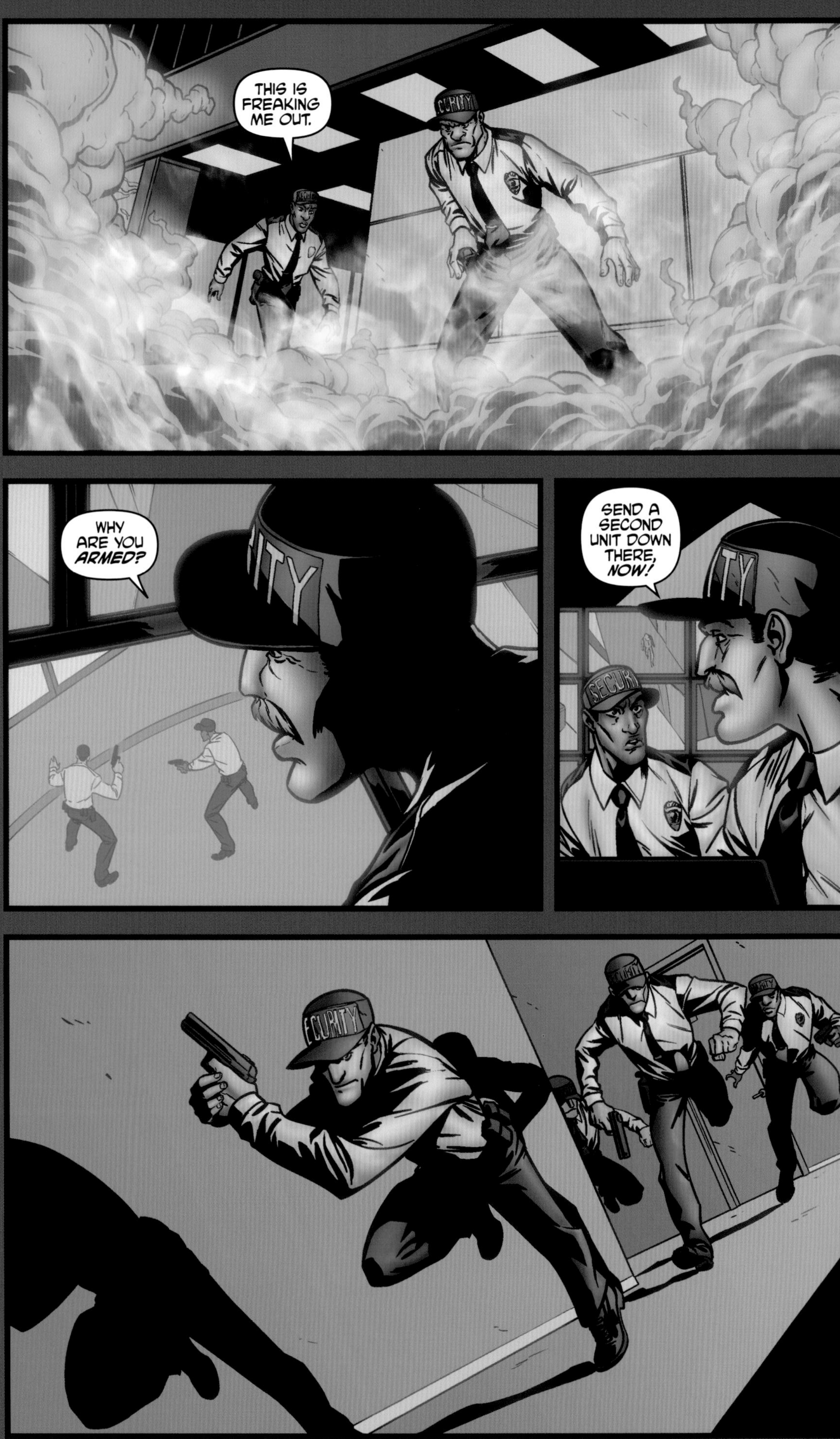
THIS IS FREAKING ME OUT.
WHY ARE YOU ARMED?
SEND A SECOND UNIT DOWN THERE, NOW!

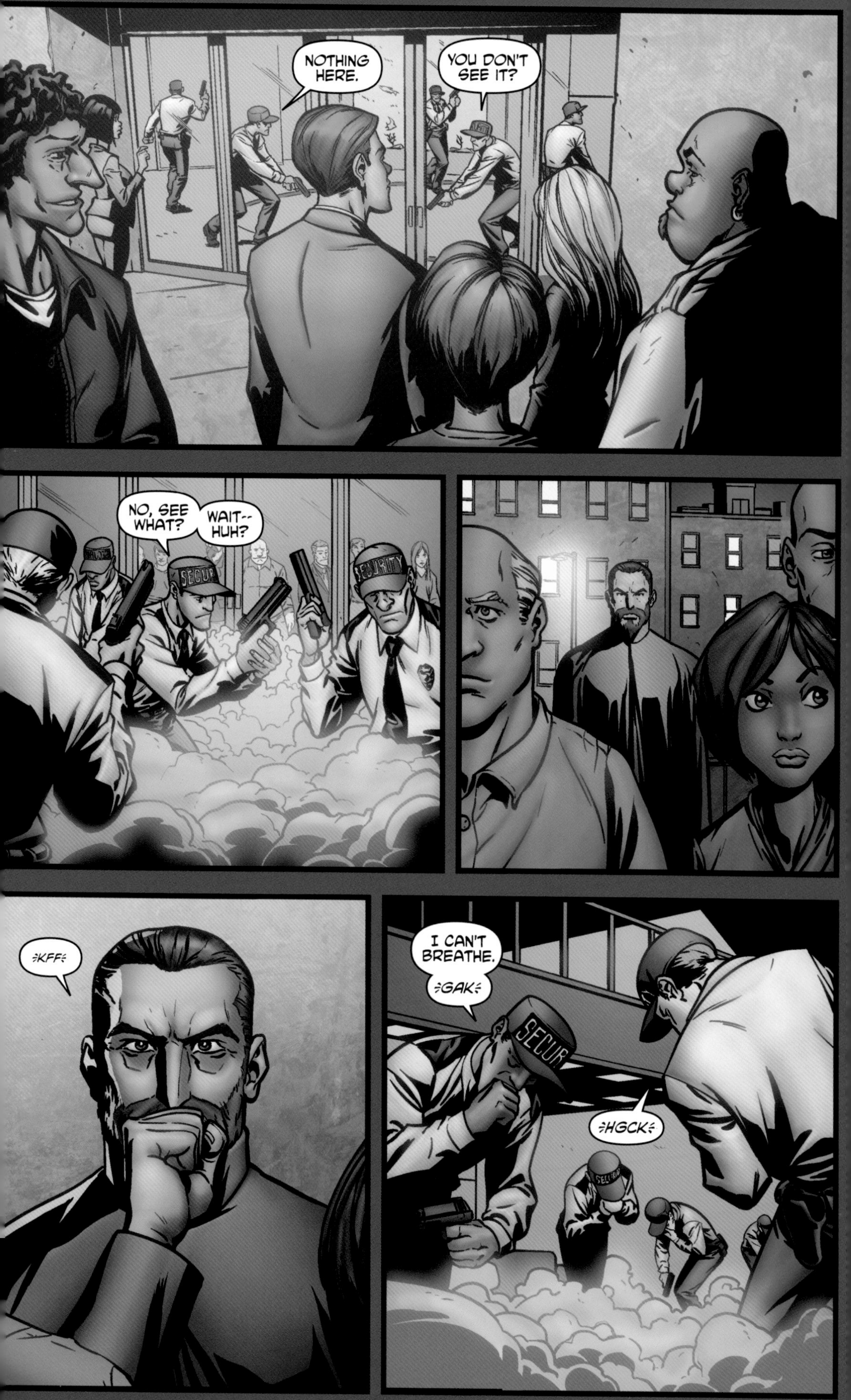
NOTHING HERE.
YOU DON'T SEE IT?
NO, SEE WHAT?
WAIT-- HUH?
KFF
I CAN'T BREATHE.
GAK
HGCK

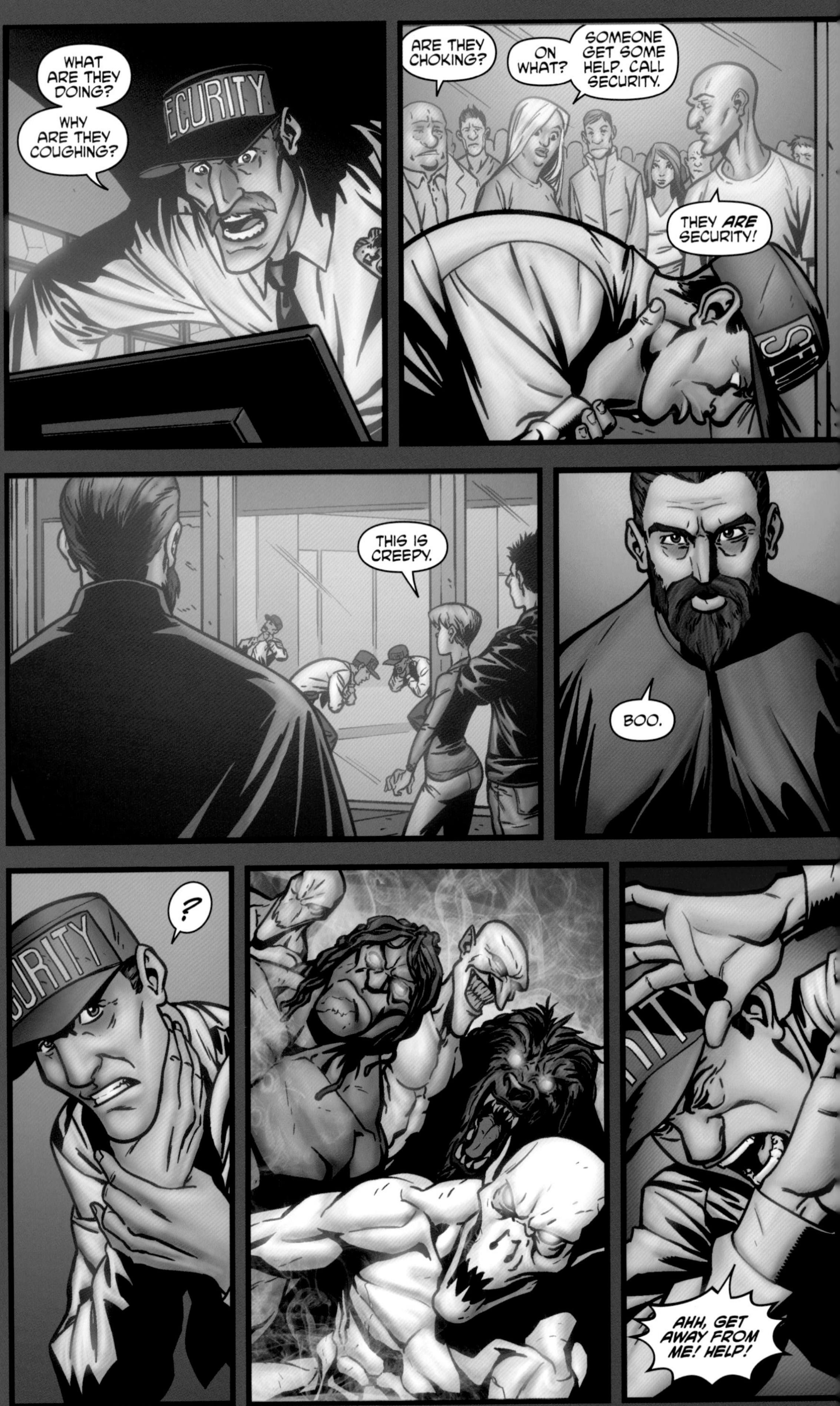
WHAT ARE THEY DOING?
WHY ARE THEY COUGHING?
ECURITY
ARE THEY CHOKING?
ON WHAT?
SOMEONE GET SOME HELP. CALL SECURITY.
THEY *ARE* SECURITY!
THIS IS CREEPY.
BOO.
?
URITY
AHH, GET AWAY FROM ME! HELP!

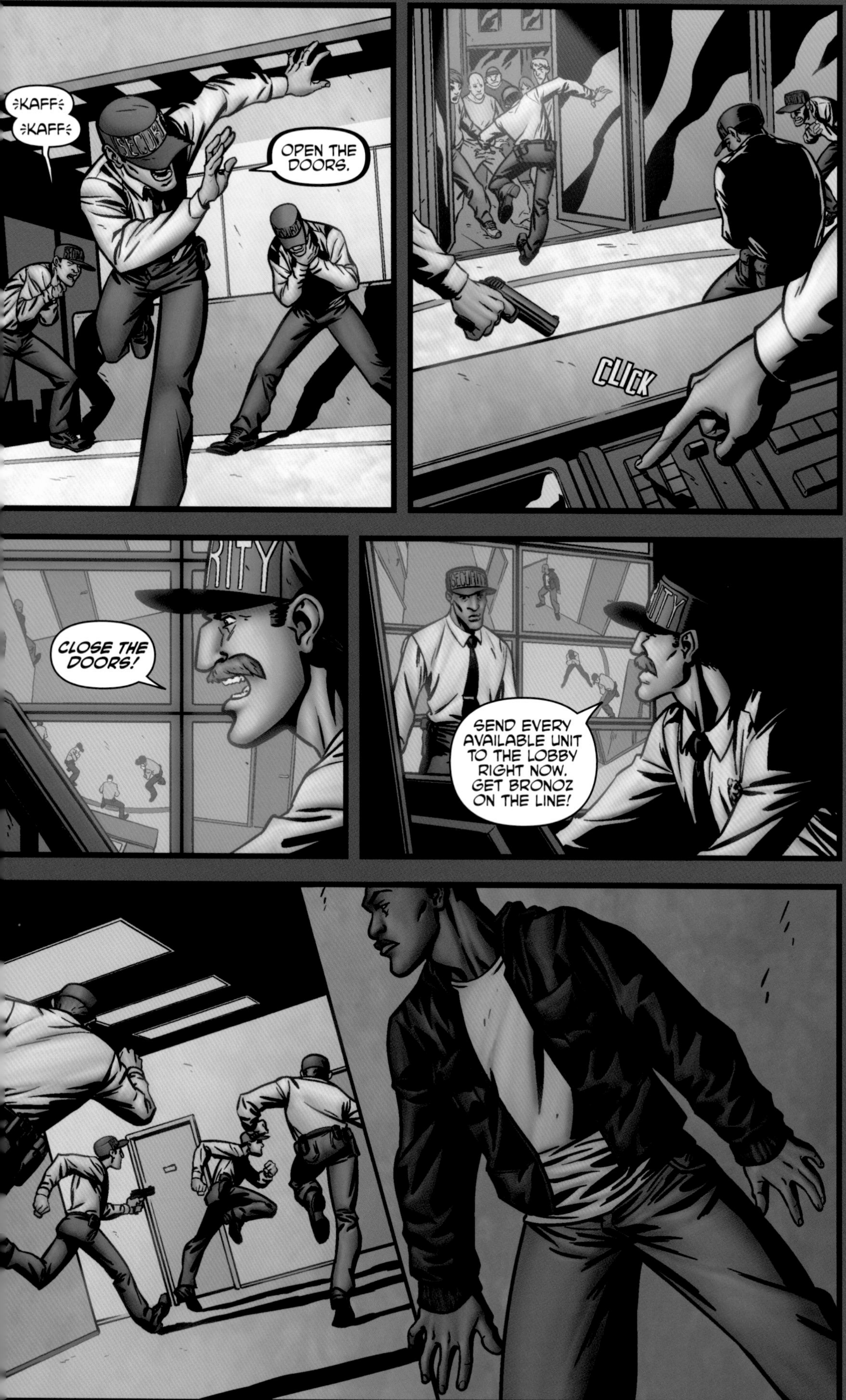
KAFF
KAFF
OPEN THE DOORS.
CLICK
CLOSE THE DOORS!
SEND EVERY AVAILABLE UNIT TO THE LOBBY RIGHT NOW. GET BRONOZ ON THE LINE!

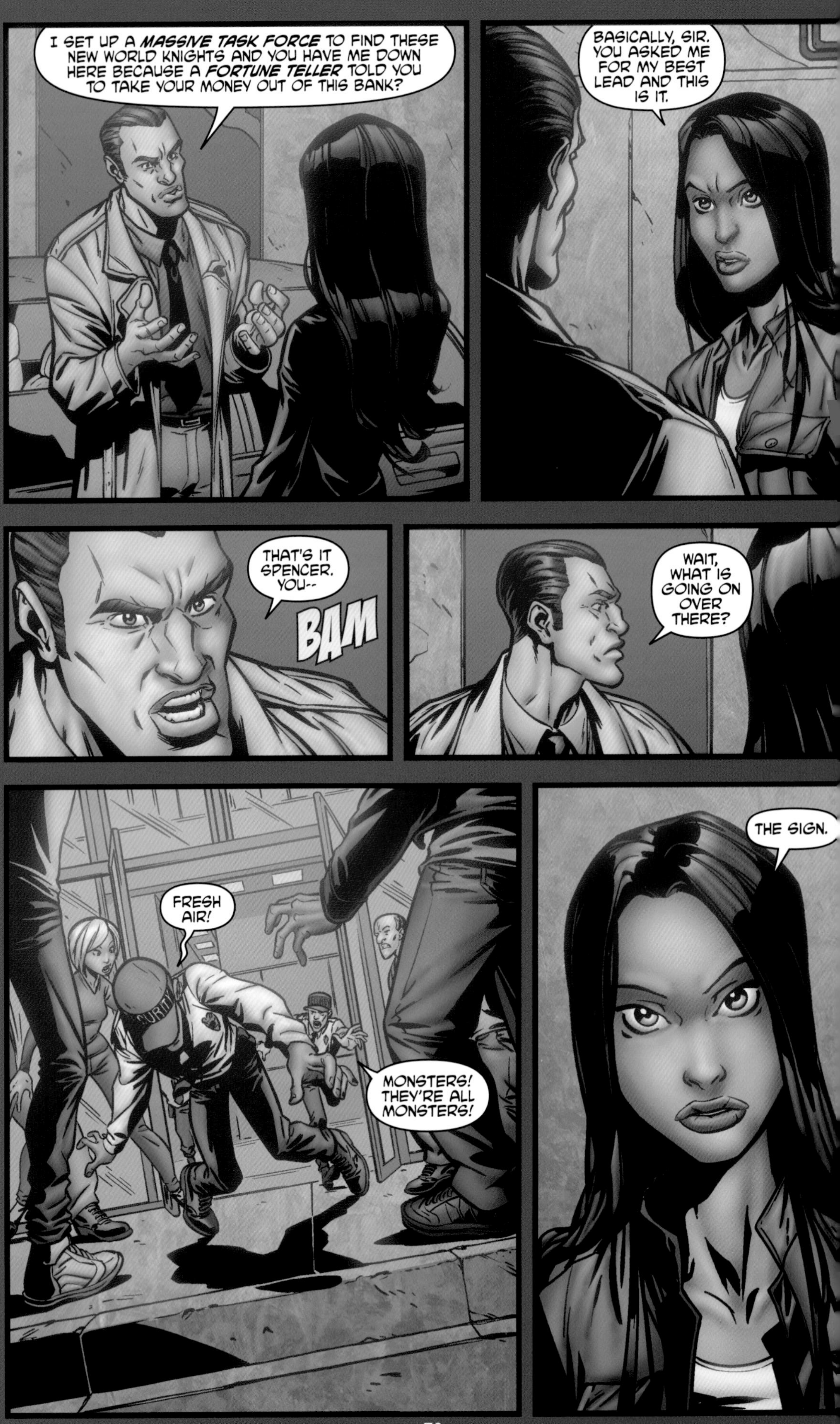
I SET UP A *MASSIVE TASK FORCE* TO FIND THESE NEW WORLD KNIGHTS AND YOU HAVE ME DOWN HERE BECAUSE A *FORTUNE TELLER* TOLD YOU TO TAKE YOUR MONEY OUT OF THIS BANK?
BASICALLY, SIR. YOU ASKED ME FOR MY BEST LEAD AND THIS IS IT.
THAT'S IT SPENCER. YOU--
BAM
WAIT, WHAT IS GOING ON OVER THERE?
FRESH AIR!
MONSTERS! THEY'RE ALL MONSTERS!
THE SIGN.

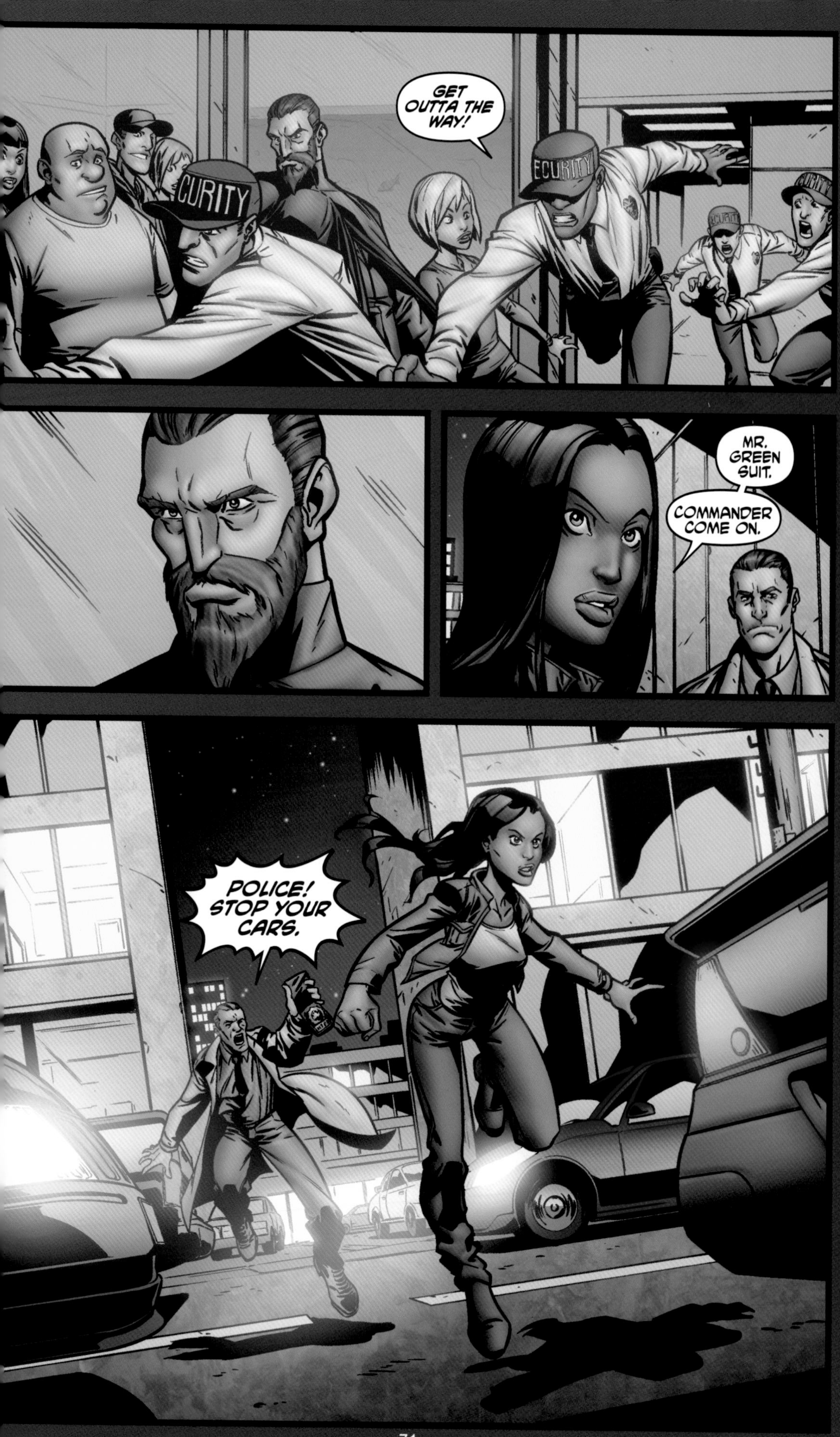
GET OUTTA THE WAY!
ECURITY
CURITY
MR. GREEN SUIT.
COMMANDER COME ON.
POLICE! STOP YOUR CARS.

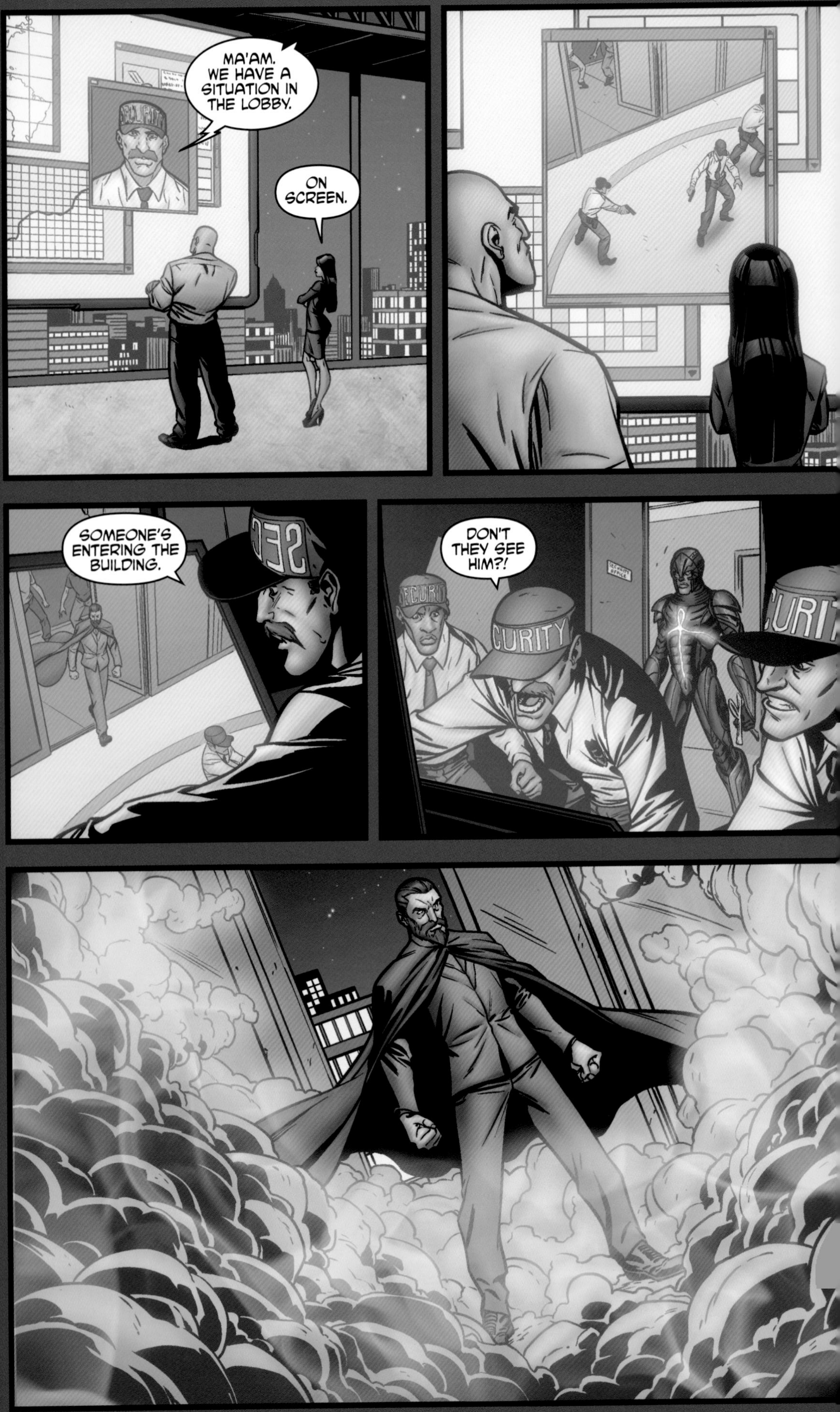
MA'AM. WE HAVE A SITUATION IN THE LOBBY.
ON SCREEN.
SOMEONE'S ENTERING THE BUILDING.
DON'T THEY SEE HIM?!

TURN AROUND! HE'S RIGHT BEHIND YOU!

WHAT ARE THEY DOING?

WAH?!

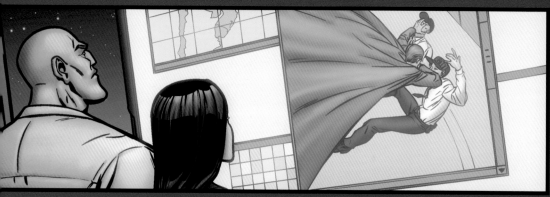

IT'S NOAH!

SECURE THE BUILDING, NOW!

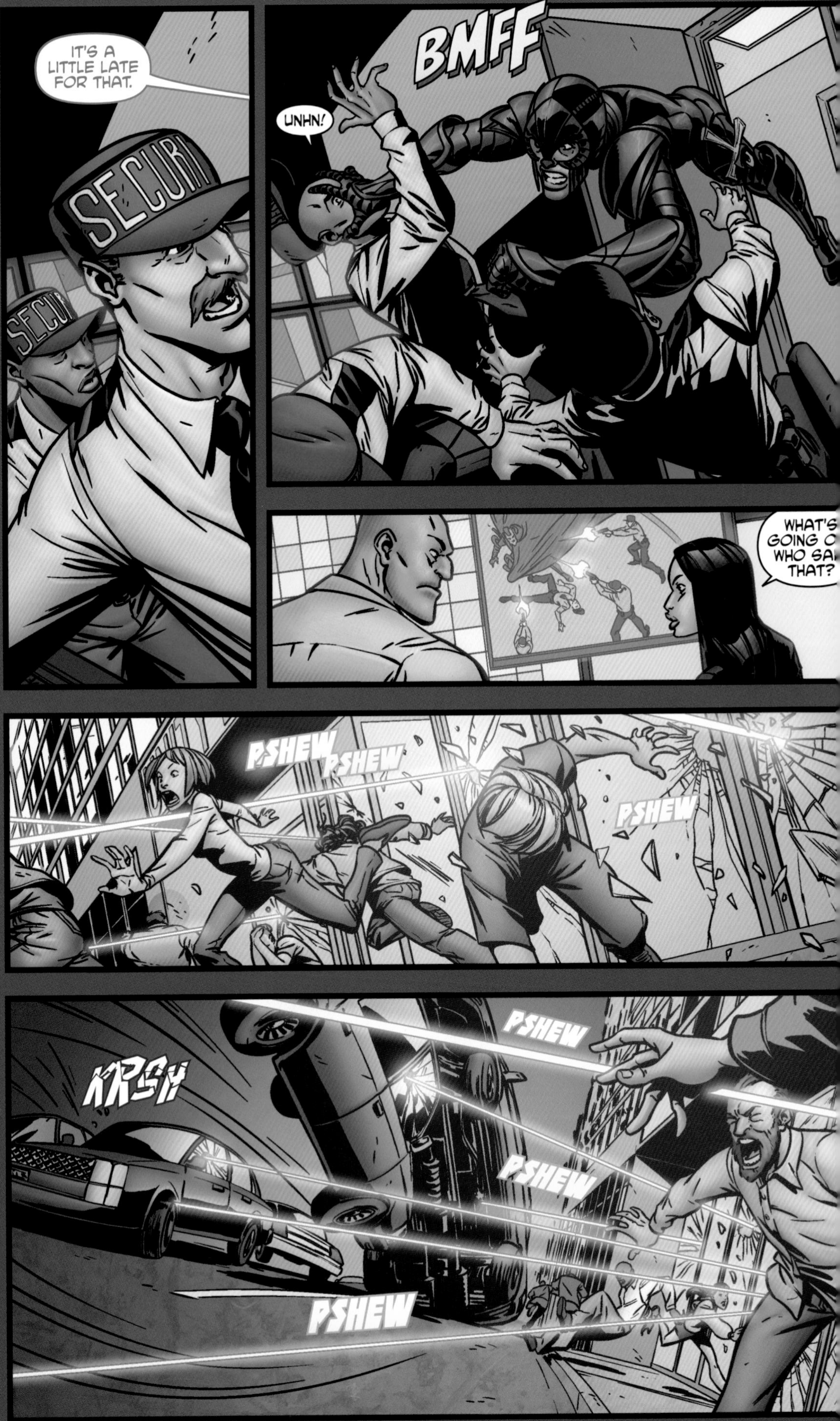

IT'S A LITTLE LATE FOR THAT.
SECURI
SECURI
BMFF
UNHN!
WHAT'S GOING O WHO SA THAT?
PSHEW
PSHEW
PSHEW
KRSH
PSHEW
PSHEW
PSHEW

PSHEW
PSHEW
VWOOP
!
KRASSH
TNK
TNK
PSHEW
BLAM
BLAM

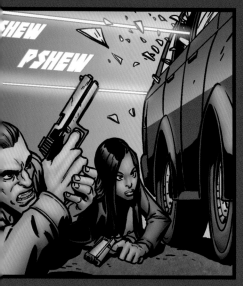

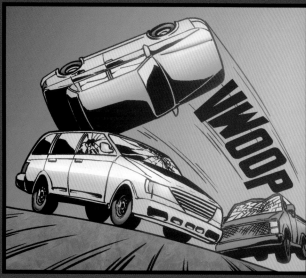

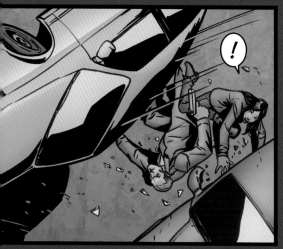

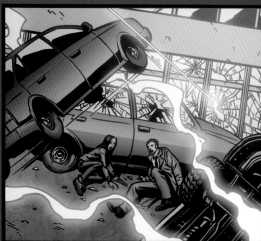

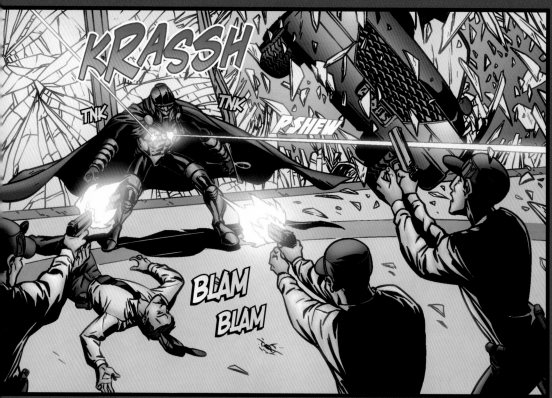

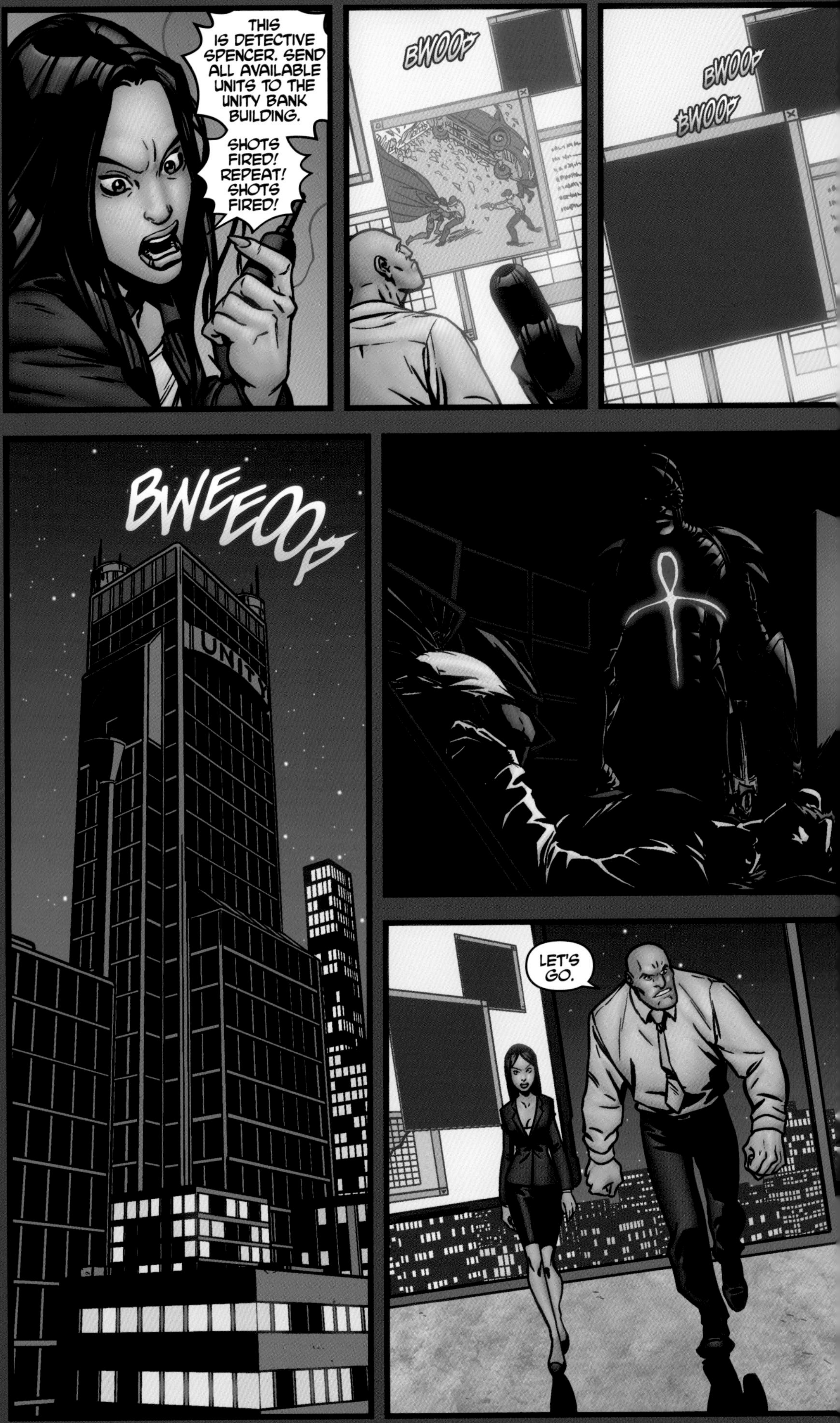
THIS IS DETECTIVE SPENCER. SEND ALL AVAILABLE UNITS TO THE UNITY BANK BUILDING.
SHOTS FIRED! REPEAT! SHOTS FIRED!
BWOOP
BWOOP
BWOOP
BWEEOOP
UNITY
LET'S GO.

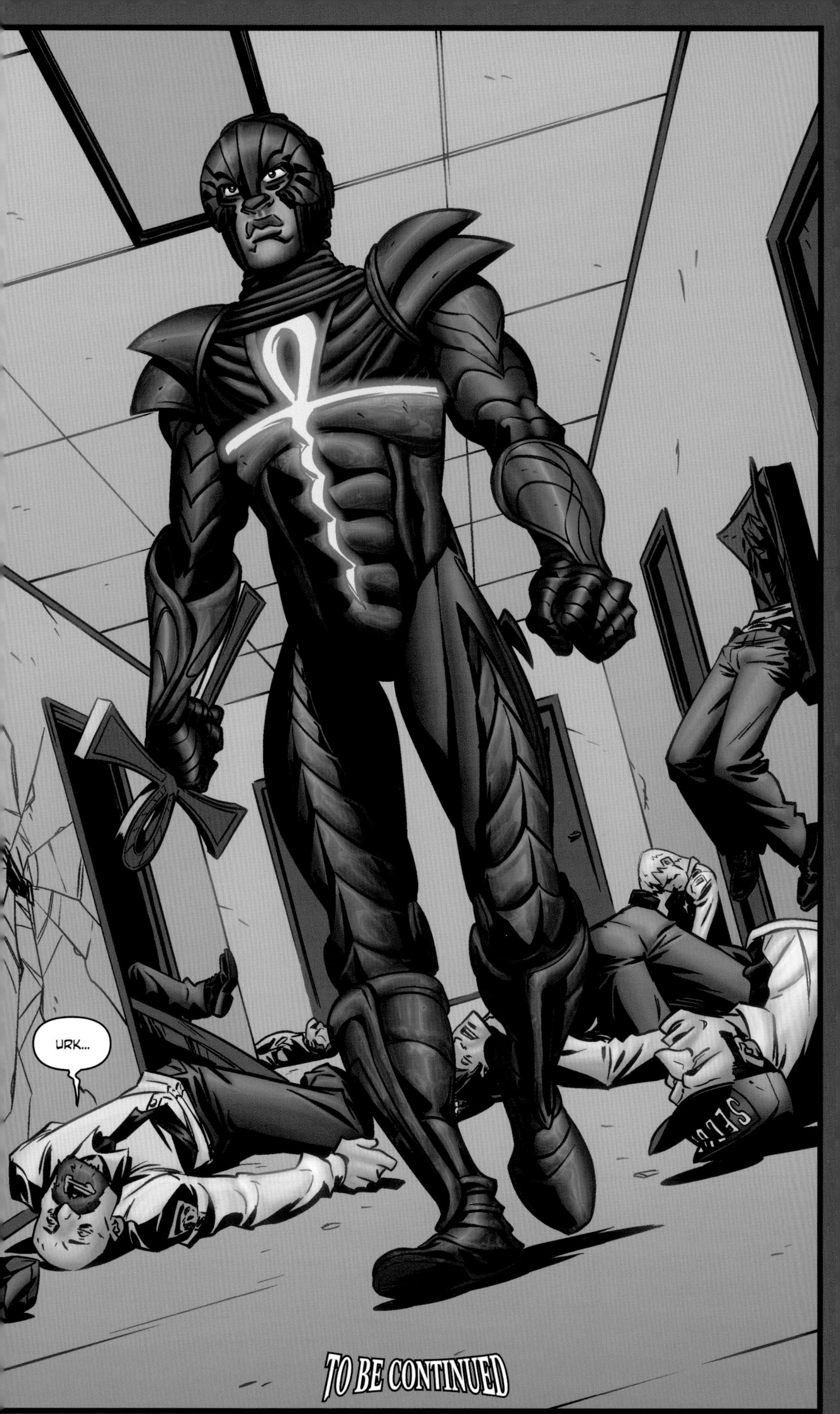
URK...
TO BE CONTINUED

CHAPTER ⑨

Sirach created abominations. They appeared as dark horsemen, and each had only one power—but it was a great and terrible power. Power so great that it burned up the human soul within, leaving only hunger and darkness behind. Many were the heroes that they killed.

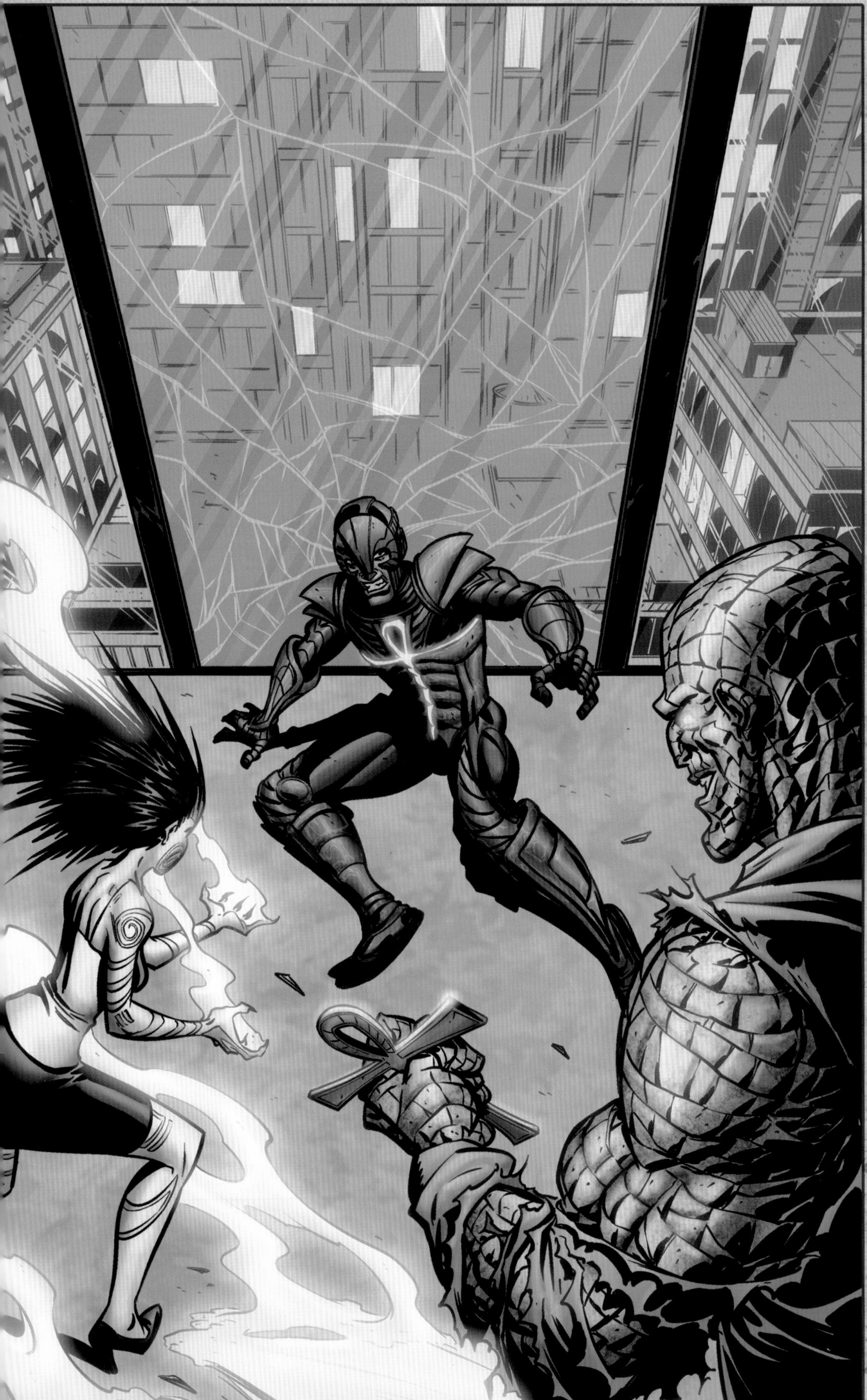

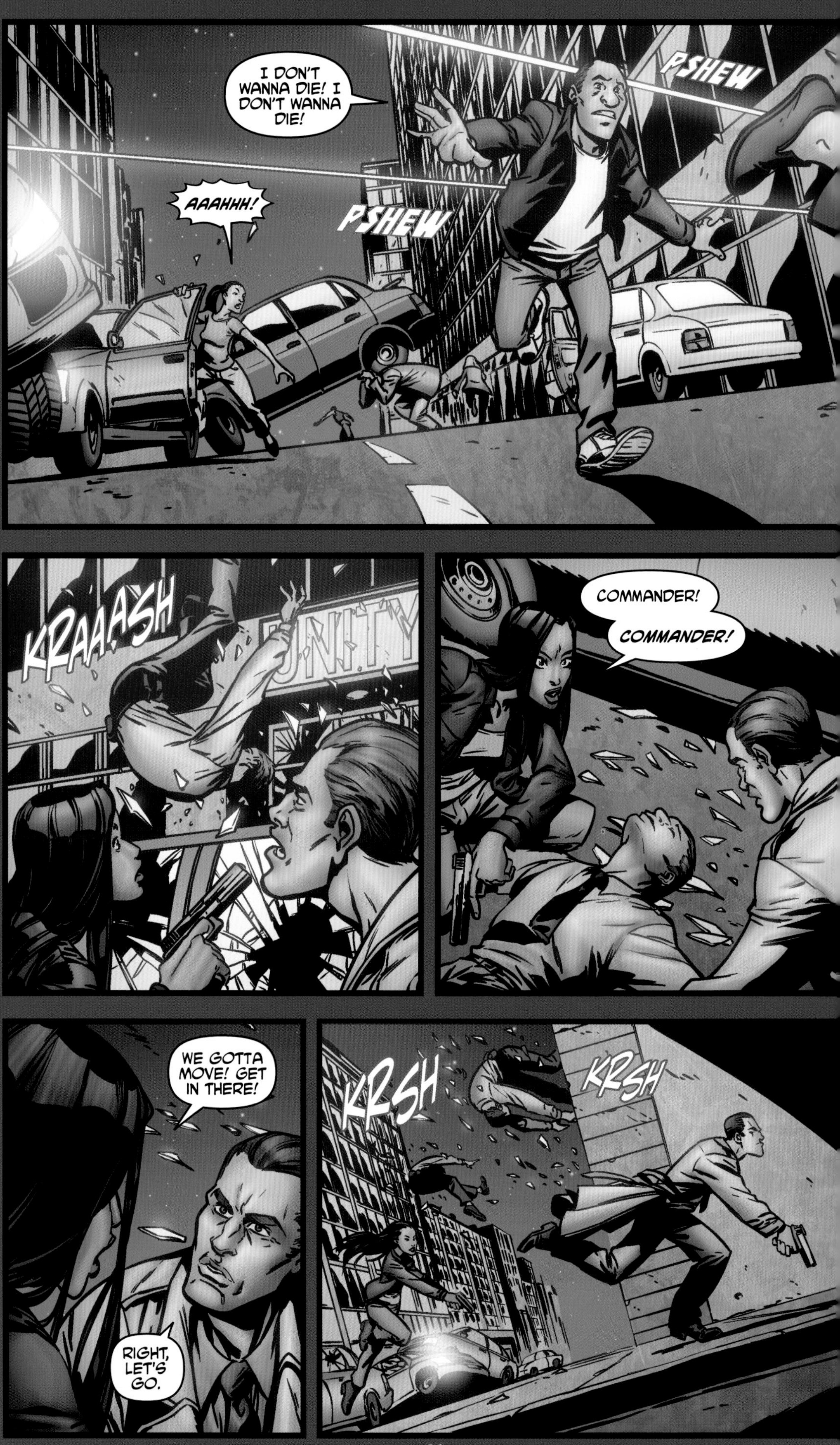
I DON'T WANNA DIE! I DON'T WANNA DIE!
PSHEW
AAAHHH!
PSHEW
KRAAASH
UNITY
COMMANDER!
COMMANDER!
WE GOTTA MOVE! GET IN THERE!
RIGHT, LET'S GO.
KRSH
KRSH

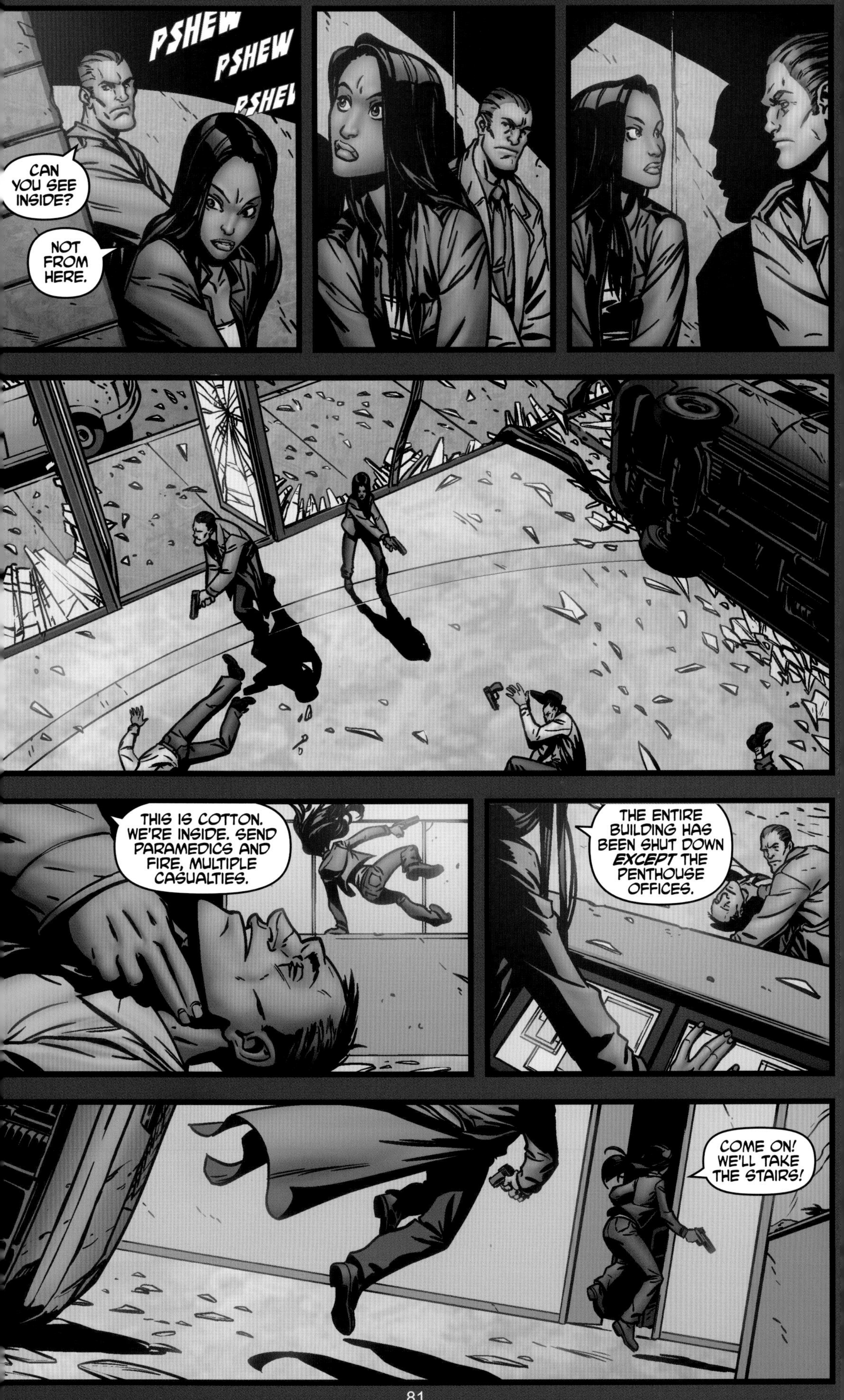
PSHEW
PSHEW
PSHEW
CAN YOU SEE INSIDE?
NOT FROM HERE.
THIS IS COTTON. WE'RE INSIDE. SEND PARAMEDICS AND FIRE, MULTIPLE CASUALTIES.
THE ENTIRE BUILDING HAS BEEN SHUT DOWN *EXCEPT* THE PENTHOUSE OFFICES.
COME ON! WE'LL TAKE THE STAIRS!

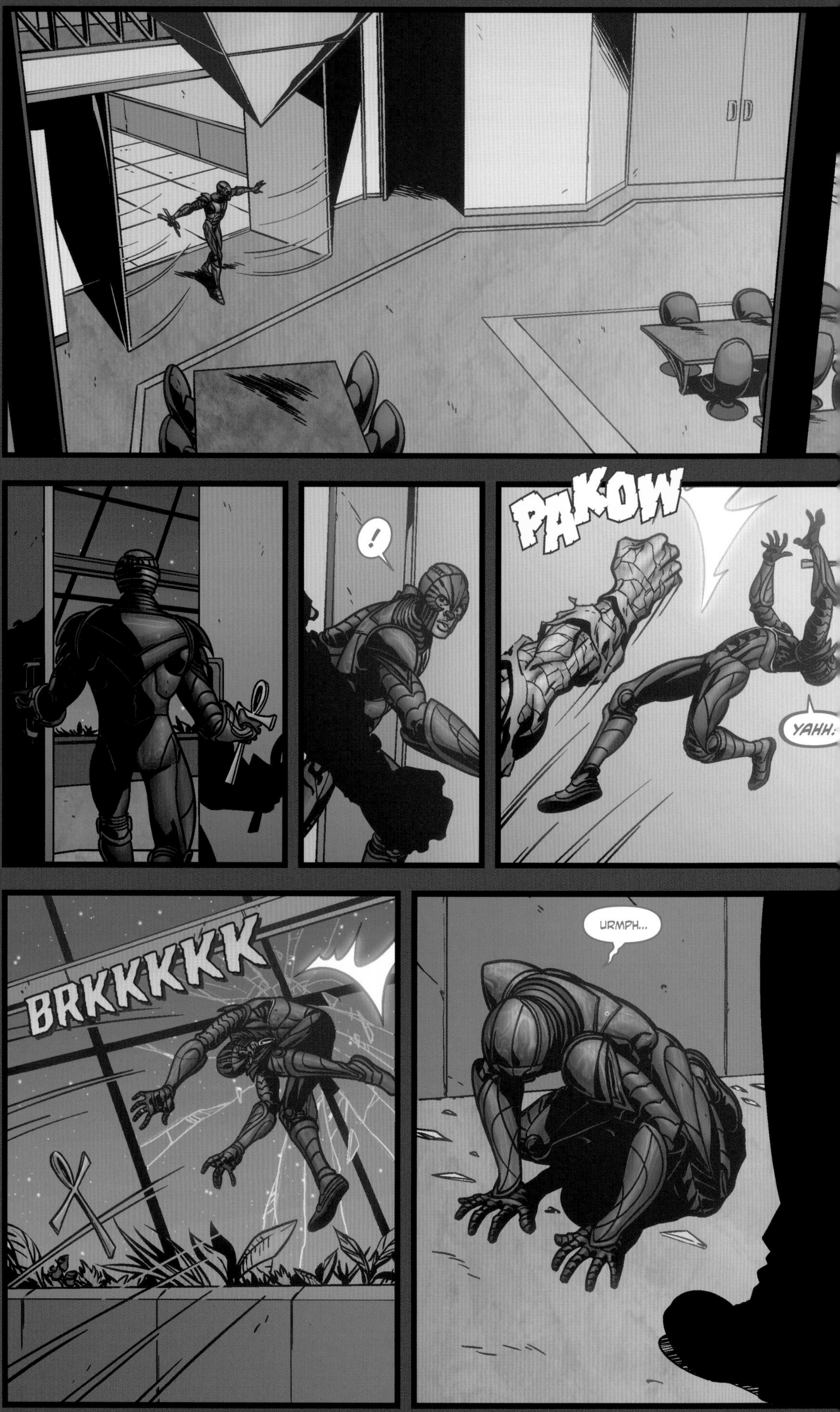
!
PAKOW
YAHH!
BRKKKKK
URMPH...

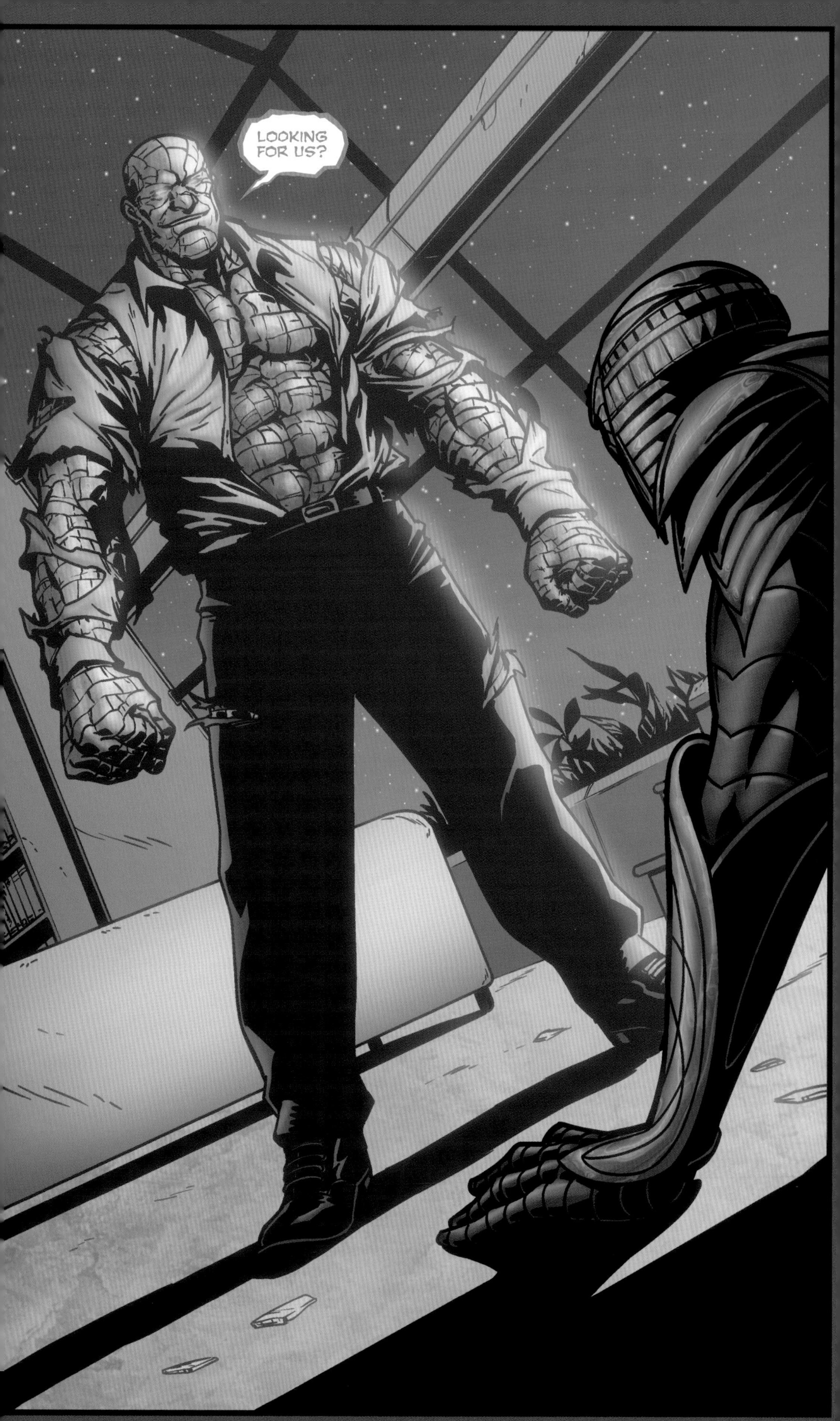
LOOKING FOR US?

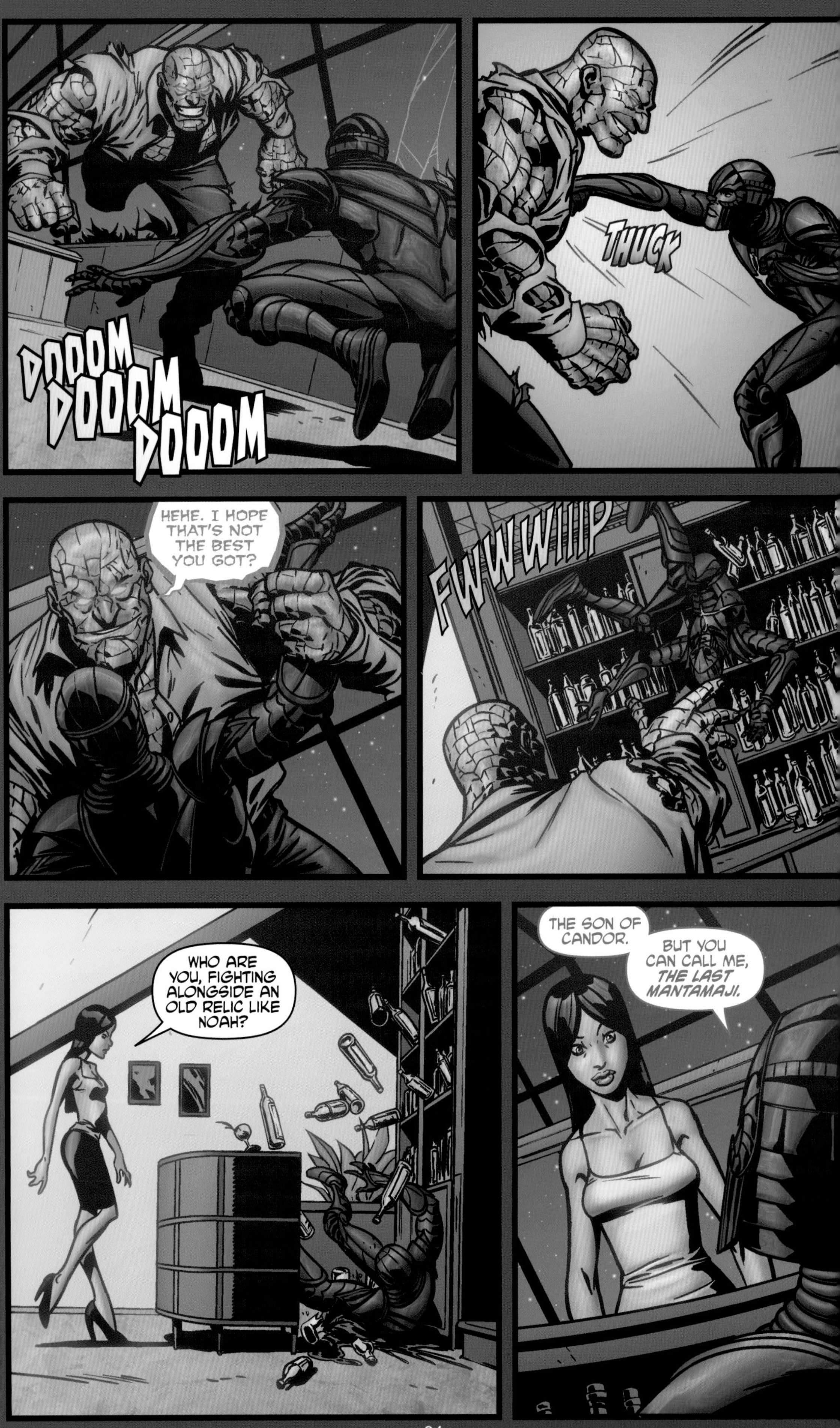
DOOOM
DOOOM
DOOOM
THUCK
HEHE. I HOPE THAT'S NOT THE BEST YOU GOT?
FWWWIIIP
WHO ARE YOU, FIGHTING ALONGSIDE AN OLD RELIC LIKE NOAH?
THE SON OF CANDOR.
BUT YOU CAN CALL ME, *THE LAST MANTAMAJI.*

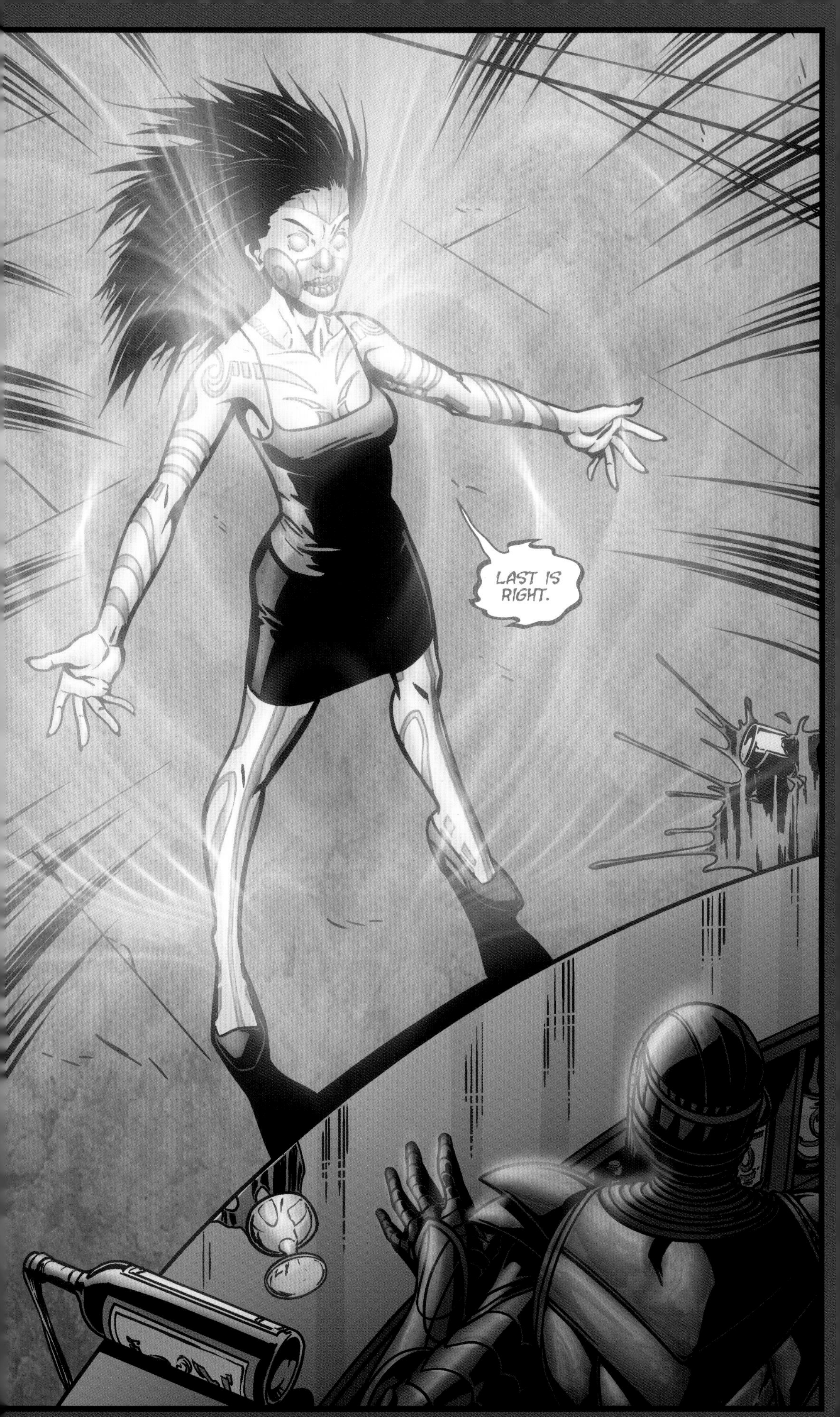
LAST IS RIGHT.

HSSSSHHHH

SHWOOM

SSSK

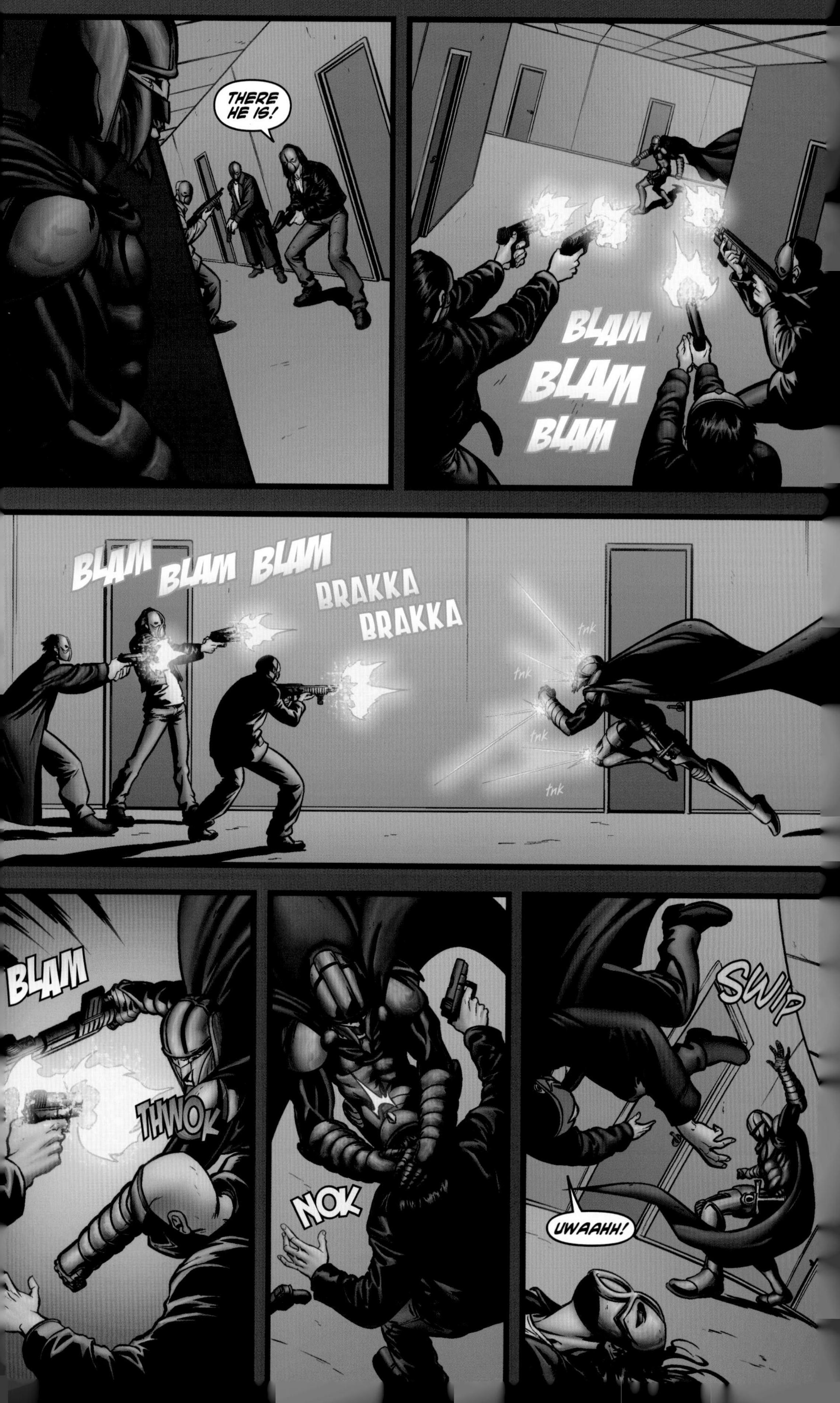
THERE HE IS!
BLAM
BLAM
BLAM
BLAM BLAM BLAM
BRAKKA BRAKKA
tnk
tnk
tnk
tnk
BLAM
THWOK
NOK
SWIP
UWAAHH!

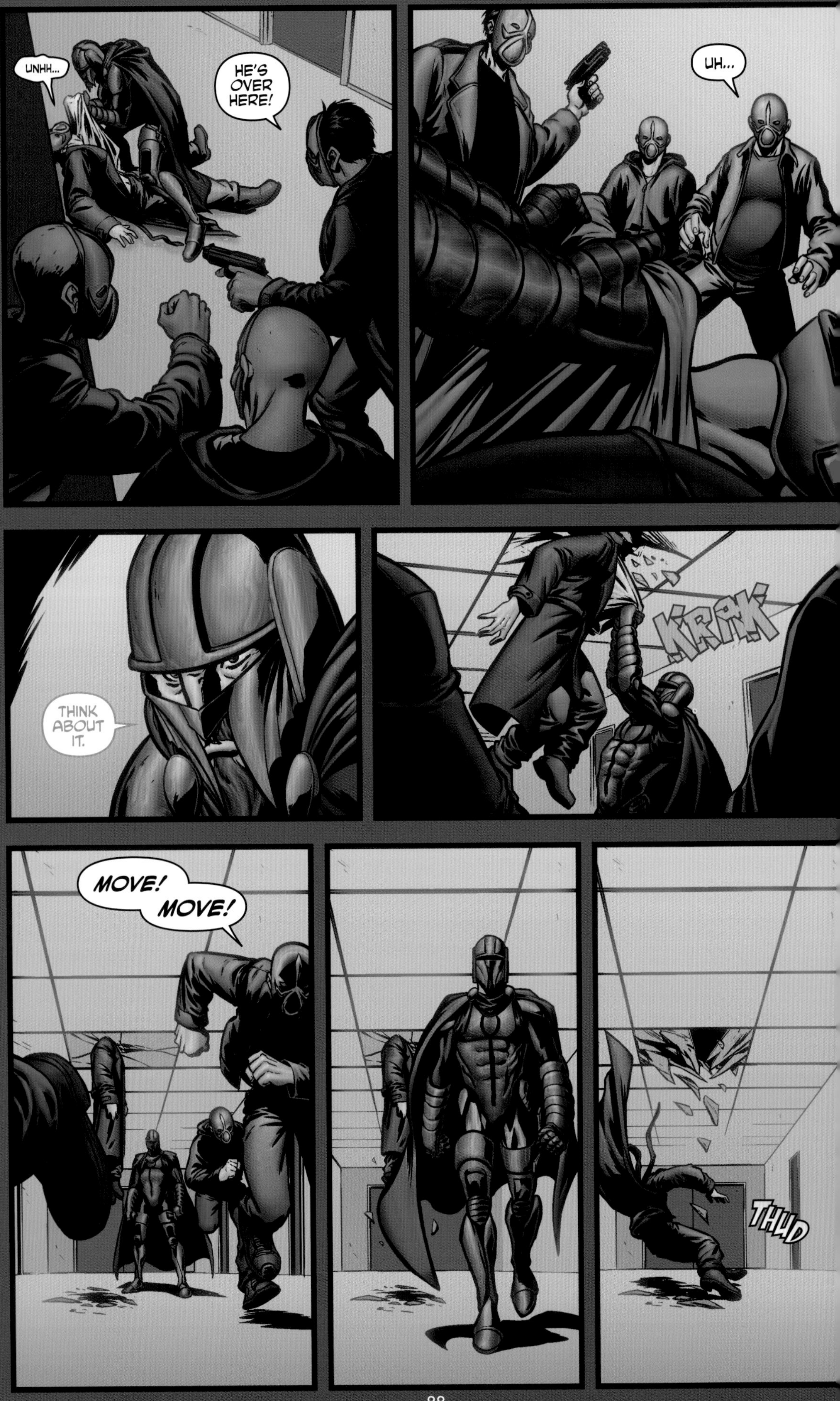
UNHH...
HE'S OVER HERE!
UH...
THINK ABOUT IT.
KRAK
MOVE! MOVE!
THUD

HEH.

FWAAP

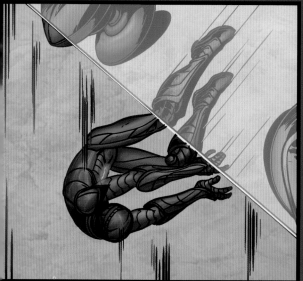

UNNGH.

PATHETIC.

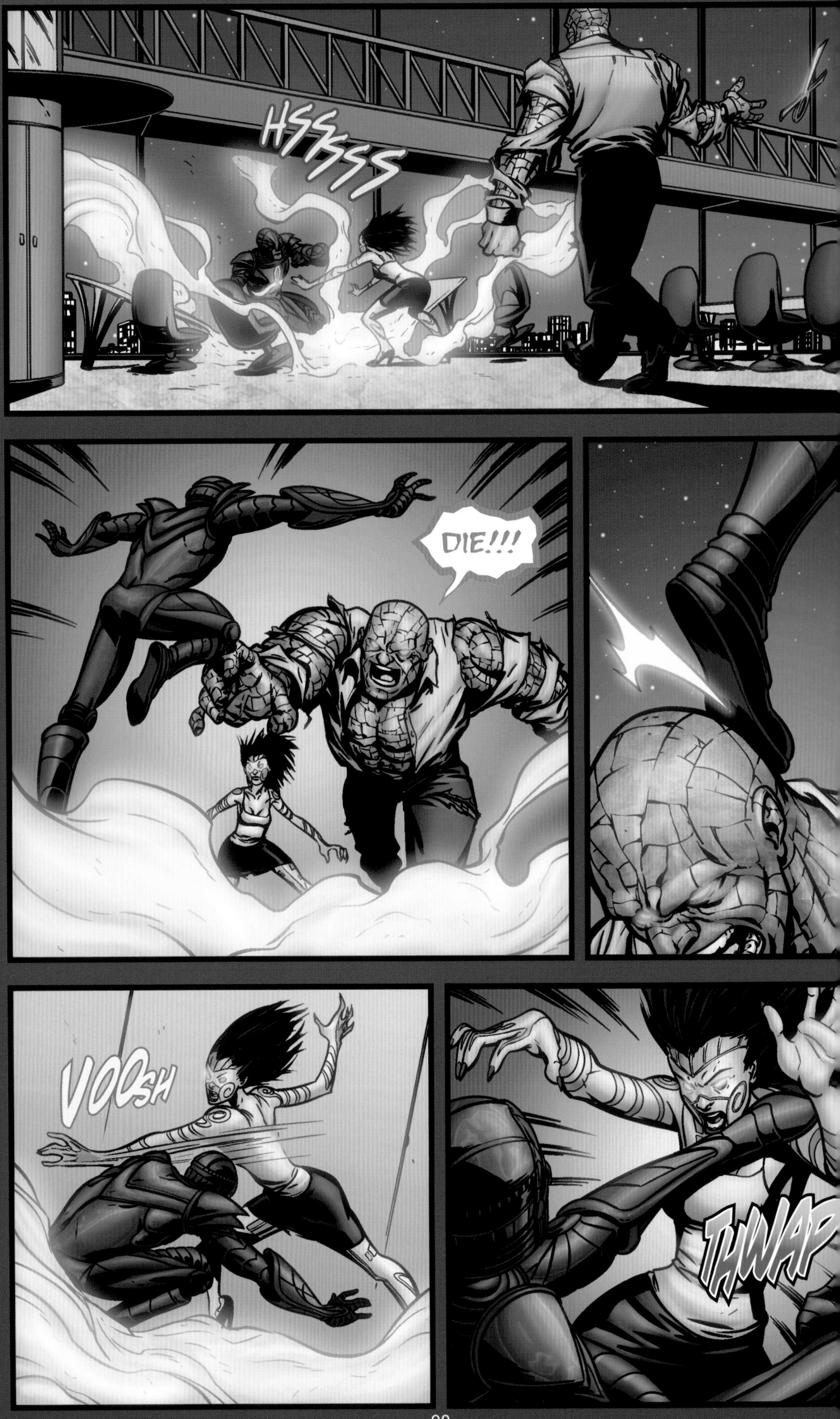
HSSSSSS
DIE!!!
VOOSH
THWAP

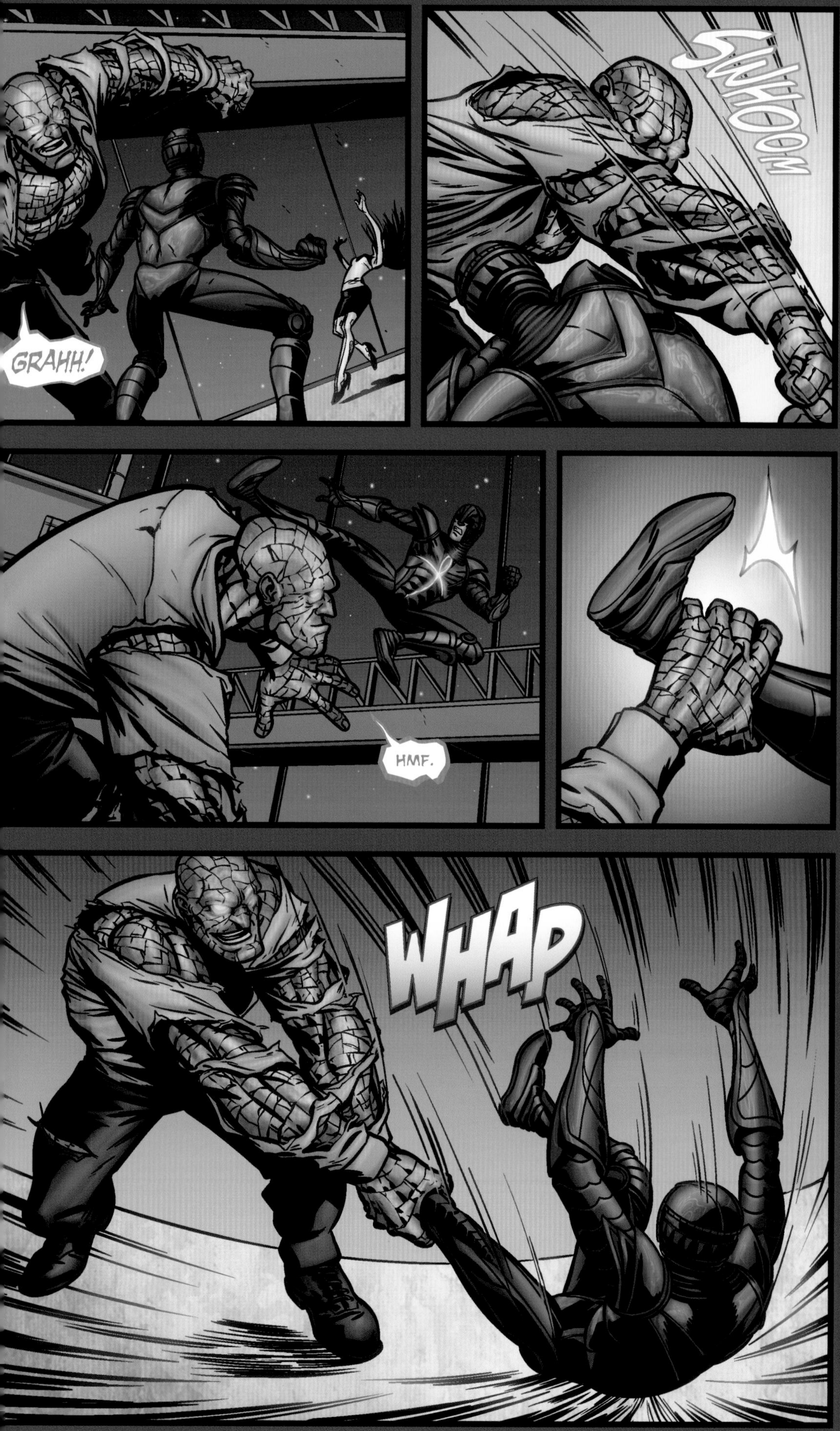
GRAHH!
SWHOOM
HMF.
WHAP

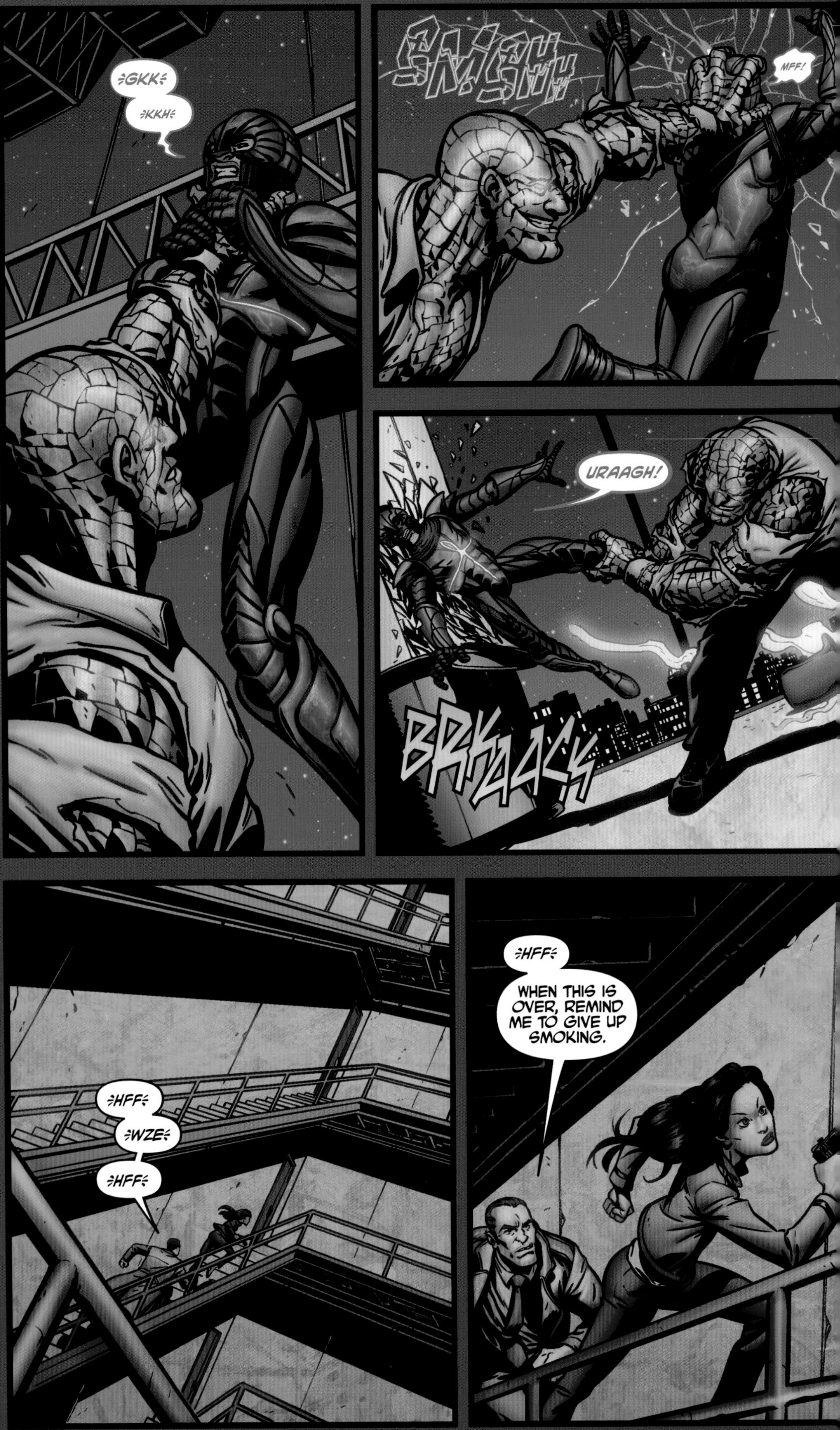

GKK
KKH
SMASH
MFF!
URAAGH!
BRKAACK
HFF
WZE
HFF
HFF
WHEN THIS IS OVER, REMIND ME TO GIVE UP SMOKING.

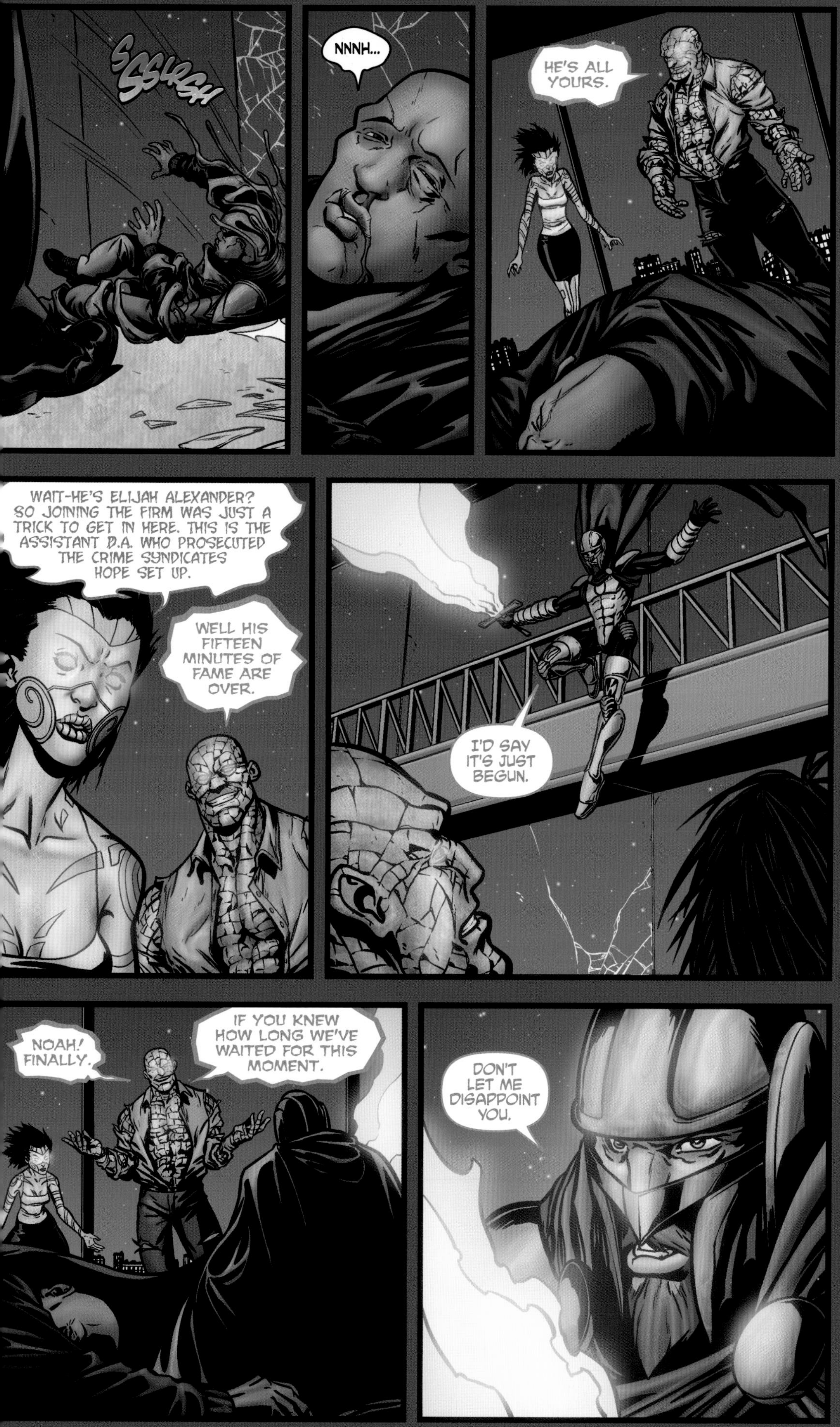

SSSLRSH
NNNH...
HE'S ALL YOURS.
WAIT-HE'S ELIJAH ALEXANDER? SO JOINING THE FIRM WAS JUST A TRICK TO GET IN HERE. THIS IS THE ASSISTANT D.A. WHO PROSECUTED THE CRIME SYNDICATES HOPE SET UP.
WELL HIS FIFTEEN MINUTES OF FAME ARE OVER.
I'D SAY IT'S JUST BEGUN.
NOAH! FINALLY.
IF YOU KNEW HOW LONG WE'VE WAITED FOR THIS MOMENT.
DON'T LET ME DISAPPOINT YOU.

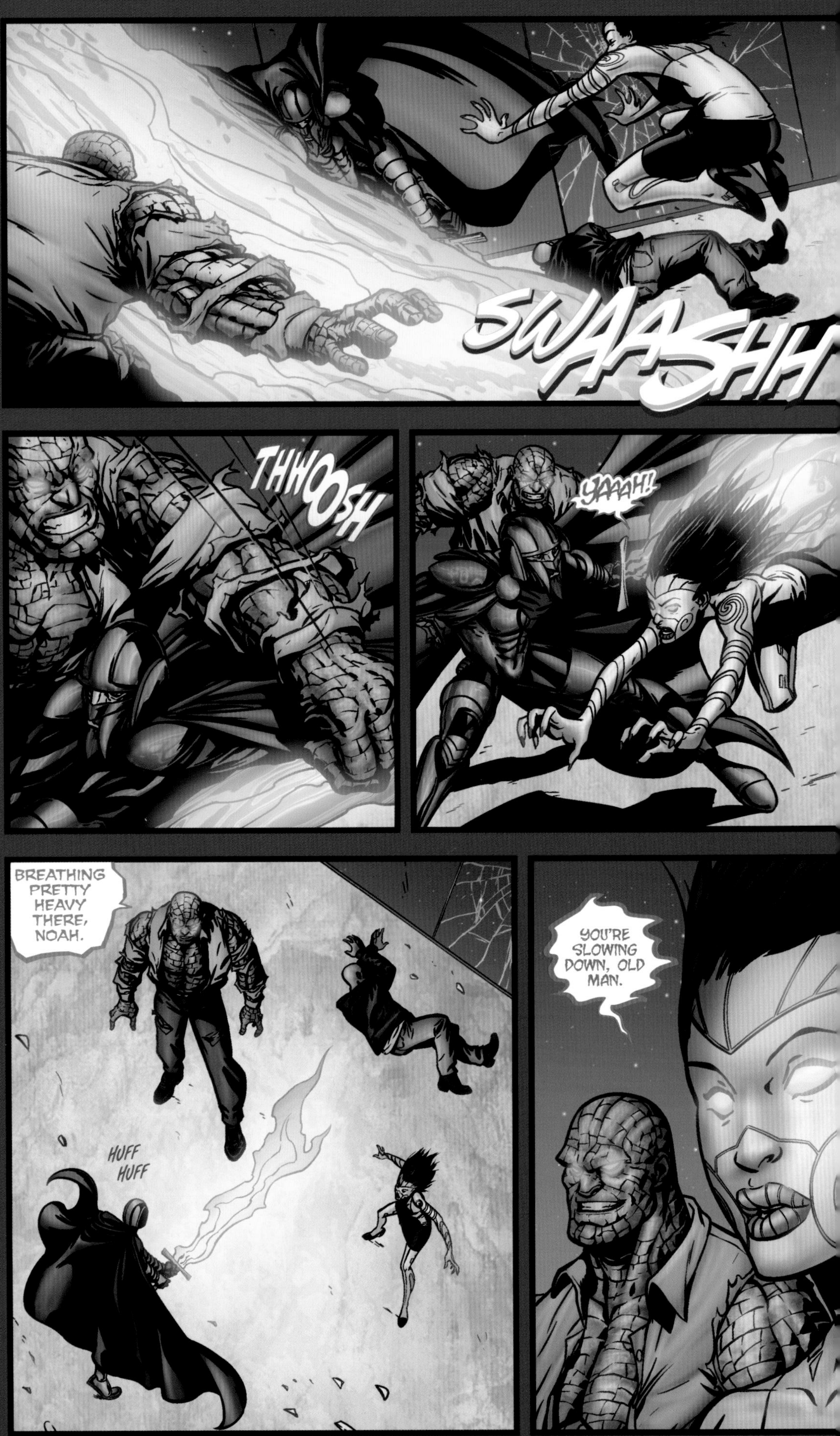
SWAASHH
THWOOSH
YAAAH!
BREATHING PRETTY HEAVY THERE, NOAH.
HUFF HUFF
YOU'RE SLOWING DOWN, OLD MAN.

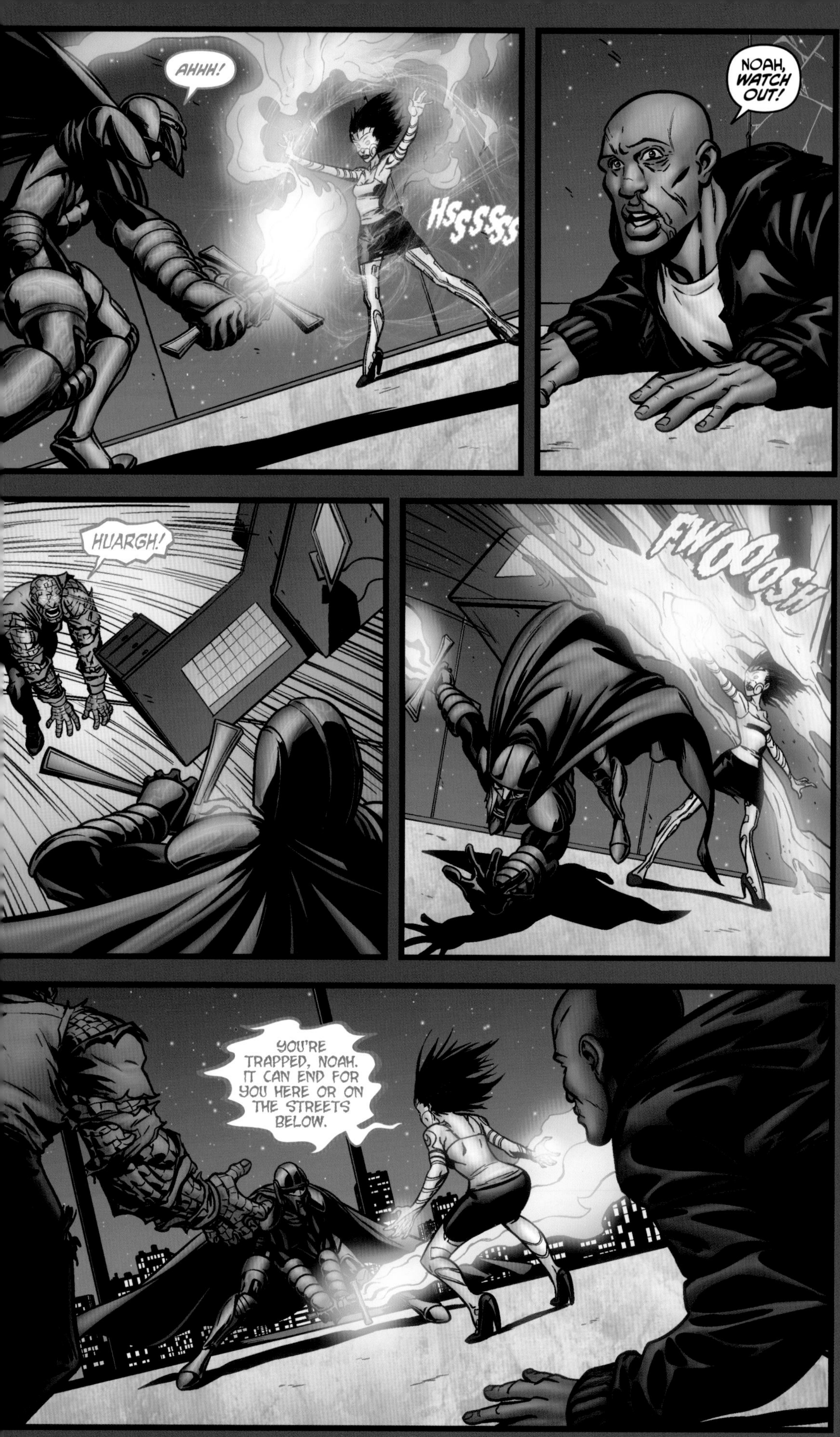
AHHH!
HSSSSSS
NOAH, WATCH OUT!
HUARGH!
FWOOOSH
YOU'RE TRAPPED, NOAH. IT CAN END FOR YOU HERE OR ON THE STREETS BELOW.

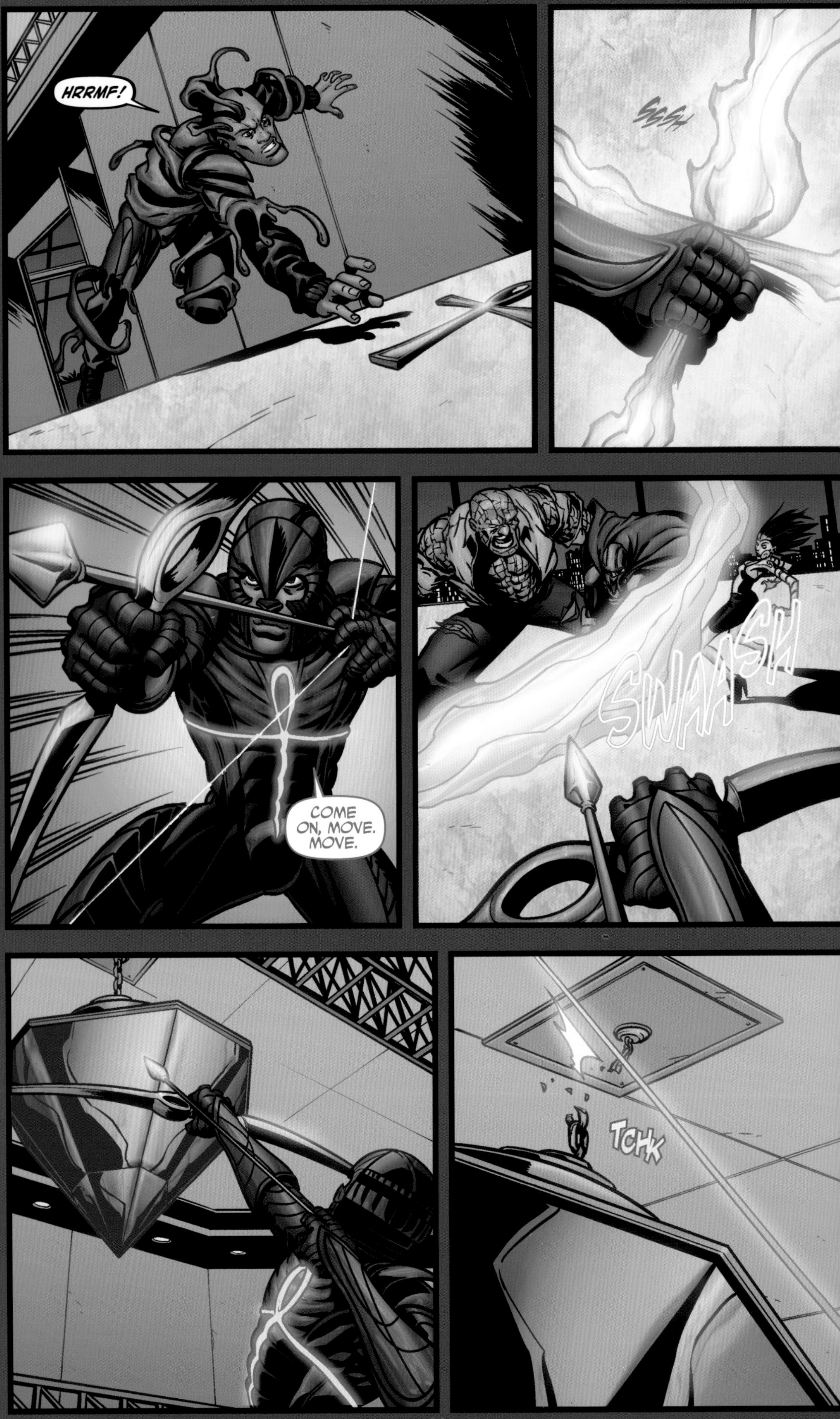
HRRMF!
SSSH
COME ON, MOVE. MOVE.
SWAASH
TCHK

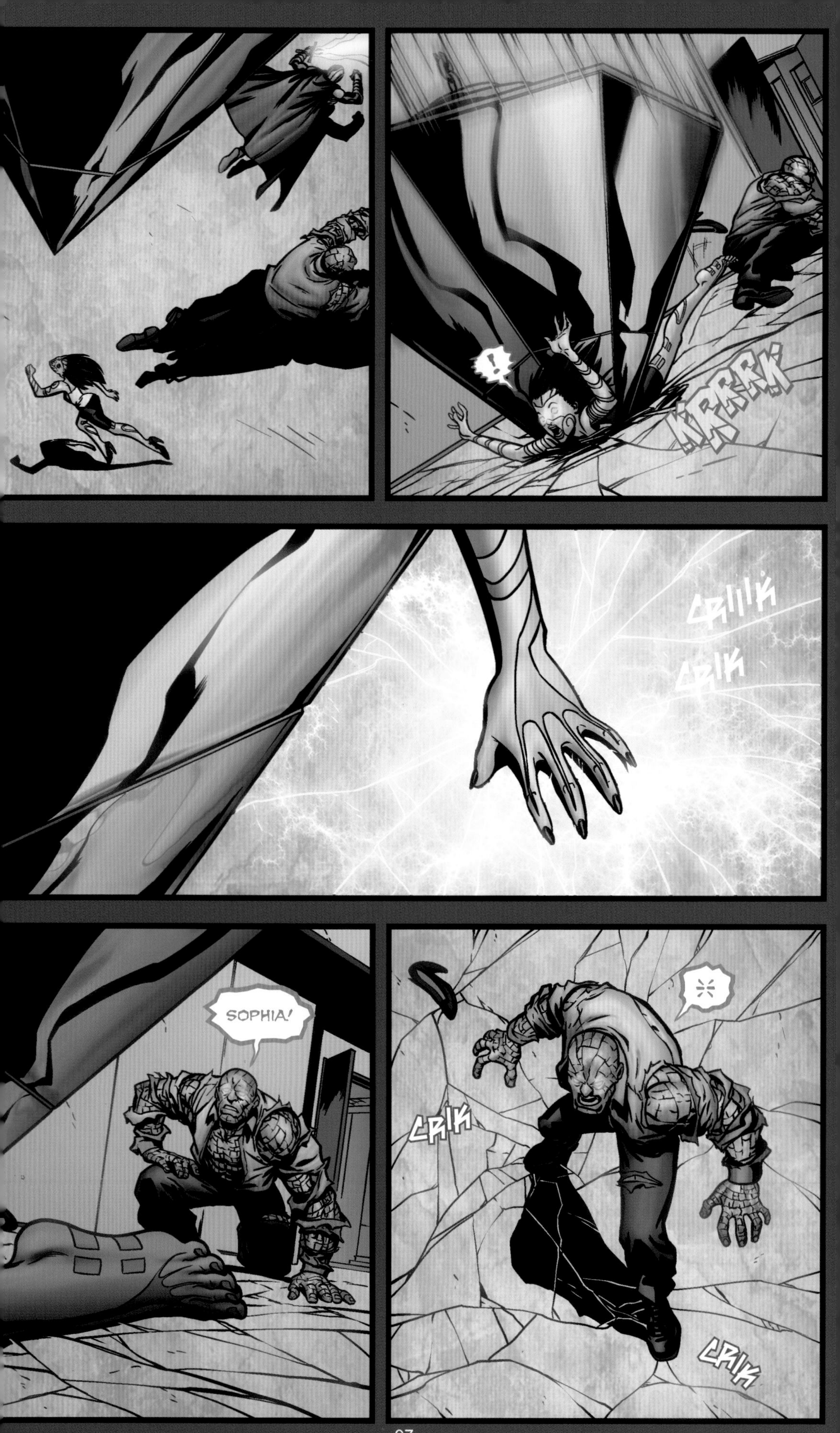
!
KRRRK
CRIIIK
CRIK
SOPHIA!
CRIK
CRIK

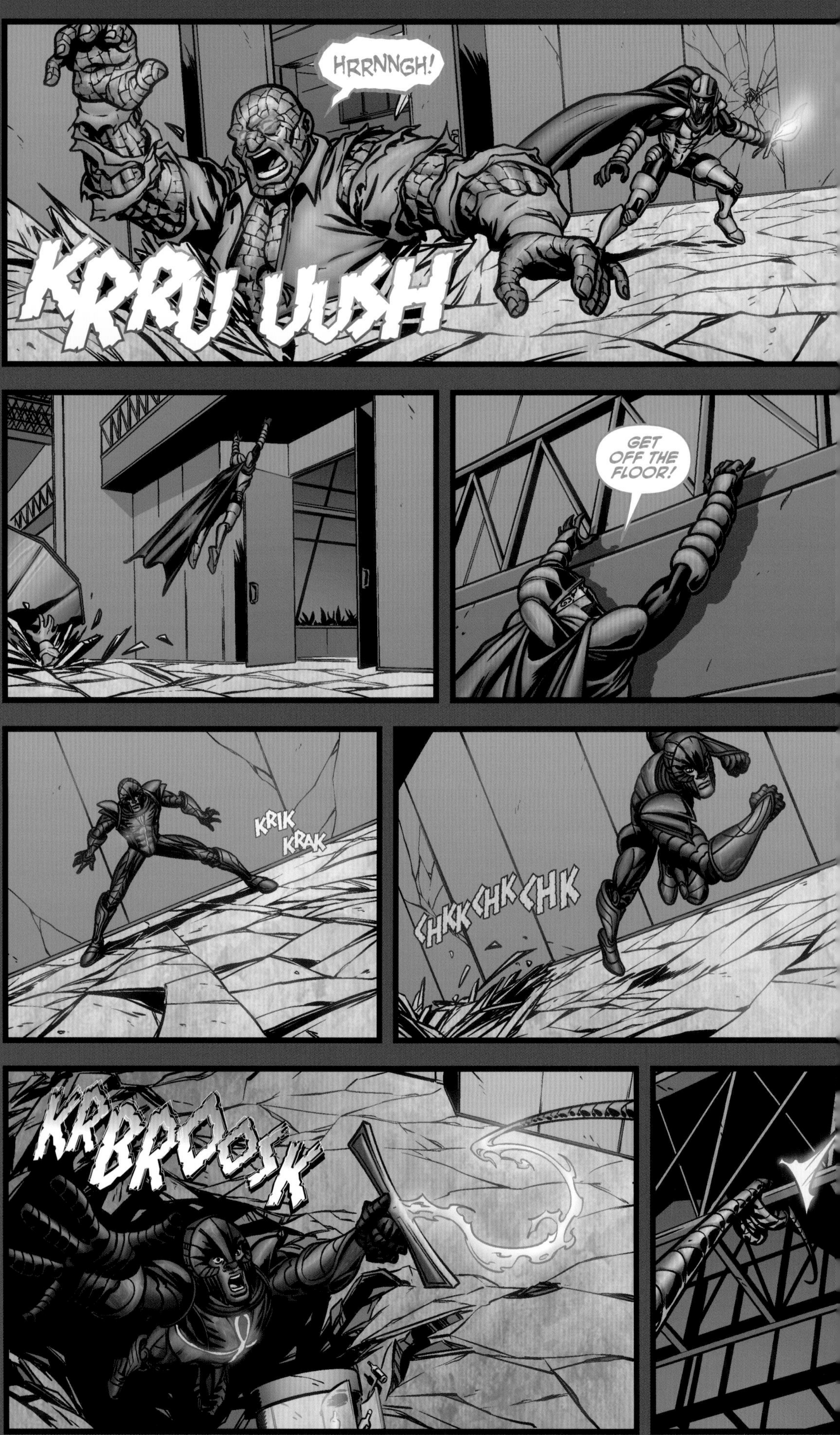
HRRNNGH!
KRRU UUSH
GET OFF THE FLOOR!
KRIK KRAK
CHKK CHK CHK
KRBROOSK

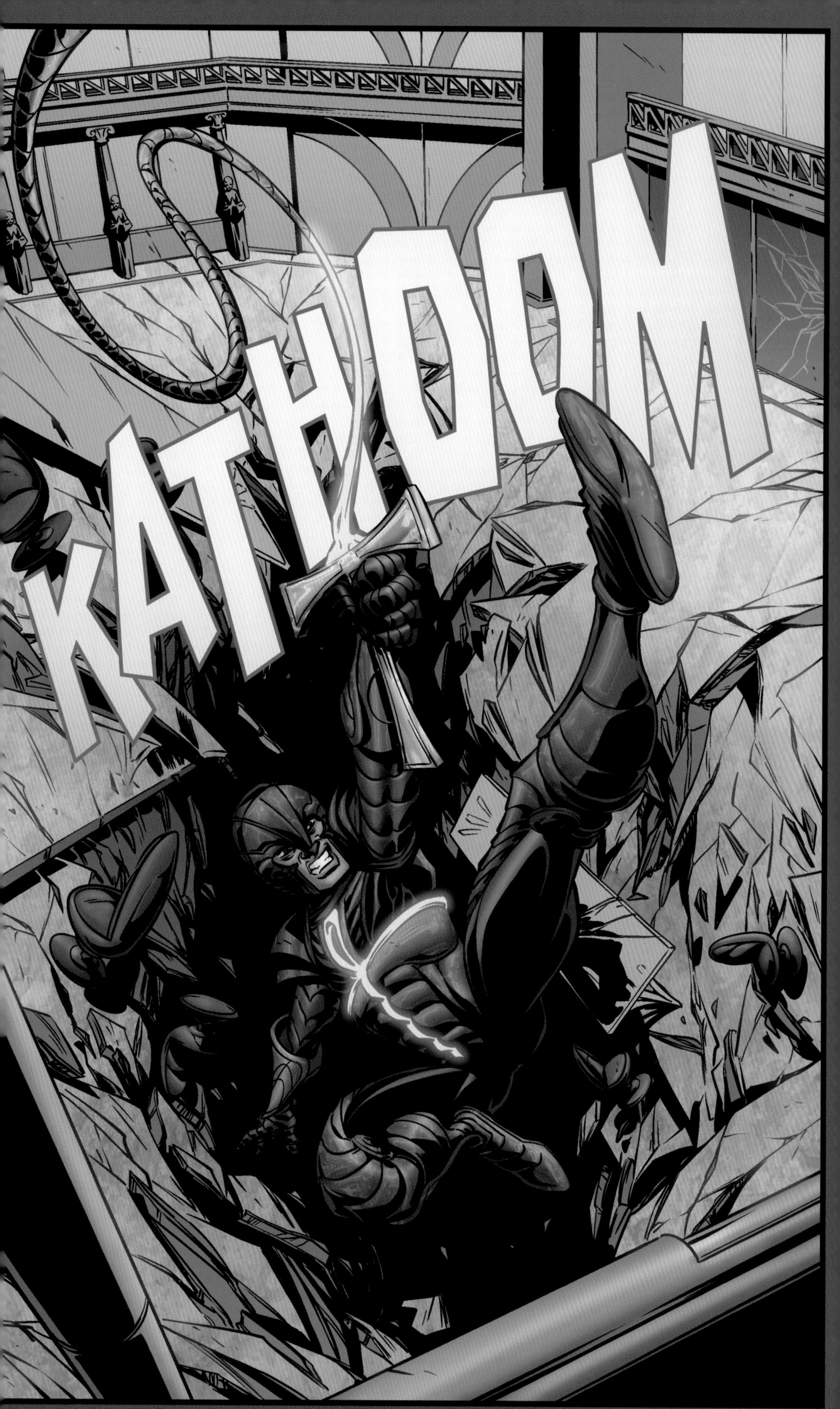
KATHOOM

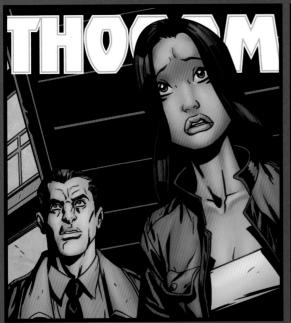

THOOOM

WHAT WAS *THAT?*

KRK

KRK

ARE YOU OKAY?

HANGING IN THERE.

LOOK, I THINK THEY WERE GOING OVER THE PLANS FOR THE LAUNCH.

HE'S STICKING HIS AHKH INTO THE CRYSTAL.

SHRKK

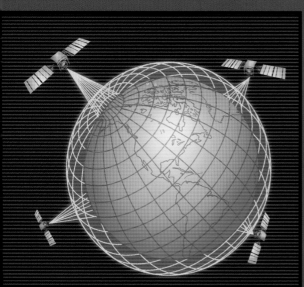

THE EYE OF CANDOR.

WITH IT, YOUR FATHER COULD INSTANTLY TRANSPORT US TO ANY LOCATION.

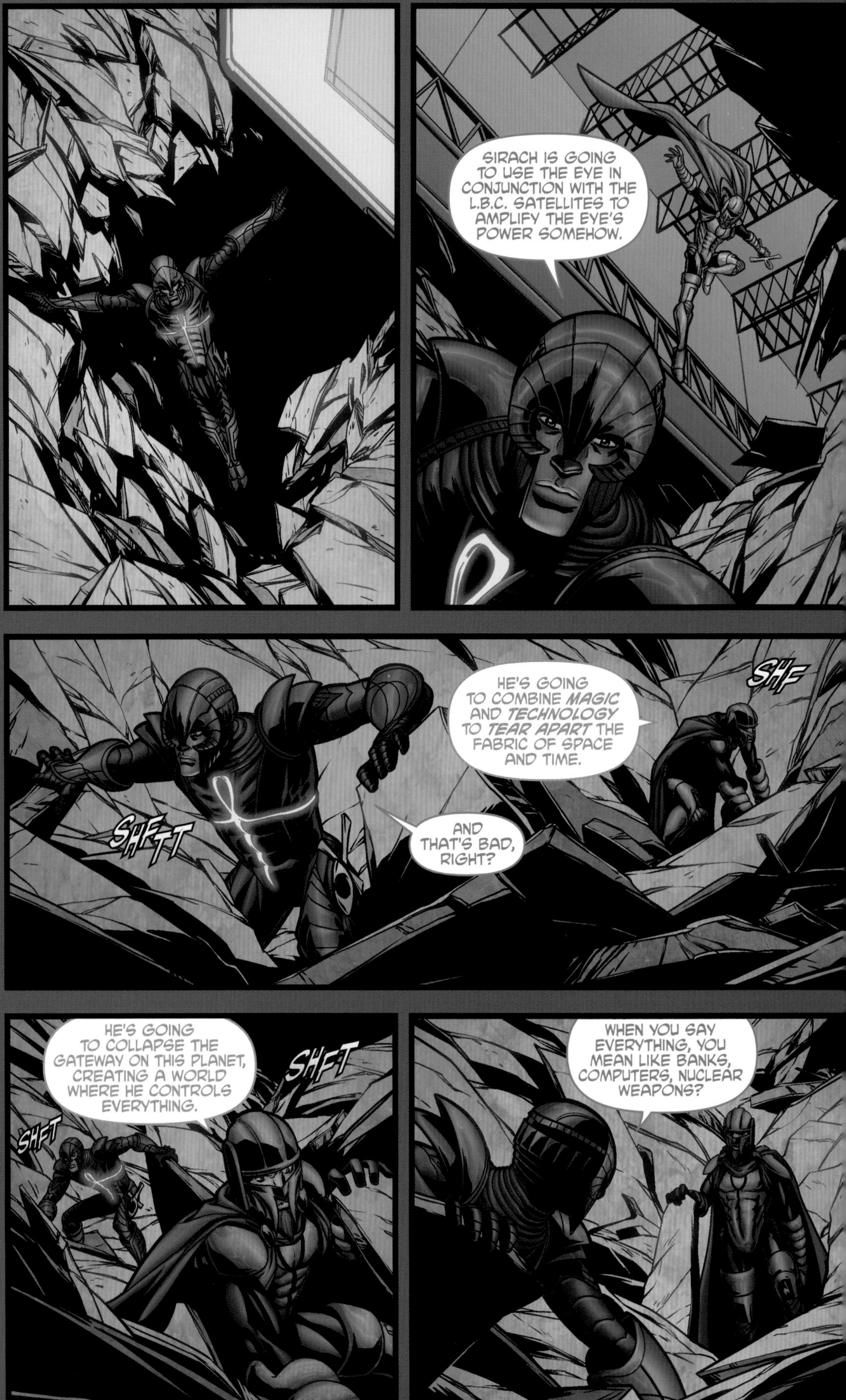
SIRACH IS GOING TO USE THE EYE IN CONJUNCTION WITH THE L.B.C. SATELLITES TO AMPLIFY THE EYE'S POWER SOMEHOW.
SHF
HE'S GOING TO COMBINE *MAGIC* AND *TECHNOLOGY* TO *TEAR APART* THE FABRIC OF SPACE AND TIME.
SHFTT
AND THAT'S BAD, RIGHT?
HE'S GOING TO COLLAPSE THE GATEWAY ON THIS PLANET, CREATING A WORLD WHERE HE CONTROLS EVERYTHING.
SHFT
SHFT
WHEN YOU SAY EVERYTHING, YOU MEAN LIKE BANKS, COMPUTERS, NUCLEAR WEAPONS?

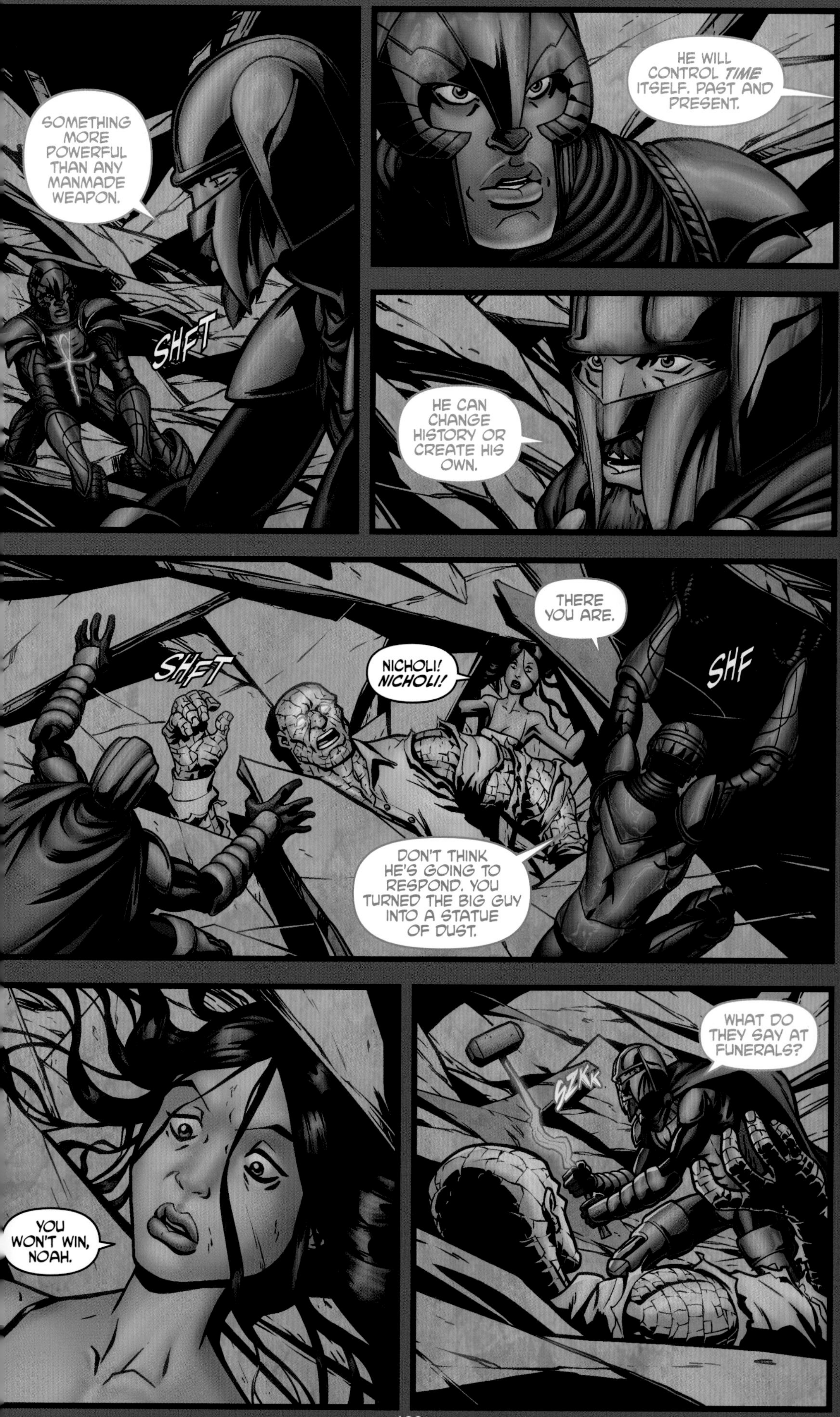
SOMETHING MORE POWERFUL THAN ANY MANMADE WEAPON.
SHFT
HE WILL CONTROL *TIME* ITSELF. PAST AND PRESENT.
HE CAN CHANGE HISTORY OR CREATE HIS OWN.
SHFT
NICHOLI! *NICHOLI!*
THERE YOU ARE.
SHF
DON'T THINK HE'S GOING TO RESPOND. YOU TURNED THE BIG GUY INTO A STATUE OF DUST.
YOU WON'T WIN, NOAH.
WHAT DO THEY SAY AT FUNERALS?
SZKK

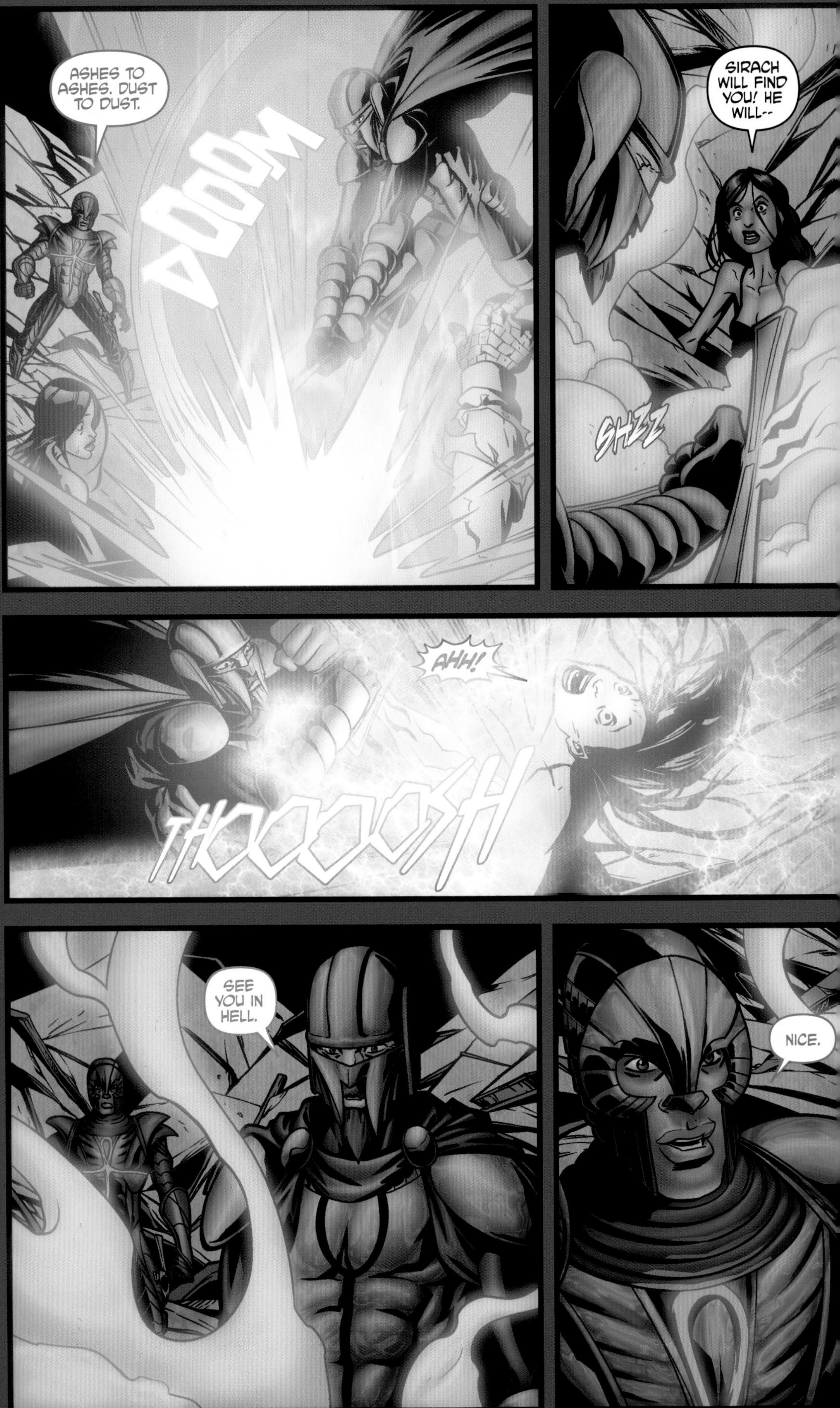
ASHES TO ASHES, DUST TO DUST.
DOOOM
SIRACH WILL FIND YOU! HE WILL--
SHZZ
AHH!
THOOOOSH
SEE YOU IN HELL.
NICE.

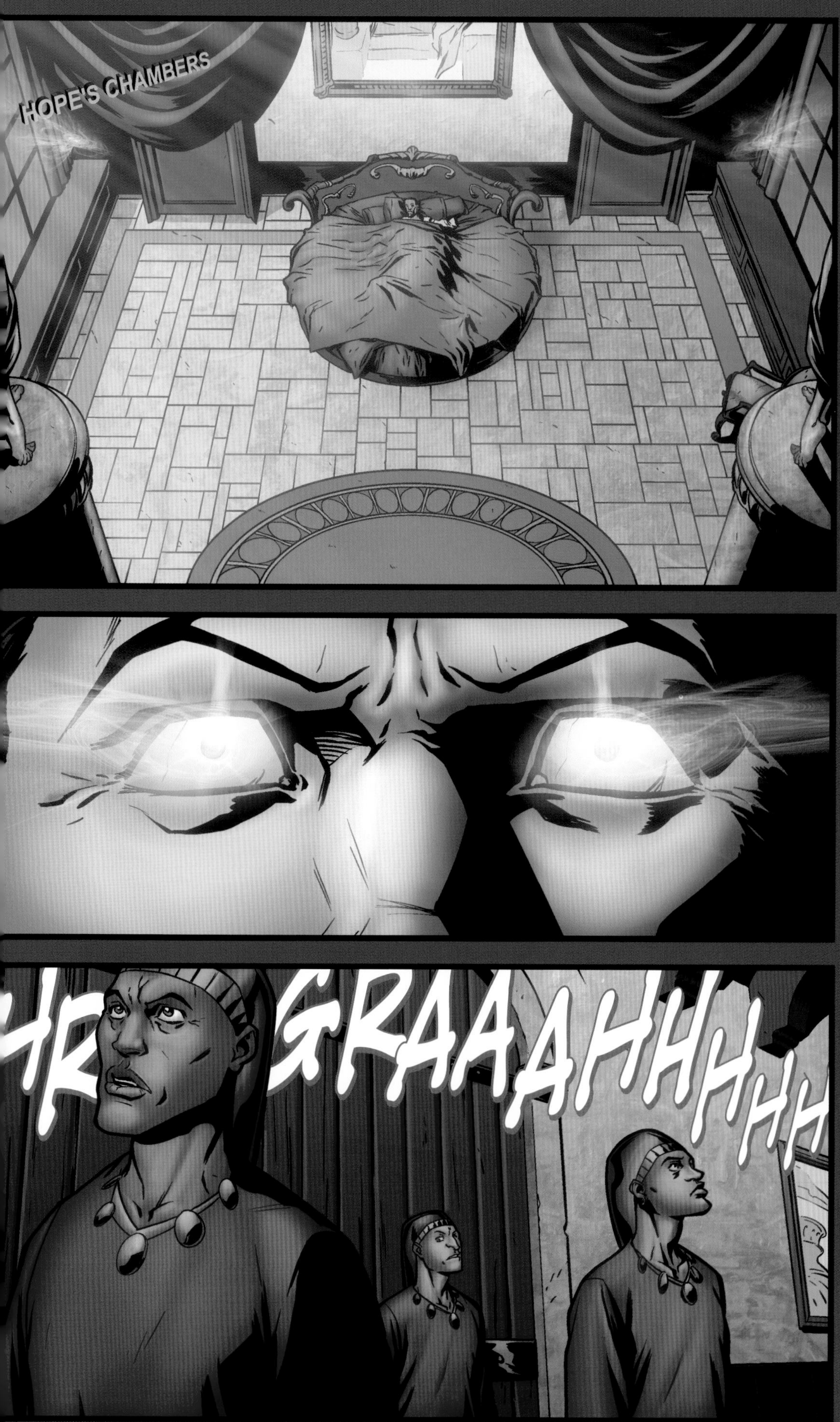
HOPE'S CHAMBERS
HRRGRAAAHHHHHH

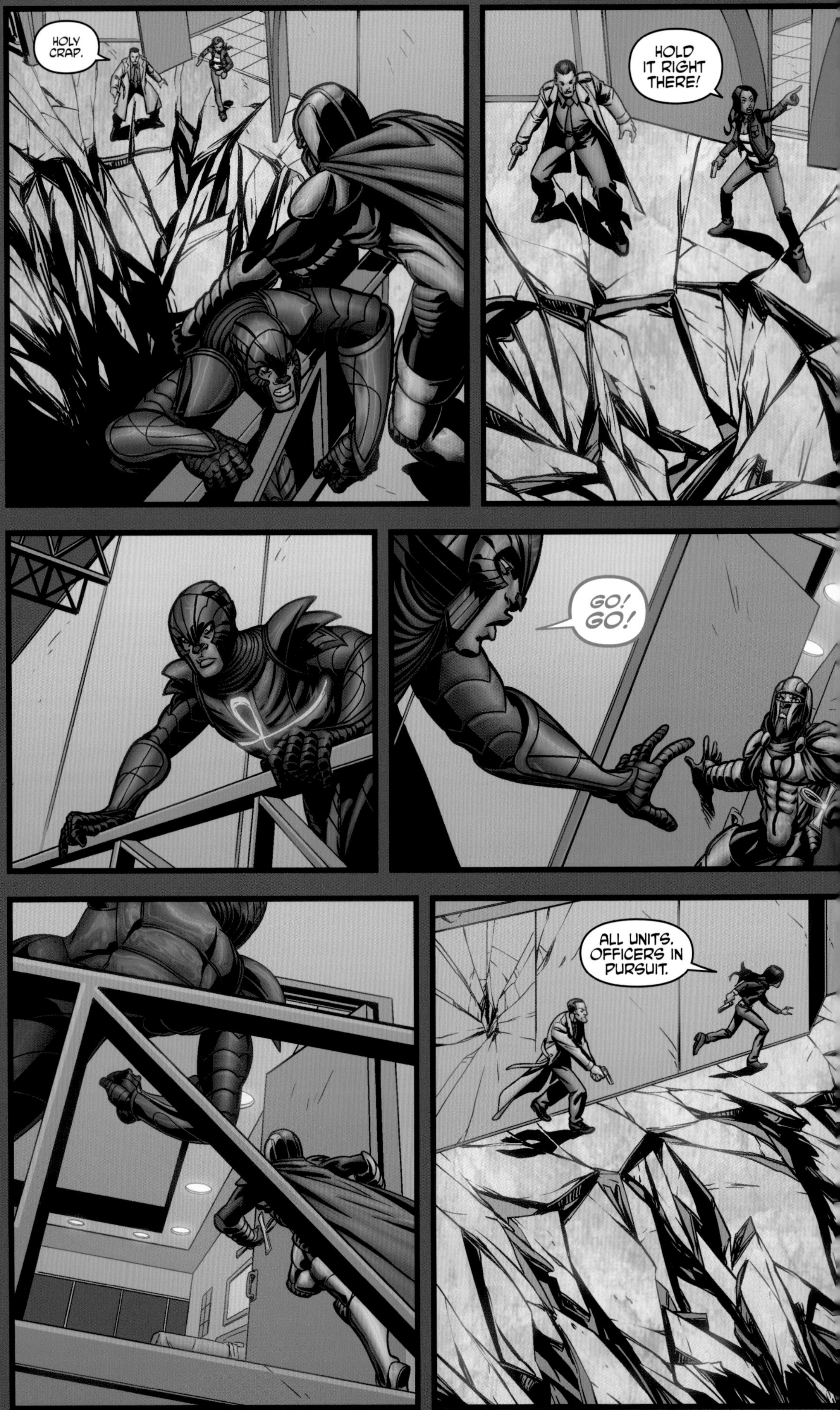
HOLY CRAP.
HOLD IT RIGHT THERE!
GO! GO!
ALL UNITS. OFFICERS IN PURSUIT.

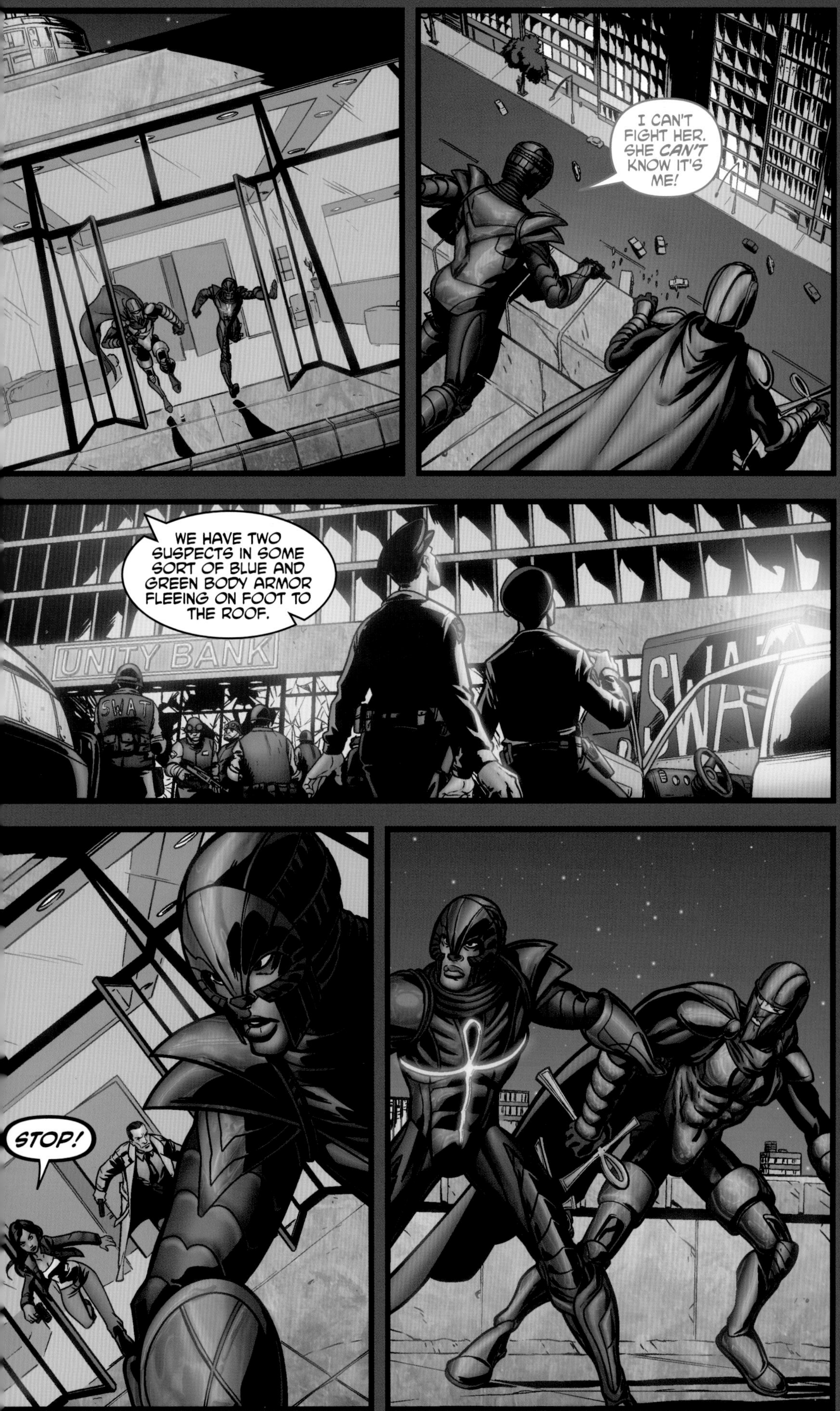
I CAN'T FIGHT HER. SHE CAN'T KNOW IT'S ME!
WE HAVE TWO SUSPECTS IN SOME SORT OF BLUE AND GREEN BODY ARMOR FLEEING ON FOOT TO THE ROOF.
UNITY BANK
SWAT
SWAT
STOP!

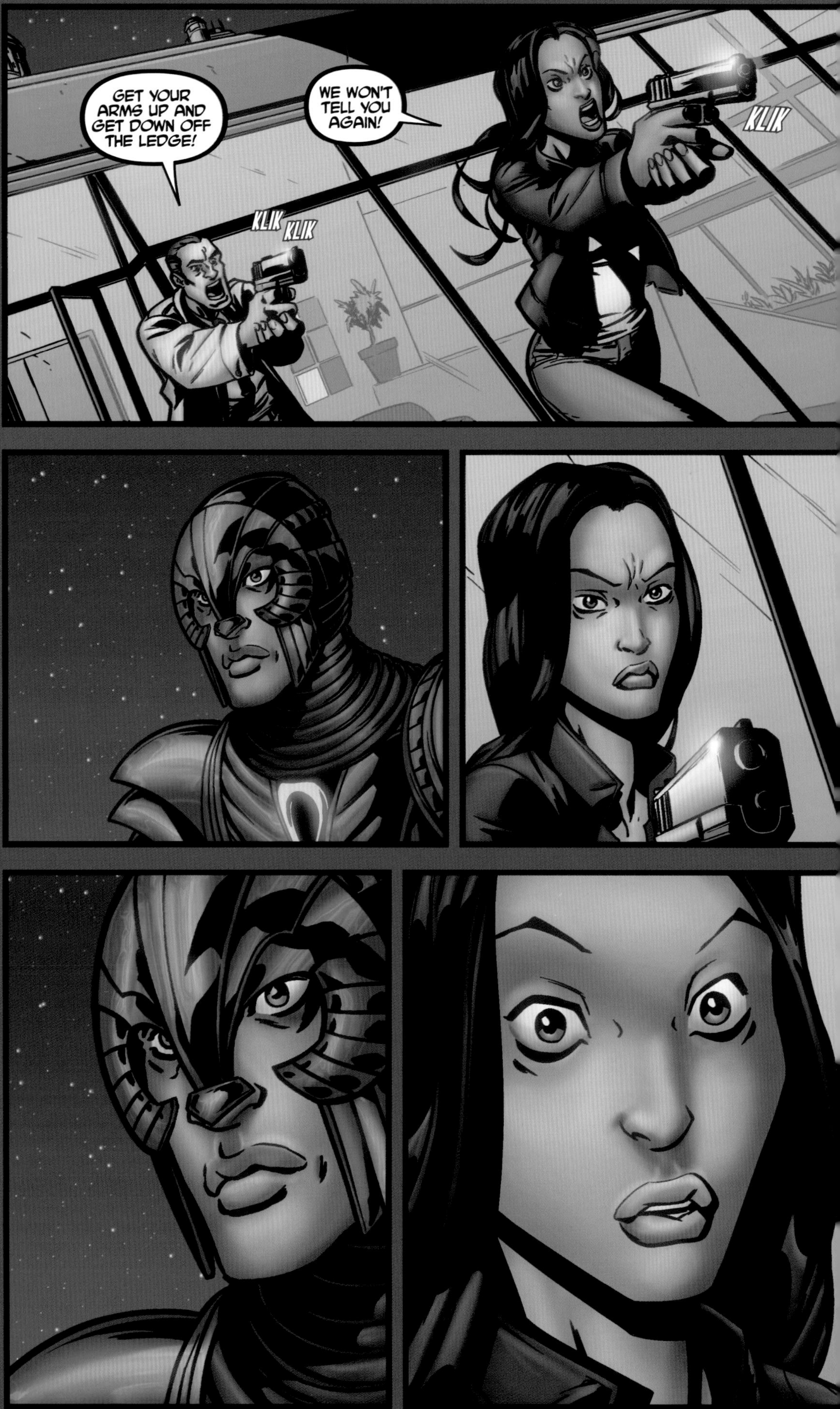
GET YOUR ARMS UP AND GET DOWN OFF THE LEDGE!
WE WON'T TELL YOU AGAIN!
KLIK
KLIK
KLIK

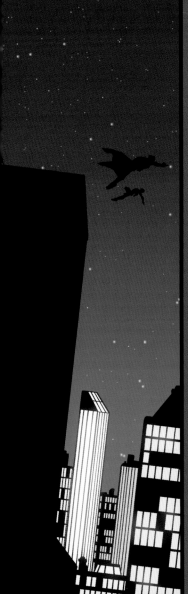

NO!

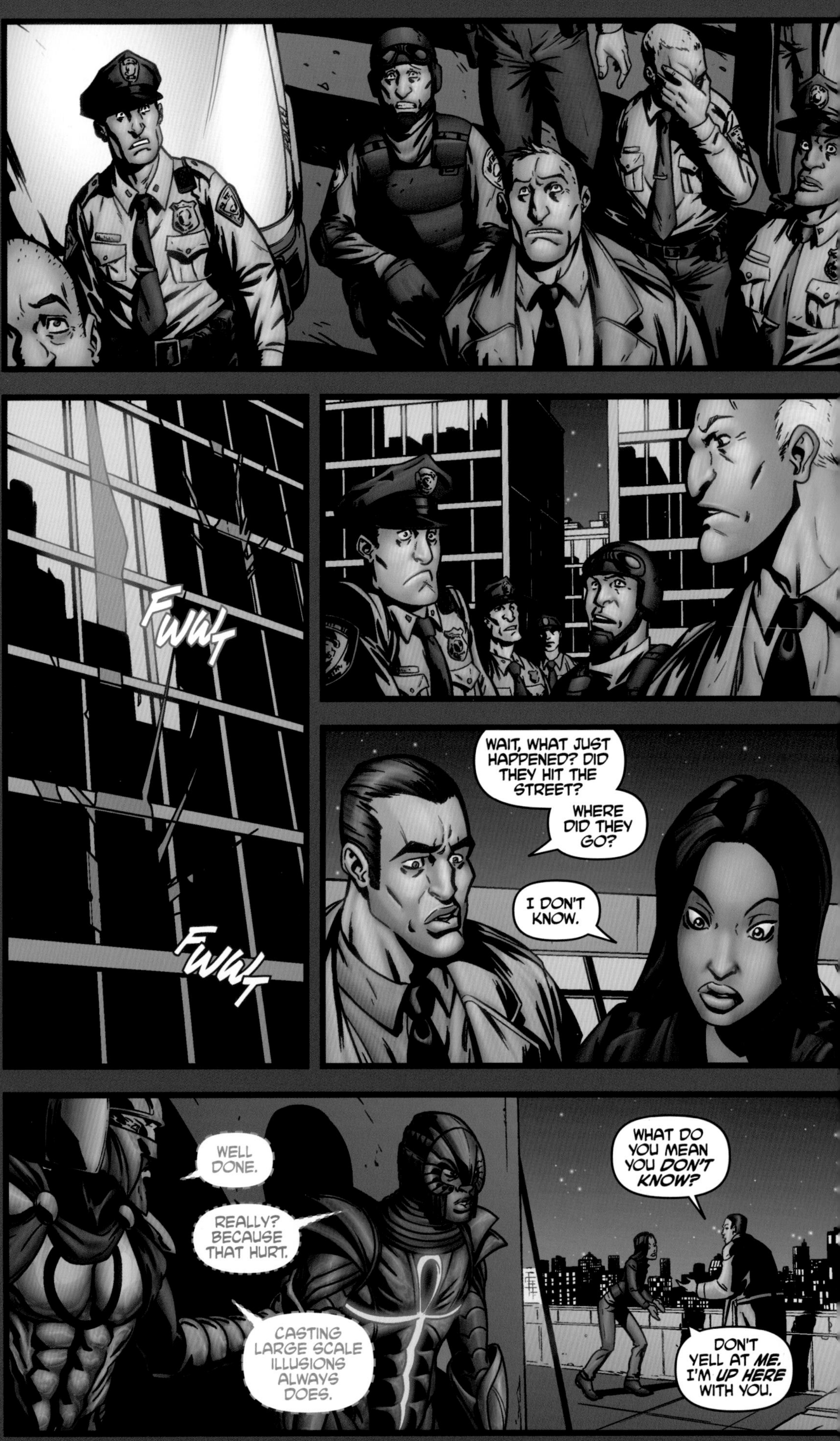
FWAT
FWAT
WAIT, WHAT JUST HAPPENED? DID THEY HIT THE STREET?
WHERE DID THEY GO?
I DON'T KNOW.
WELL DONE.
REALLY? BECAUSE THAT HURT.
CASTING LARGE SCALE ILLUSIONS ALWAYS DOES.
WHAT DO YOU MEAN YOU *DON'T KNOW*?
DON'T YELL AT *ME.* I'M *UP HERE* WITH YOU.

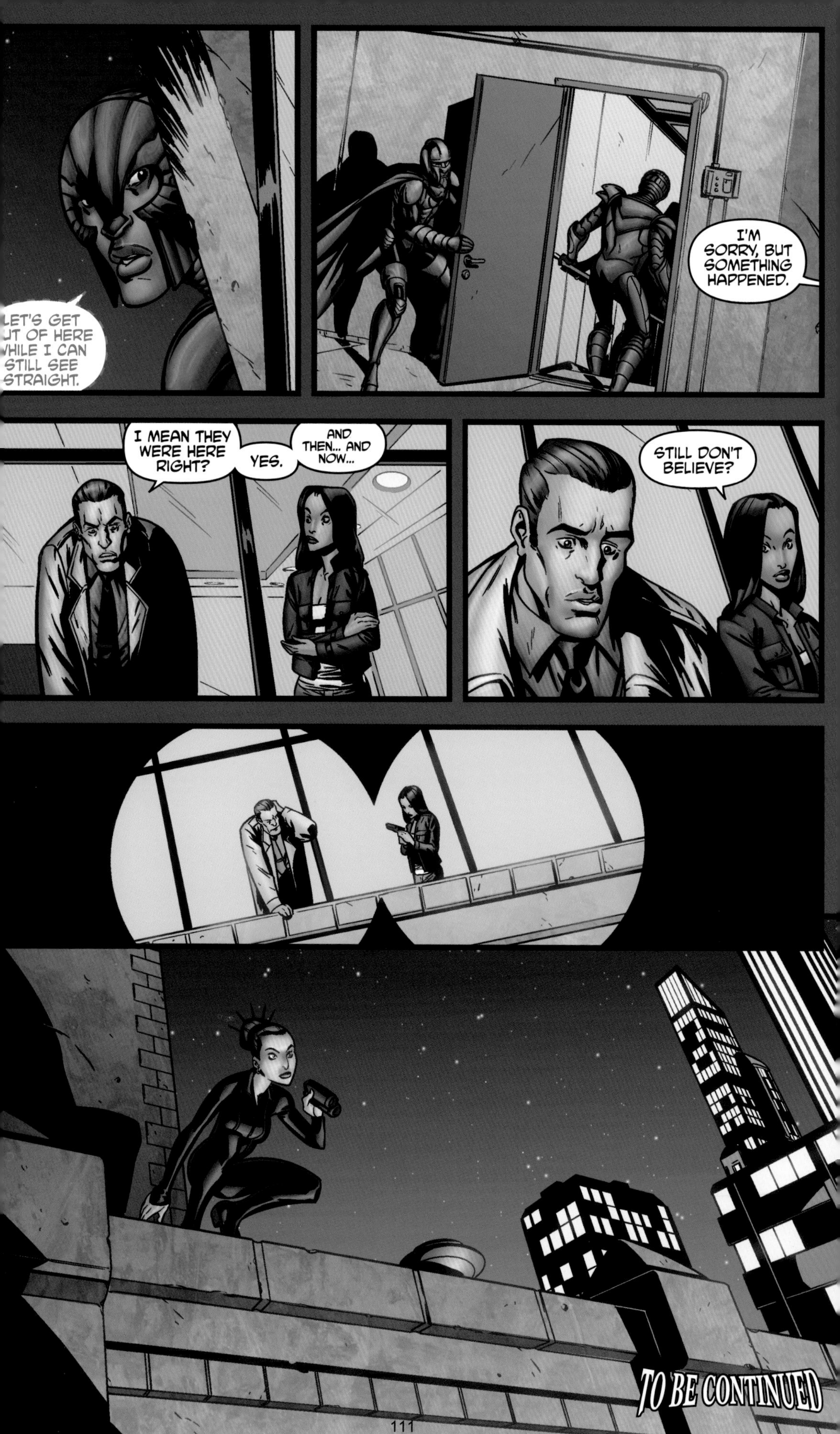
LET'S GET
...UT OF HERE
...HILE I CAN
STILL SEE
STRAIGHT.
I'M SORRY, BUT SOMETHING HAPPENED.
I MEAN THEY WERE HERE RIGHT?
YES.
AND THEN... AND NOW...
STILL DON'T BELIEVE?
TO BE CONTINUED

CHAPTER ⑩

The Mantamaji fought best from the shadows. For it is said that they fought darkness by becoming like water: quiet, unpredictable, slipping in through every crack. The power of water is the power of surprise. Sometimes only that surprise kept the Mantamaji from death.

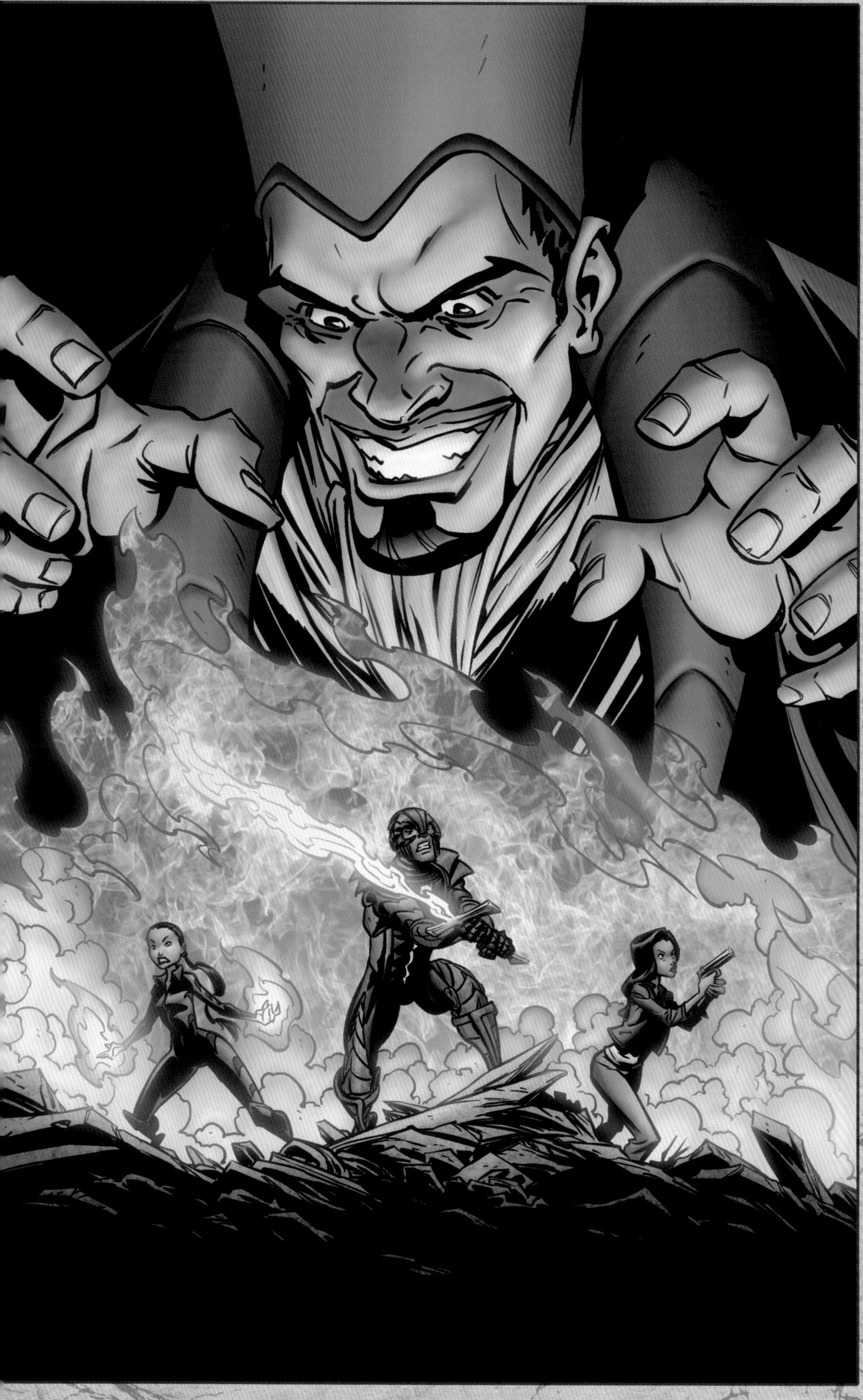

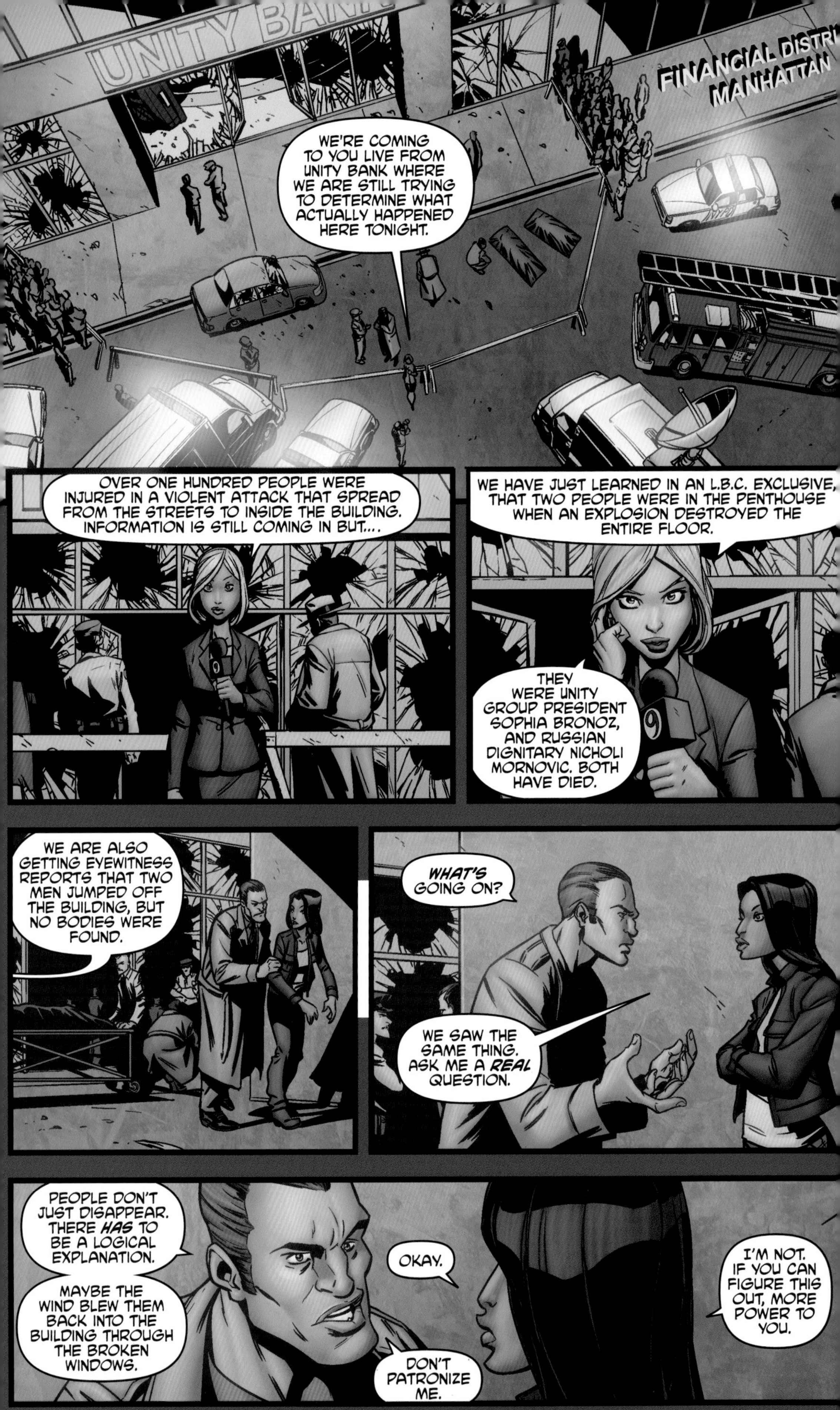
UNITY BANK
FINANCIAL DISTRI
MANHATTAN
WE'RE COMING TO YOU LIVE FROM UNITY BANK WHERE WE ARE STILL TRYING TO DETERMINE WHAT ACTUALLY HAPPENED HERE TONIGHT.
OVER ONE HUNDRED PEOPLE WERE INJURED IN A VIOLENT ATTACK THAT SPREAD FROM THE STREETS TO INSIDE THE BUILDING. INFORMATION IS STILL COMING IN BUT....
WE HAVE JUST LEARNED IN AN L.B.C. EXCLUSIVE, THAT TWO PEOPLE WERE IN THE PENTHOUSE WHEN AN EXPLOSION DESTROYED THE ENTIRE FLOOR.
THEY WERE UNITY GROUP PRESIDENT SOPHIA BRONOZ, AND RUSSIAN DIGNITARY NICHOLI MORNOVIC. BOTH HAVE DIED.
WE ARE ALSO GETTING EYEWITNESS REPORTS THAT TWO MEN JUMPED OFF THE BUILDING, BUT NO BODIES WERE FOUND.
WHAT'S GOING ON?
WE SAW THE SAME THING. ASK ME A REAL QUESTION.
PEOPLE DON'T JUST DISAPPEAR. THERE HAS TO BE A LOGICAL EXPLANATION.
MAYBE THE WIND BLEW THEM BACK INTO THE BUILDING THROUGH THE BROKEN WINDOWS.
OKAY.
DON'T PATRONIZE ME.
I'M NOT. IF YOU CAN FIGURE THIS OUT, MORE POWER TO YOU.

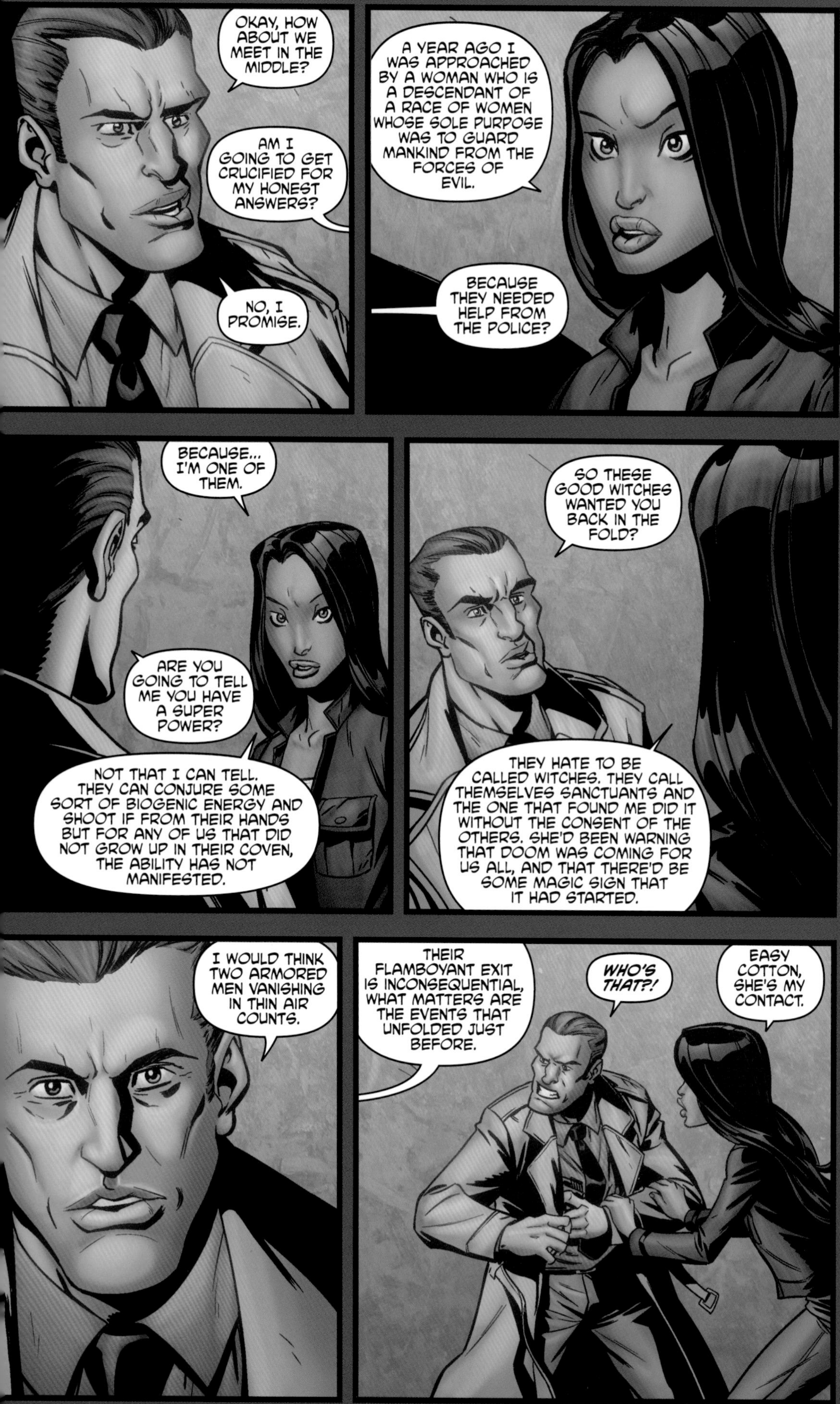

OKAY, HOW ABOUT WE MEET IN THE MIDDLE?
AM I GOING TO GET CRUCIFIED FOR MY HONEST ANSWERS?
NO, I PROMISE.
A YEAR AGO I WAS APPROACHED BY A WOMAN WHO IS A DESCENDANT OF A RACE OF WOMEN WHOSE SOLE PURPOSE WAS TO GUARD MANKIND FROM THE FORCES OF EVIL.
BECAUSE THEY NEEDED HELP FROM THE POLICE?
BECAUSE... I'M ONE OF THEM.
ARE YOU GOING TO TELL ME YOU HAVE A SUPER POWER?
NOT THAT I CAN TELL. THEY CAN CONJURE SOME SORT OF BIOGENIC ENERGY AND SHOOT IF FROM THEIR HANDS BUT FOR ANY OF US THAT DID NOT GROW UP IN THEIR COVEN, THE ABILITY HAS NOT MANIFESTED.
SO THESE GOOD WITCHES WANTED YOU BACK IN THE FOLD?
THEY HATE TO BE CALLED WITCHES. THEY CALL THEMSELVES SANCTUANTS AND THE ONE THAT FOUND ME DID IT WITHOUT THE CONSENT OF THE OTHERS. SHE'D BEEN WARNING THAT DOOM WAS COMING FOR US ALL, AND THAT THERE'D BE SOME MAGIC SIGN THAT IT HAD STARTED.
I WOULD THINK TWO ARMORED MEN VANISHING IN THIN AIR COUNTS.
THEIR FLAMBOYANT EXIT IS INCONSEQUENTIAL, WHAT MATTERS ARE THE EVENTS THAT UNFOLDED JUST BEFORE.
WHO'S THAT?!
EASY COTTON, SHE'S MY CONTACT.

COMMANDER COTTON, MEET CORNERSTONE.

SORRY BUT IT'S BETTER YOU DON'T KNOW WHAT I LOOK LIKE.

FOR YOUR SAFETY?

NO, YOURS.

WHAT HAPPENED HERE TONIGHT?

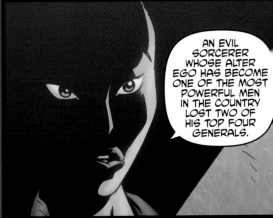

AN EVIL SORCERER WHOSE ALTER EGO HAS BECOME ONE OF THE MOST POWERFUL MEN IN THE COUNTRY LOST TWO OF HIS TOP FOUR GENERALS.

YOU MEAN BROTHER HOPE?

HIS REAL NAME IS SIRACH. THE TWO MEN THAT ATTACKED HIS EMPIRE TONIGHT ARE LEGENDARY WARRIORS CALLED THE MANTAMAJI. THOUSANDS OF YEARS AGO THEY MADE A DIFFERENCE IN THIS WORLD.

SO THEY ARE HERE TO HELP?

I ONLY KNOW THAT THEIR APPEARANCE MEANS AN ENDGAME HAS BEEN PUT IN MOTION BUT THE OUTCOME MAY NOT BE IN OUR FAVOR.

ENDGAME?

WHAT IS HOPE'S PLAN?

THIS IS CRAZY.

SIRACH THINKS THE WORLD IS BEYOND REDEMPTION, SO HE AIMS TO DESTROY EVERYTHING AND REBUILD IT IN HIS OWN IMAGE.

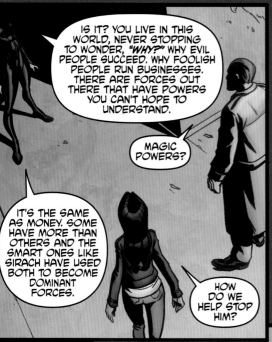

IS IT? YOU LIVE IN THIS WORLD, NEVER STOPPING TO WONDER, *"WHY?"* WHY EVIL PEOPLE SUCCEED. WHY FOOLISH PEOPLE RUN BUSINESSES. THERE ARE FORCES OUT THERE THAT HAVE POWERS YOU CAN'T HOPE TO UNDERSTAND.

MAGIC POWERS?

IT'S THE SAME AS MONEY. SOME HAVE MORE THAN OTHERS AND THE SMART ONES LIKE SIRACH HAVE USED BOTH TO BECOME DOMINANT FORCES.

HOW DO WE HELP STOP HIM?

BE READY FOR ANYTHING. THE HORSEMEN HOLD A MYSTICAL KEY TO SIRACH'S POWERS. WITH TWO OF THEM GONE, THE OTHERS WILL BE OUT FOR BLOOD.

THERE WILL BE COLLATERAL DAMAGE. LOTS OF INNOCENT PEOPLE ARE ABOUT TO BE PUT IN HARM'S WAY.

I'M GOING BACK TO THE OFFICE TO CHECK IN WITH THE TASK FORCE AND PULL EVERY REFERENCE THE NEW WORLD KNIGHTS MADE ABOUT THE MANTAMAJI. I WANT YOU TO TRY AND LEARN MORE ABOUT THESE GENERALS SHE TALKED ABOUT. WHAT WERE BRONOZ AND MORNOVIC UP TO? WHO THE OTHER TWO COULD BE? WHAT CAN WE DO TO HELP STOP THEM?

COME SUNRISE YOU AND I WILL BECOME A PERSONAL POLICE ESCORTS FOR BROTHER HOPE OR SIRACH OR WHATEVER HE CALLS HIMSELF. LET'S SEE HOW FAR HE GETS WITH THE TWO OF US ATTACHED TO HIS HIP.

HOPE'S CHAMBER
GREENWICH VILLAGE.
LOOK AT ME!
LOOK WHAT HE'S DONE TO ME.
I WANT NOAH'S SOUL!
WE MIGHT HAVE *ANOTHER* PROBLEM. WE ERASED ALL THE COMPUTERS BEFORE THE POLICE LOCKED DOWN THE BOARDROOM, BUT TOUCH AND FORCE WERE WORKING ON THE FINAL PREPARATIONS FOR THE *DAY OF RETRIBUTION.*
THAT'S WHY NOAH WAS THERE. HE'S TRYING *TO WEAKEN* ME BY DESTROYING *ALL OF YOU* BEFORE IT'S TOO LATE.
THE TWO OF YOU WILL BE HIS NEXT TARGET. TONIGHT, AT THE RECEPTION.
THEN WE SHOULD CANCEL IT.
YOUR BROTHER AND SISTER ARE DEAD, AND YOU DON'T WANT VENGEANCE?
IT'S JUST THAT WE ARE SO CLOSE TO OUR ULTIMATE GOAL. CAN'T VENGEANCE WAIT?
I'VE WAITED FOR THREE THOUSA YEARS. I WILL N WAIT A MOME LONGER.

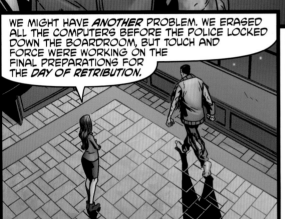

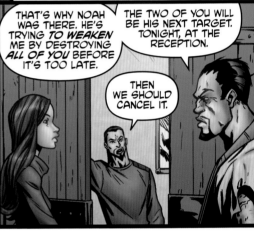

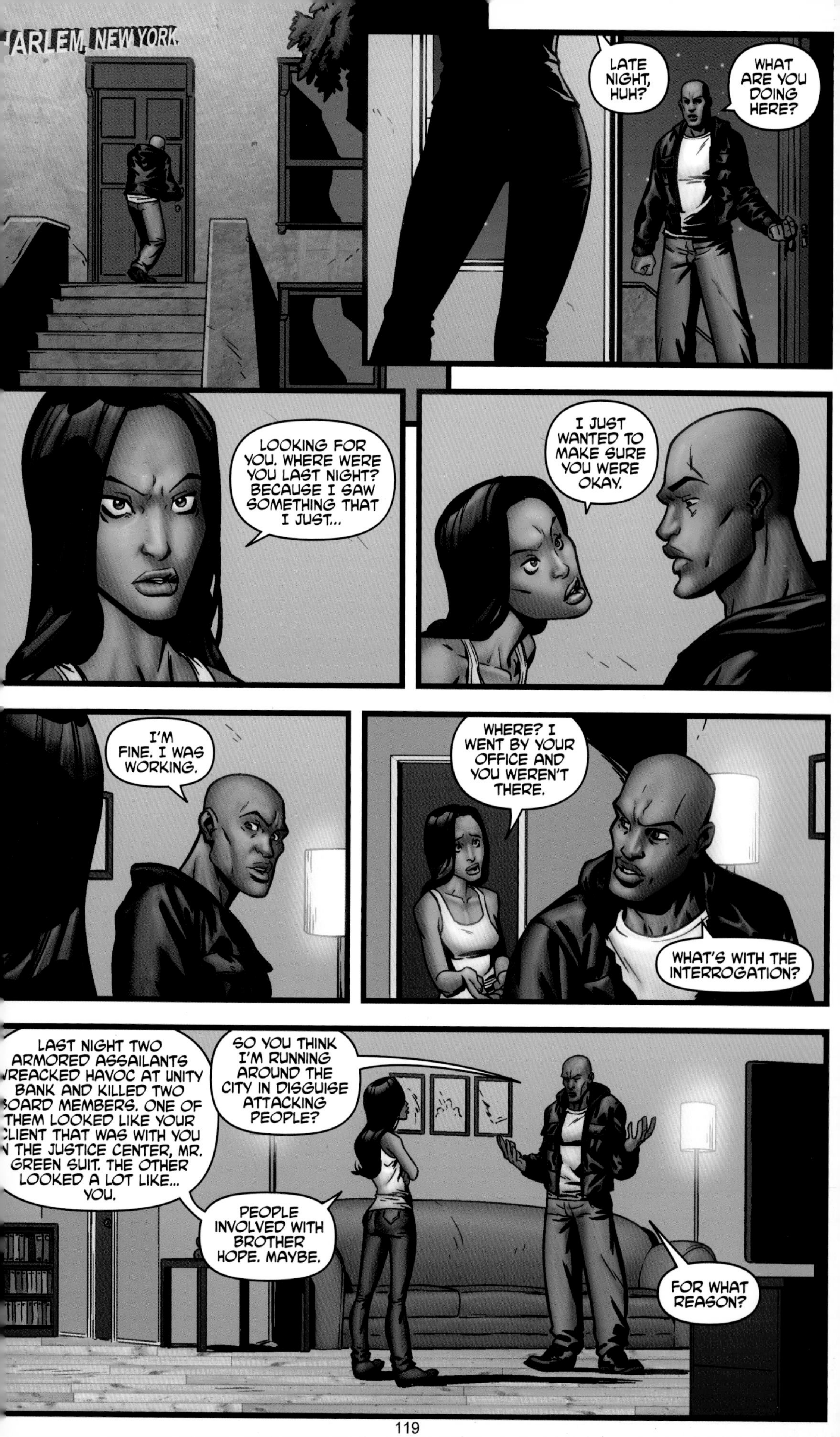
HARLEM, NEW YORK
LATE NIGHT, HUH?
WHAT ARE YOU DOING HERE?
LOOKING FOR YOU. WHERE WERE YOU LAST NIGHT? BECAUSE I SAW SOMETHING THAT I JUST...
I JUST WANTED TO MAKE SURE YOU WERE OKAY.
I'M FINE. I WAS WORKING.
WHERE? I WENT BY YOUR OFFICE AND YOU WEREN'T THERE.
WHAT'S WITH THE INTERROGATION?
LAST NIGHT TWO ARMORED ASSAILANTS WREACKED HAVOC AT UNITY BANK AND KILLED TWO BOARD MEMBERS. ONE OF THEM LOOKED LIKE YOUR CLIENT THAT WAS WITH YOU IN THE JUSTICE CENTER, MR. GREEN SUIT. THE OTHER LOOKED A LOT LIKE... YOU.
SO YOU THINK I'M RUNNING AROUND THE CITY IN DISGUISE ATTACKING PEOPLE?
PEOPLE INVOLVED WITH BROTHER HOPE. MAYBE.
FOR WHAT REASON?

BECAUSE HOPE IS THE LEADER OF THE NEW WORLD KNIGHTS AND I BELIEVE HE WAS BEHIND YOUR MOTHER'S MURDER.

AND YOU CAN PROVE THIS?

NOT YET, BUT I'M TRYING.

WELL LET ME KNOW WHEN YOU CAN.

THAT'S *IT*? I JUST TOLD YOU I THINK I KNOW WHO MURDERED YOUR MOTHER AND THAT'S ALL YOU GOT?

WHAT DO YOU WANT FROM ME? I NEED PROOF BEFORE I RELIVE THAT NIGHTMARE.

THEN HELP ME FIND IT.

I WISH I COULD, BUT I'M TRYING TO GET MY LIFE TOGETHER HERE.

ARE YOU REALLY? BECAUSE IT DOESN'T SEEM LIKE YOU'RE PUTTING FORTH MUCH OF AN EFFORT.

AND YOU'RE AN EXPERT BECAUSE YOUR MOTHER DIED TWO DAYS AGO OR TWENTY-EIGHT YEARS AGO?

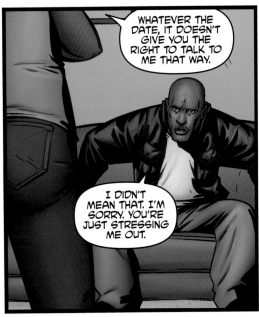

WHATEVER THE DATE, IT DOESN'T GIVE YOU THE RIGHT TO TALK TO ME THAT WAY.

I DIDN'T MEAN THAT. I'M SORRY. YOU'RE JUST STRESSING ME OUT.

WHAT HAPPENED TO US? THERE IS SO MUCH I WANT TO SHARE WITH YOU. THINGS I'VE SEEN, THINGS THAT ARE GOING ON RIGHT NOW BUT SINCE YOU CAN'T COME CLEAN WITH ME, I CAN'T TRUST YOU.

YOU CAN TRUST ME.

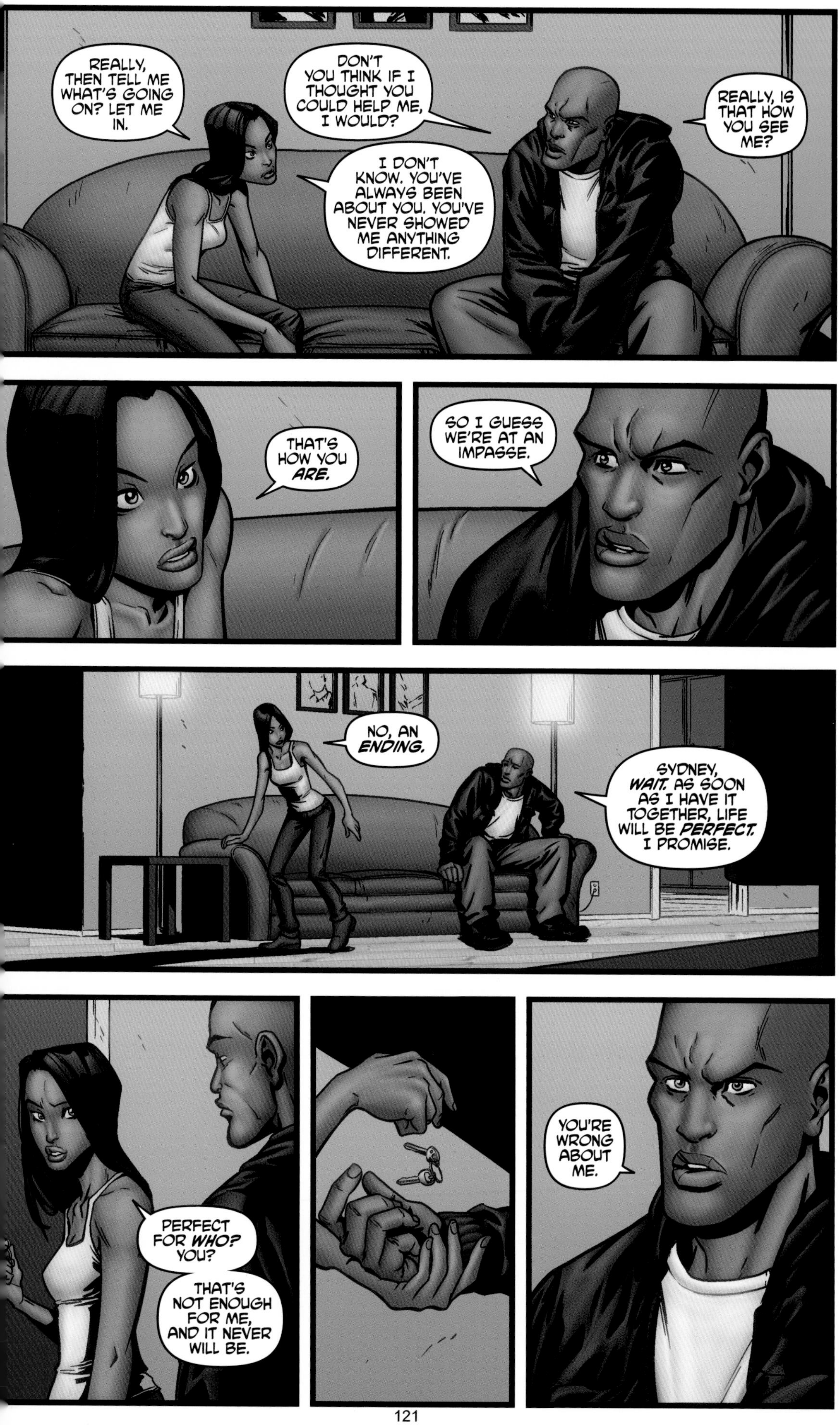
REALLY, THEN TELL ME WHAT'S GOING ON? LET ME IN.
DON'T YOU THINK IF I THOUGHT YOU COULD HELP ME, I WOULD?
I DON'T KNOW. YOU'VE ALWAYS BEEN ABOUT YOU. YOU'VE NEVER SHOWED ME ANYTHING DIFFERENT.
REALLY, IS THAT HOW YOU SEE ME?
THAT'S HOW YOU ARE.
SO I GUESS WE'RE AT AN IMPASSE.
NO, AN ENDING.
SYDNEY, WAIT. AS SOON AS I HAVE IT TOGETHER, LIFE WILL BE PERFECT. I PROMISE.
PERFECT FOR WHO? YOU?
THAT'S NOT ENOUGH FOR ME, AND IT NEVER WILL BE.
YOU'RE WRONG ABOUT ME.

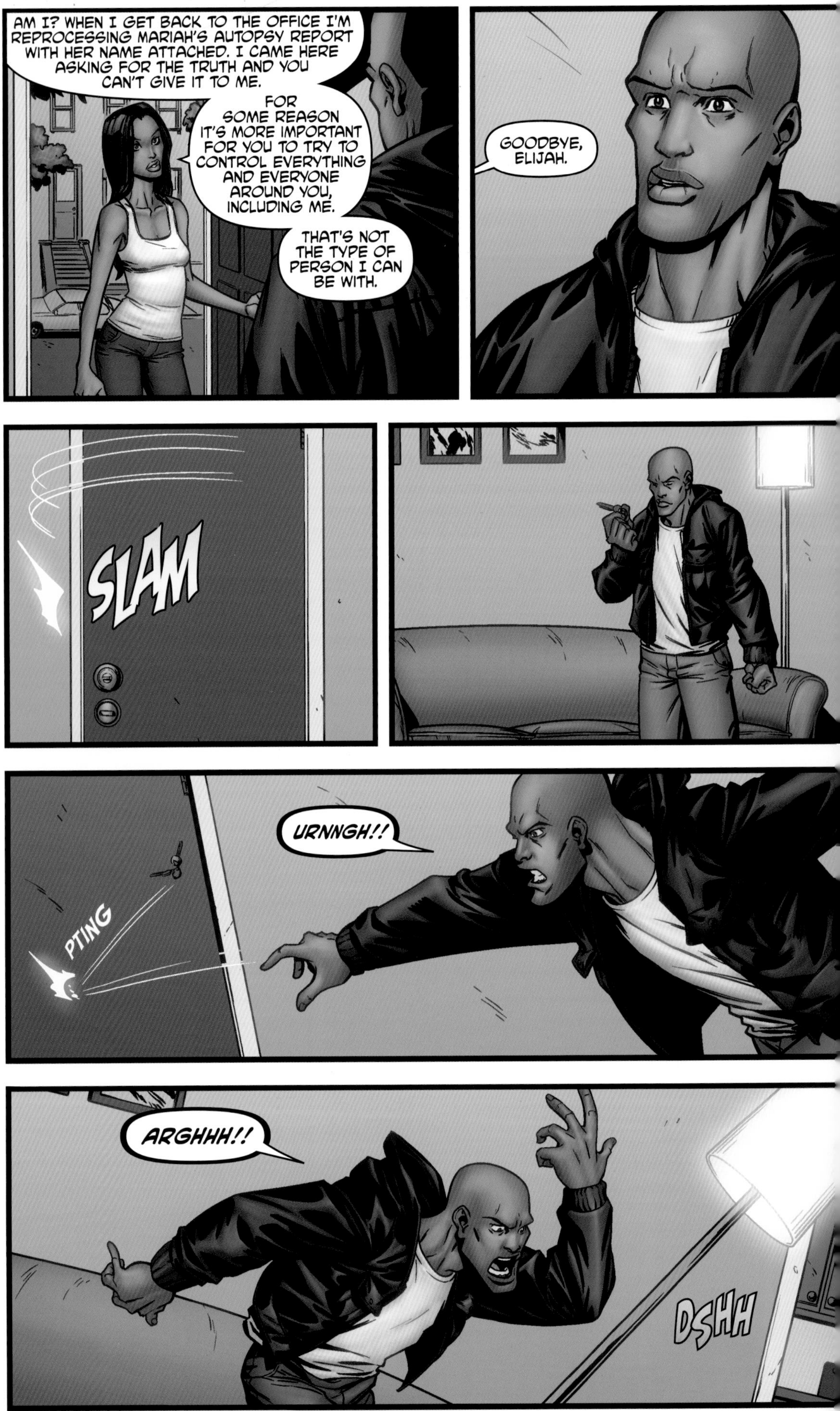

AM I? WHEN I GET BACK TO THE OFFICE I'M REPROCESSING MARIAH'S AUTOPSY REPORT WITH HER NAME ATTACHED. I CAME HERE ASKING FOR THE TRUTH AND YOU CAN'T GIVE IT TO ME.
FOR SOME REASON IT'S MORE IMPORTANT FOR YOU TO TRY TO CONTROL EVERYTHING AND EVERYONE AROUND YOU, INCLUDING ME.
THAT'S NOT THE TYPE OF PERSON I CAN BE WITH.
GOODBYE, ELIJAH.
SLAM
URNNGH!!
PTING
ARGHHH!!
DSHH

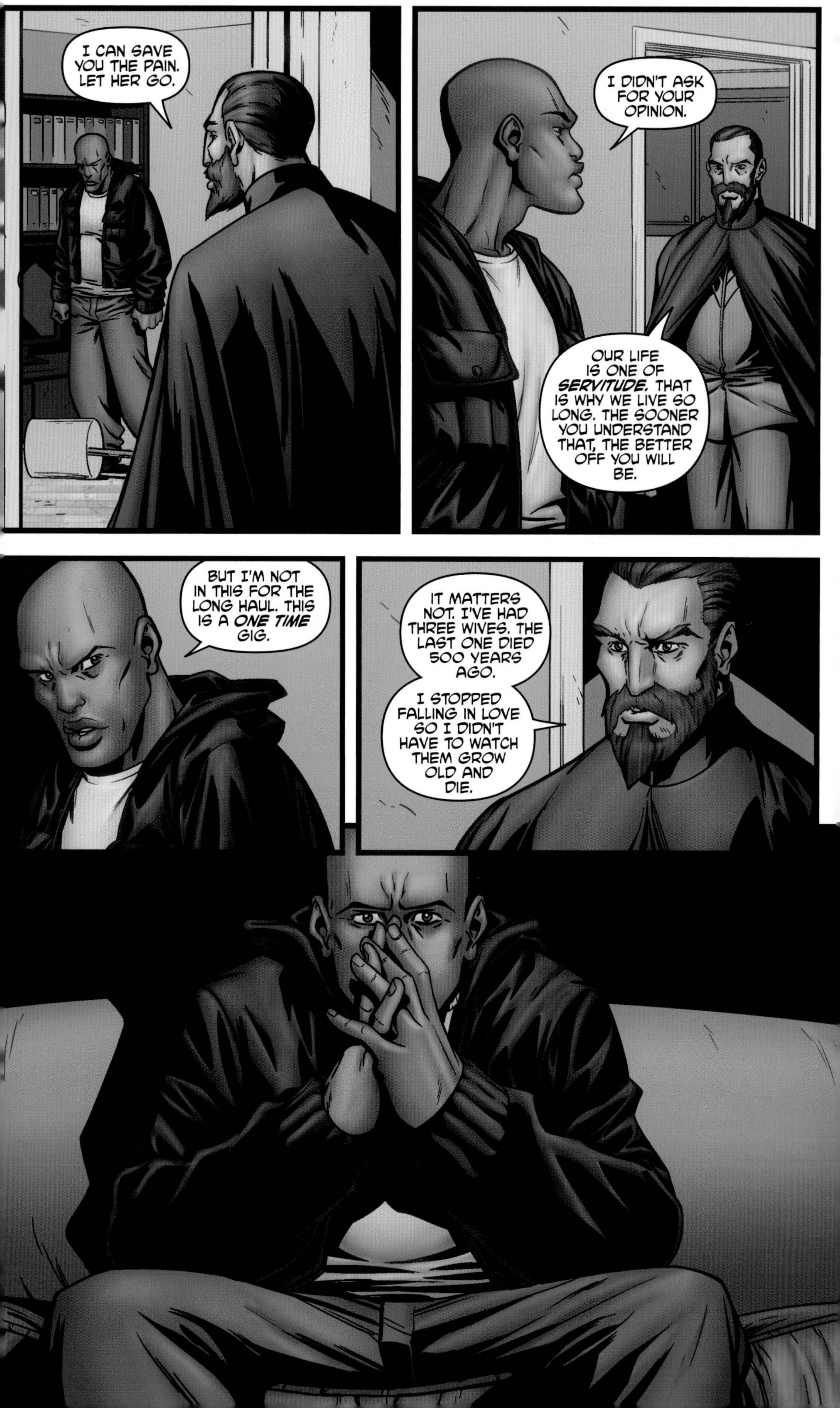
I CAN SAVE YOU THE PAIN. LET HER GO.
I DIDN'T ASK FOR YOUR OPINION.
OUR LIFE IS ONE OF *SERVITUDE.* THAT IS WHY WE LIVE SO LONG. THE SOONER YOU UNDERSTAND THAT, THE BETTER OFF YOU WILL BE.
BUT I'M NOT IN THIS FOR THE LONG HAUL. THIS IS A *ONE TIME* GIG.
IT MATTERS NOT. I'VE HAD THREE WIVES. THE LAST ONE DIED 500 YEARS AGO.
I STOPPED FALLING IN LOVE SO I DIDN'T HAVE TO WATCH THEM GROW OLD AND DIE.

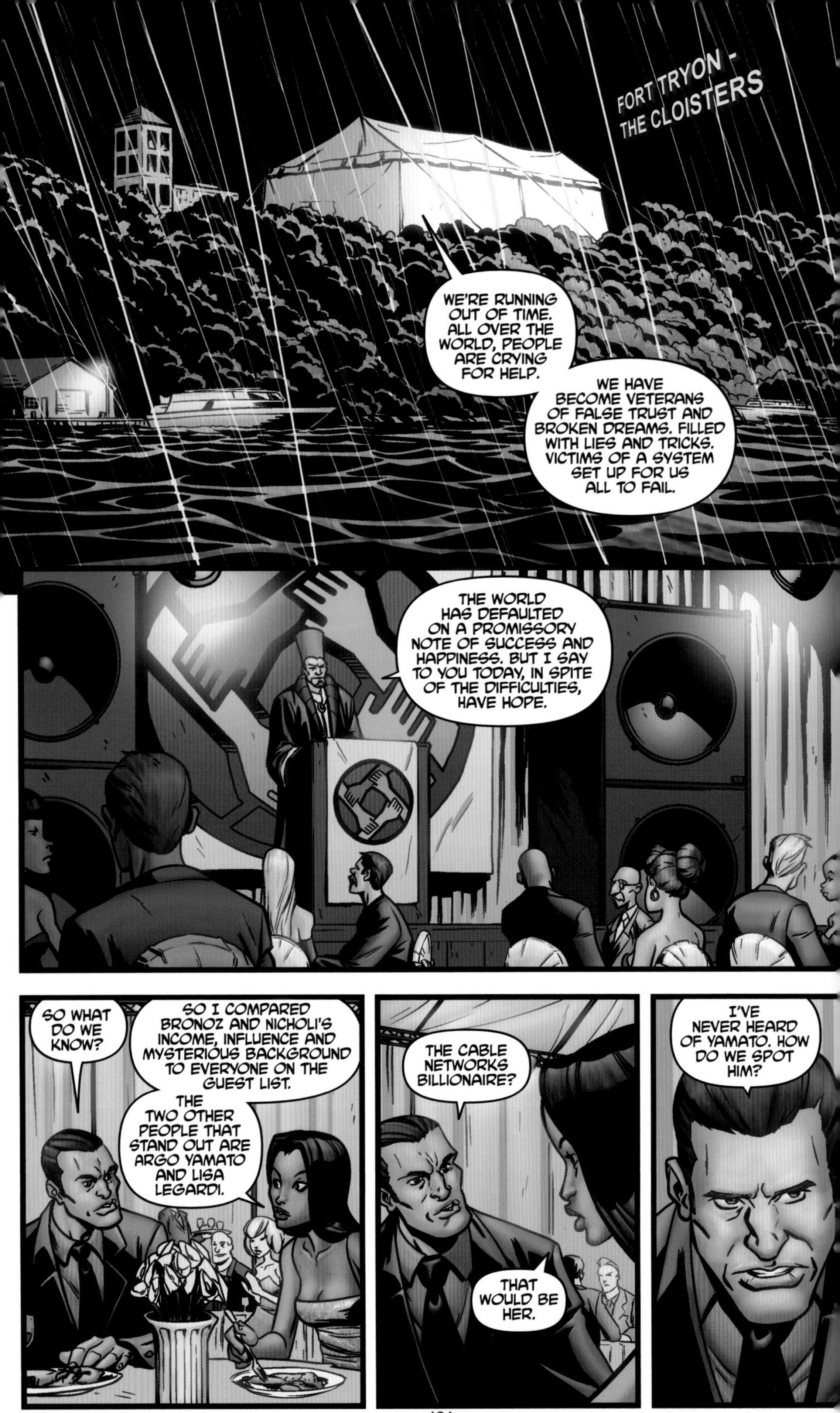
FORT TRYON - THE CLOISTERS
WE'RE RUNNING OUT OF TIME. ALL OVER THE WORLD, PEOPLE ARE CRYING FOR HELP.
WE HAVE BECOME VETERANS OF FALSE TRUST AND BROKEN DREAMS. FILLED WITH LIES AND TRICKS. VICTIMS OF A SYSTEM SET UP FOR US ALL TO FAIL.
THE WORLD HAS DEFAULTED ON A PROMISSORY NOTE OF SUCCESS AND HAPPINESS. BUT I SAY TO YOU TODAY, IN SPITE OF THE DIFFICULTIES, HAVE HOPE.
SO WHAT DO WE KNOW?
SO I COMPARED BRONOZ AND NICHOLI'S INCOME, INFLUENCE AND MYSTERIOUS BACKGROUND TO EVERYONE ON THE GUEST LIST.
THE TWO OTHER PEOPLE THAT STAND OUT ARE ARGO YAMATO AND LISA LEGARDI.
THE CABLE NETWORKS BILLIONAIRE?
THAT WOULD BE HER.
I'VE NEVER HEARD OF YAMATO. HOW DO WE SPOT HIM?

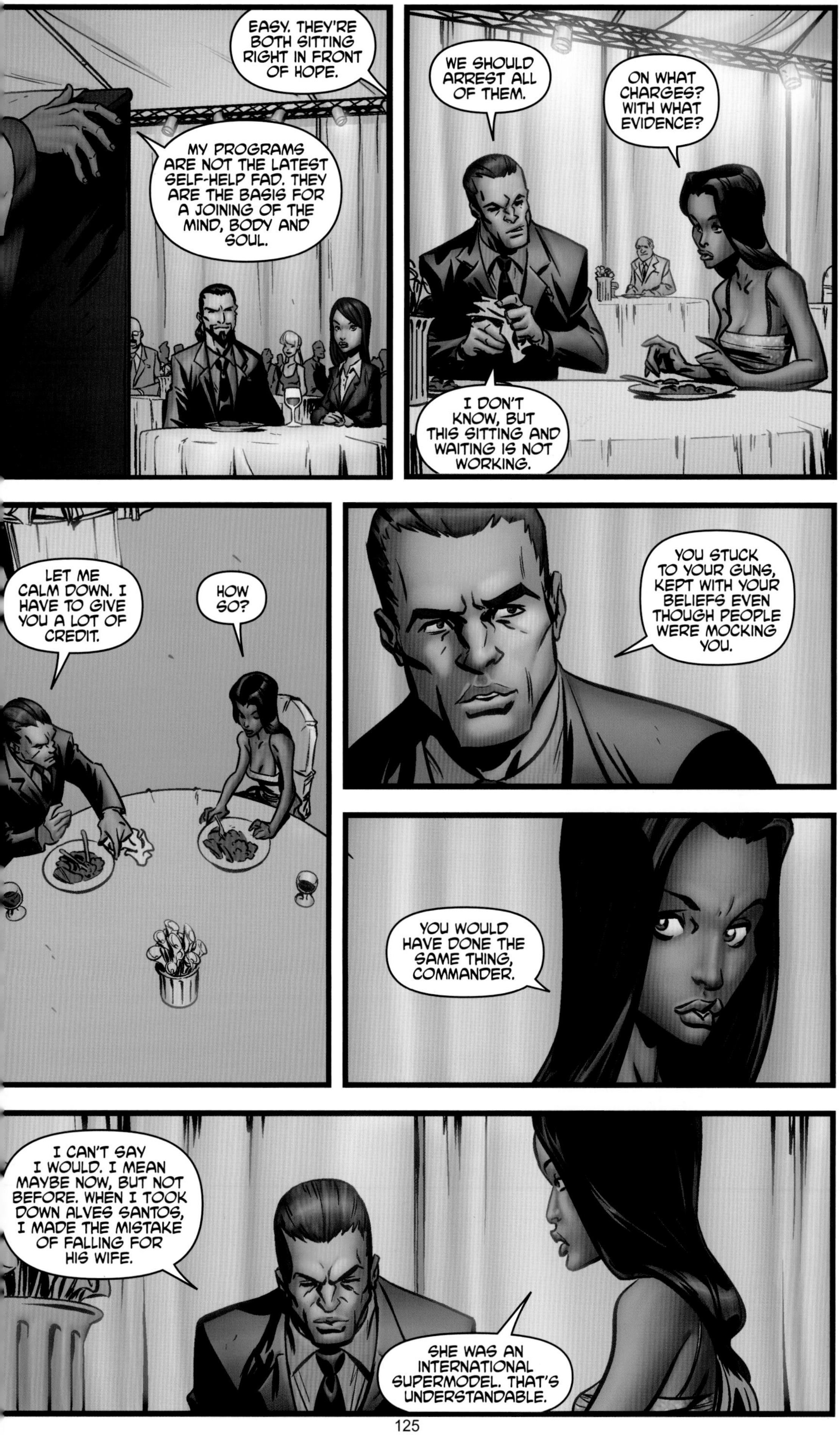
EASY. THEY'RE BOTH SITTING RIGHT IN FRONT OF HOPE.
MY PROGRAMS ARE NOT THE LATEST SELF-HELP FAD. THEY ARE THE BASIS FOR A JOINING OF THE MIND, BODY AND SOUL.
WE SHOULD ARREST ALL OF THEM.
ON WHAT CHARGES? WITH WHAT EVIDENCE?
I DON'T KNOW, BUT THIS SITTING AND WAITING IS NOT WORKING.
LET ME CALM DOWN. I HAVE TO GIVE YOU A LOT OF CREDIT.
HOW SO?
YOU STUCK TO YOUR GUNS, KEPT WITH YOUR BELIEFS EVEN THOUGH PEOPLE WERE MOCKING YOU.
YOU WOULD HAVE DONE THE SAME THING, COMMANDER.
I CAN'T SAY I WOULD. I MEAN MAYBE NOW, BUT NOT BEFORE. WHEN I TOOK DOWN ALVES SANTOS, I MADE THE MISTAKE OF FALLING FOR HIS WIFE.
SHE WAS AN INTERNATIONAL SUPERMODEL. THAT'S UNDERSTANDABLE.

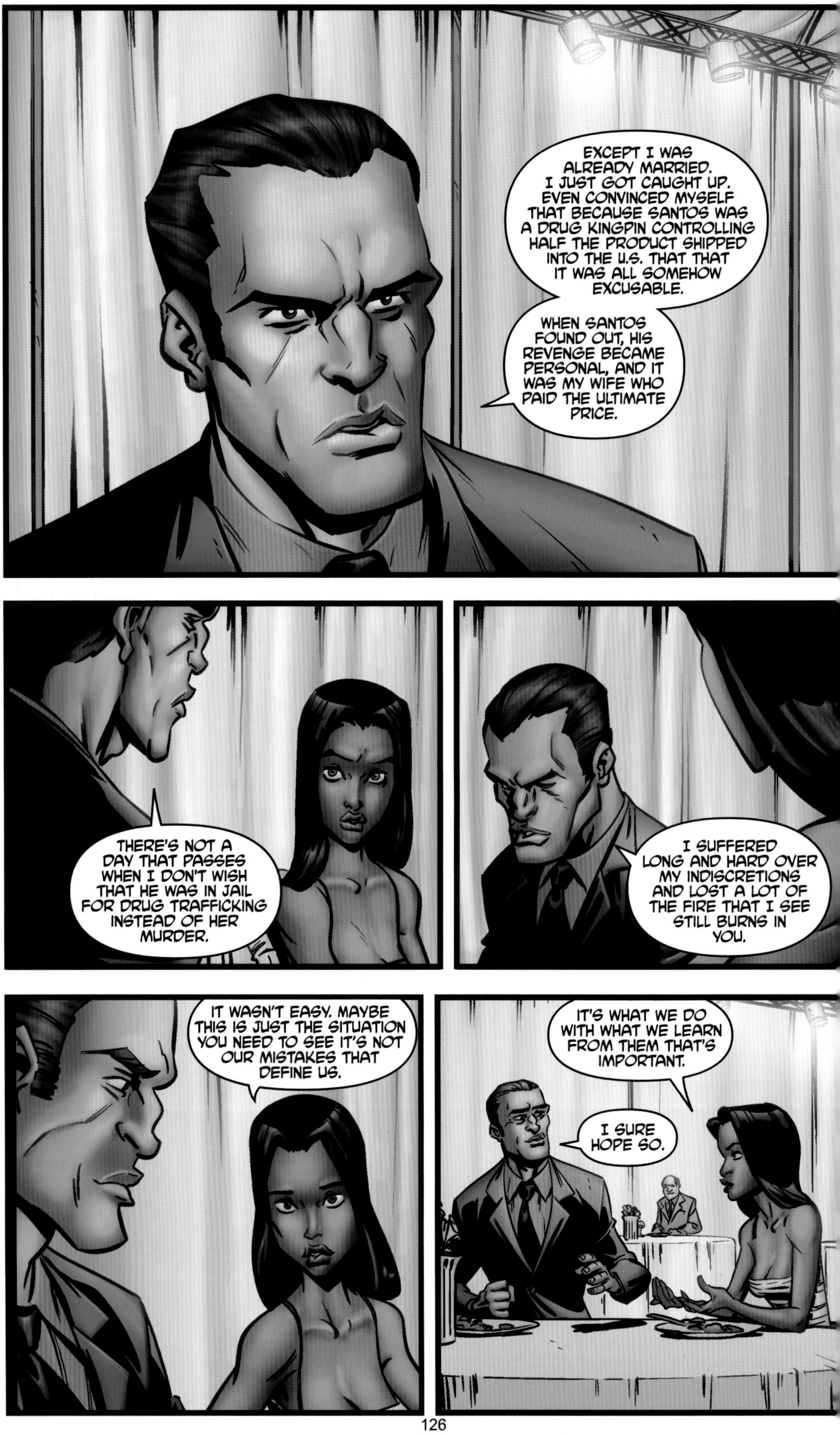
EXCEPT I WAS ALREADY MARRIED. I JUST GOT CAUGHT UP. EVEN CONVINCED MYSELF THAT BECAUSE SANTOS WAS A DRUG KINGPIN CONTROLLING HALF THE PRODUCT SHIPPED INTO THE U.S. THAT THAT IT WAS ALL SOMEHOW EXCUSABLE.
WHEN SANTOS FOUND OUT, HIS REVENGE BECAME PERSONAL, AND IT WAS MY WIFE WHO PAID THE ULTIMATE PRICE.
THERE'S NOT A DAY THAT PASSES WHEN I DON'T WISH THAT HE WAS IN JAIL FOR DRUG TRAFFICKING INSTEAD OF HER MURDER.
I SUFFERED LONG AND HARD OVER MY INDISCRETIONS AND LOST A LOT OF THE FIRE THAT I SEE STILL BURNS IN YOU.
IT WASN'T EASY. MAYBE THIS IS JUST THE SITUATION YOU NEED TO SEE IT'S NOT OUR MISTAKES THAT DEFINE US.
IT'S WHAT WE DO WITH WHAT WE LEARN FROM THEM THAT'S IMPORTANT.
I SURE HOPE SO.

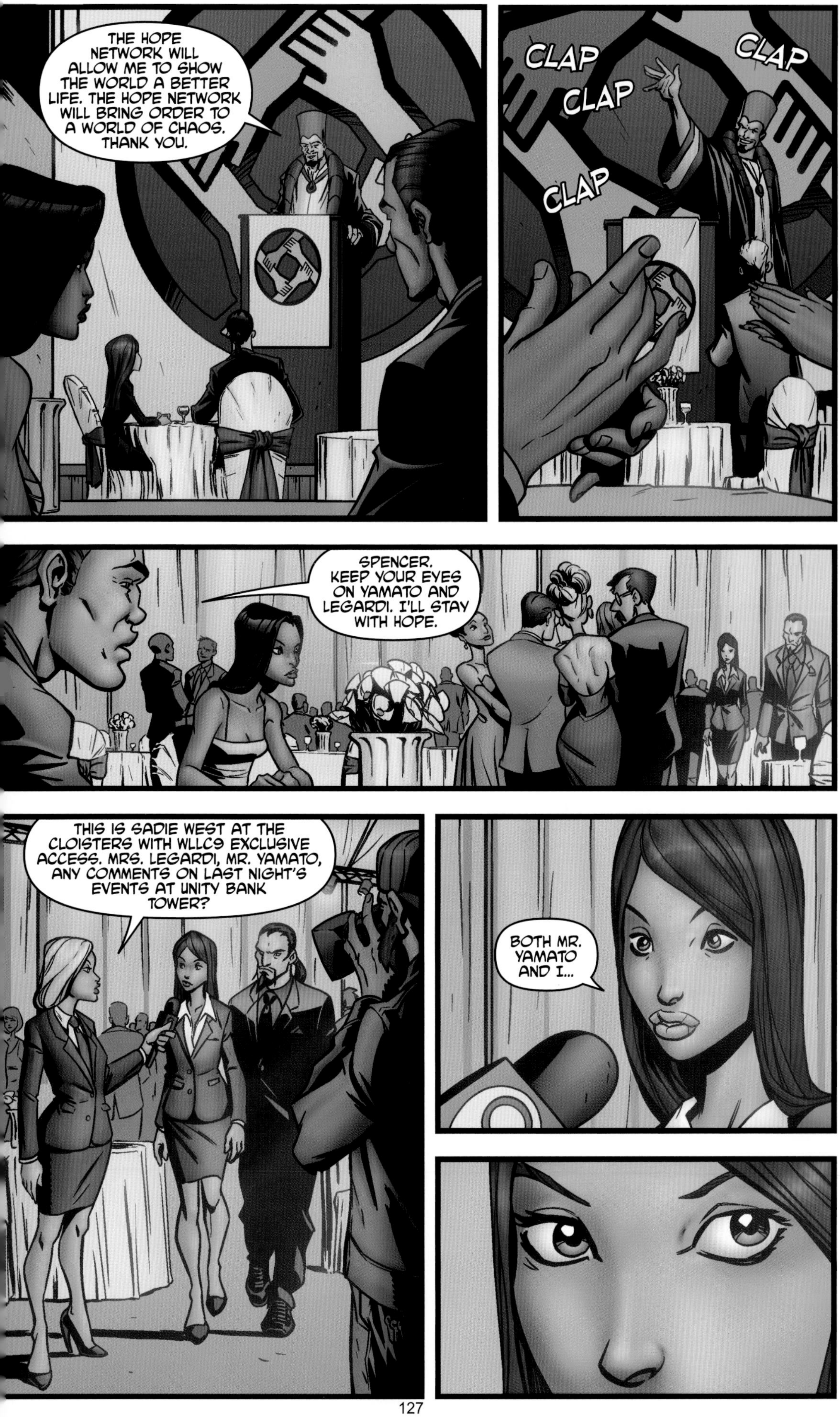
THE HOPE NETWORK WILL ALLOW ME TO SHOW THE WORLD A BETTER LIFE. THE HOPE NETWORK WILL BRING ORDER TO A WORLD OF CHAOS. THANK YOU.
CLAP
CLAP
CLAP
CLAP
SPENCER. KEEP YOUR EYES ON YAMATO AND LEGARDI. I'LL STAY WITH HOPE.
THIS IS SADIE WEST AT THE CLOISTERS WITH WLLC9 EXCLUSIVE ACCESS. MRS. LEGARDI, MR. YAMATO, ANY COMMENTS ON LAST NIGHT'S EVENTS AT UNITY BANK TOWER?
BOTH MR. YAMATO AND I...

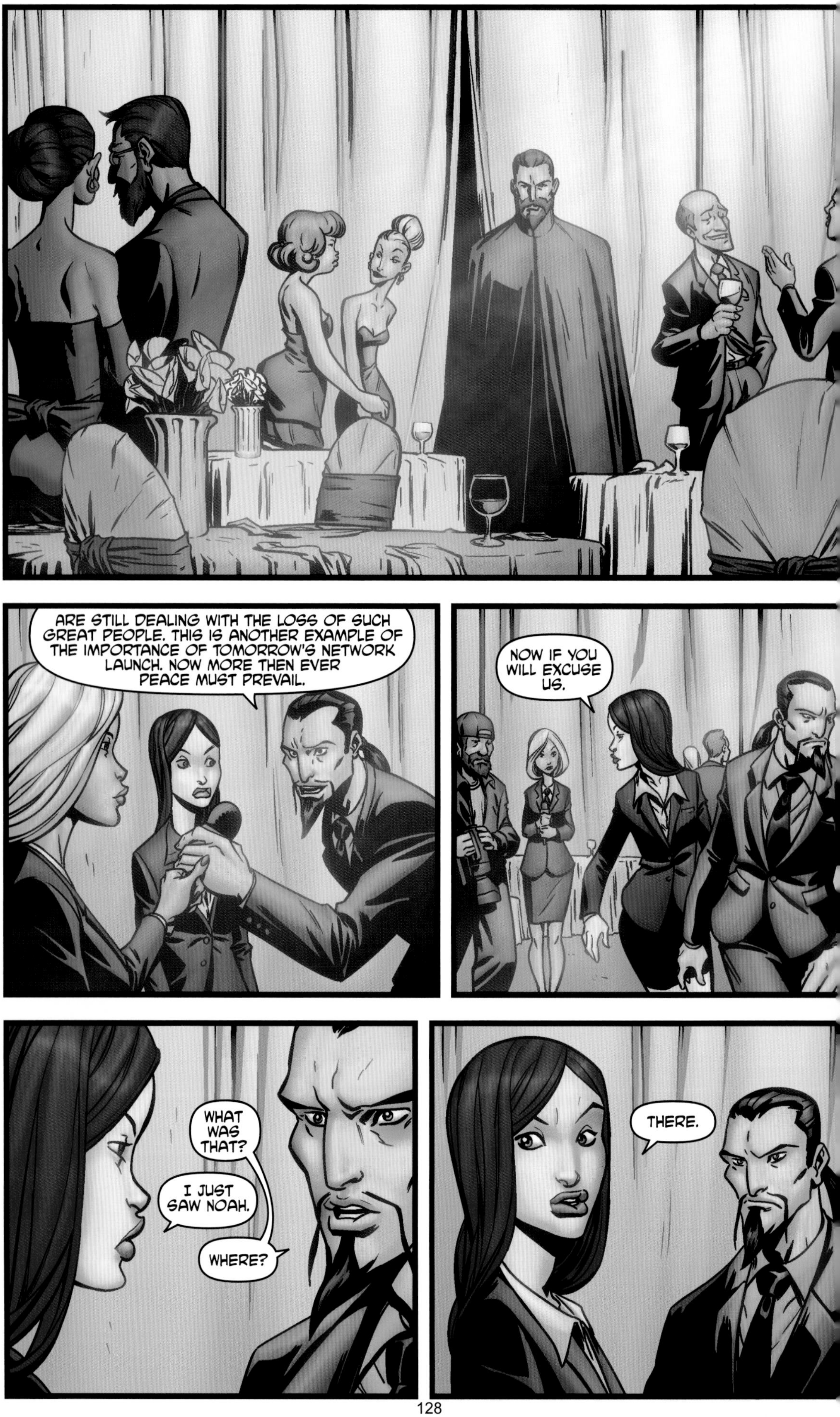
ARE STILL DEALING WITH THE LOSS OF SUCH GREAT PEOPLE. THIS IS ANOTHER EXAMPLE OF THE IMPORTANCE OF TOMORROW'S NETWORK LAUNCH. NOW MORE THEN EVER PEACE MUST PREVAIL.
NOW IF YOU WILL EXCUSE US.
WHAT WAS THAT?
I JUST SAW NOAH.
WHERE?
THERE.

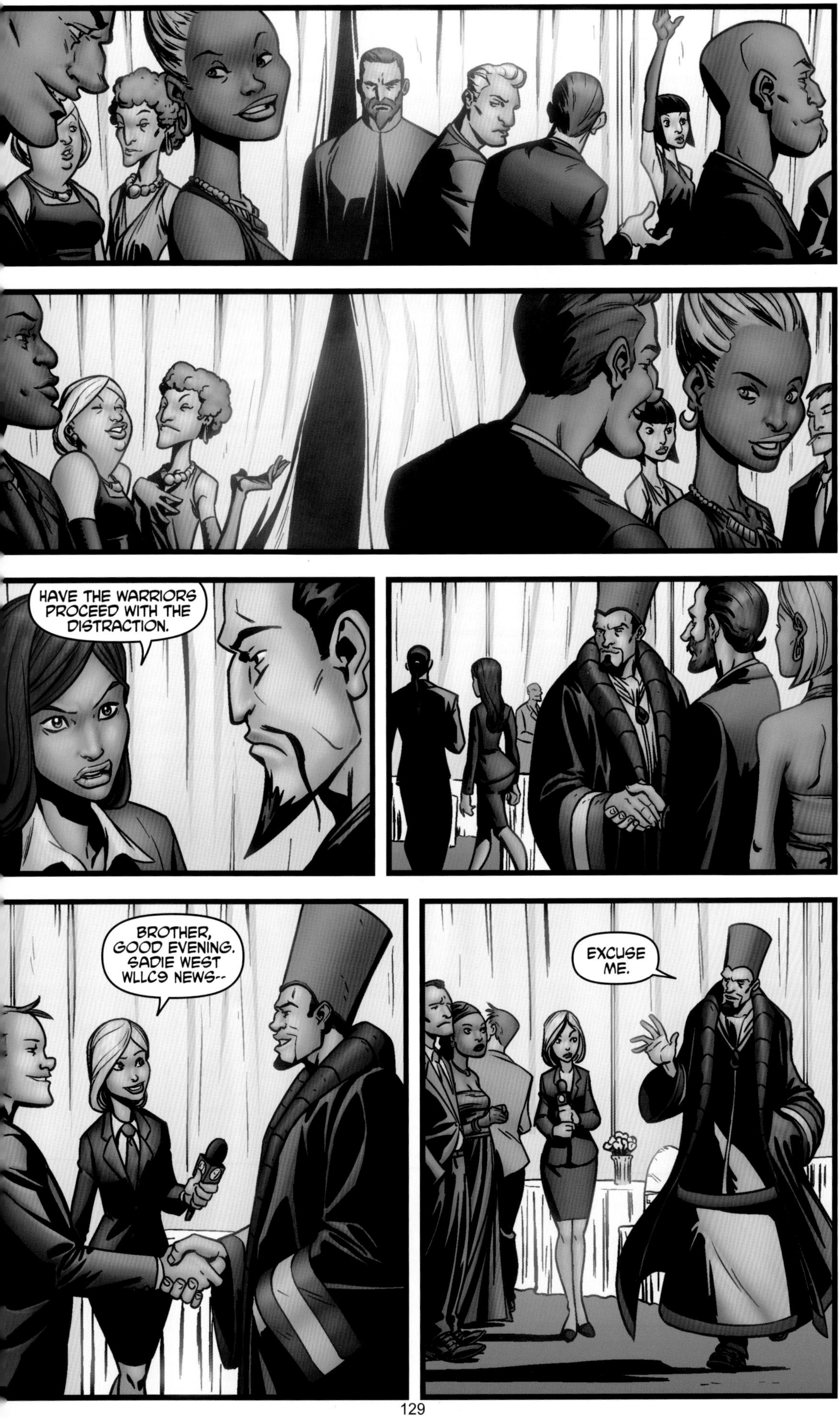
HAVE THE WARRIORS PROCEED WITH THE DISTRACTION.
BROTHER, GOOD EVENING. SADIE WEST WLLC9 NEWS--
EXCUSE ME.

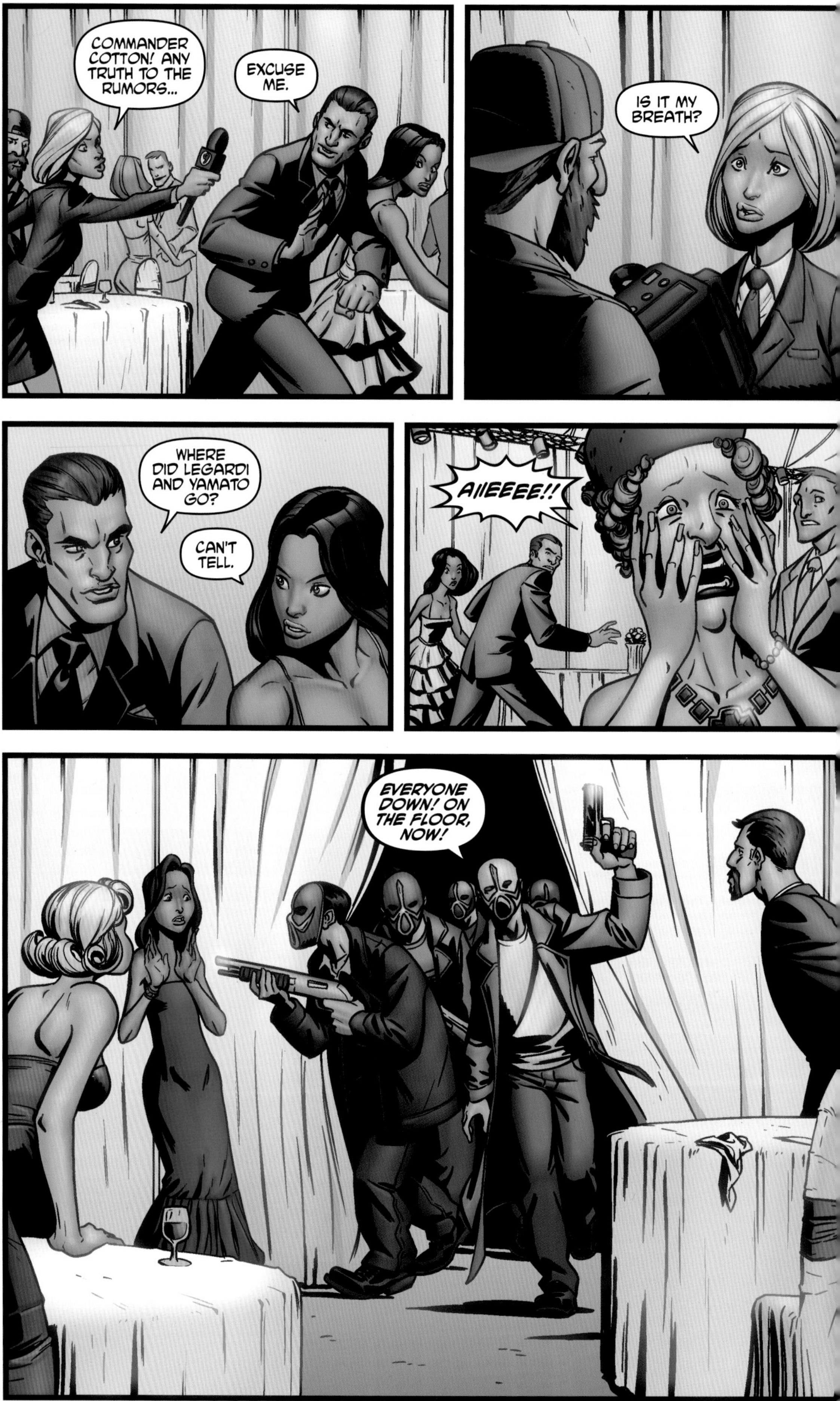
COMMANDER COTTON! ANY TRUTH TO THE RUMORS...
EXCUSE ME.
IS IT MY BREATH?
WHERE DID LEGARDI AND YAMATO GO?
CAN'T TELL.
AIIEEEE!!
EVERYONE DOWN! ON THE FLOOR, NOW!

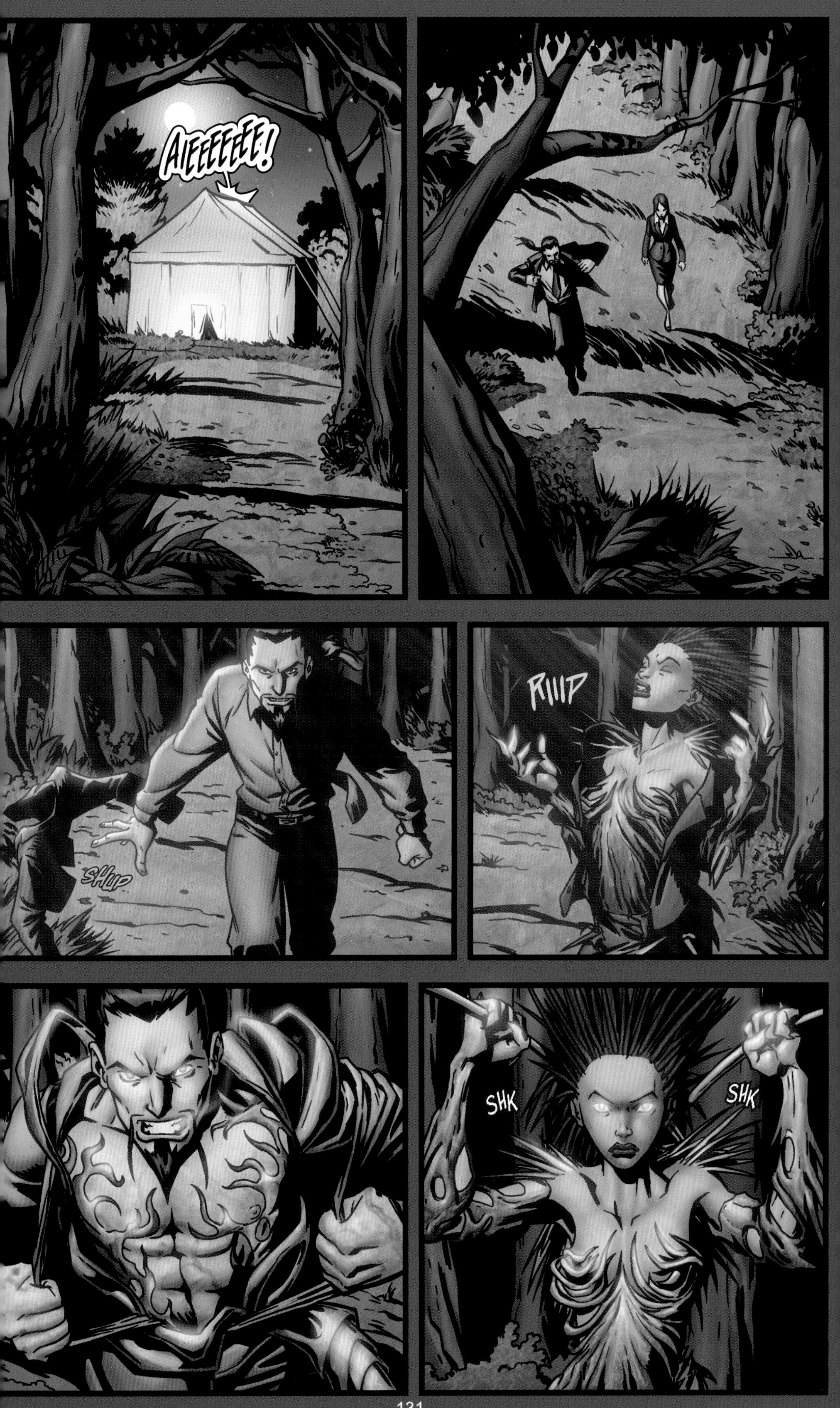
AIEEEEEEE!
SHLIP
RIIIP
SHK
SHK

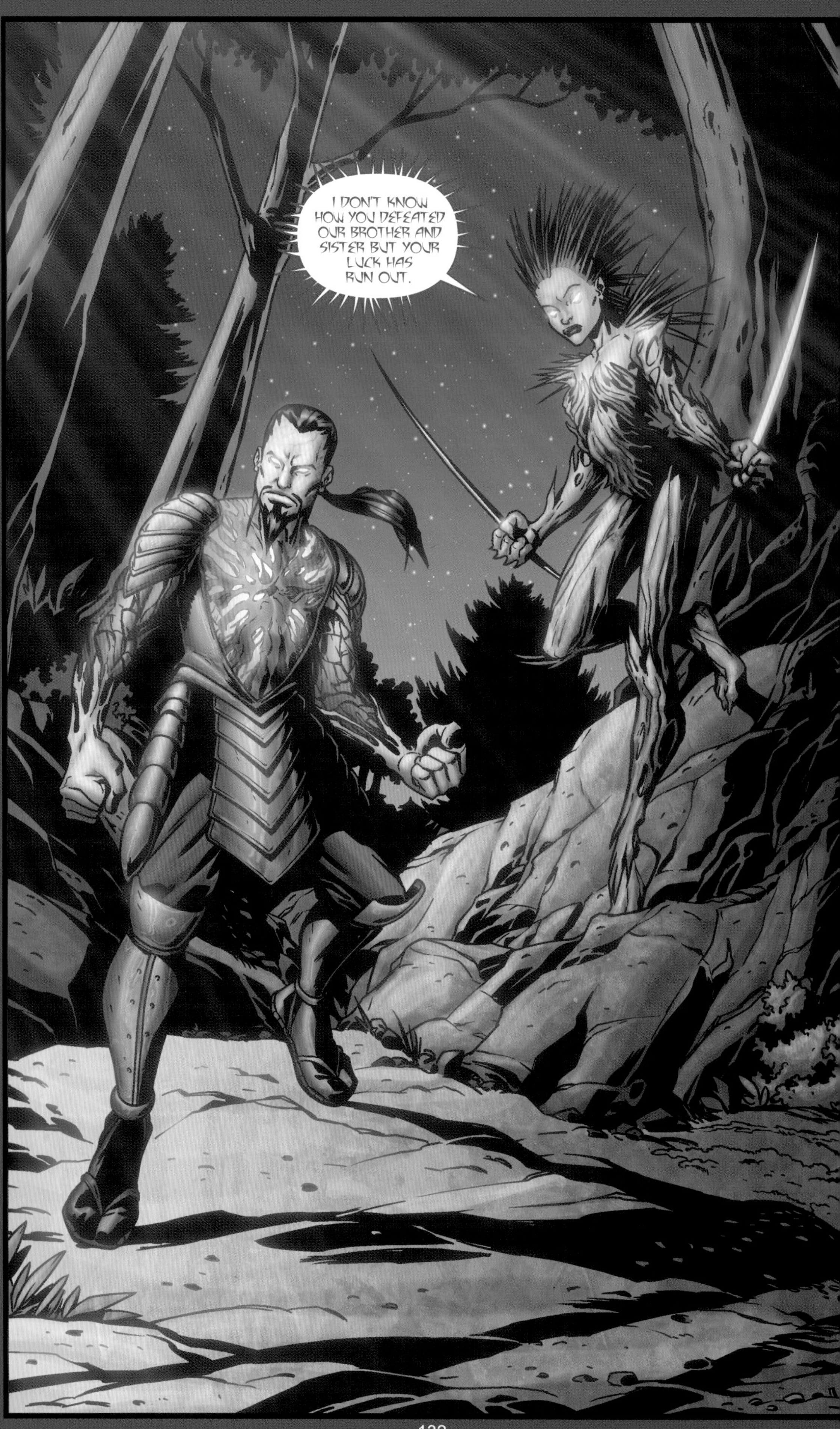
I DON'T KNOW HOW YOU DEFEATED OUR BROTHER AND SISTER BUT YOUR LUCK HAS RUN OUT.

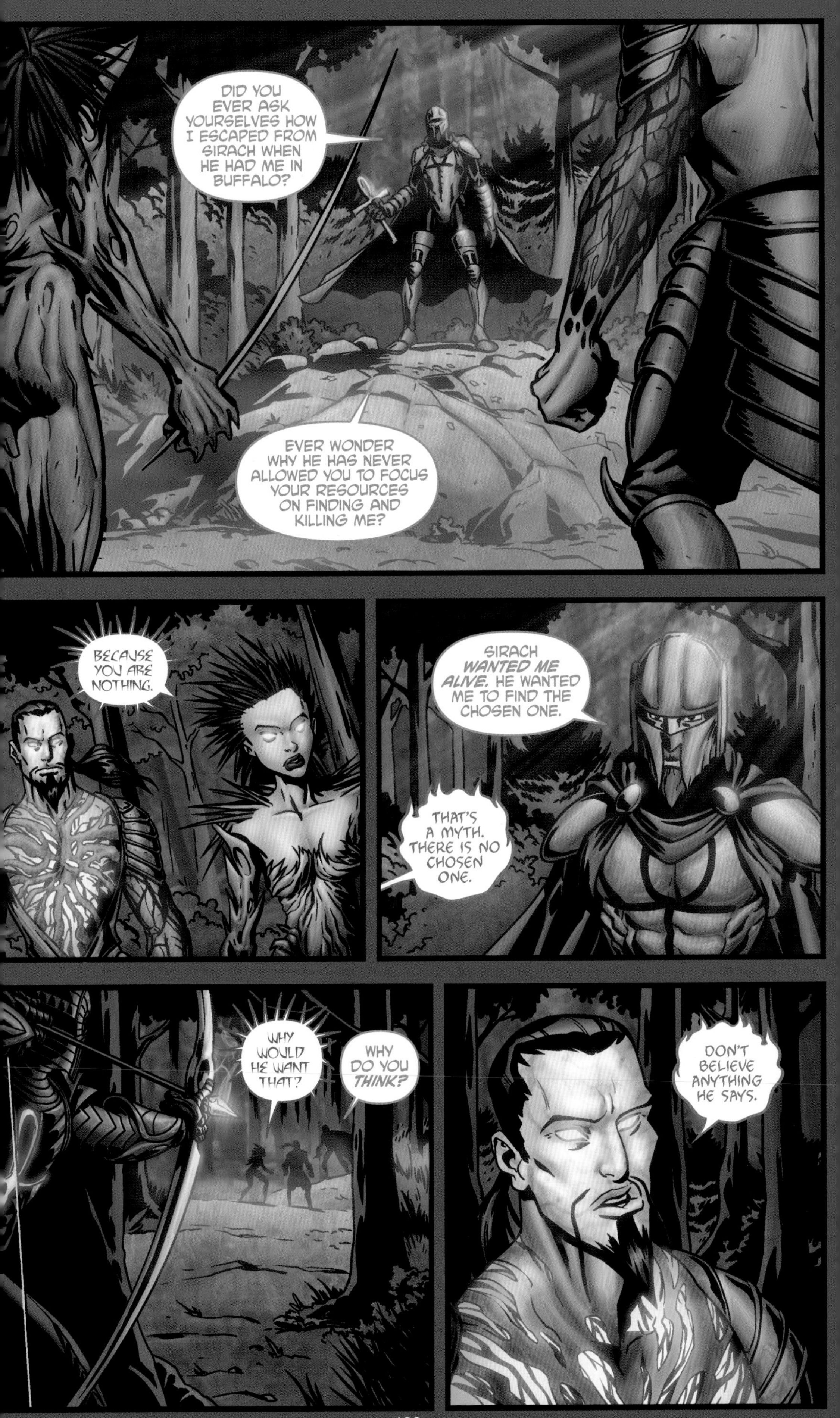
DID YOU EVER ASK YOURSELVES HOW I ESCAPED FROM SIRACH WHEN HE HAD ME IN BUFFALO?
EVER WONDER WHY HE HAS NEVER ALLOWED YOU TO FOCUS YOUR RESOURCES ON FINDING AND KILLING ME?
BECAUSE YOU ARE NOTHING.
SIRACH *WANTED ME ALIVE.* HE WANTED ME TO FIND THE CHOSEN ONE.
THAT'S A MYTH. THERE IS NO CHOSEN ONE.
WHY WOULD HE WANT THAT?
WHY DO YOU *THINK?*
DON'T BELIEVE ANYTHING HE SAYS.

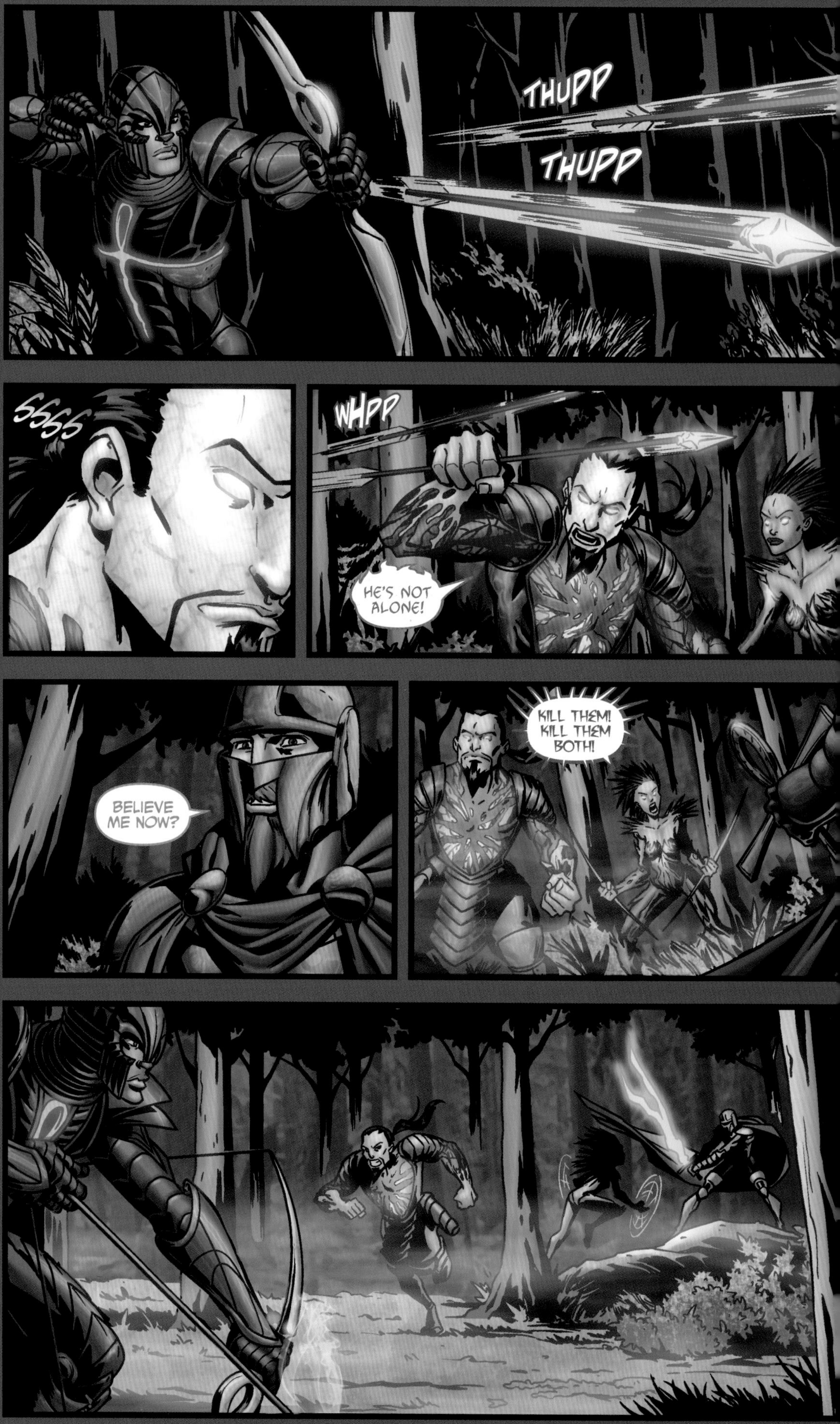
THUPP
THUPP
SSSS
WHPP
HE'S NOT ALONE!
BELIEVE ME NOW?
KILL THEM! KILL THEM BOTH!

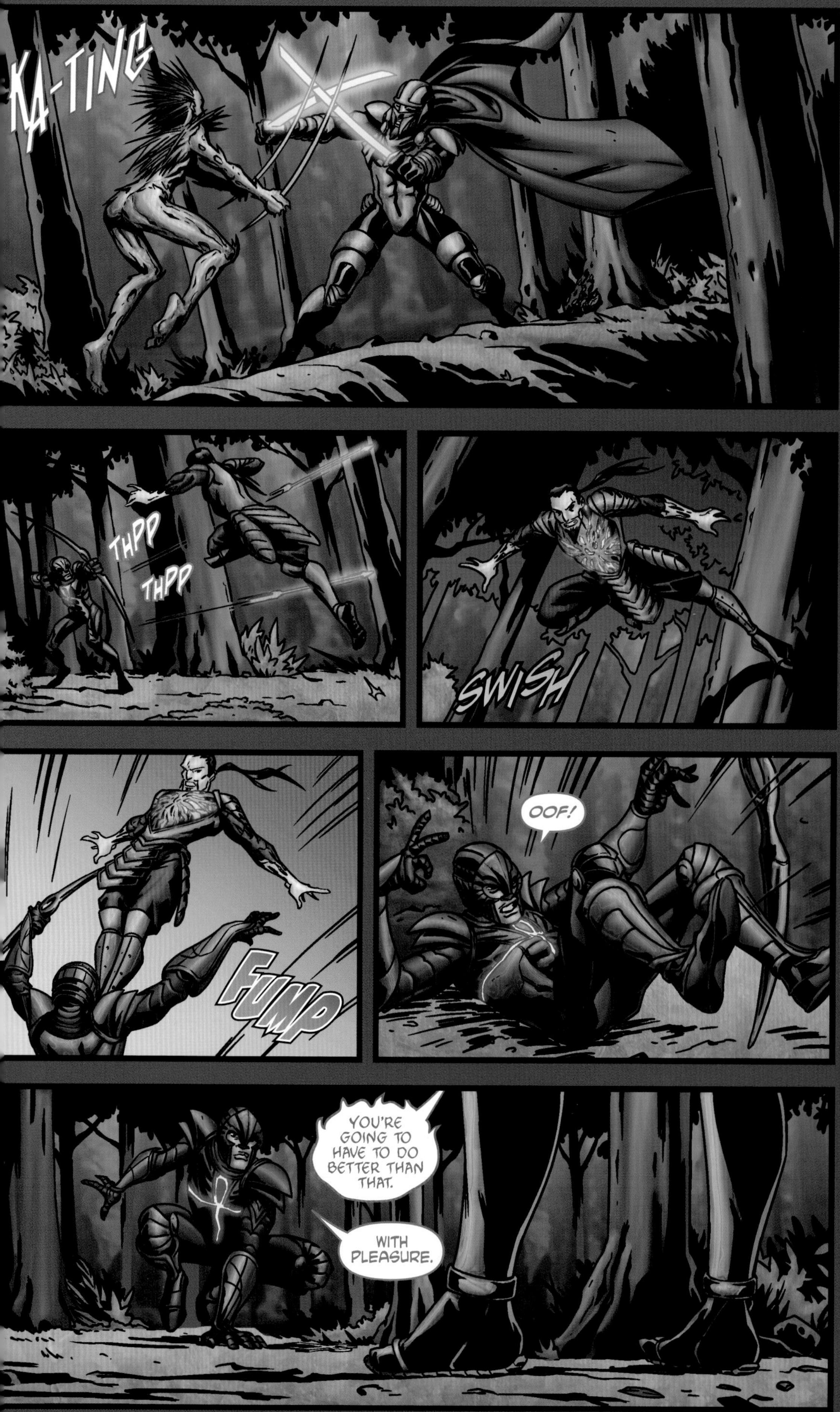
KA-TING
THPP
THPP
SWISH
FUMP
OOF!
YOU'RE GOING TO HAVE TO DO BETTER THAN THAT.
WITH PLEASURE.

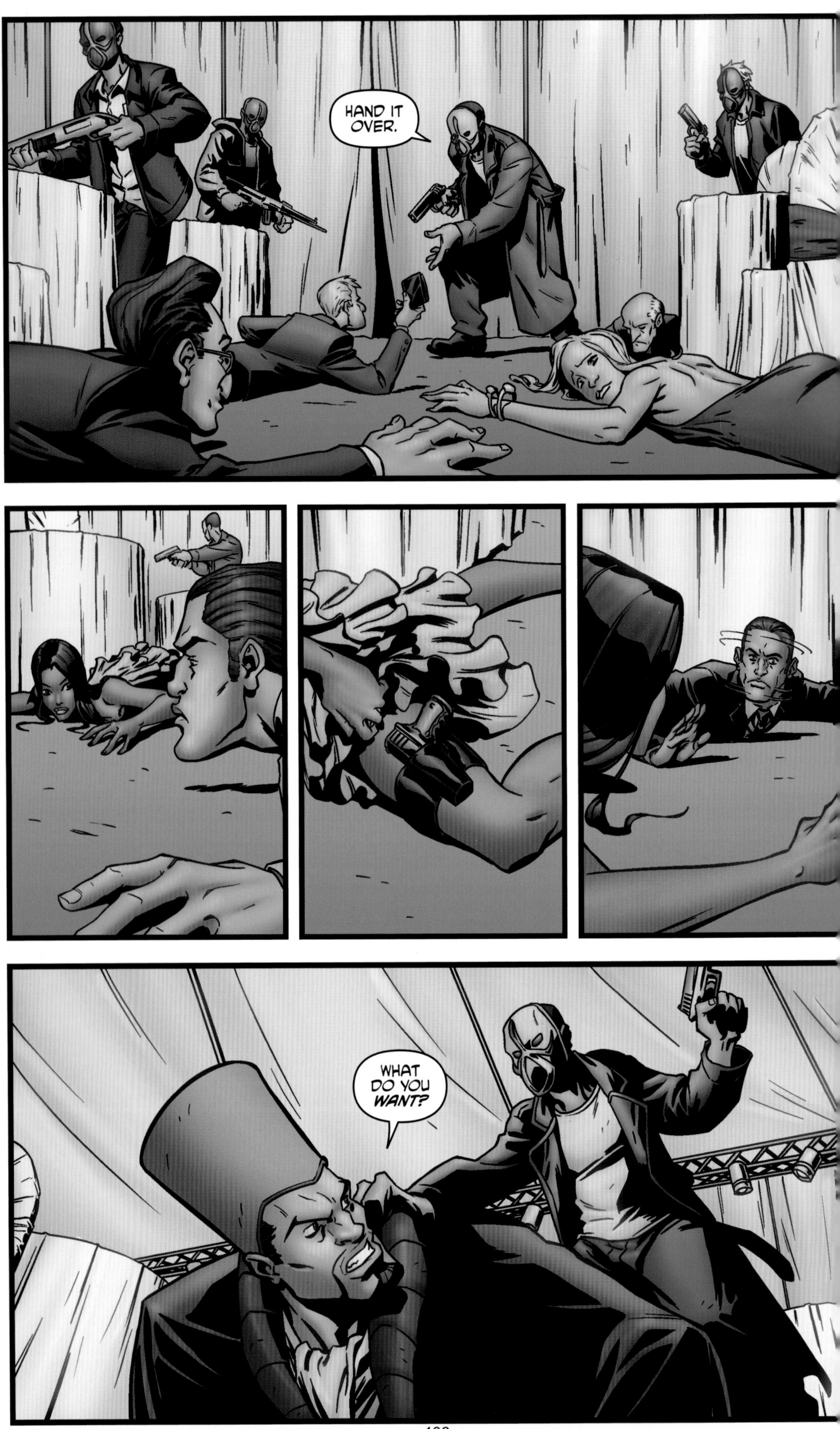
HAND IT OVER.
WHAT DO YOU *WANT?*

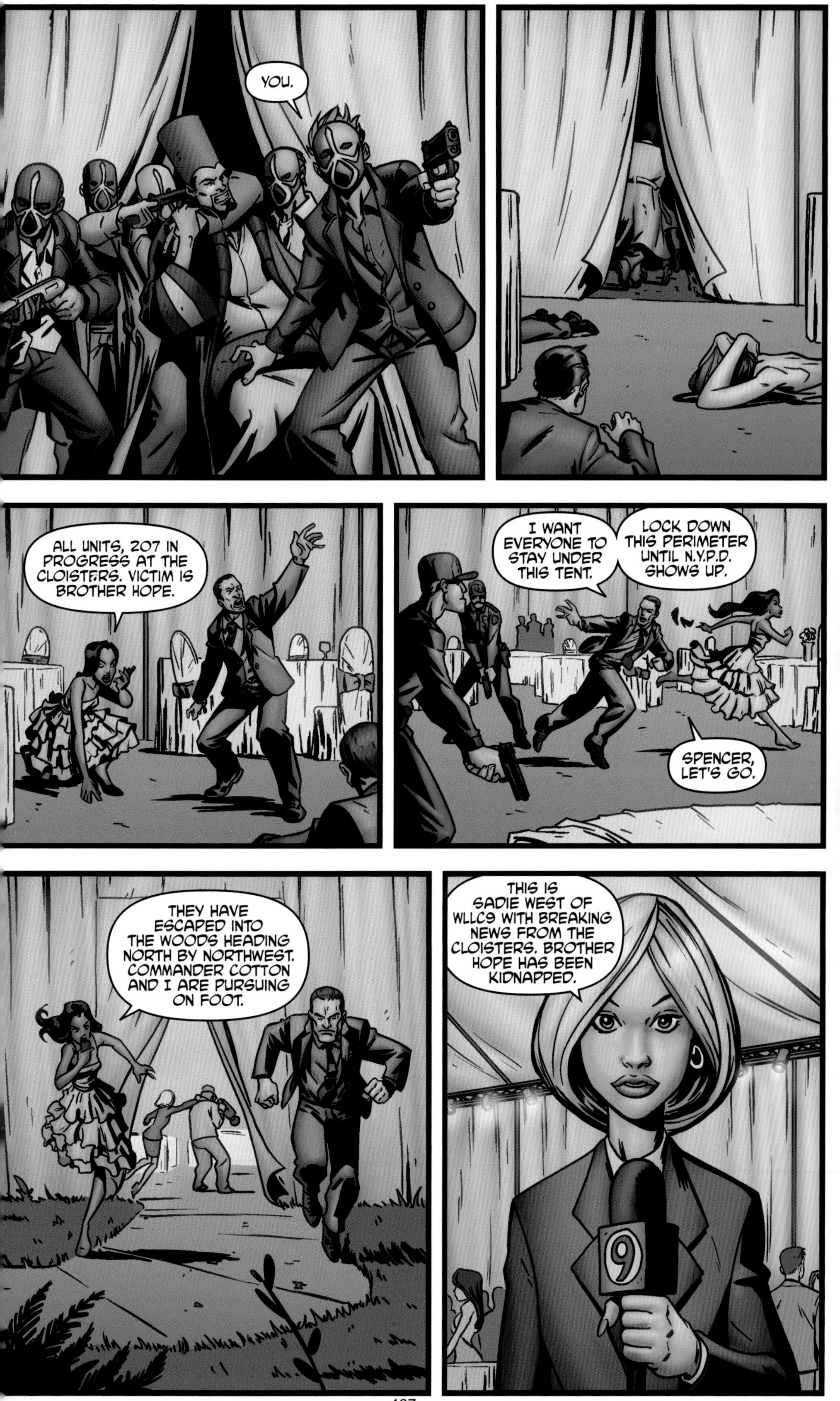
YOU.
ALL UNITS, 207 IN PROGRESS AT THE CLOISTERS. VICTIM IS BROTHER HOPE.
I WANT EVERYONE TO STAY UNDER THIS TENT.
LOCK DOWN THIS PERIMETER UNTIL N.Y.P.D. SHOWS UP.
SPENCER, LET'S GO.
THEY HAVE ESCAPED INTO THE WOODS HEADING NORTH BY NORTHWEST. COMMANDER COTTON AND I ARE PURSUING ON FOOT.
THIS IS SADIE WEST OF WLLC9 WITH BREAKING NEWS FROM THE CLOISTERS. BROTHER HOPE HAS BEEN KIDNAPPED.
9

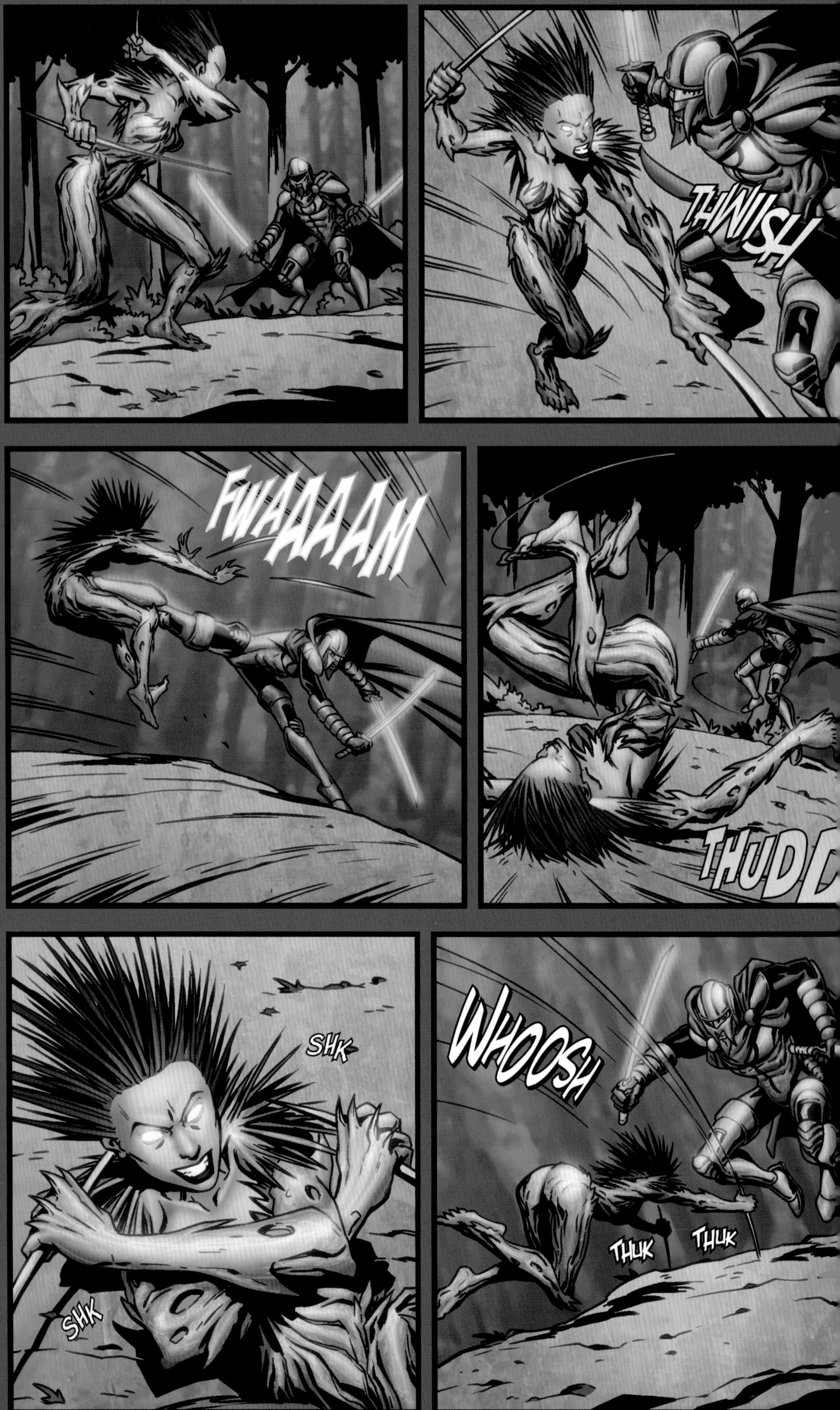
THWISH
FWAAAAM
THUDD
SHK
SHK
WHOOSH
THUK
THUK

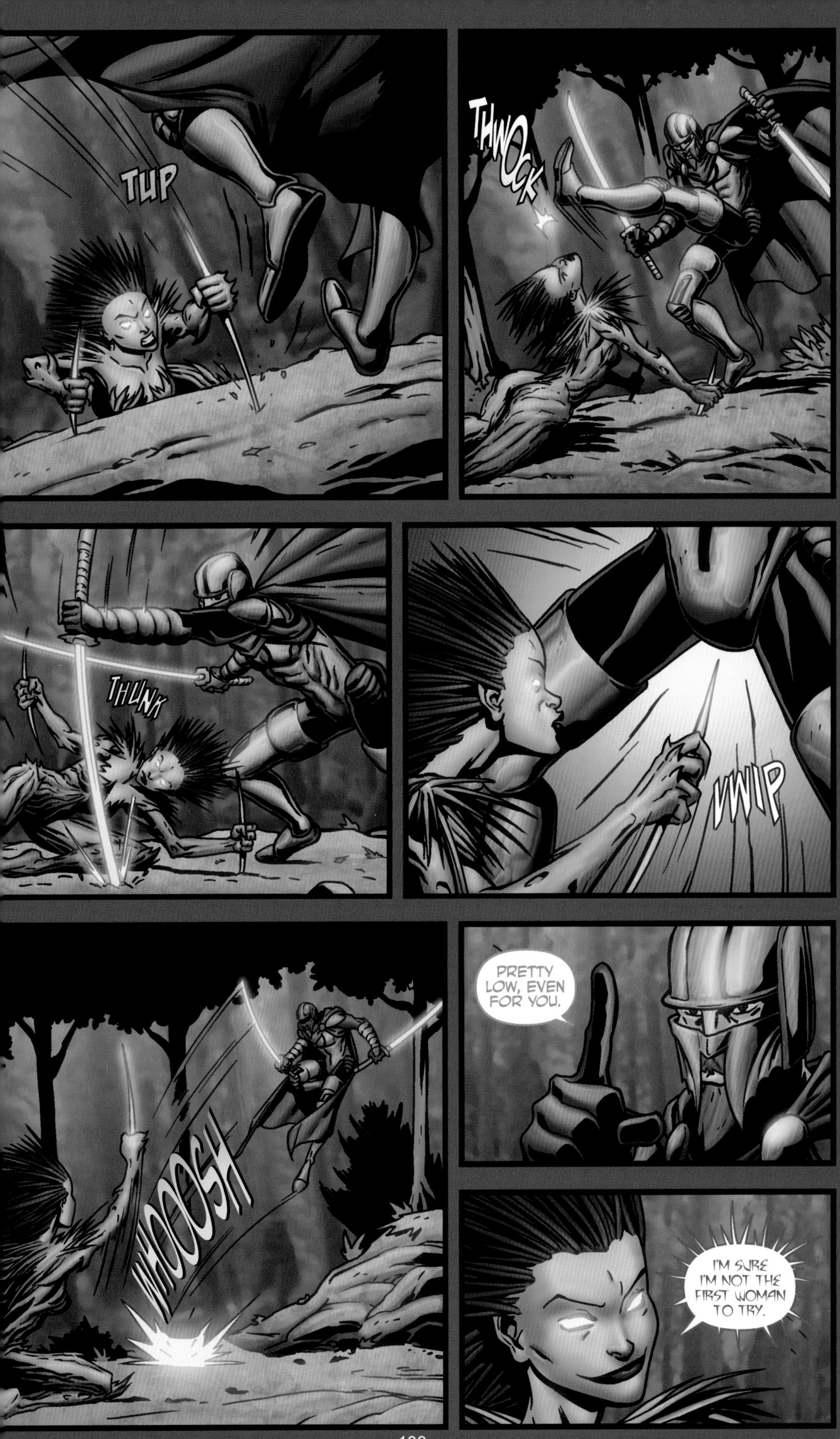

TUP
THWOCK
THUNK
VWIP
WHOOOSH
PRETTY LOW, EVEN FOR YOU.
I'M SURE I'M NOT THE FIRST WOMAN TO TRY.

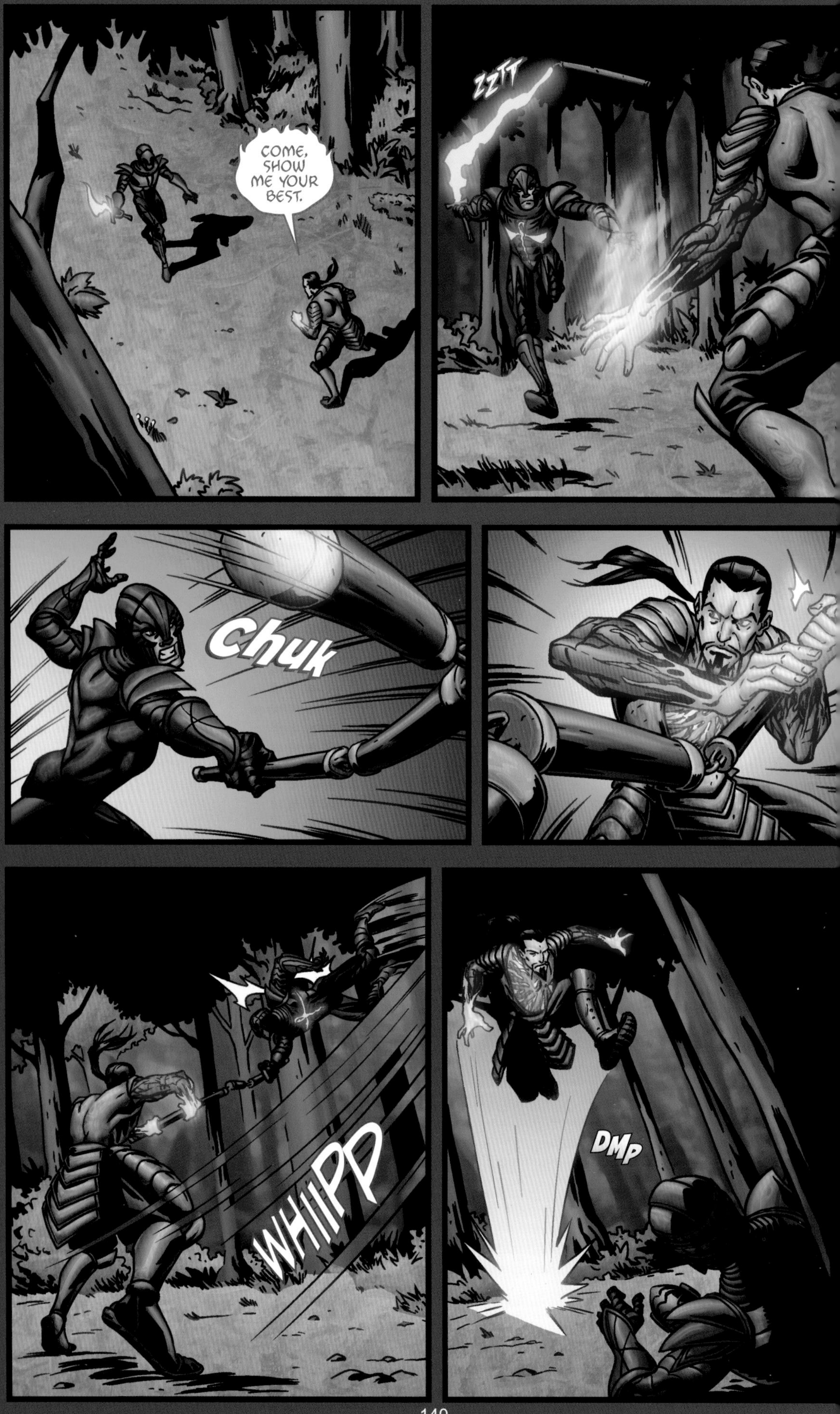
COME, SHOW ME YOUR BEST.
ZZTT
Chuk
WHIPP
DMP

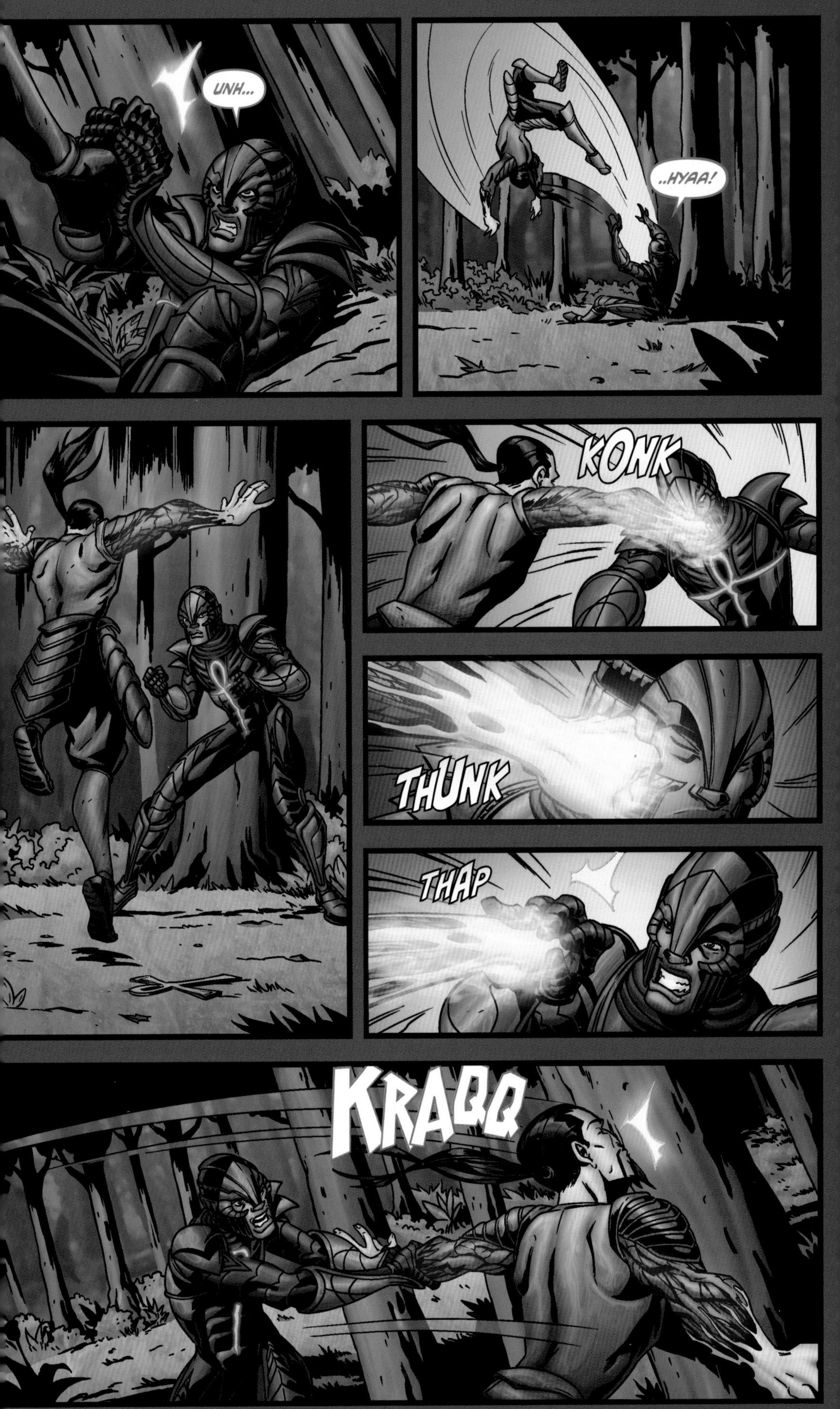

UNH...
..HYAA!
KONK
THUNK
THAP
KRAQQ

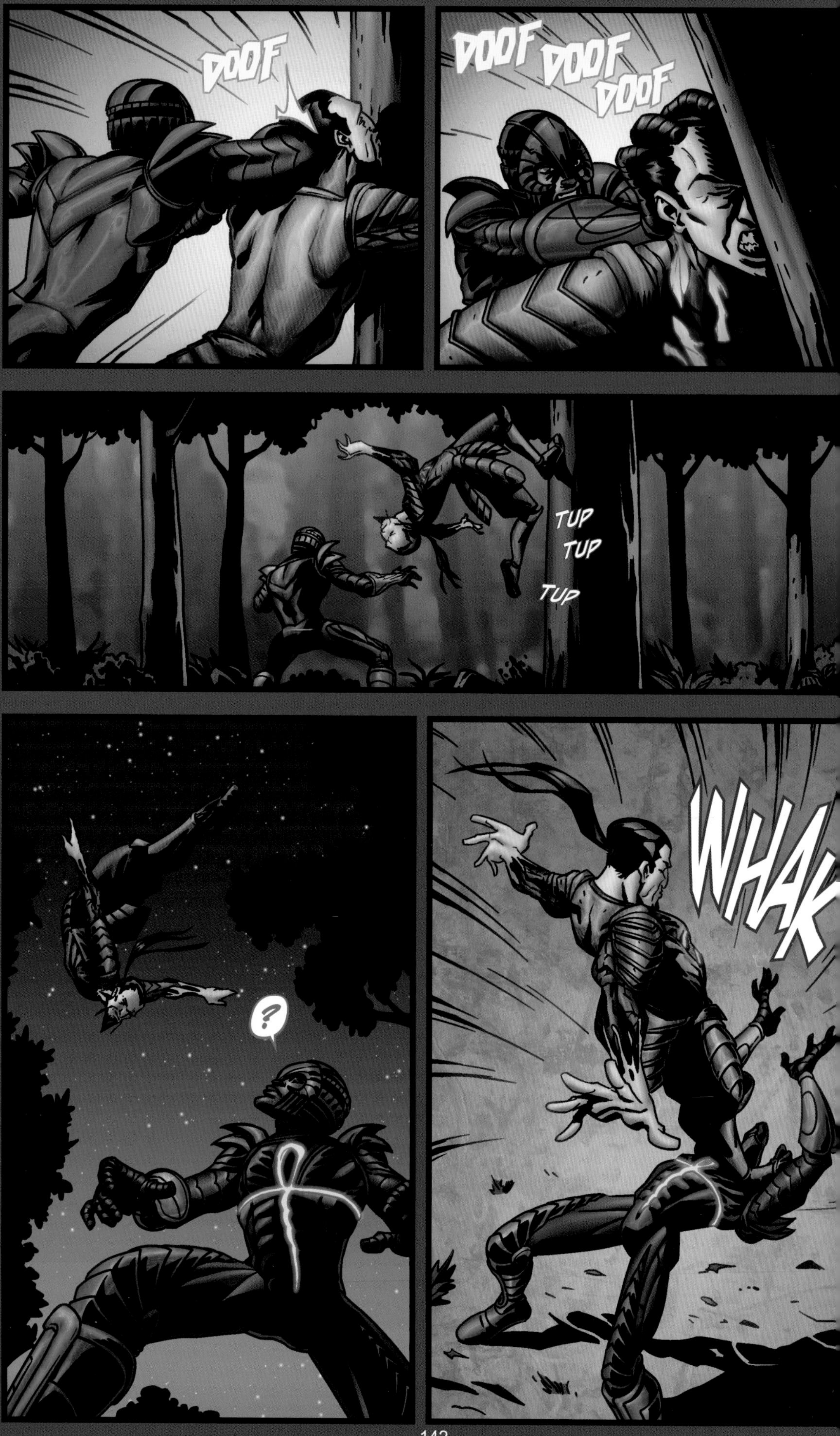
DOOF
DOOF DOOF DOOF
TUP TUP TUP
?
WHAK

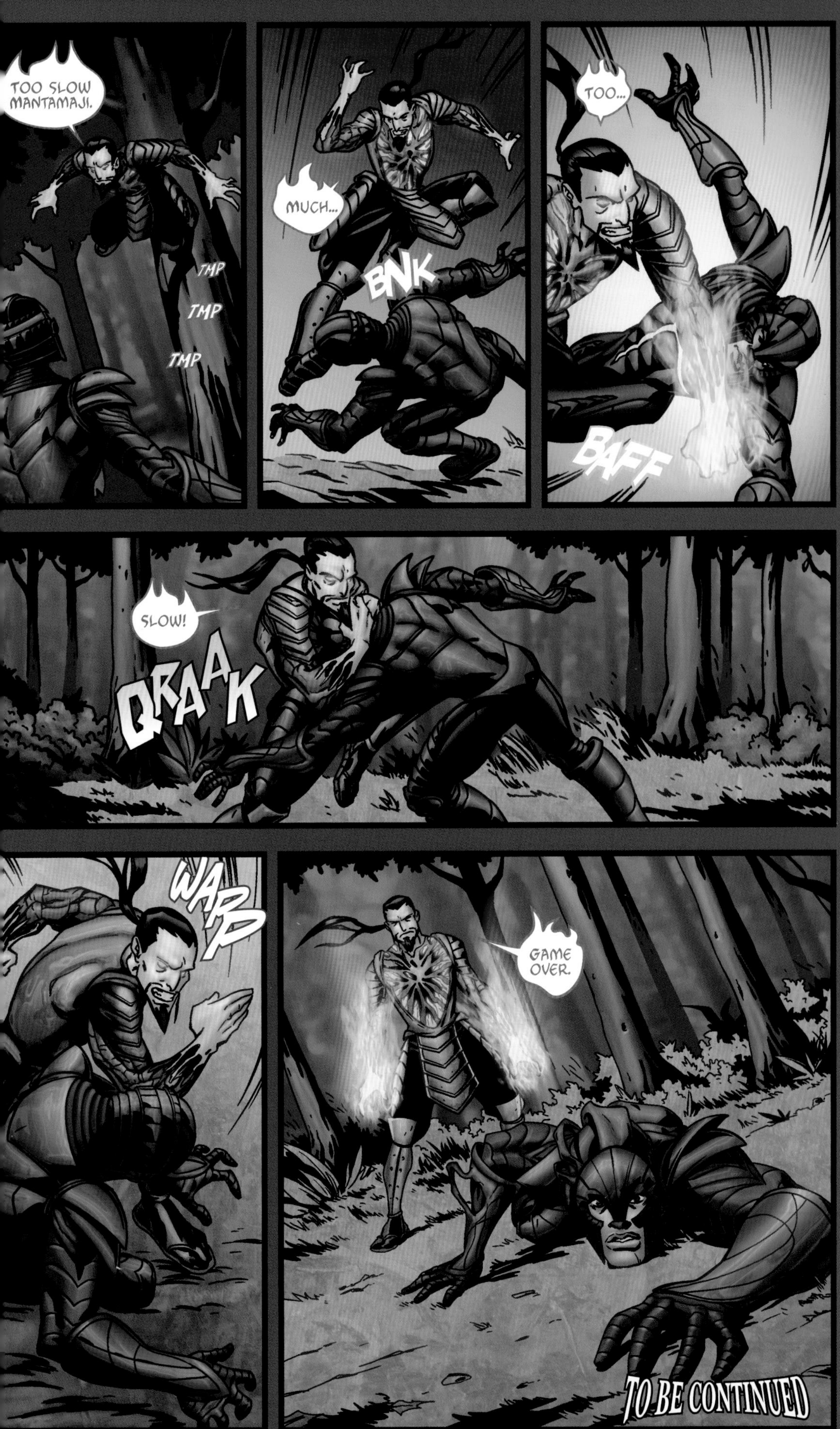
TOO SLOW
MANTAMAJI.
TMP
TMP
TMP
MUCH...
BNK
TOO...
BAFF
SLOW!
QRAAK
WAPP
GAME
OVER.
TO BE CONTINUED

CHAPTER ⑪

In their first appearing, the Mantamaji were only defeated when a blow cracked their armor. But when the road is long, the burden grows heavy, and the Mantamaji carried a great burden of responsibility. Over so many years, the worst adversary was not the flashing blade but the loss of focus; the temptation to blink.

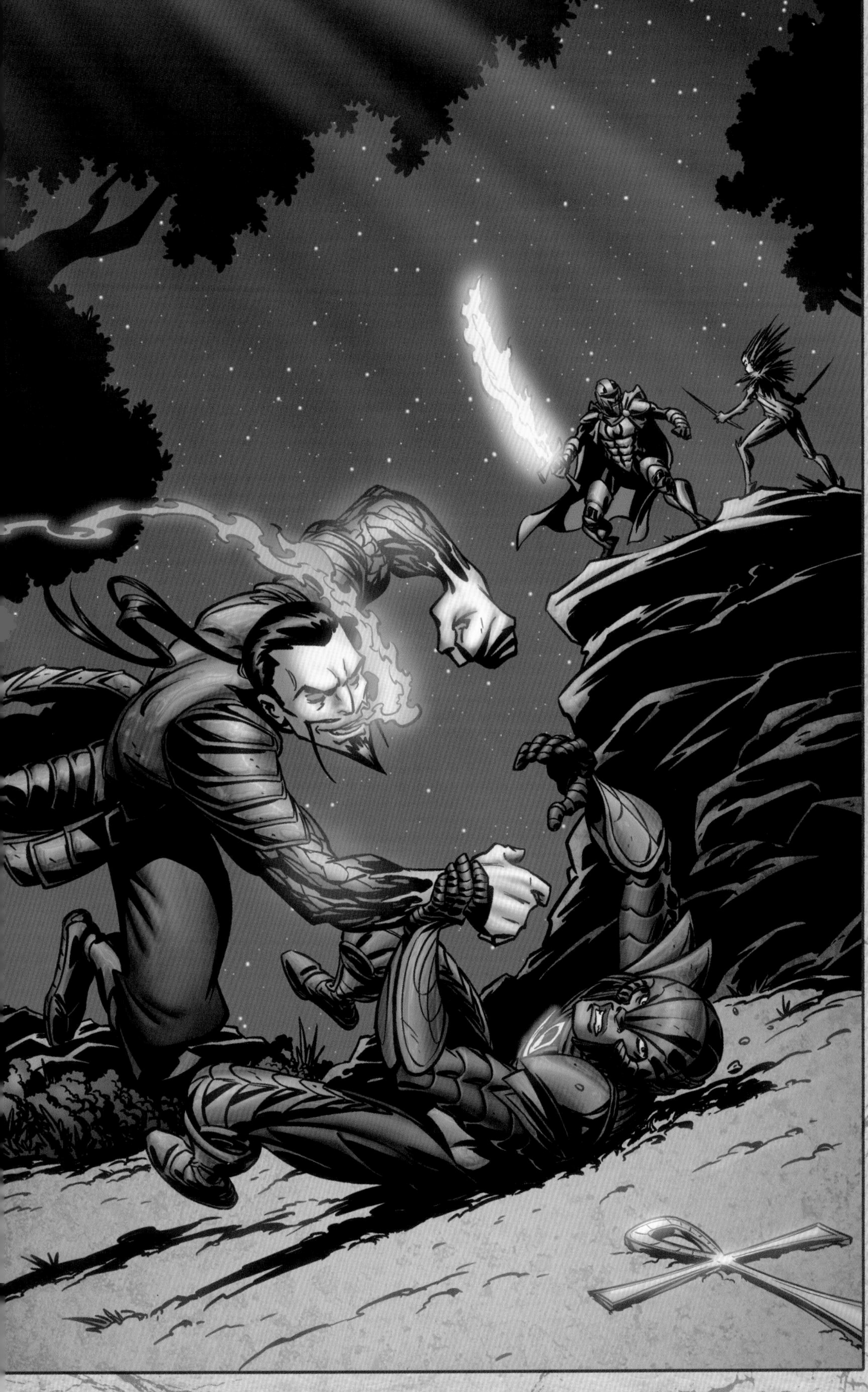

FOCUS, FOCUS.

SLFF

SLF

KRIIK

YOUR MIND IS SUCH A GLARING WEAKNESS.

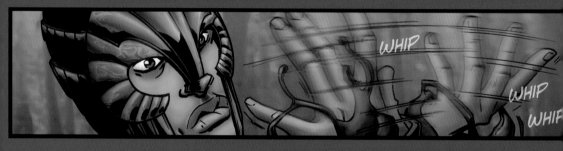

WHIP

WHIP

WHIP

PAP

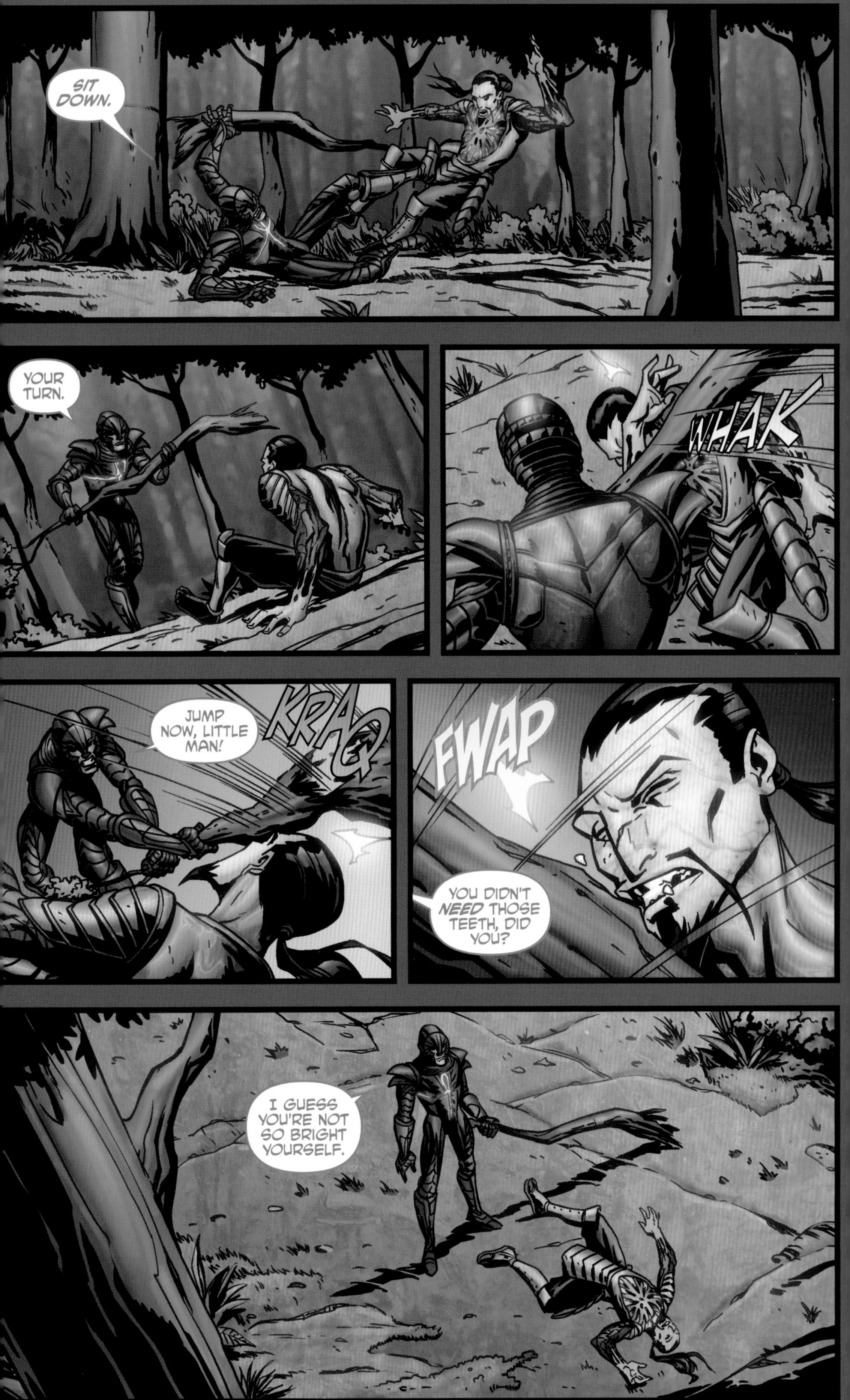
SIT DOWN.
YOUR TURN.
WHAK
JUMP NOW, LITTLE MAN!
KRAQ
FWAP
YOU DIDN'T *NEED* THOSE TEETH, DID YOU?
I GUESS YOU'RE NOT SO BRIGHT YOURSELF.

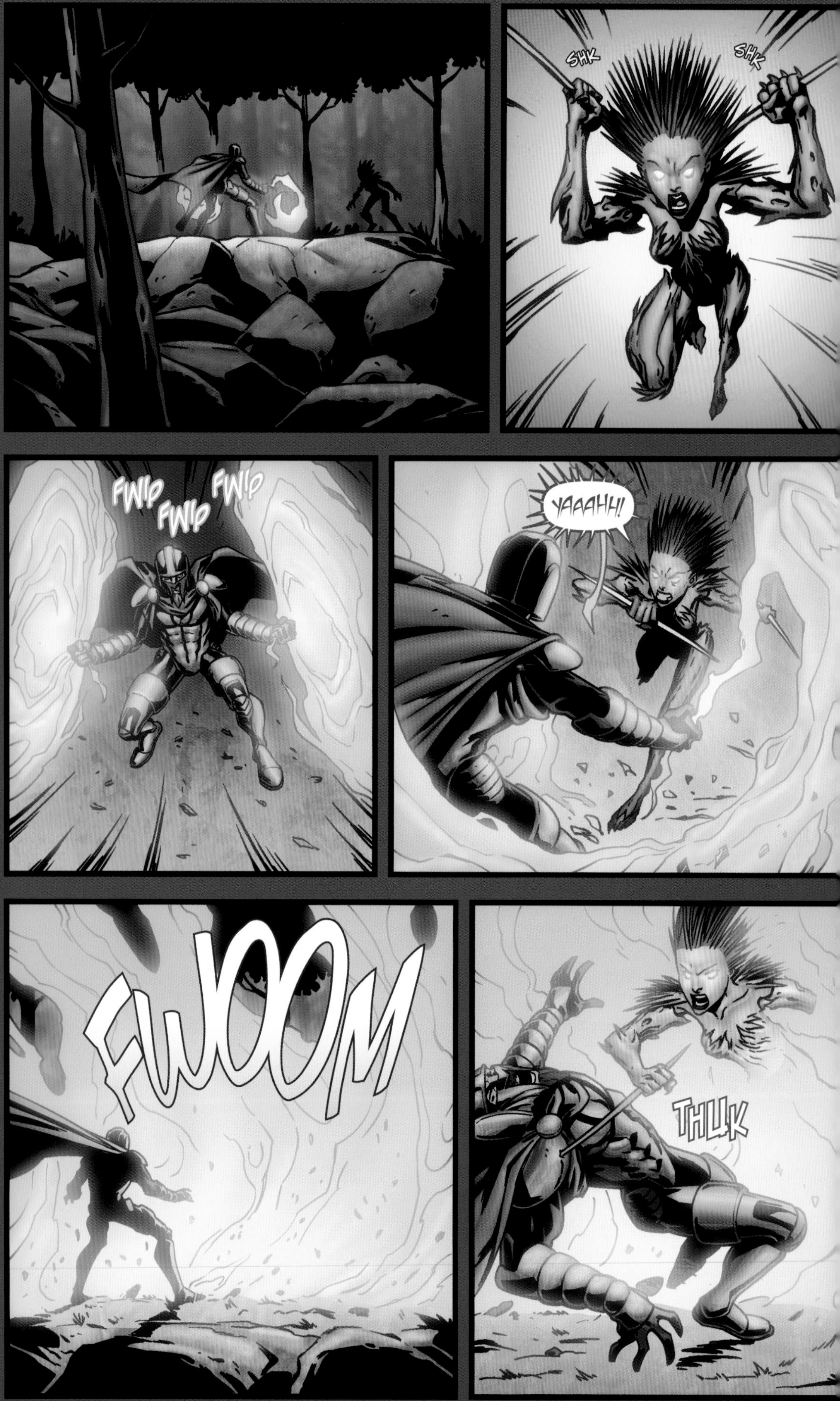
SHK
SHK
FWIP
FWIP
FWIP
YAAAHH!
FWOOM
THUK

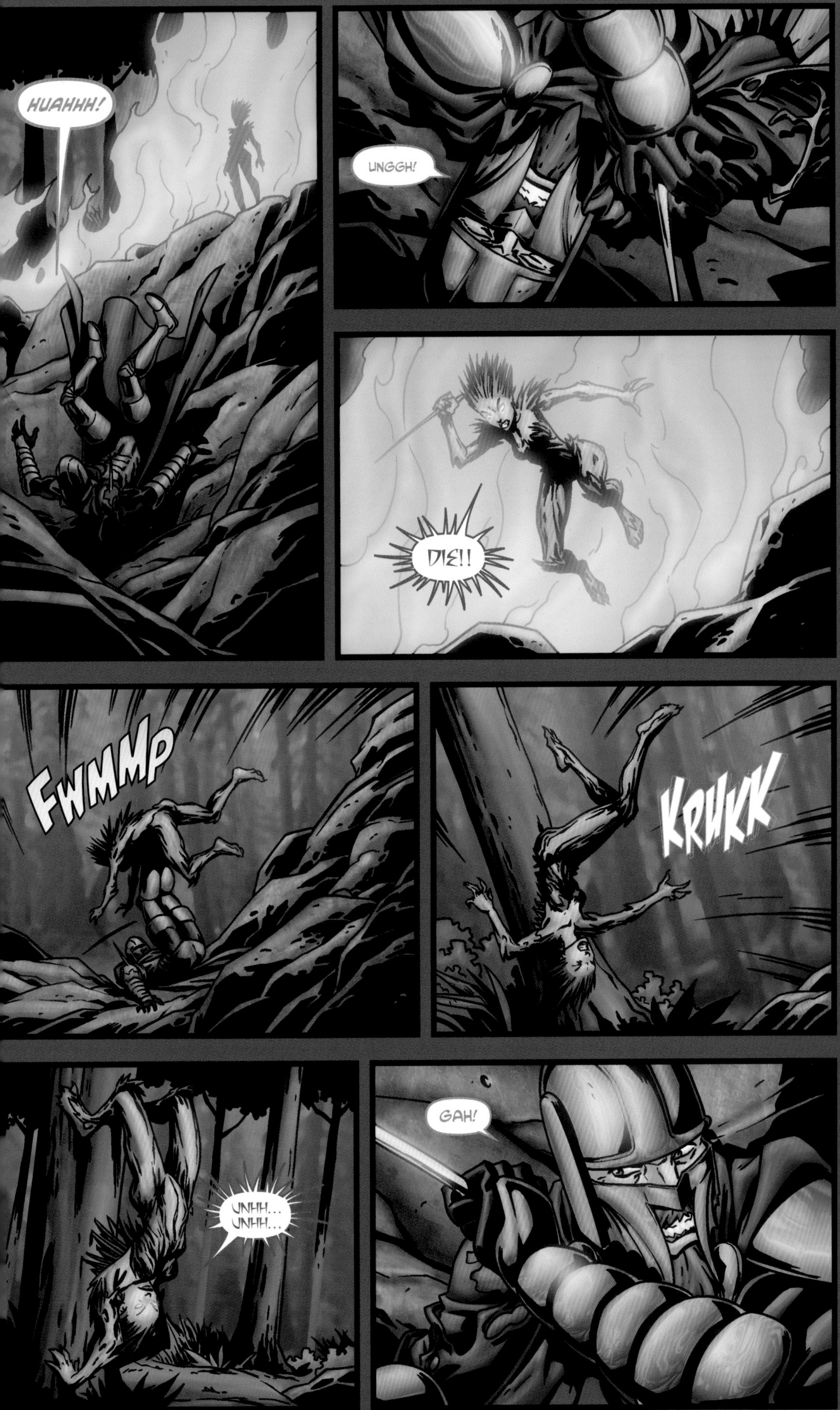
HUAHHH!
UNGGH!
DIE!!
FWMMP
KRUKK
UNHH... UNHH...
GAH!

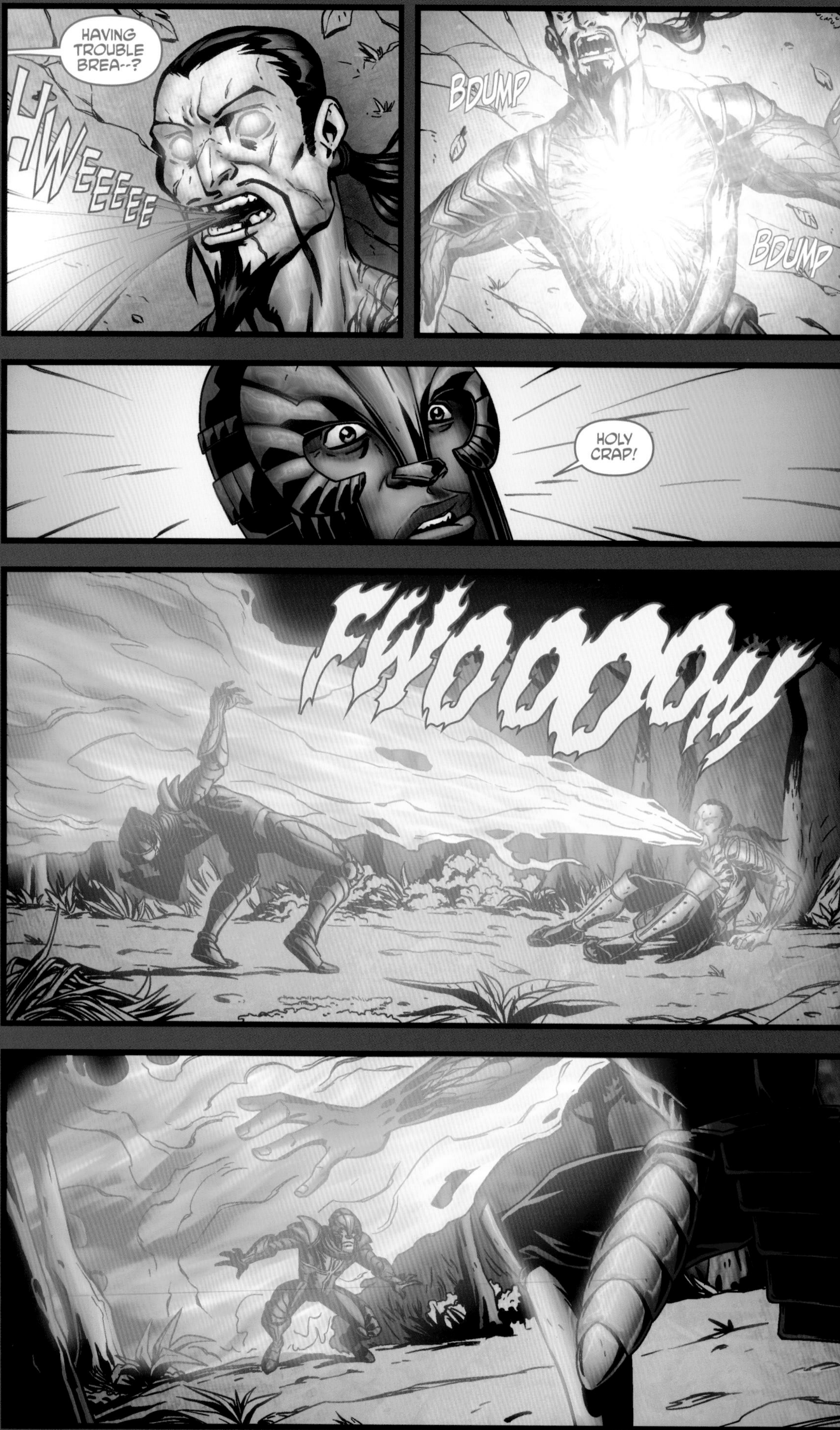
HAVING TROUBLE BREA--?
HWEEEEEE
BDUMP
BDUMP
HOLY CRAP!
FFHOOOOM

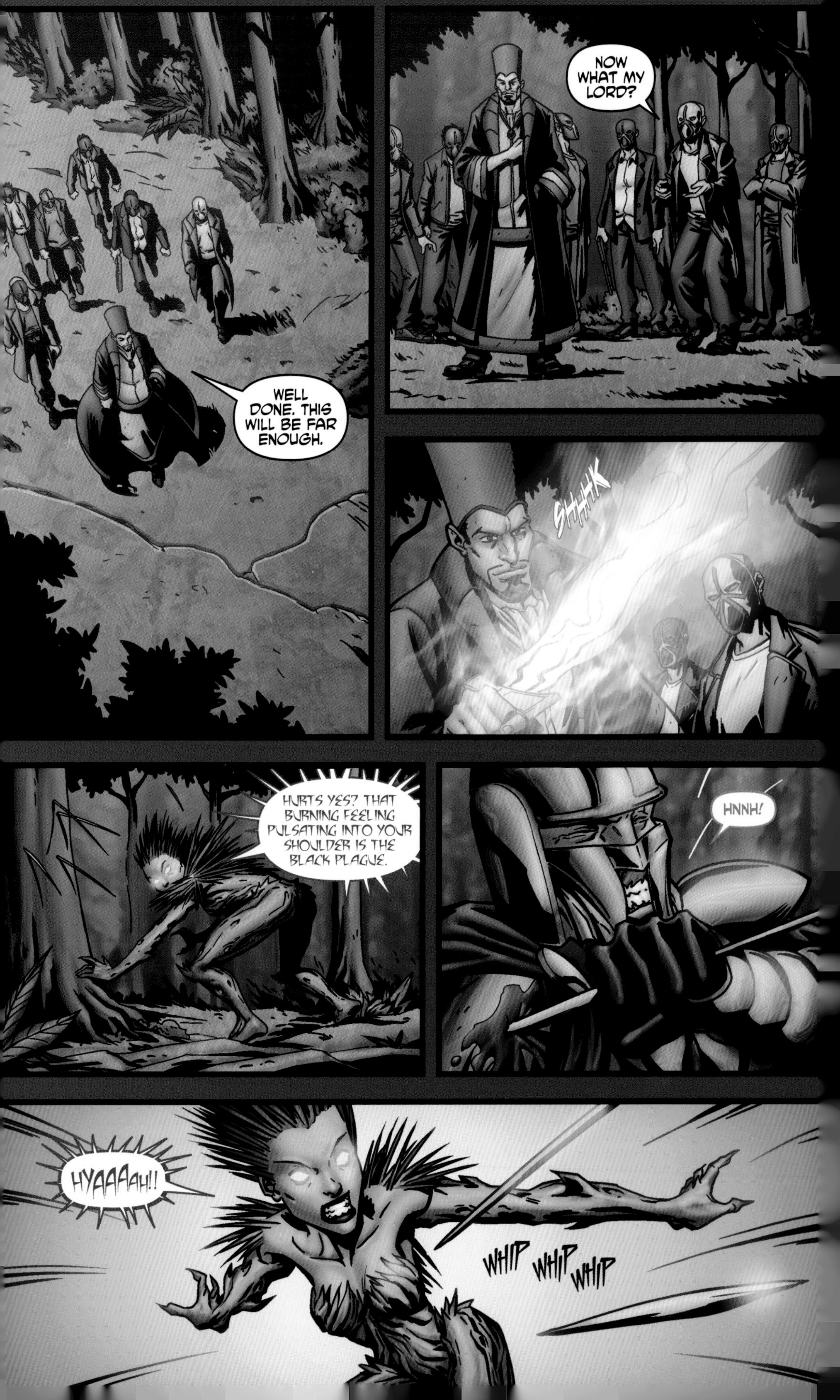
WELL DONE. THIS WILL BE FAR ENOUGH.
NOW WHAT MY LORD?
SHHK
HURTS YES? THAT BURNING FEELING PULSATING INTO YOUR SHOULDER IS THE BLACK PLAGUE.
HNNH!
HYAAAAH!!
WHIP WHIP WHIP

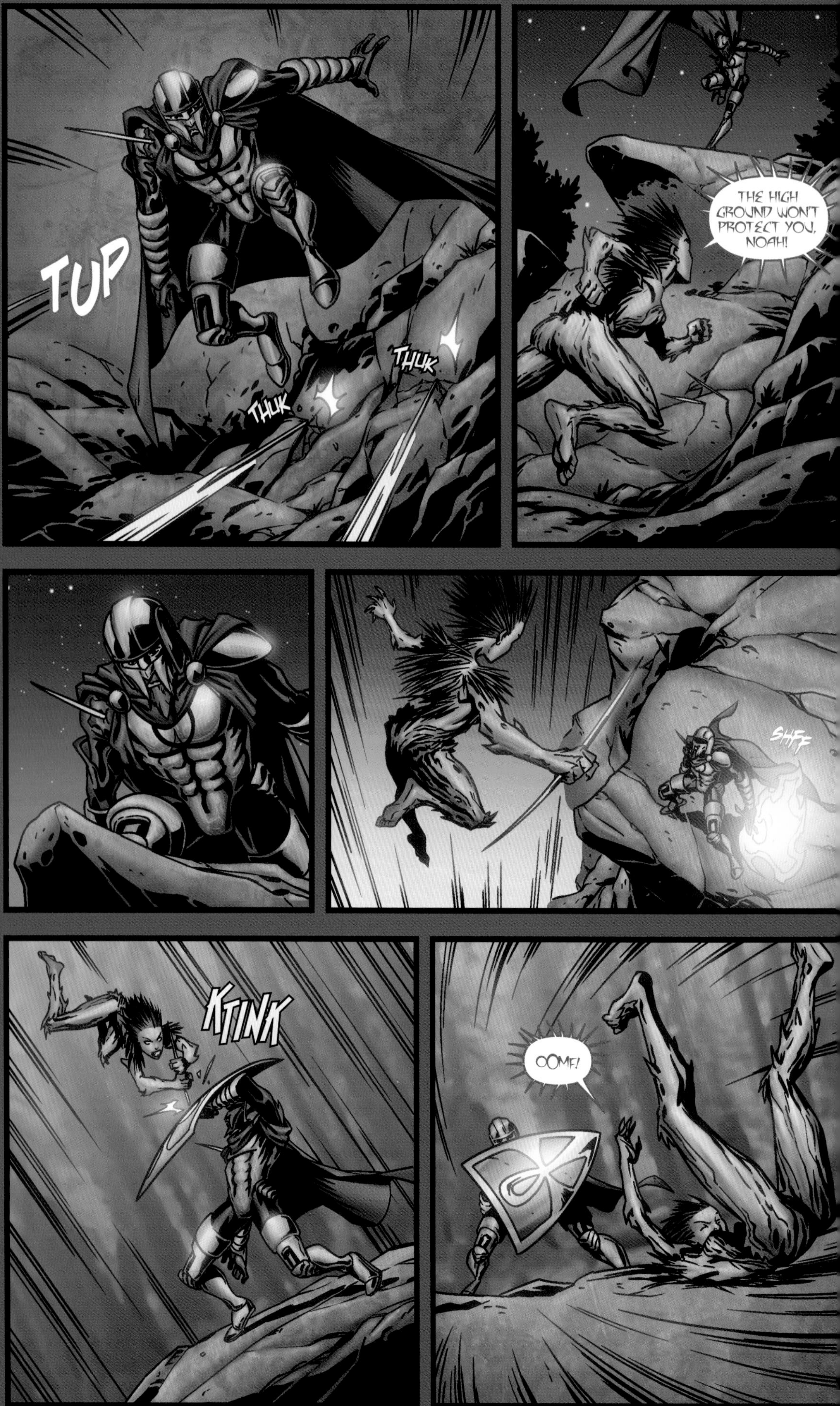
TUP
THUK
THUK
THE HIGH GROUND WON'T PROTECT YOU, NOAH!
SHFF
KTINK
OOMF!

FWOOSH

FWUT

HWOOOO O

HWOO OO O O

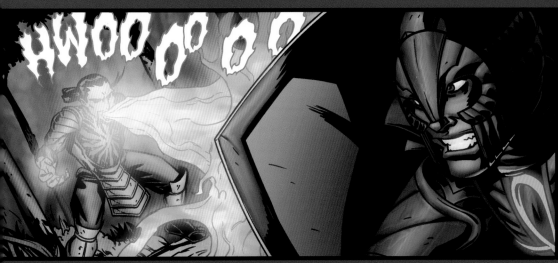

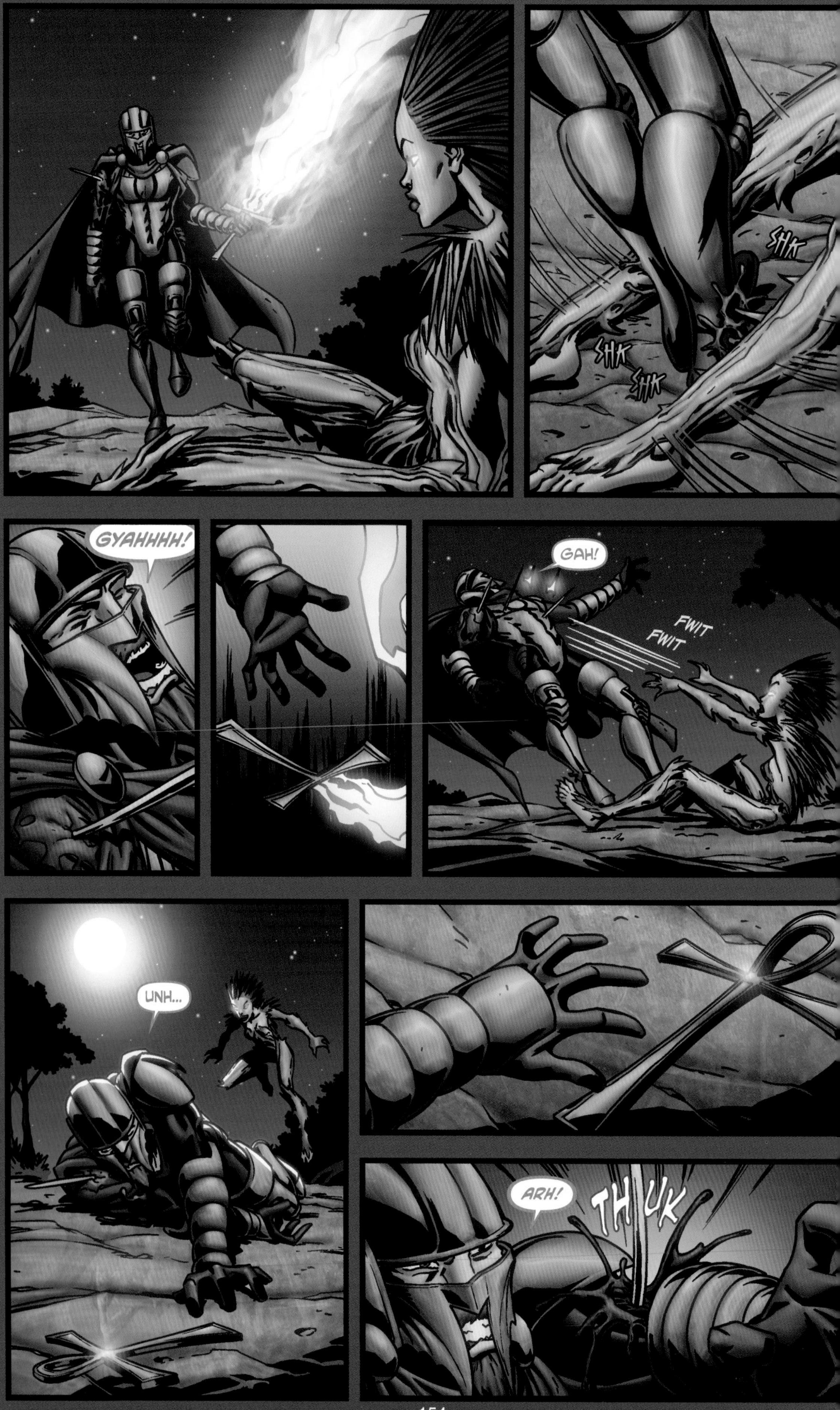
SHK
SHK
SHK
GYAHHHH!
GAH!
FWIT
FWIT
UNH...
ARH!
THUK

HEY, PORCUPINE!

WHIPP

HAAAH!!

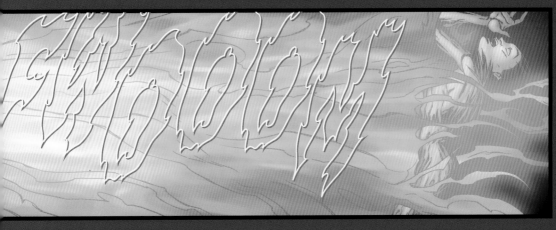

THUK

THUK

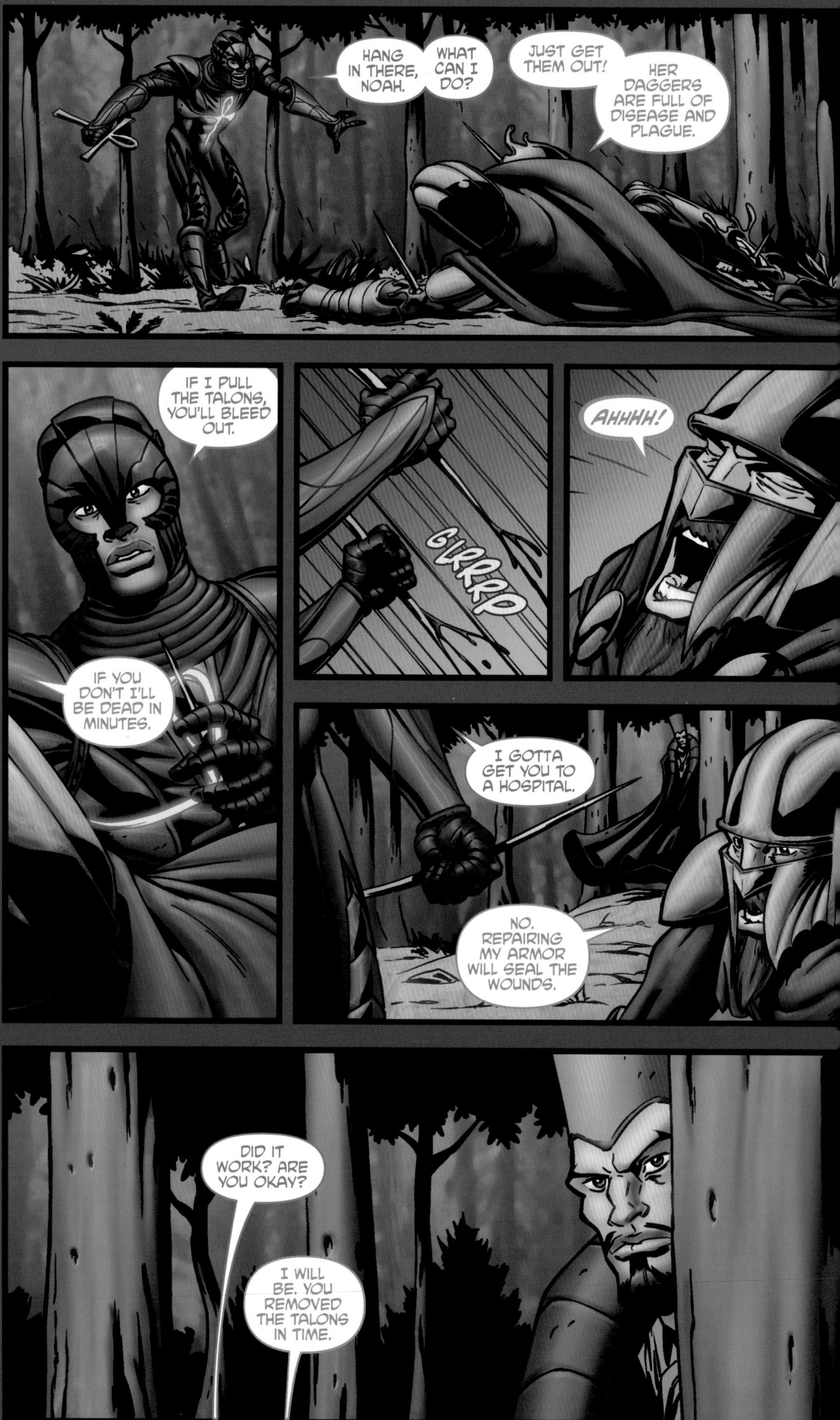
HANG IN THERE, NOAH.
WHAT CAN I DO?
JUST GET THEM OUT!
HER DAGGERS ARE FULL OF DISEASE AND PLAGUE.
IF I PULL THE TALONS, YOU'LL BLEED OUT.
IF YOU DON'T I'LL BE DEAD IN MINUTES.
GLRRP
AHHHH!
I GOTTA GET YOU TO A HOSPITAL.
NO. REPAIRING MY ARMOR WILL SEAL THE WOUNDS.
DID IT WORK? ARE YOU OKAY?
I WILL BE. YOU REMOVED THE TALONS IN TIME.

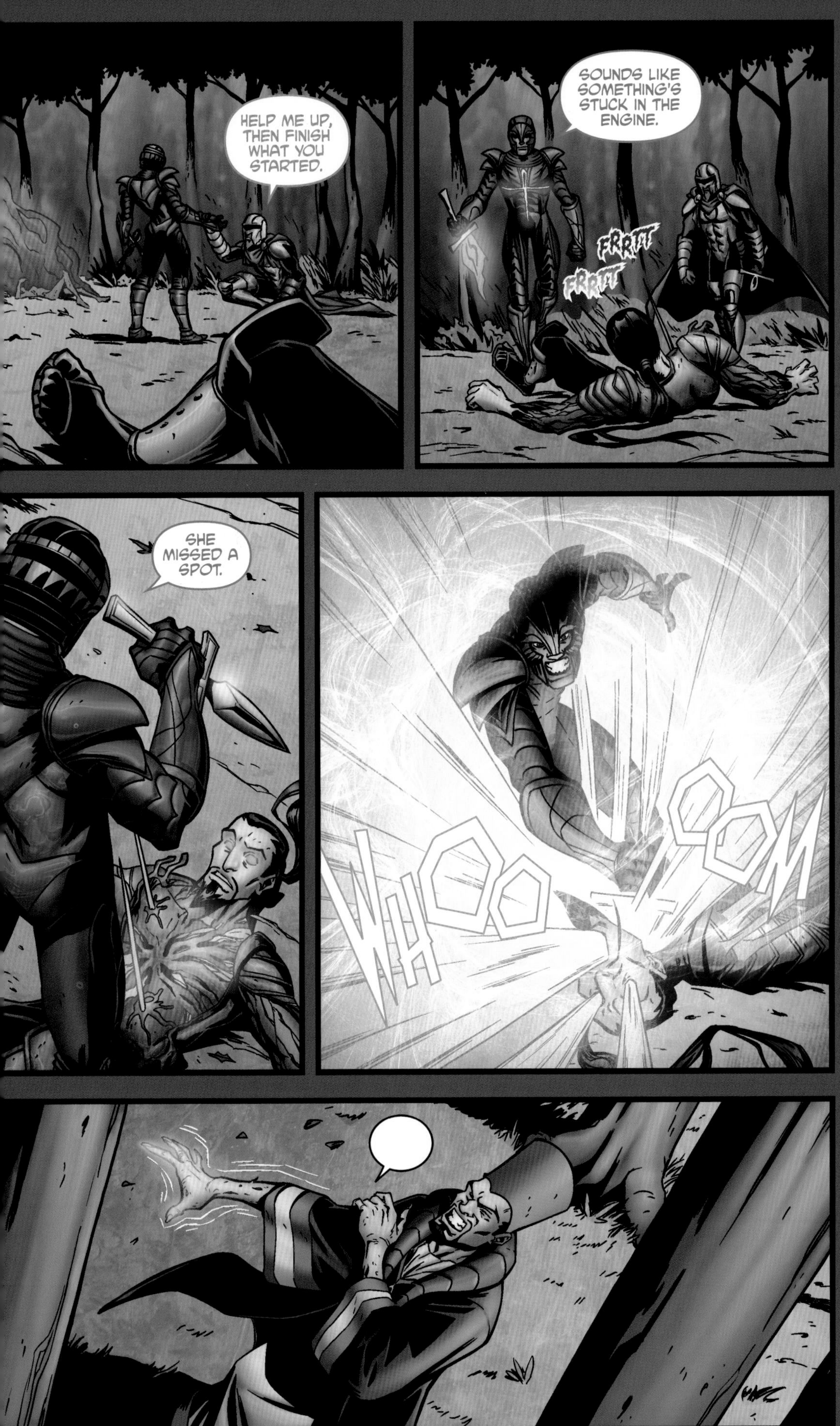
HELP ME UP, THEN FINISH WHAT YOU STARTED.
SOUNDS LIKE SOMETHING'S STUCK IN THE ENGINE.
FRRTT
FRRTT
SHE MISSED A SPOT.
WHOO-OOM

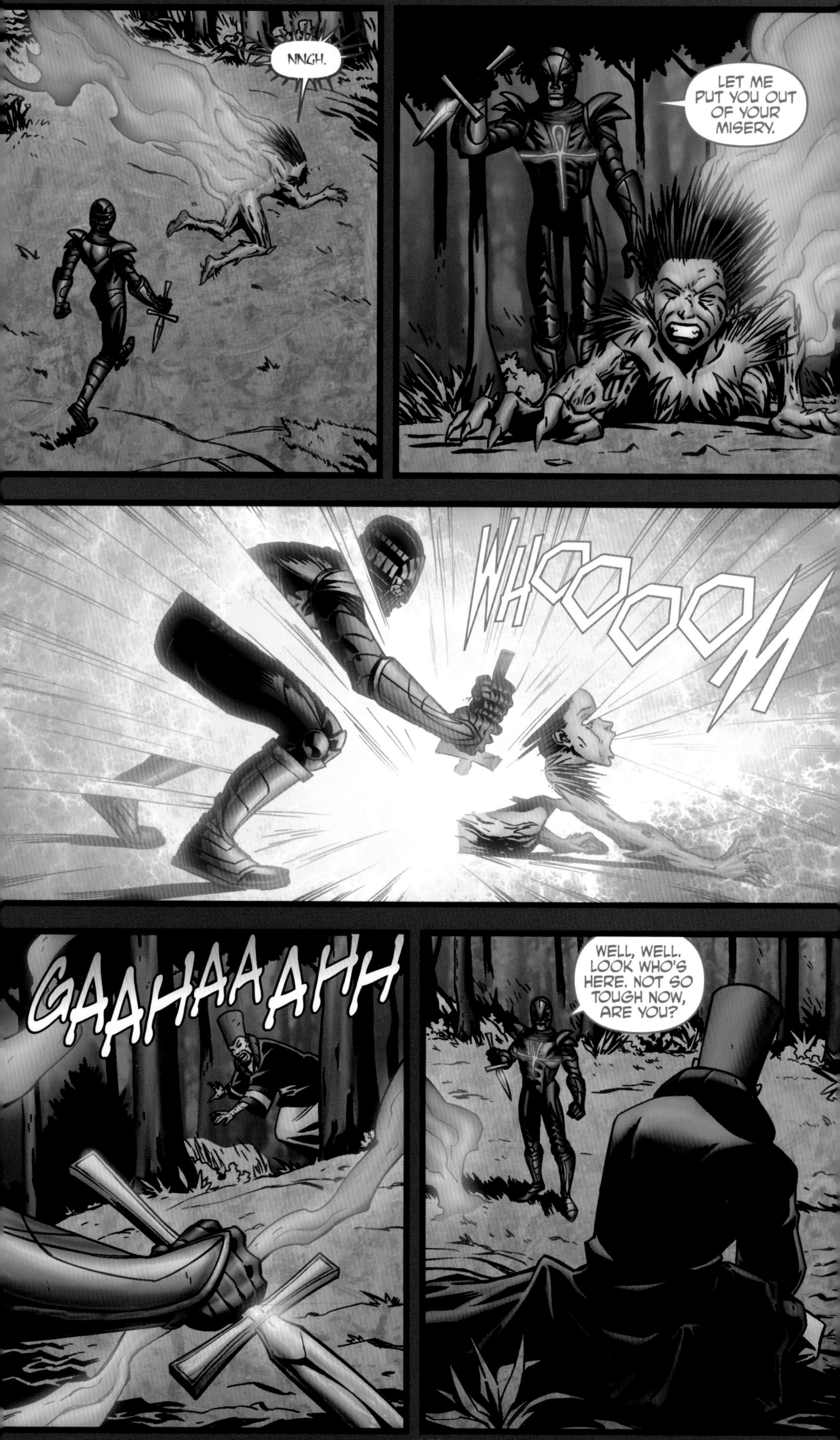

NNGH.
LET ME PUT YOU OUT OF YOUR MISERY.
WHOOOOOM
GAAHAAAAHH
WELL, WELL. LOOK WHO'S HERE. NOT SO TOUGH NOW, ARE YOU?

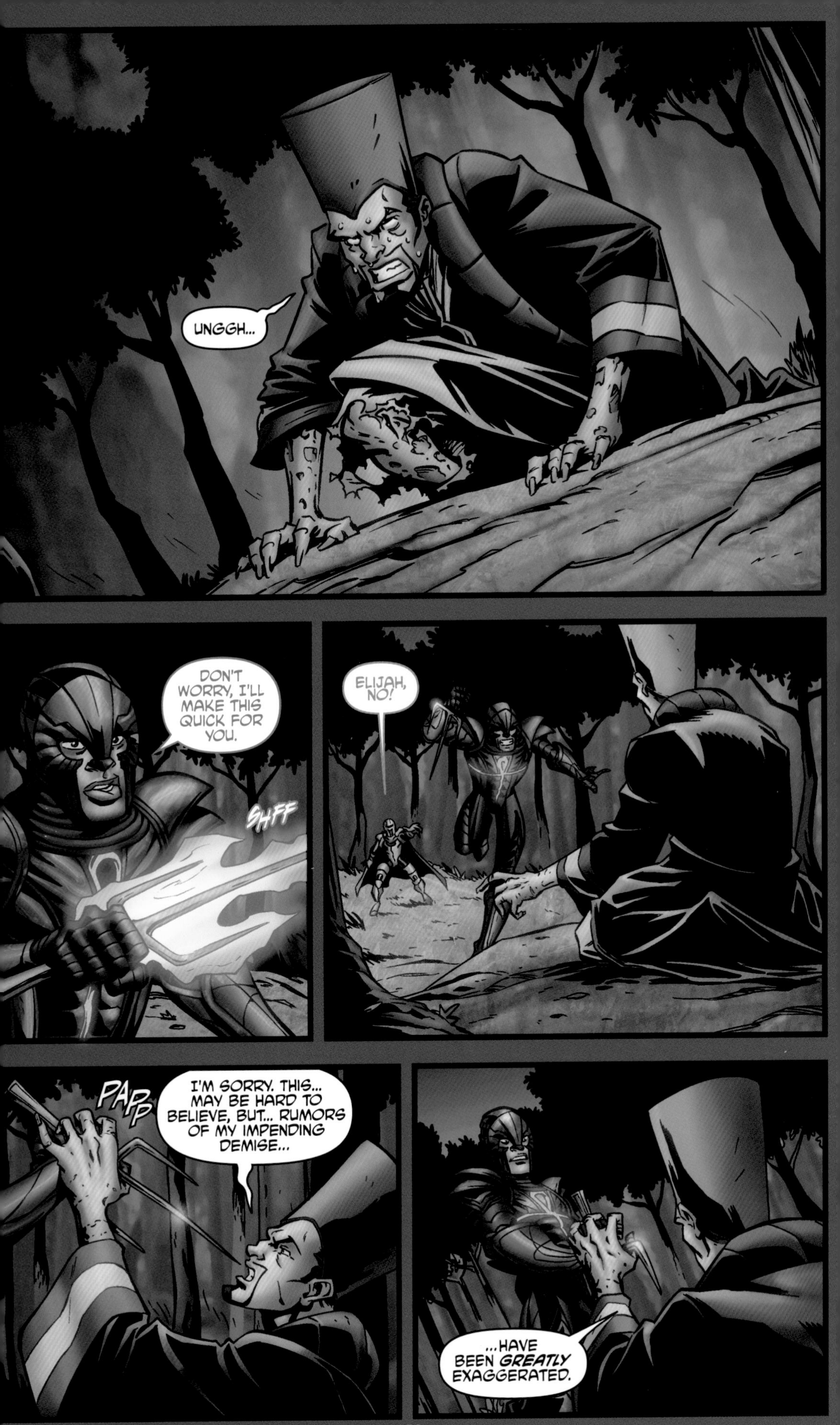
UNGGH...
DON'T WORRY, I'LL MAKE THIS QUICK FOR YOU.
SHFF
ELIJAH, NO!
PAPP
I'M SORRY. THIS... MAY BE HARD TO BELIEVE, BUT... RUMORS OF MY IMPENDING DEMISE...
...HAVE BEEN *GREATLY* EXAGGERATED.

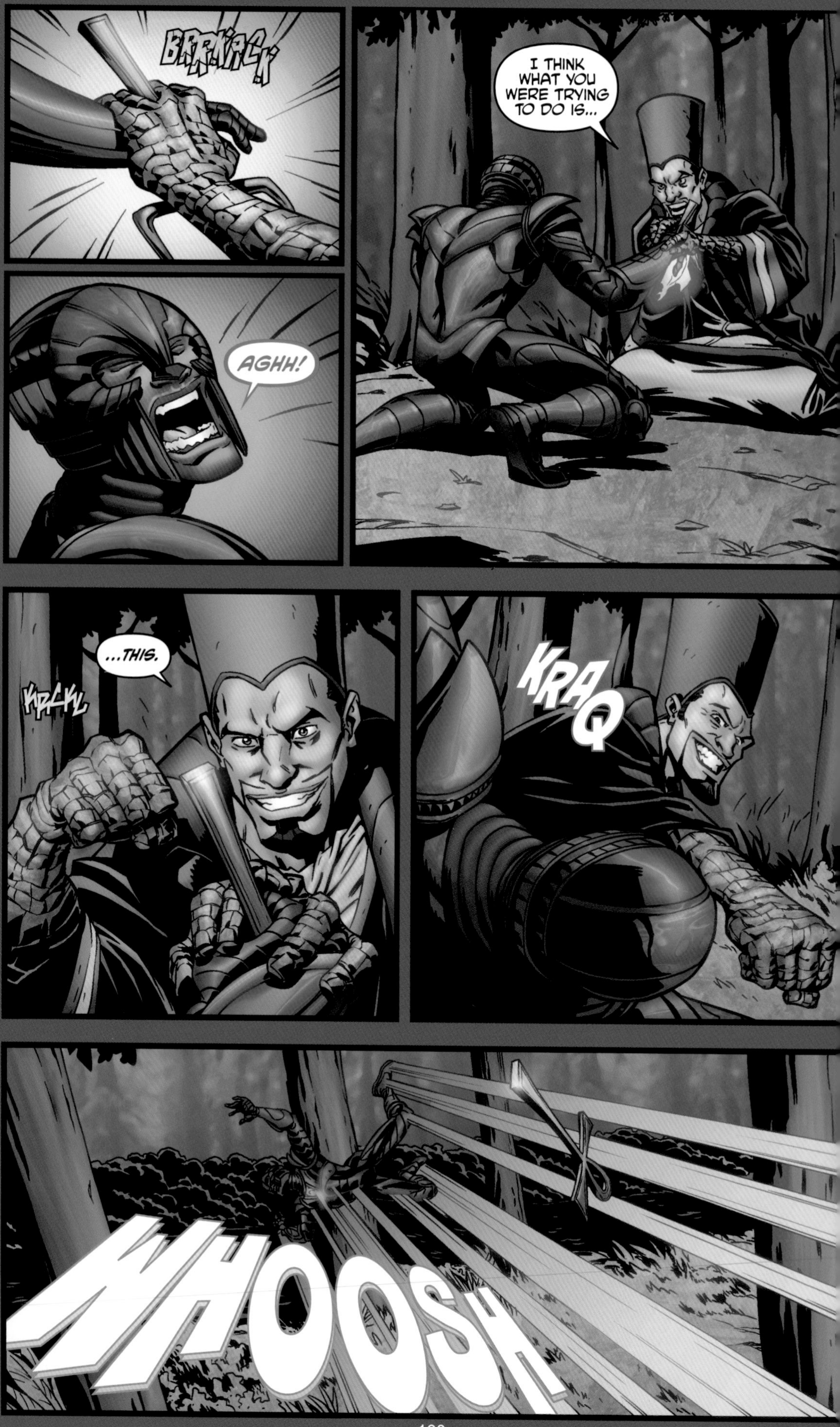
BRRKRCK
I THINK WHAT YOU WERE TRYING TO DO IS...
AGHH!
...THIS.
KRCKL
KRAQ
WHOOSH

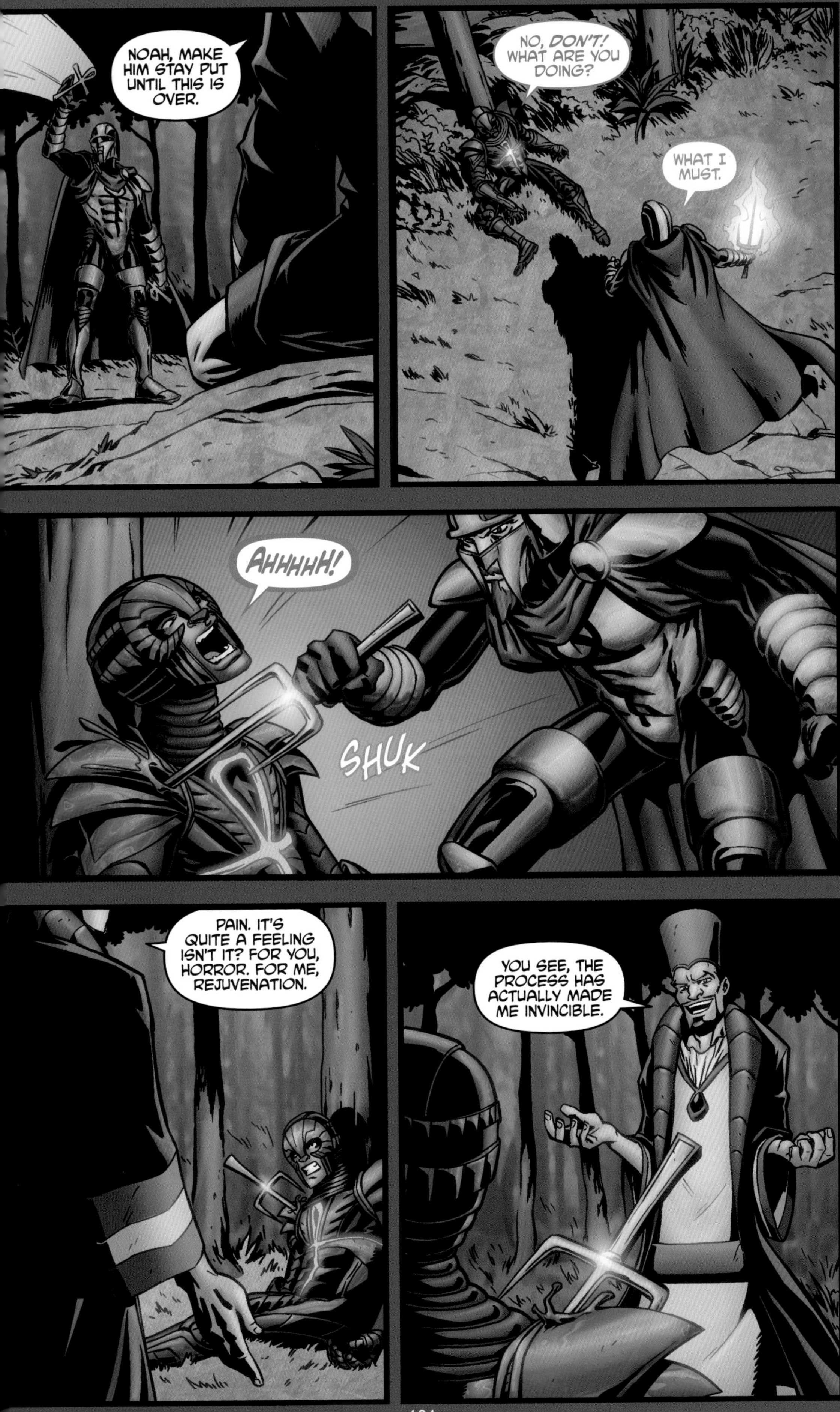
NOAH, MAKE HIM STAY PUT UNTIL THIS IS OVER.
NO, DON'T! WHAT ARE YOU DOING?
WHAT I MUST.
AHHHHH!
SHUK
PAIN. IT'S QUITE A FEELING ISN'T IT? FOR YOU, HORROR. FOR ME, REJUVENATION.
YOU SEE, THE PROCESS HAS ACTUALLY MADE ME INVINCIBLE.

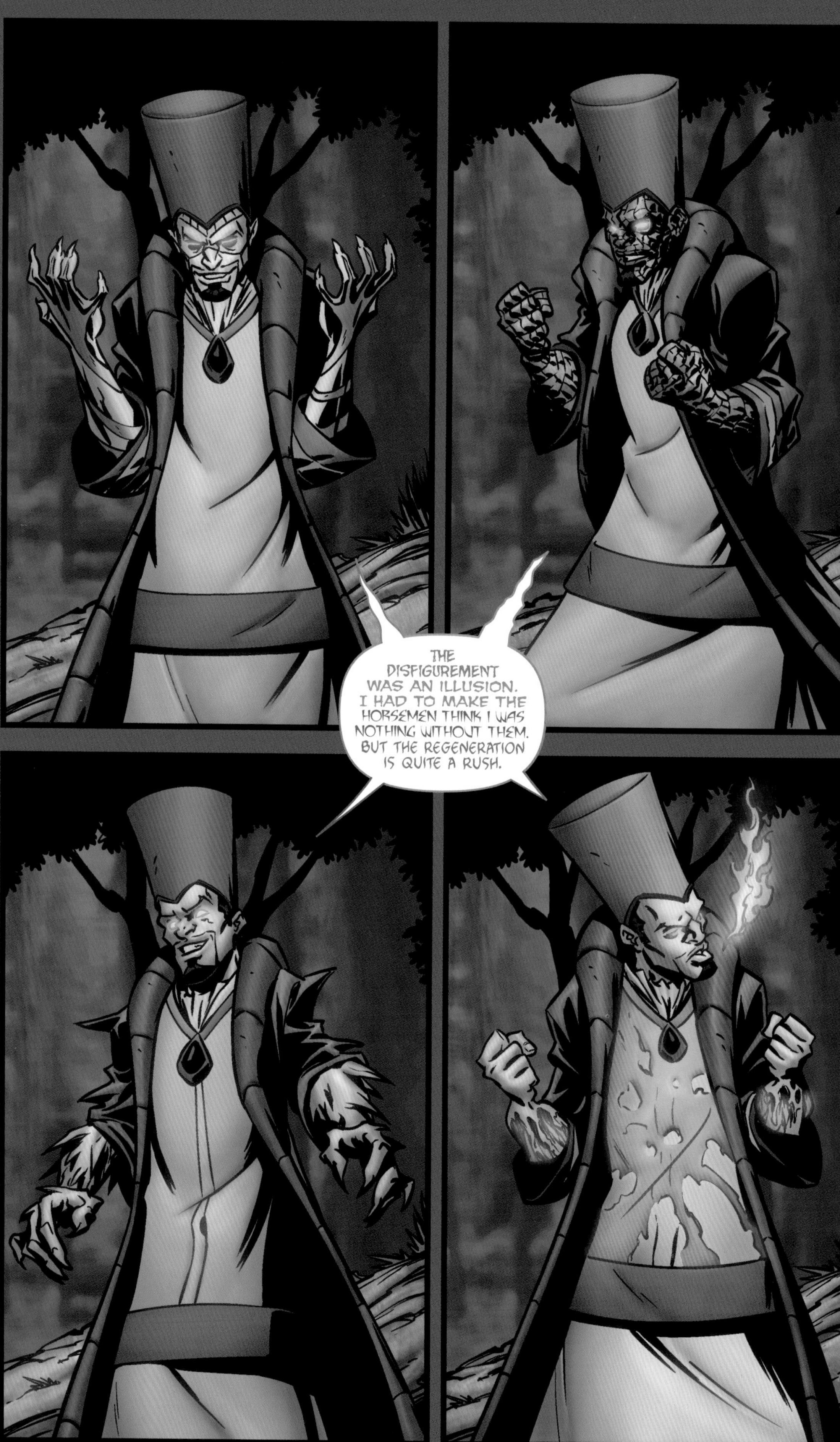
THE DISFIGUREMENT WAS AN ILLUSION. I HAD TO MAKE THE HORSEMEN THINK I WAS NOTHING WITHOUT THEM. BUT THE REGENERATION IS QUITE A RUSH.

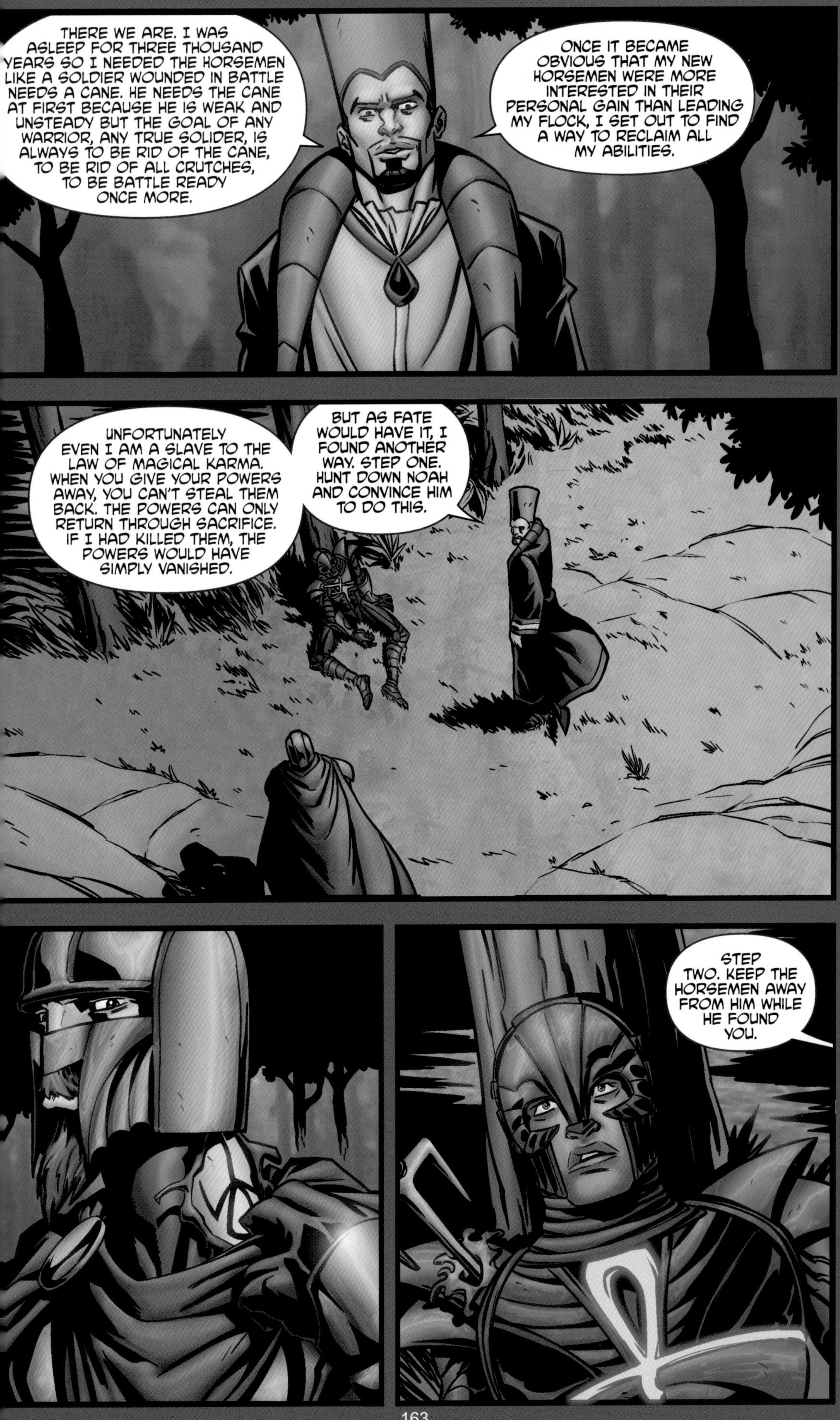
THERE WE ARE. I WAS ASLEEP FOR THREE THOUSAND YEARS SO I NEEDED THE HORSEMEN LIKE A SOLDIER WOUNDED IN BATTLE NEEDS A CANE. HE NEEDS THE CANE AT FIRST BECAUSE HE IS WEAK AND UNSTEADY BUT THE GOAL OF ANY WARRIOR, ANY TRUE SOLIDER, IS ALWAYS TO BE RID OF THE CANE, TO BE RID OF ALL CRUTCHES, TO BE BATTLE READY ONCE MORE.
ONCE IT BECAME OBVIOUS THAT MY NEW HORSEMEN WERE MORE INTERESTED IN THEIR PERSONAL GAIN THAN LEADING MY FLOCK, I SET OUT TO FIND A WAY TO RECLAIM ALL MY ABILITIES.
UNFORTUNATELY EVEN I AM A SLAVE TO THE LAW OF MAGICAL KARMA. WHEN YOU GIVE YOUR POWERS AWAY, YOU CAN'T STEAL THEM BACK. THE POWERS CAN ONLY RETURN THROUGH SACRIFICE. IF I HAD KILLED THEM, THE POWERS WOULD HAVE SIMPLY VANISHED.
BUT AS FATE WOULD HAVE IT, I FOUND ANOTHER WAY. STEP ONE. HUNT DOWN NOAH AND CONVINCE HIM TO DO THIS.
STEP TWO. KEEP THE HORSEMEN AWAY FROM HIM WHILE HE FOUND YOU.

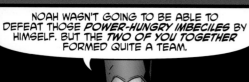

NOAH WASN'T GOING TO BE ABLE TO DEFEAT THOSE *POWER-HUNGRY IMBECILES* BY HIMSELF. BUT THE *TWO OF YOU TOGETHER* FORMED QUITE A TEAM.

HOW COULD YOU DO THIS? I TRUSTED YOU!

I HAD LOST AND AFTER THREE THOUSAND YEARS OF FIGHTING, I JUST DIDN'T WANT TO DIE.

JOIN US, ELIJAH. TOGETHER WE CAN RULE THE WORLD.

I'D RATHER... BURN IN HELL.

AS YOU WISH.

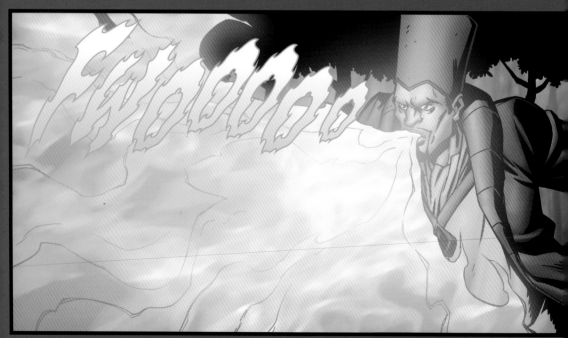

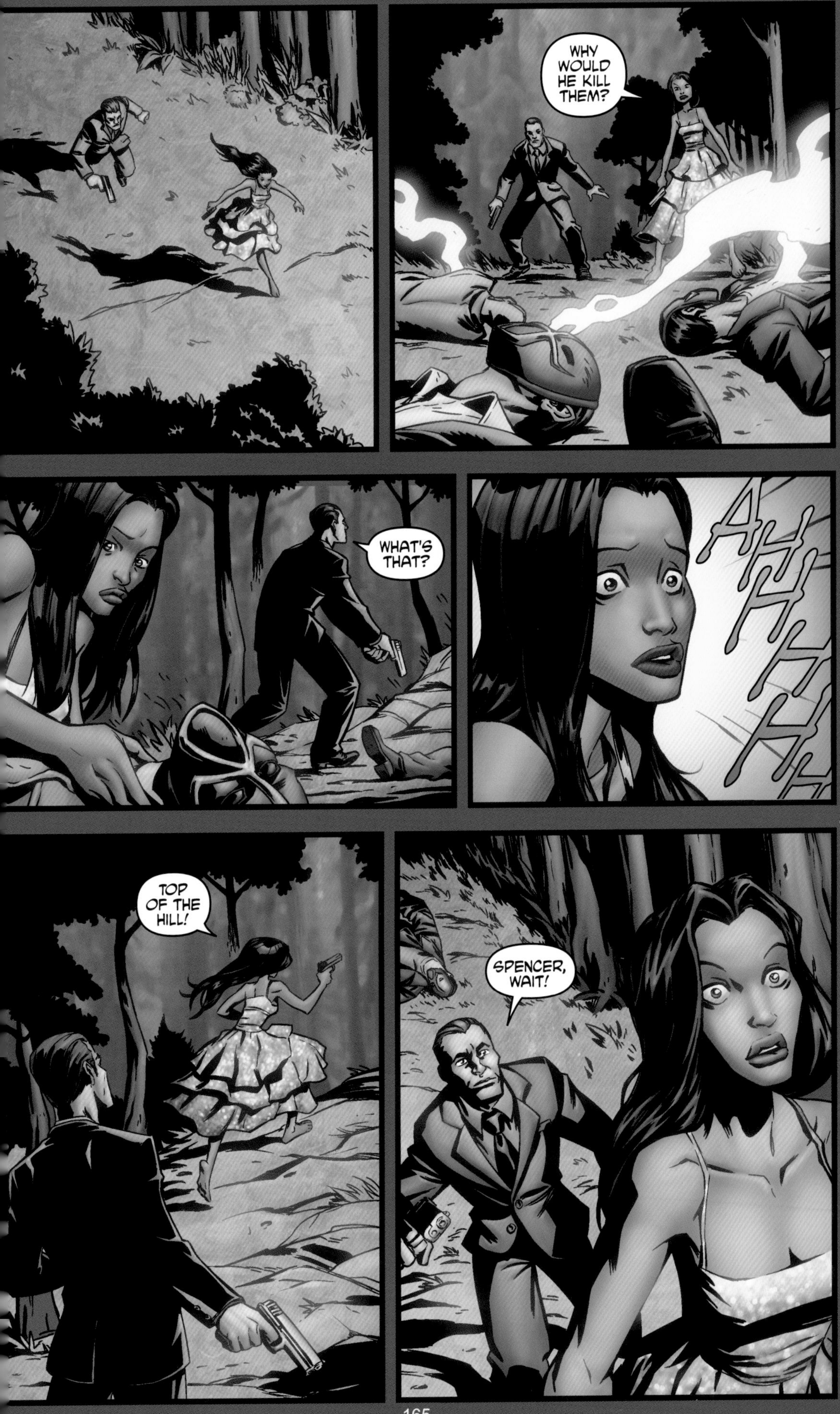
WHY WOULD HE KILL THEM?
WHAT'S THAT?
AHHHHH
TOP OF THE HILL!
SPENCER, WAIT!

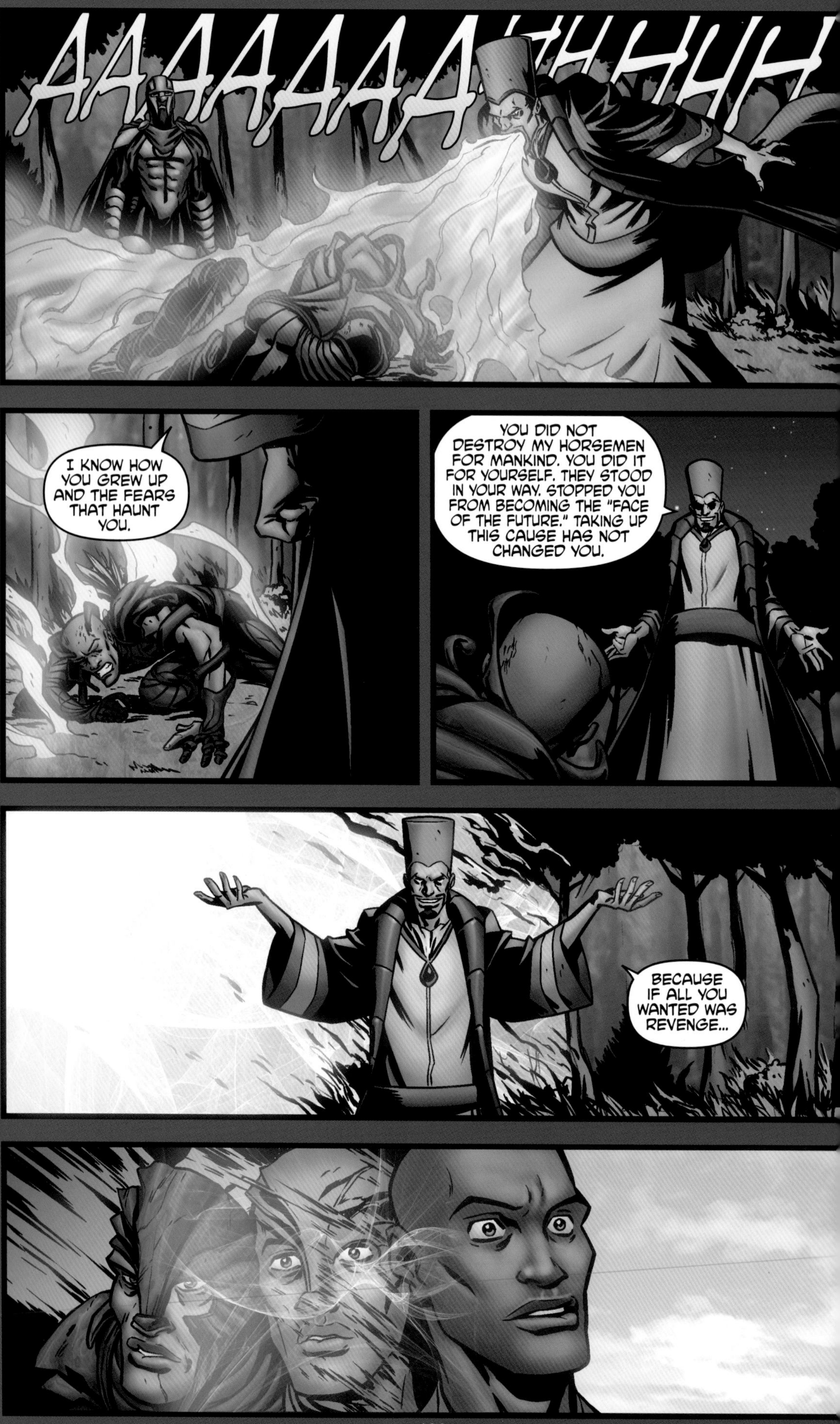
AAAAAAAHHHHH
I KNOW HOW YOU GREW UP AND THE FEARS THAT HAUNT YOU.
YOU DID NOT DESTROY MY HORSEMEN FOR MANKIND. YOU DID IT FOR YOURSELF. THEY STOOD IN YOUR WAY. STOPPED YOU FROM BECOMING THE "FACE OF THE FUTURE." TAKING UP THIS CAUSE HAS NOT CHANGED YOU.
BECAUSE IF ALL YOU WANTED WAS REVENGE...

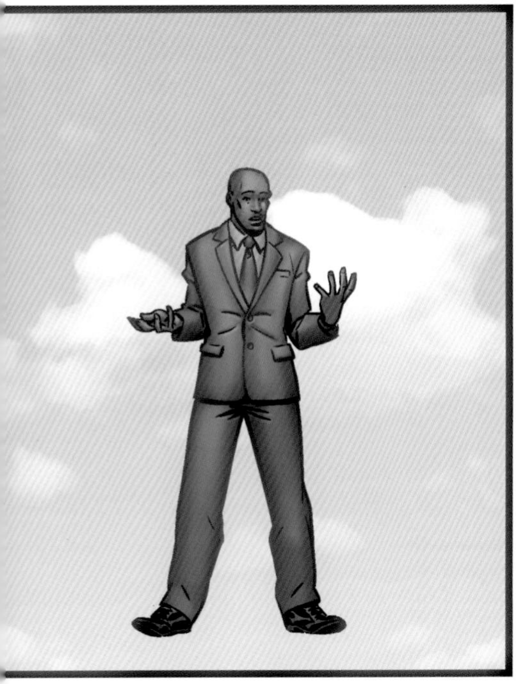

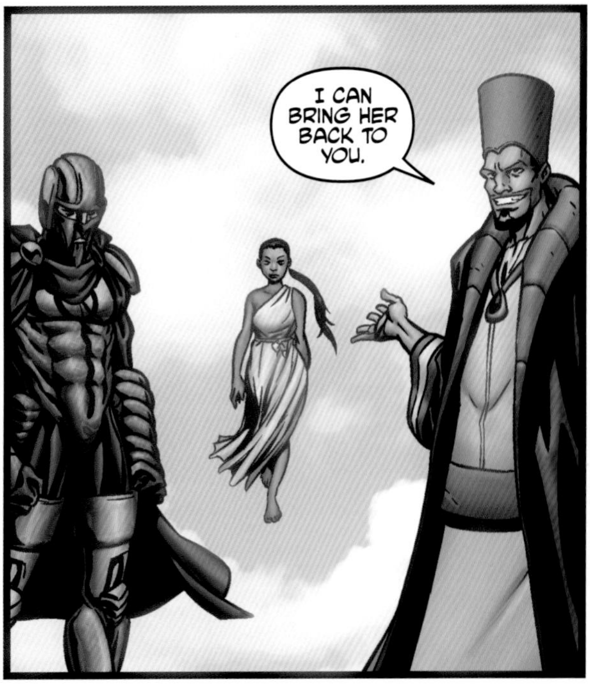
I CAN BRING HER BACK TO YOU.

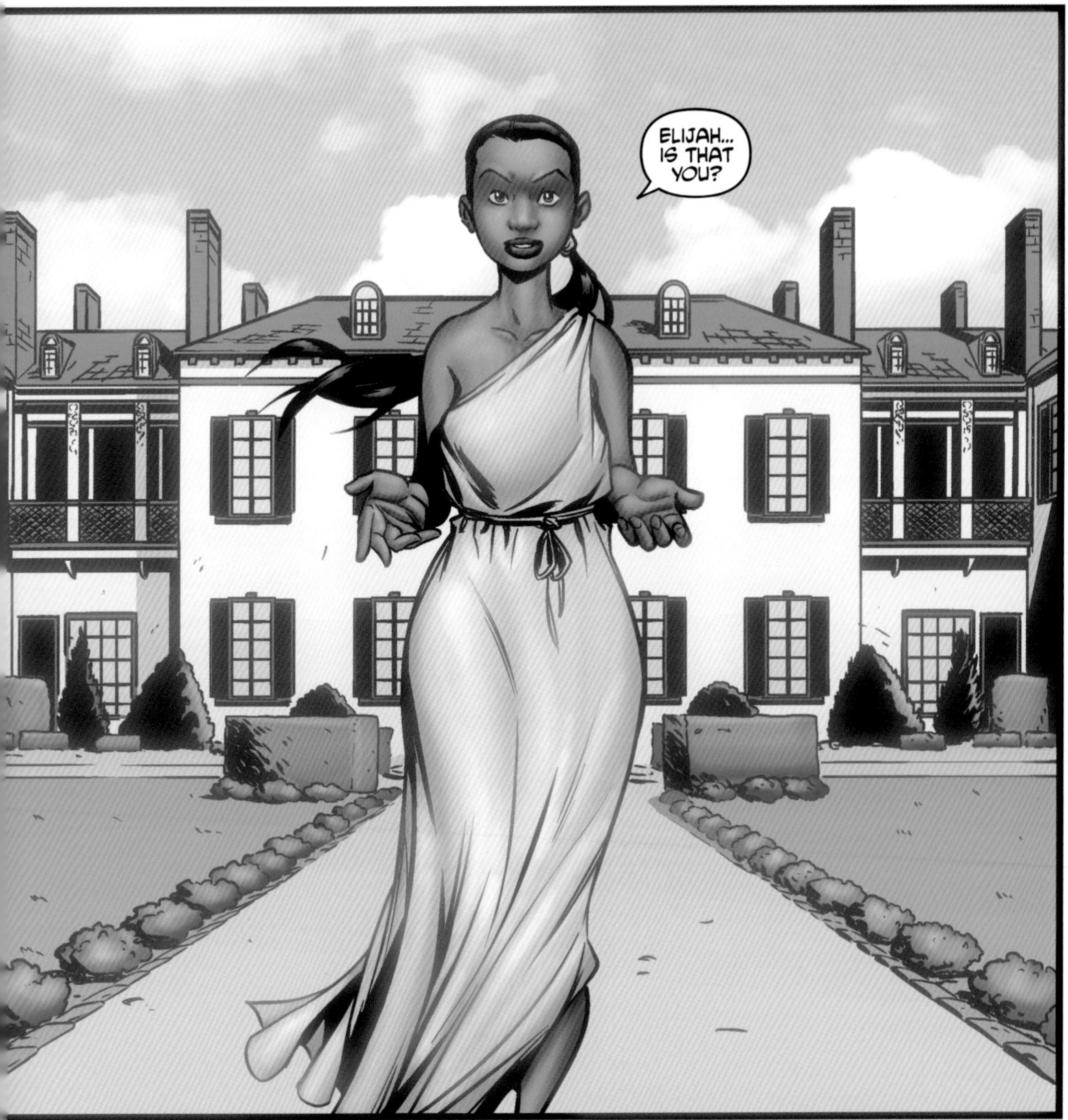
ELIJAH... IS THAT YOU?

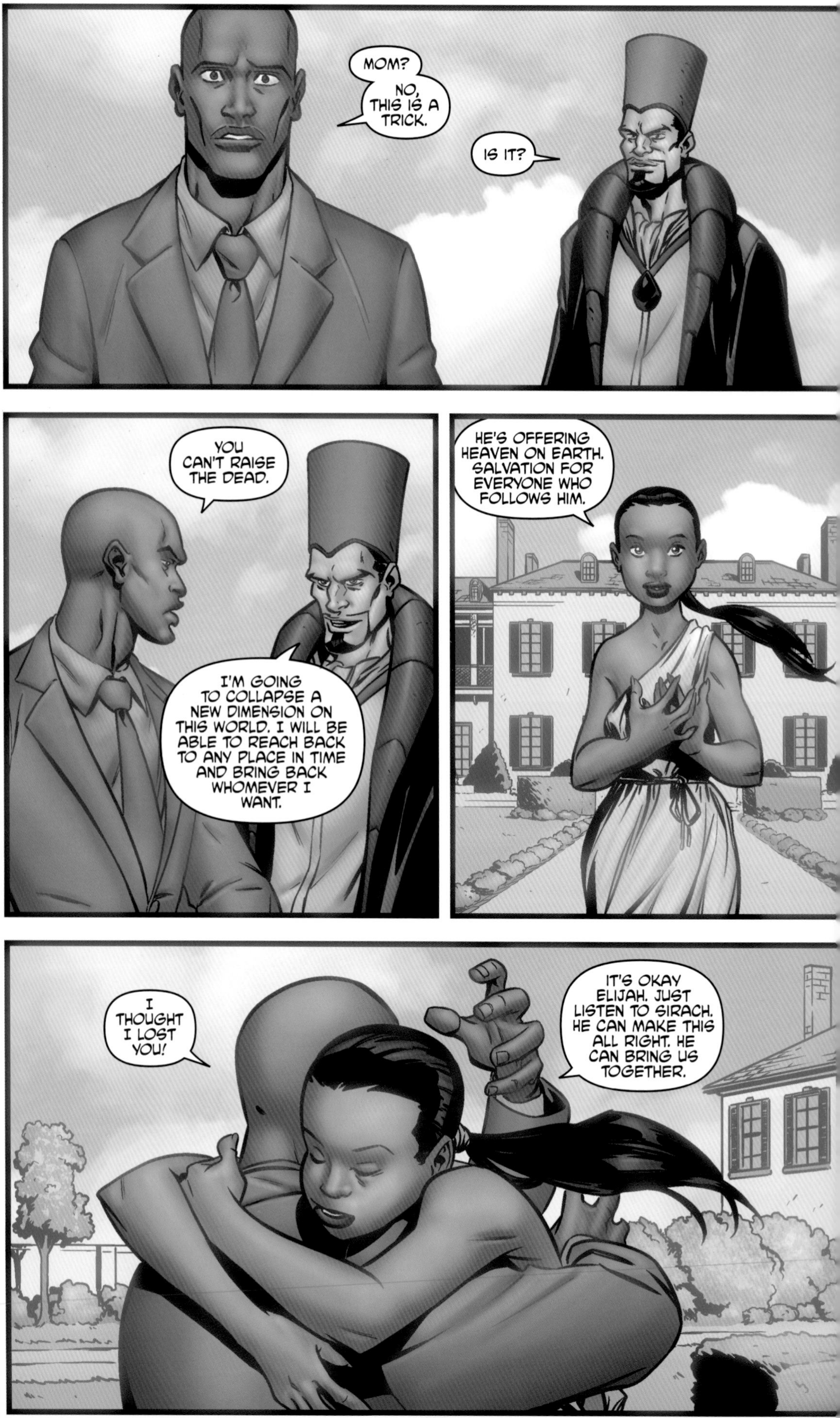
MOM?
NO, THIS IS A TRICK.
IS IT?
YOU CAN'T RAISE THE DEAD.
I'M GOING TO COLLAPSE A NEW DIMENSION ON THIS WORLD. I WILL BE ABLE TO REACH BACK TO ANY PLACE IN TIME AND BRING BACK WHOMEVER I WANT.
HE'S OFFERING HEAVEN ON EARTH. SALVATION FOR EVERYONE WHO FOLLOWS HIM.
I THOUGHT I LOST YOU!
IT'S OKAY ELIJAH. JUST LISTEN TO SIRACH. HE CAN MAKE THIS ALL RIGHT. HE CAN BRING US TOGETHER.

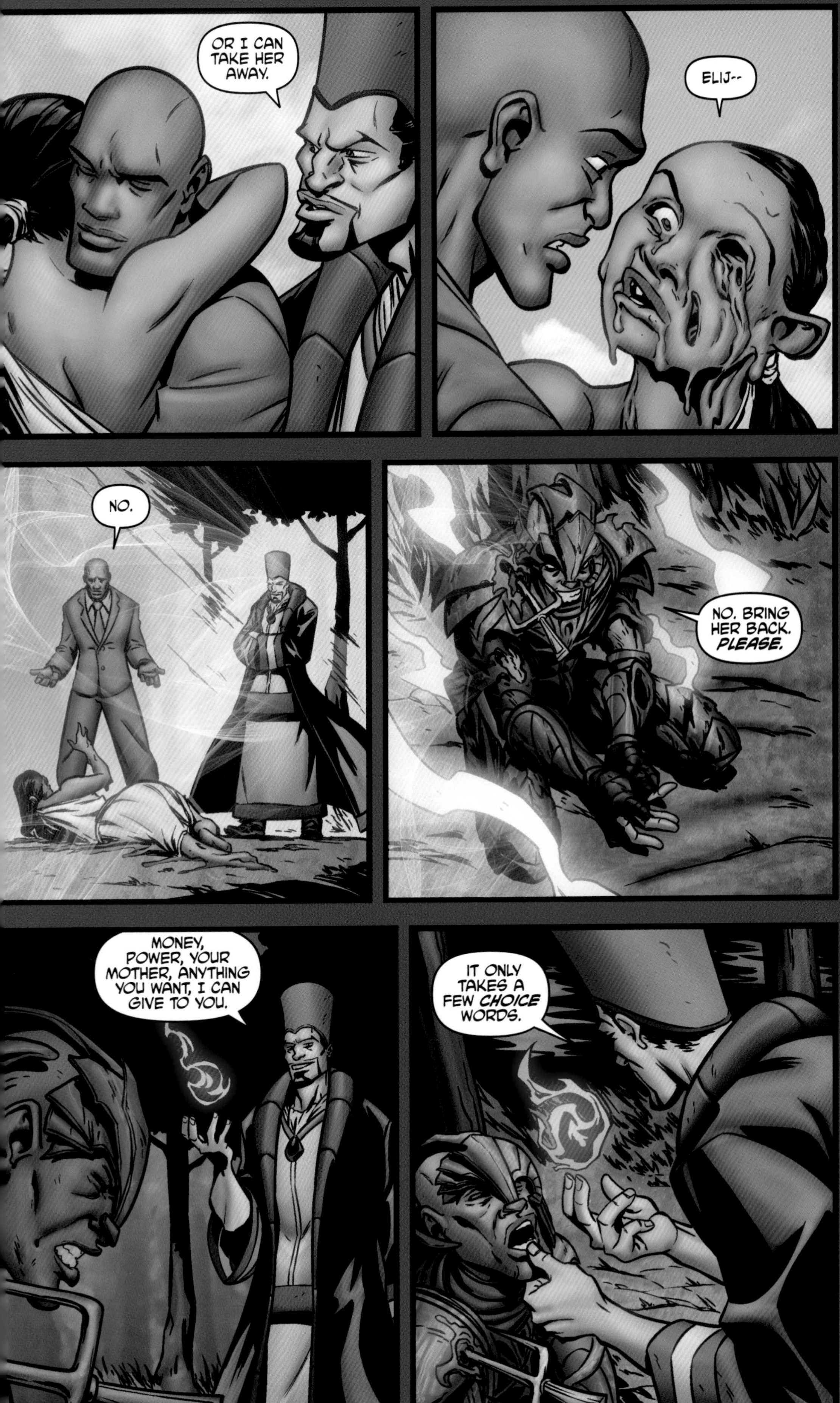
OR I CAN TAKE HER AWAY.
ELIJ--
NO.
NO. BRING HER BACK. *PLEASE.*
MONEY, POWER, YOUR MOTHER, ANYTHING YOU WANT, I CAN GIVE TO YOU.
IT ONLY TAKES A FEW *CHOICE* WORDS.

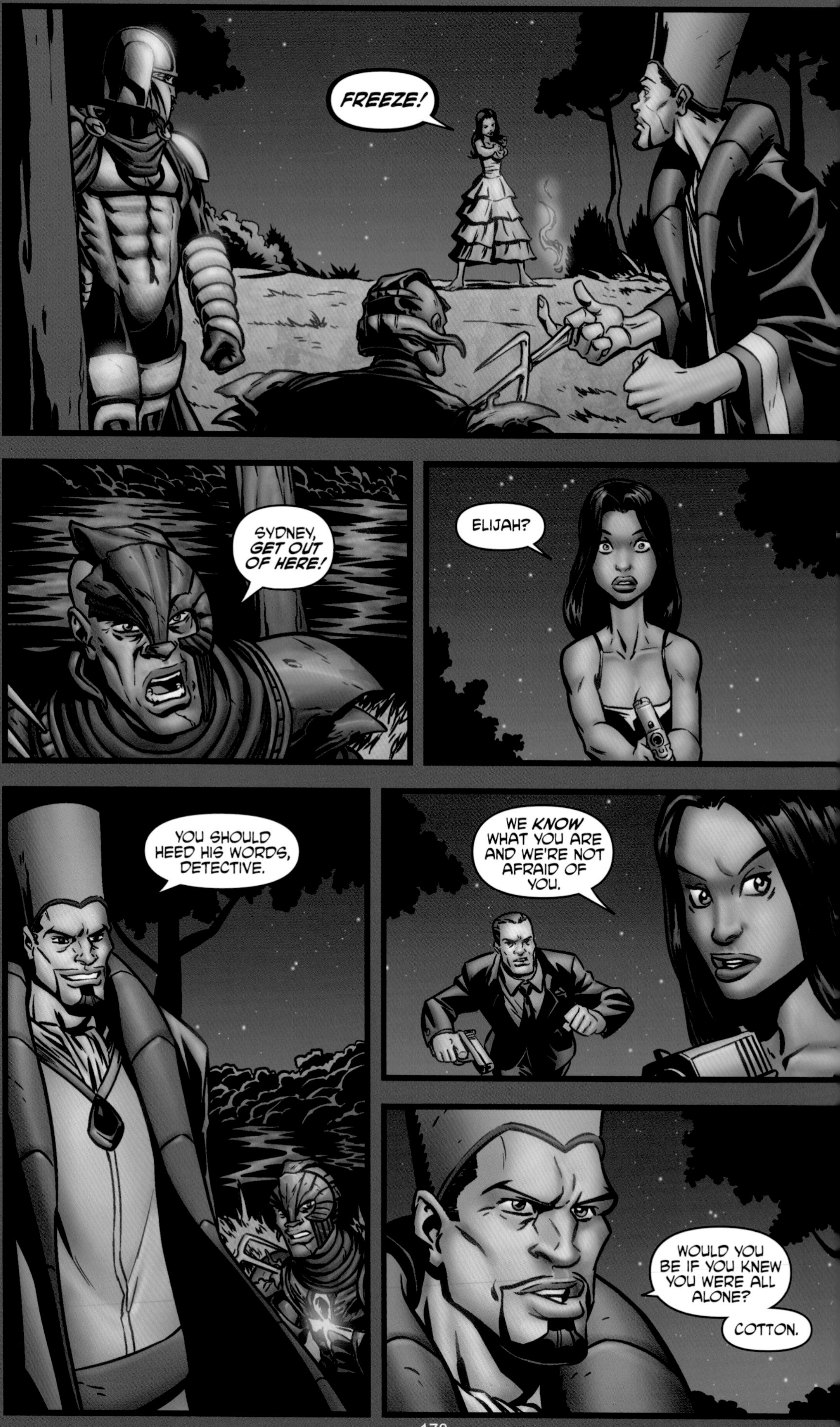
FREEZE!
SYDNEY, GET OUT OF HERE!
ELIJAH?
YOU SHOULD HEED HIS WORDS, DETECTIVE.
WE KNOW WHAT YOU ARE AND WE'RE NOT AFRAID OF YOU.
WOULD YOU BE IF YOU KNEW YOU WERE ALL ALONE?
COTTON.

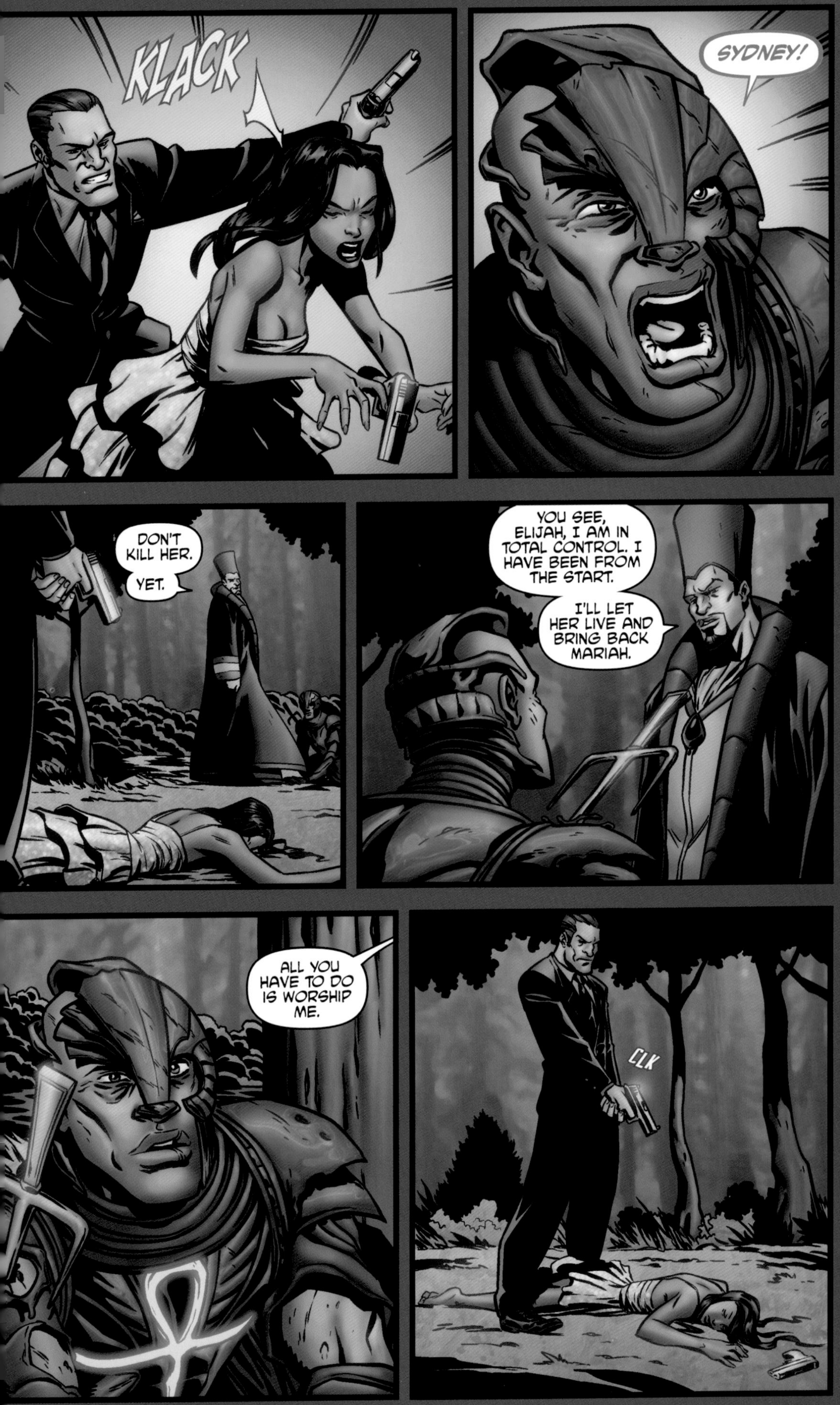
KLACK
SYDNEY!
DON'T KILL HER.
YET.
YOU SEE, ELIJAH, I AM IN TOTAL CONTROL. I HAVE BEEN FROM THE START.
I'LL LET HER LIVE AND BRING BACK MARIAH.
ALL YOU HAVE TO DO IS WORSHIP ME.
CLK

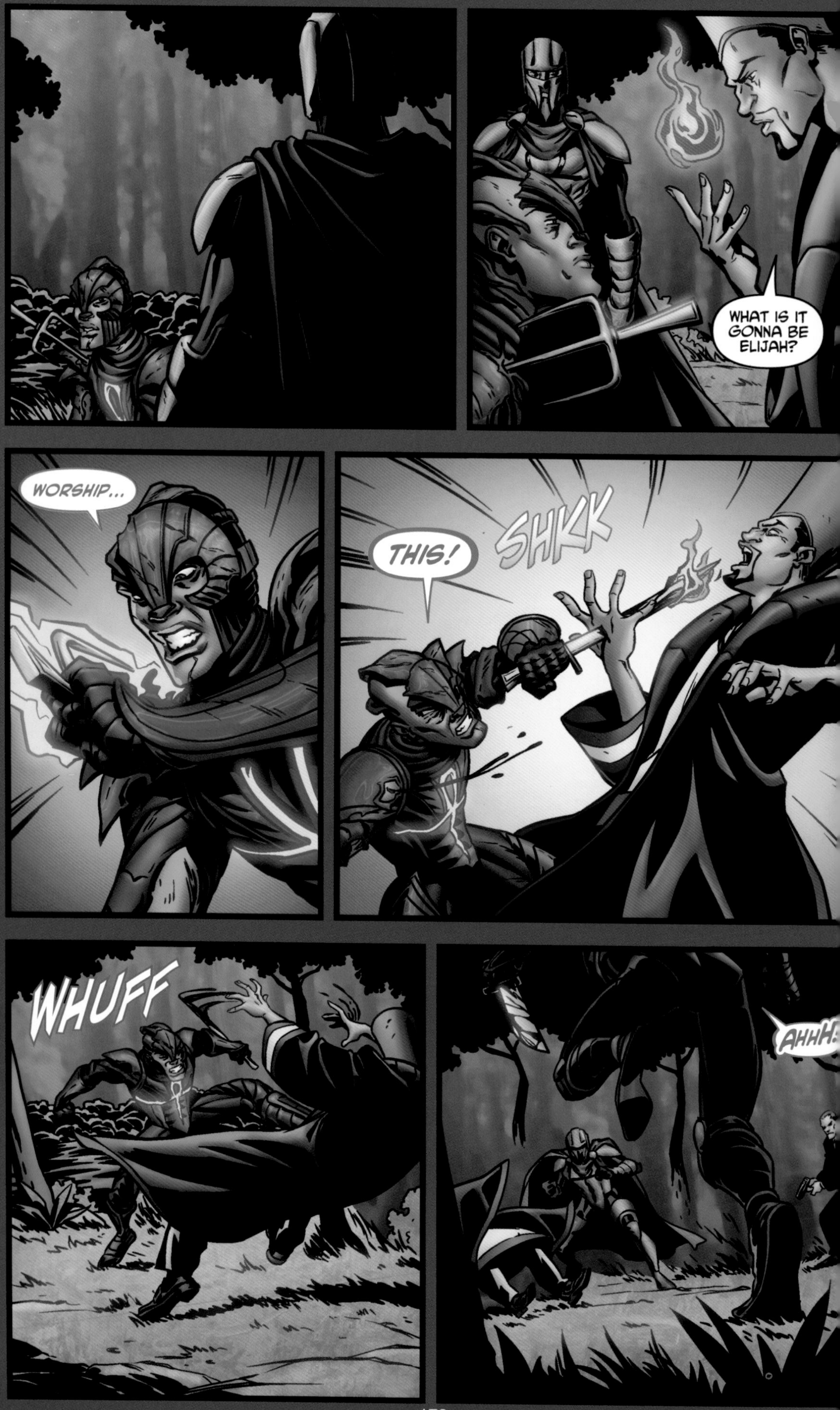
WHAT IS IT GONNA BE ELIJAH?
WORSHIP...
THIS!
SHKK
WHUFF
AHHH

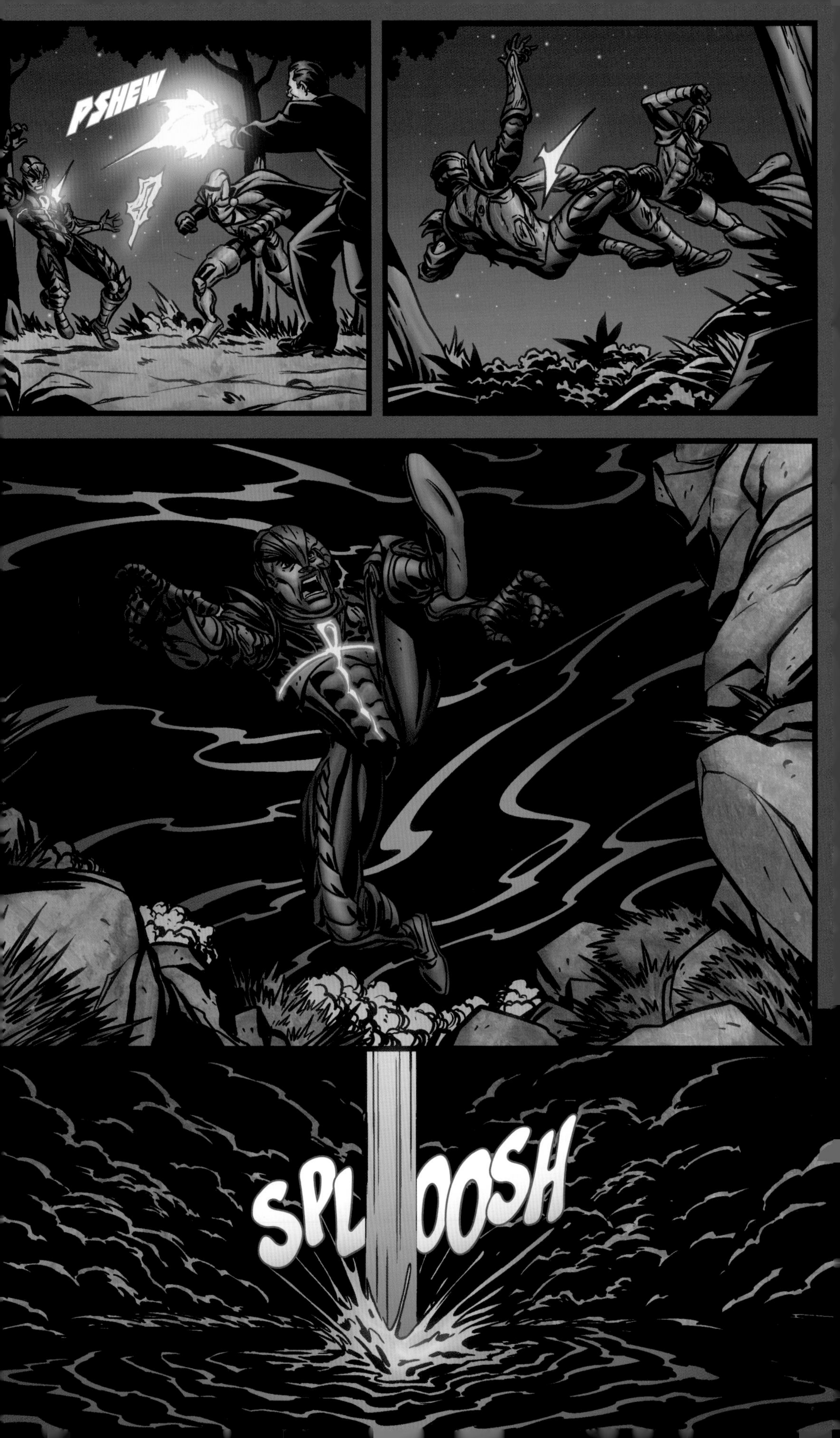
PSHEW
SPLOOSH

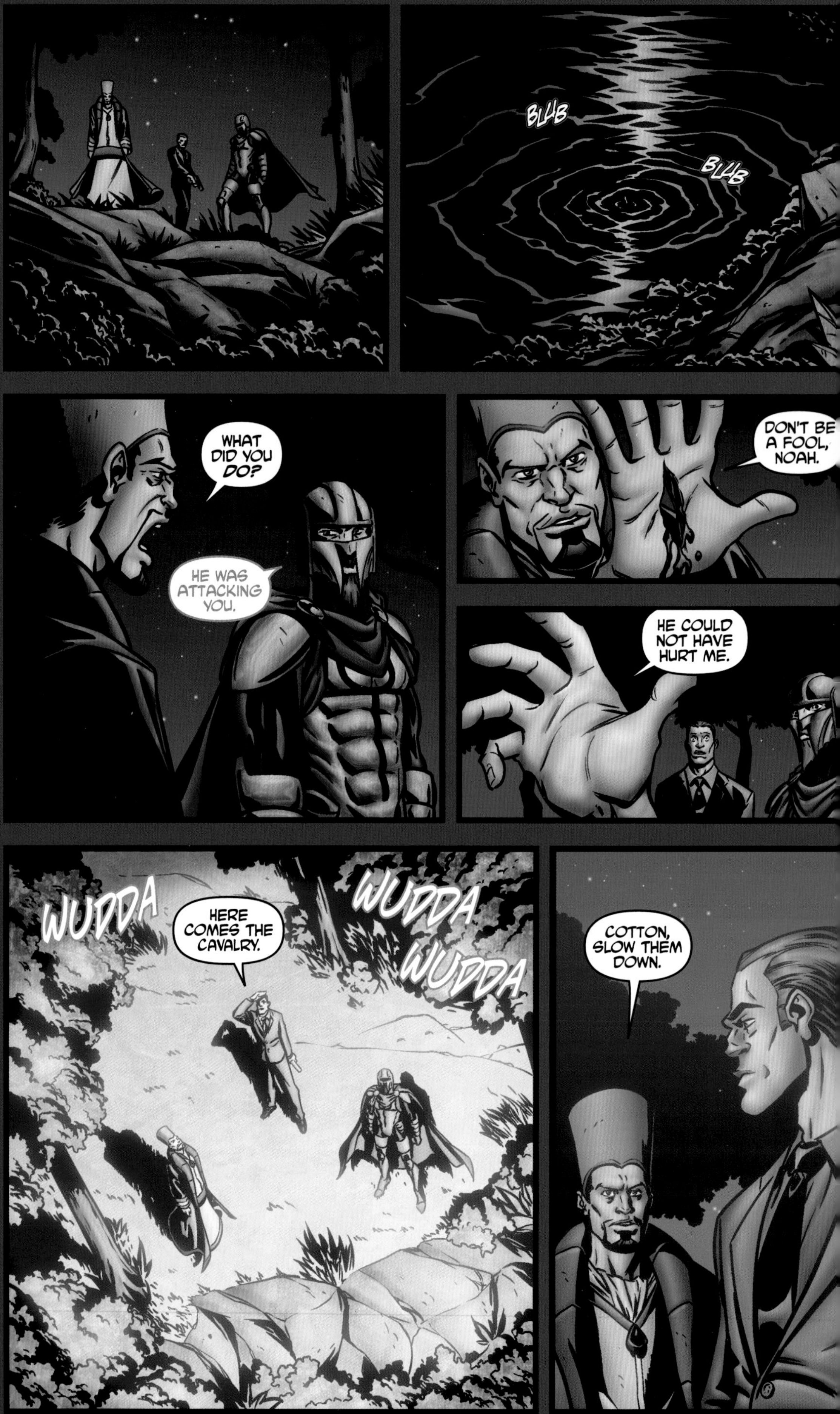
BLUB
BLUB
WHAT DID YOU DO?
HE WAS ATTACKING YOU.
DON'T BE A FOOL, NOAH.
HE COULD NOT HAVE HURT ME.
WUDDA
HERE COMES THE CAVALRY.
WUDDA WUDDA
COTTON, SLOW THEM DOWN.

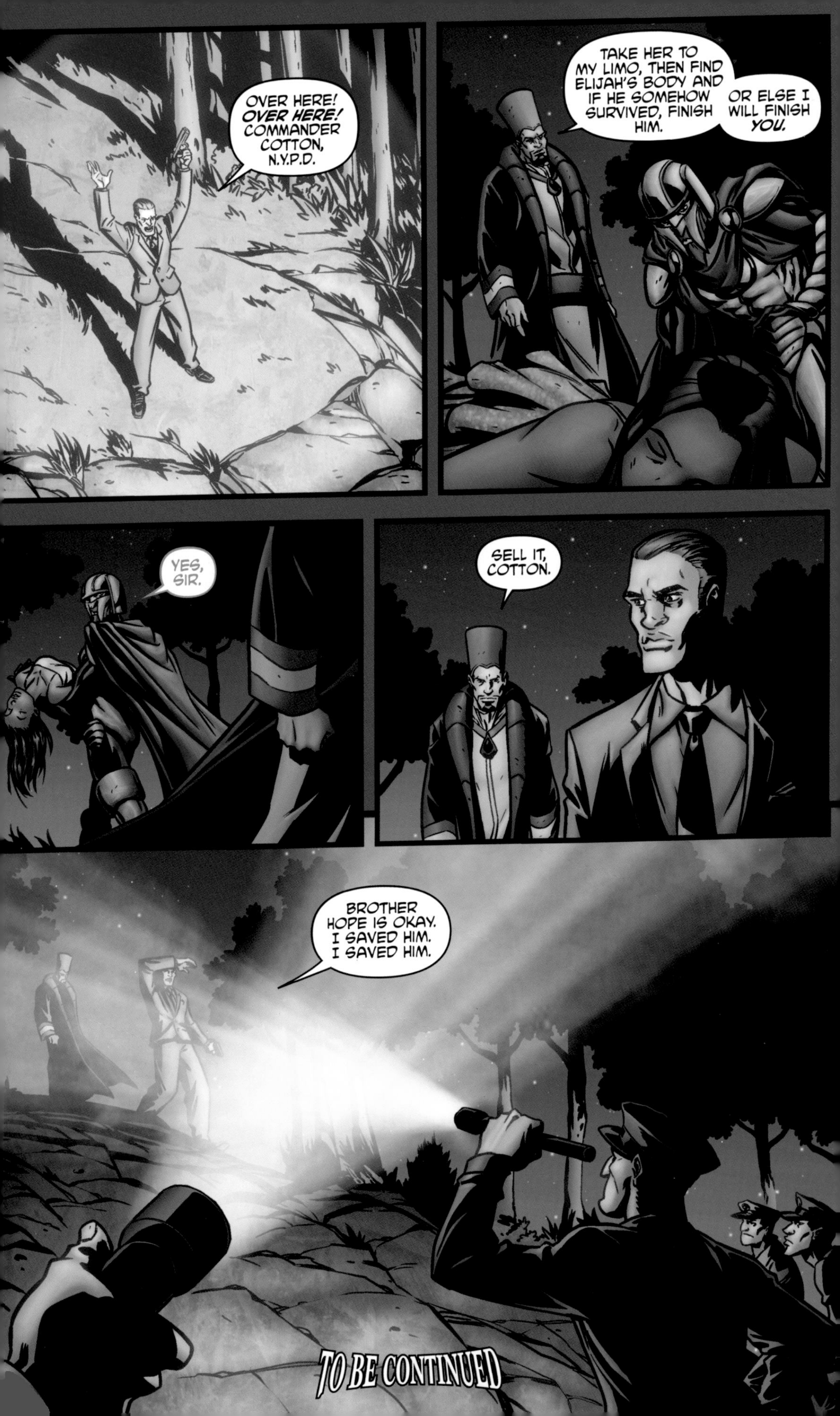
OVER HERE! *OVER HERE!* COMMANDER COTTON, N.Y.P.D.
TAKE HER TO MY LIMO, THEN FIND ELIJAH'S BODY AND IF HE SOMEHOW SURVIVED, FINISH HIM.
OR ELSE I WILL FINISH *YOU.*
YES, SIR.
SELL IT, COTTON.
BROTHER HOPE IS OKAY. I SAVED HIM. I SAVED HIM.
TO BE CONTINUED

LEGEND OF THE MANTAMAJI: BOOK 3

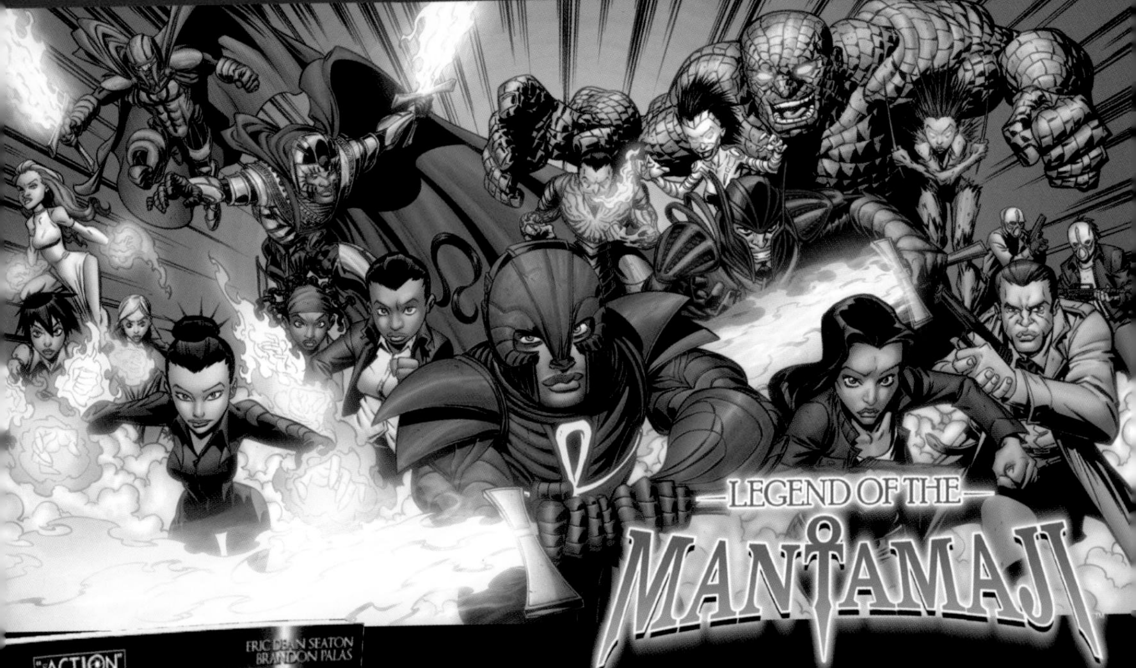
LEGEND OF THE
MANTAMAJI

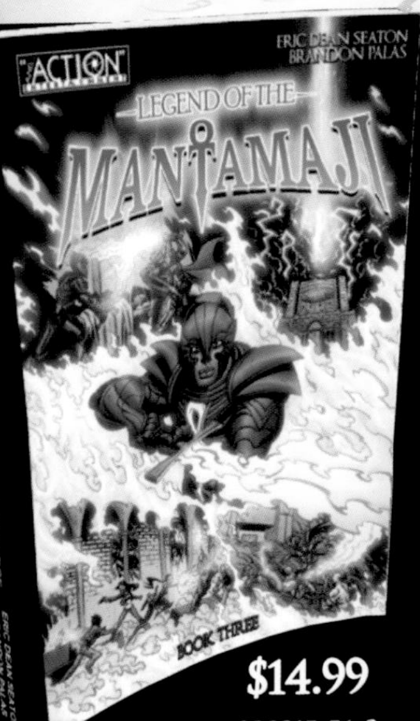
ERIC DEAN SEATON
BRANDON PALAS
ACTION
LEGEND OF THE
MANTAMAJI
BOOK THREE

$14.99

ISBN 978-1-930315-56-3

Beaten, betrayed, and left for dead, Elijah Alexander, the last Mantamaji, knows the end of the world is at hand. Soon Sirach will carry out his plan to open the Gates of Time and alter Earth's history to suit his purposes. How can Elijah stop Sirach, when he's already failed before? To succeed, he will have to put aside vengeance, ignore his pain, and listen to a wisdom he's forgotten. But he, and the world, are running out of time.

ON SALE FEBRUARY 11, 2015

STORY BY ERIC DEAN SEATON
FULL COLOR
184 PAGES

ART BY BRANDON PALAS
LETTERS BY DERON BENNETT
COLORS BY ANDREW DALHOUSE

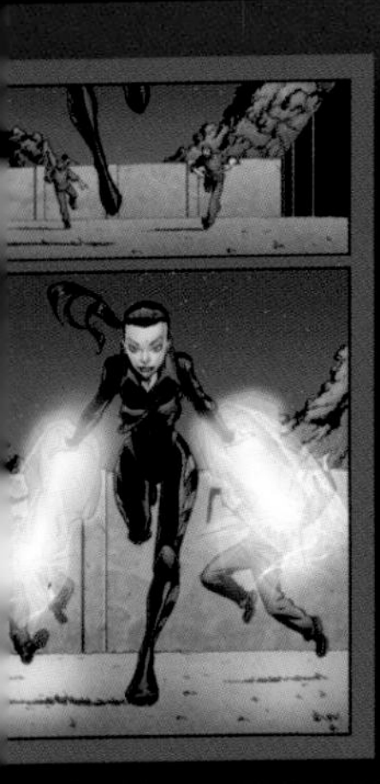

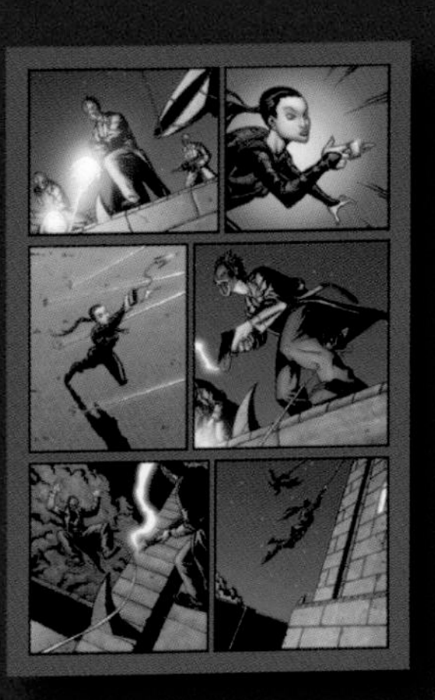

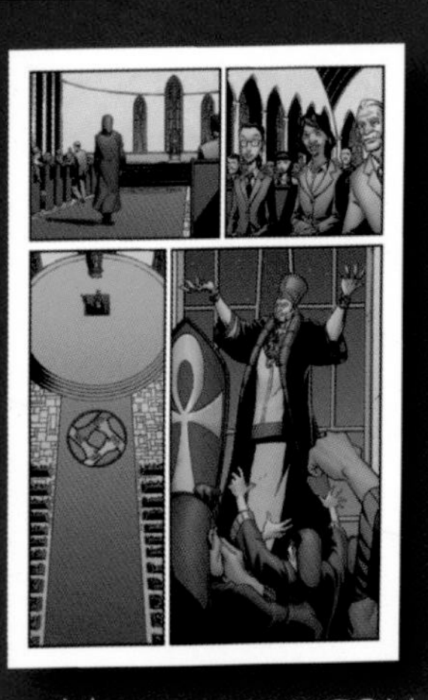

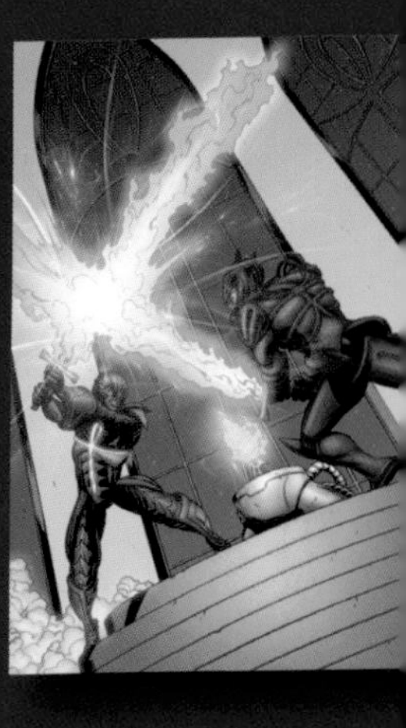

WWW.LEGENDOFTHEMANTAMAJI.COM

LEGEND OF THE MANTAMAJI

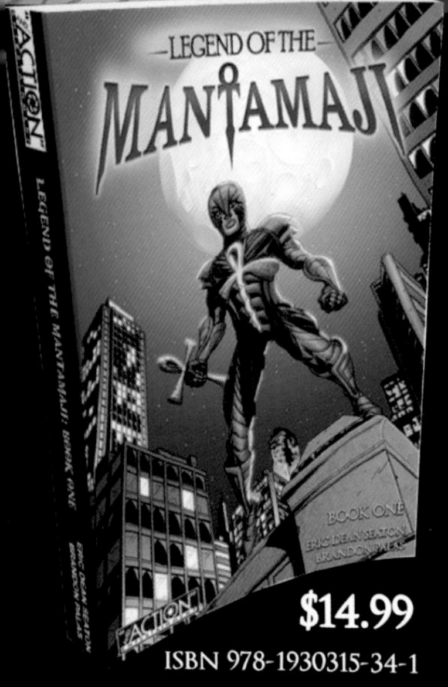

Elijah Alexander, New York's hottest, cockiest, and most media-hungry ADA, is about to learn something shocking: h is not even human. He's the last of the Mantamaji, a long-lo race of warriors who once protected humanity when the world was young. Now another Mantamaji—the worst of al their kind—has reawakened to visit doom on all of humanit Can Elijah accept his past, reject his present life, and learn about his talents, in time to defeat the villain who killed all the other Mantamaji before him?

AVAILABLE NOW!

STORY BY ERIC DEAN SEATON
FULL COLOR
216 PAGES

ART BY BRANDON PALAS
LETTERS BY DERON BENNETT
COLORS BY ANDREW DALHOUSE

$14.99
ISBN 978-1930315-34-1

WWW.LEGENDOFTHEMANTAMAJI.COM

LEGEND OF THE MANTAMAJI

In a single week, Elijah Alexander has gone from being a famous and successful ADA in New York, to a hunted, haunted renegade on a mission of vengeance. Because Elijah is the last of a race of ancient warriors called the Mantamaji who once fought the world's greatest evils. And now the greatest evil of all has just reappeared and seeks to destroy the world as we know it. Elijah's the only one who knows how to stop this, and the only one with the power to get it done—because it takes a warrior to kill a mystical being. Or four of them.

AVAILABLE NOW!

$14.99

ISBN 978-1930315-37-2

STORY BY ERIC DEAN SEATON
FULL COLOR
184 PAGES

ART BY BRANDON PALAS
LETTERS BY DERON BENNETT
COLORS BY ANDREW DALHOUSE

WWW.LEGENDOFTHEMANTAMAJI.COM

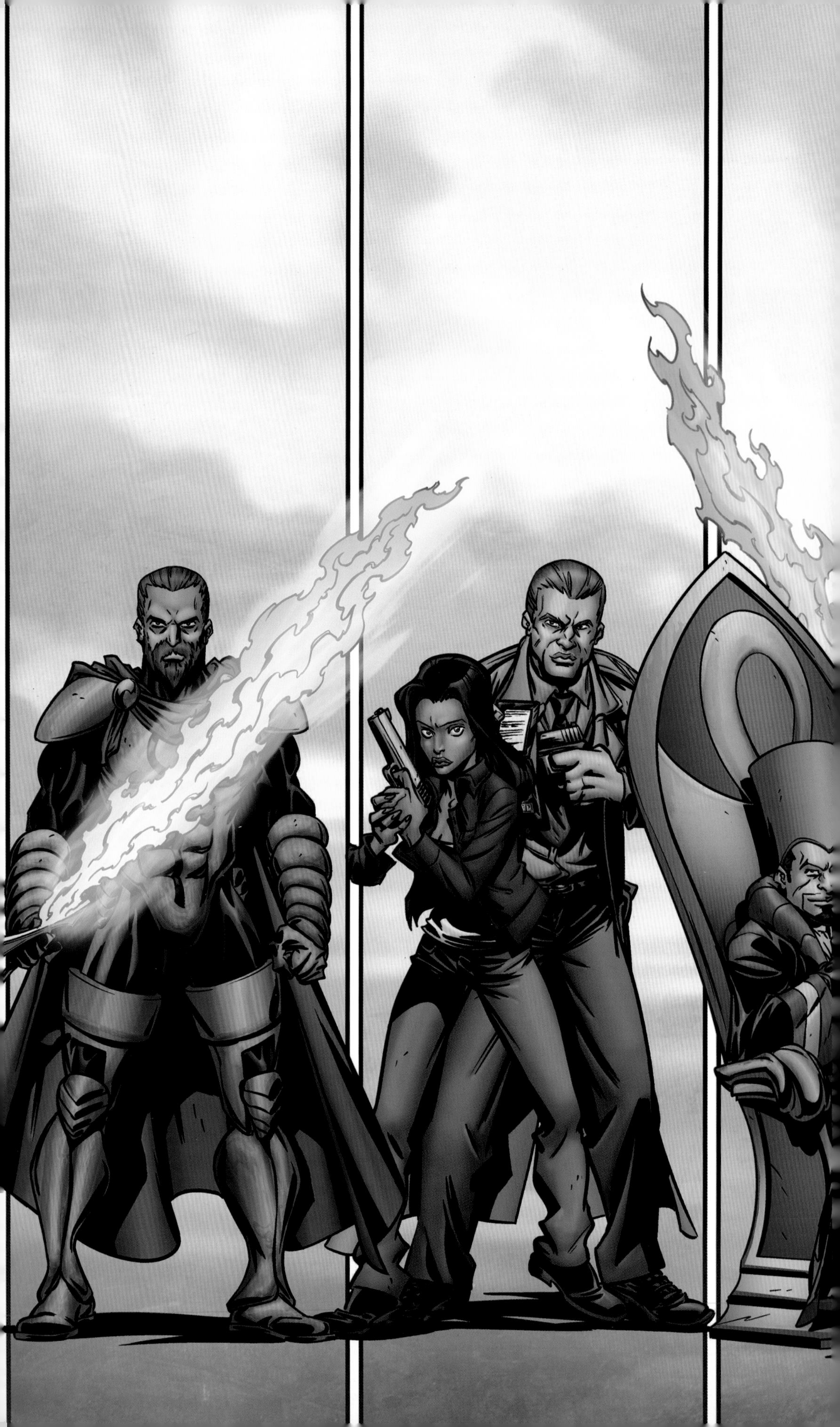

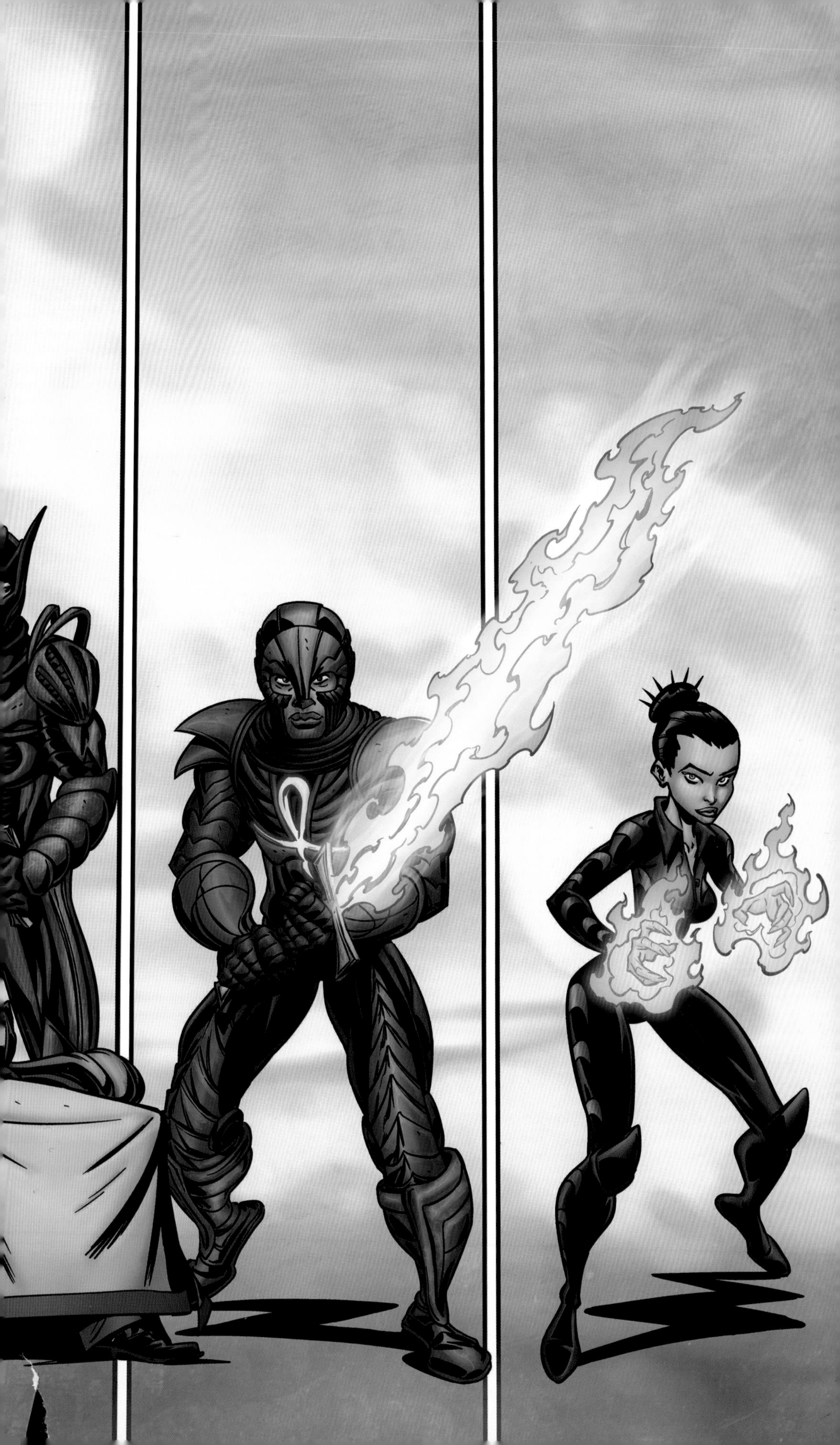

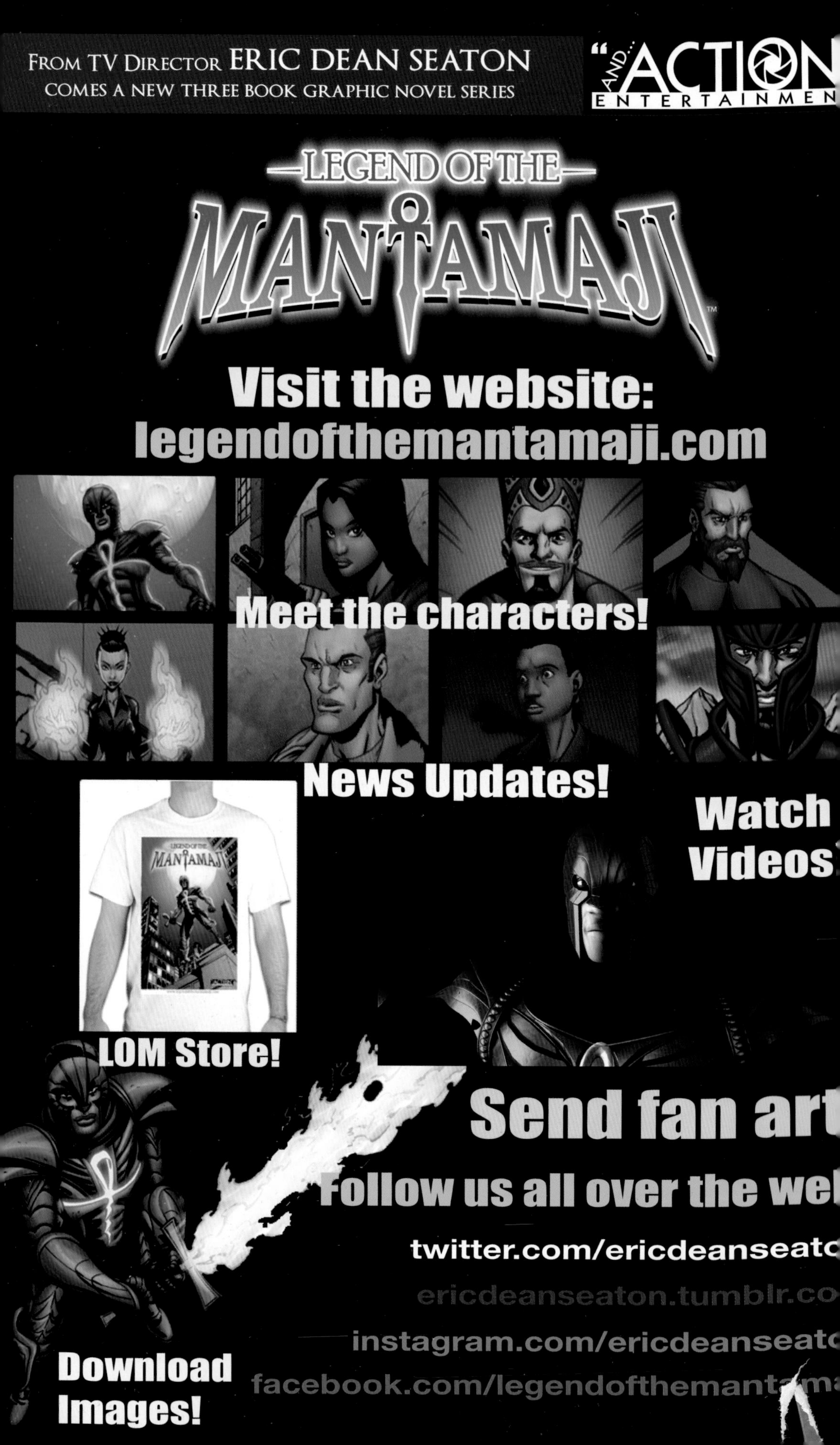
FROM TV DIRECTOR ERIC DEAN SEATON
COMES A NEW THREE BOOK GRAPHIC NOVEL SERIES
"AND... ACTION ENTERTAINMEN
LEGEND OF THE
MANTAMAJI
Visit the website:
legendofthemantamaji.com
Meet the characters!
News Updates!
Watch
Videos
LOM Store!
Send fan ar
Follow us all over the we
twitter.com/ericdeanseat
ericdeanseaton.tumblr.co
instagram.com/ericdeanseat
facebook.com/legendofthemant
Download
Images!